THE CHALLENGE OF ORIGINALISM

Originalism is a force to be reckoned with in constitutional interpretation. At one time a monolithic theory of constitutional interpretation, contemporary originalism has developed into a sophisticated family of theories about how to interpret and reason with a constitution. Contemporary originalists harness the resources of linguistic, moral, and political philosophy to propose methodologies for the interpretation of constitutional texts and provide reasons for fidelity to those texts.

The essays in this volume, which includes contributions from the flag bearers of several competing schools of constitutional interpretation, provide an introduction to the development of originalist thought, showcase the great range of contemporary originalist constitutional scholarship, and situate competing schools of thought in dialogue with each other. They also make new contributions to the methodological and normative disputes between originalists and non-originalists, and among originalists themselves.

Grant Huscroft is a Professor of Law at the University of Western Ontario and is a member of Western Law's Public Law and Legal Philosophy research group. He was a member of the Faculty of Law at the University of Auckland, New Zealand, from 1992 to 2002, and has been a visiting Professor at McGill University. Professor Huscroft has written extensively about constitutional rights and judicial review and his work has been published in Canada, the United States, the United Kingdom, New Zealand, and Australia. He is the co-author of the treatise, *The New Zealand Bill of Rights* (2003), and has edited or co-edited six collections of essays.

Bradley W. Miller is an Associate Professor in the Faculty of Law at University of Western Ontario and is a member of Western Law's Public Law and Legal Philosophy research group. He is called to the bars of British Columbia and Ontario and has appeared before all levels of court in Ontario, including the Supreme Court of Canada. His research is focused on theories of constitutional interpretation and the place of moral reasoning in legal reasoning. His papers have been published in edited collections and in the *American Journal of Jurisprudence*, the *Canadian Journal of Law and Jurisprudence*, *Public Law Review*, and *Res Publica*.

The Challenge of Originalism

Theories of Constitutional Interpretation

Edited by

GRANT HUSCROFT
Faculty of Law, University of Western Ontario

BRADLEY W. MILLER
Faculty of Law, University of Western Ontario

CAMBRIDGE
UNIVERSITY PRESS

CAMBRIDGE
UNIVERSITY PRESS

University Printing House, Cambridge CB2 8BS, United Kingdom

One Liberty Plaza, 20th Floor, New York, NY 10006, USA

477 Williamstown Road, Port Melbourne, VIC 3207, Australia

314-321, 3rd Floor, Plot 3, Splendor Forum, Jasola District Centre, New Delhi - 110025, India

79 Anson Road, #06-04/06, Singapore 079906

Cambridge University Press is part of the University of Cambridge.

It furthers the University's mission by disseminating knowledge in the pursuit of education, learning and research at the highest international levels of excellence.

www.cambridge.org
Information on this title: www.cambridge.org/9781107013254

First published 2011

A catalogue record for this publication is available from the British Library

Library of Congress Cataloging in Publication data
The challenge of originalism : Theories of Constitutional Interpretation / [edited by] Grant Huscroft, Bradley Miller.
p. cm.
Includes bibliographical references and index.
ISBN 978-1-107-01325-4 (hardback)
1. Constitutional law – Philosophy. 2. Law – Interpretation and construction. 3. Origin (Philosophy) I. Huscroft, Grant. II. Miller, Bradley W. III. Title.
K3165.C428 2011
342.001–dc22 2011015740

ISBN 978-1-107-01325-4 Hardback
ISBN 978-1-107-61304-1 Paperback

Contents

Preface

This volume originates from a colloquium on originalist constitutional theory hosted in the autumn of 2008 by the Public Law and Legal Philosophy Research Group at the Faculty of Law at the University of Western Ontario. Constitutional scholars and legal philosophers – proponents of originalism, sceptics, and critics – drew from different jurisdictions and intellectual traditions to address the challenge of originalism. Following standard practice at PLLP colloquia, the entirety of the colloquium was given over to the exchange of ideas in informal discussion. The fruit is evident in this volume, which is the product of scholars engaging with each other to identify common ground, refine disagreement, and provoke questions for future discussion.

We are grateful to the University of Western Ontario, which has provided financial support for public law and legal philosophy since 2007, and in particular to Dr. Ted Hewitt, Vice-President (Research & International Relations), who supported the creation of the Public Law and Legal Philosophy Research Group.

Essays arising out of the 2006 Public Law and Legal Philosophy colloquium on law and morality were published by Cambridge University Press as *Expounding the Constitution: Essays in Constitutional Theory*, Grant Huscroft (ed) (2008), and it has been our great pleasure to work once again with Cambridge and in particular with general editor John Berger.

Grant Huscroft
Bradley W. Miller

Faculty of Law
University of Western Ontario
May, 2011

Contributors

Larry Alexander, Warren Distinguished Professor of Law, University of San Diego

James Allan, Garrick Professor of Law, University of Queensland

Mitchell N. Berman, Richard Dale Endowed Chair in Law, University of Texas at Austin

Brian H. Bix, Frederick W. Thomas Professor of Law and Philosophy, University of Minnesota

Stanley Fish, Davidson-Kahn Distinguished University Professor of Humanities and Law, Florida International University

Jeffrey Goldsworthy, Professor of Law, Monash University

Grant Huscroft, Professor of Law, University of Western Ontario

Bradley W. Miller, Associate Professor of Law, University of Western Ontario

Steven D. Smith, Warren Distinguished Professor of Law, University of San Diego

Lawrence B. Solum, Professor of Law, Georgetown University

Grégoire C. N. Webber, Lecturer in Law, Department of Law, London School of Economics and Political Science

Keith E. Whittington, William Nelson Cromwell Professor of Politics, Princeton University

The Challenge of Originalism: Theories of Constitutional Interpretation

Originalism is a force to be reckoned with in American constitutional theory. From its origins as a monolithic theory of constitutional interpretation, originalism has developed into a sophisticated family of theories about how to interpret and reason with a constitution.[1] Contemporary originalists have harnessed the resources of linguistic, moral, and political philosophy in responding to critics. Recent work is characterized by methodological concerns about how to identify the meaning of constitutional texts as well as the development of normative arguments for fidelity to them.

Despite these developments, originalism is sometimes dismissed out of hand. Critics of originalism often rely on stock arguments that neither addressed nor anticipated the arguments of contemporary originalists. Many are persuaded that originalism was dealt a fatal blow by the criticism of Paul Brest[2] and Jefferson Powell[3] in the 1980s, culminating in the failure of Judge Robert Bork's nomination to the United States Supreme Court.[4] But originalism has moved on considerably since that time. The multiplicity and complexity of the new variants of originalism require interlocutors to make a considerable investment in order to participate in the debate. The essays in this volume, which includes contributions from the flag bearers of several competing schools of constitutional interpretation, provide an introduction to the development of originalist thought, showcase the great range of contemporary originalist

[1] The history of modern originalism is discussed in Steven G. Calabresi (ed.), *Originalism: A Quarter-Century of Debate* (2007); Johnathan O'Neill, *Originalism in American Law and Politics: A Constitutional History* (2005).

[2] Paul Brest, "The Misconceived Quest for the Original Understanding", 60 B.U.L. Rev. 204 (1980).

[3] H. Jefferson Powell, "The Original Understanding of Original Intent", 98 Harv. L. Rev 885 (1984).

[4] Robert H. Bork, *The Tempting of America: The Political Seduction of the Law* (1990).

constitutional scholarship, and situate competing schools of thought in dialogue with each other. They also make new contributions to the methodological and normative disputes between originalists and non-originalists, and among originalists themselves.

The essays are grouped around four themes.

I

The essays in Part I, "Exposition and Defense," set the stage by introducing the basic tenets of originalism and the commitments that lay at its core. They also raise the question of whether it is, in fact, reasonable to speak of an originalist orthodoxy.

Lawrence Solum's contribution, "What Is Originalism? The Evolution of Contemporary Originalist Theory," provides an intellectual history of originalism from the 1930s onward. He identifies the key move made by some originalists in the mid-1980s to abandon the search for original intentions in favor of original public meaning. Original public meaning – the idea that the constitution means what its intended audience would have understood the text to have meant when it was adopted – became a cornerstone of the "new originalism" propounded by Jeffrey Goldsworthy in Australia, and Solum, Keith Whittington, and Randy Barnett in the United States. Solum vividly displays the fault lines between the so-called old originalism (with its focus on original intentions), the new originalism, and living constitutionalism, through a reading of the decision of the U.S. Supreme Court in *District of Columbia v. Heller*,[5] in which the Court provided its first in-depth consideration of the Second Amendment.

New originalists characteristically approach a constitutional text with two distinct tasks in mind: constitutional interpretation and constitutional construction. Although "interpretation" is often used compendiously to refer to the whole of legal reasoning in constitutional adjudication, new originalists limit the application of the term to the task of discovering the meaning of constitutional text. Once interpretation is complete, "construction" is the task of developing rules and principles necessary to fill the gaps left by vague or underdeterminate constitutional text in order to resolve concrete disputes.[6]

[5] 554 U.S 570 (2008).

[6] Whittington develops his conception of construction in a way that emphasizes the role played by the non-judicial branches of government. See Keith E. Whittington, *Constitutional Interpretation: Textual Meaning, Original Intent, and Judicial Review* (1999), and *Constitutional Construction: Divided Powers and Constitutional Meaning* (1999).

On Solum's account, the originalists' acknowledgment of vagueness, underdeterminacy, and the necessity for construction allows for the possible reconciliation of originalist and living constitutional approaches, an intriguing possibility to which we will return.

Working independently of the American originalist scholars, Jeffrey Goldsworthy's research in the Australian constitutional context arrived at many of the same conclusions and principles of constitutional interpretation as Solum and Whittington. In "The Case for Originalism," Goldsworthy identifies eight propositions about the nature of constitutions and the rule of law that support the originalist project:

1. A constitution necessarily has a meaning prior to judicial interpretation of it.
2. To change the meaning of a law is to change the law.
3. The original meaning of a constitution is its "utterance meaning," which must be distinguished from its original literal meaning and its originally intended meaning.
4. Constitutional amending formulas bind judges as well as other officials and preclude change through judicial "interpretation."
5. Change to the constitution through interpretation undermines the constitution, the rule of law, the principle of democracy, and the principle of federalism.
6. Judges are duty-bound to determine and clarify the pre-existing meaning of the constitution but can supplement that meaning when it is not sufficiently determinate to resolve the problem at hand.
7. Although judges cannot deliberately change the constitution, constitutional law can and does legitimately evolve over time (and to this extent, originalism is perfectly consistent with "common law constitutionalism" and "living constitutionalism").
8. Consistent application of any constitutional theory, including originalism, might lead to grave injustice in a particular case and if it does, judges might be morally bound to disobey the constitution, but this has nothing to do with the true meaning of the constitution.

Goldsworthy elaborates on each of these principles, drawing on Canadian and Australian law to illustrate. He engages with Solum and Whittington in stating the case for originalism and defending it against critics, most notably Mitchell Berman, whose recent criticism of originalism has attracted considerable attention.[7] Goldsworthy argues for a moderate form of originalism

[7] Mitchell N. Berman, "Originalism is Bunk" 84 N.Y.U. L. Rev 1 (2009).

that is flexible enough to adapt to meet contemporary needs and values – the very claim usually made in support of arguments for living constitutionalism. Goldsworthy appears to go further than Solum in reconciling originalism and living constitutionalism, arguing that "[a]s both theories are purged of their weaknesses, they are moderated and eventually merge. Originalists wonder what more, by way of flexibility and capacity for 'evolution', non-originalists could possibly want."[8]

In "On Pluralism within Originalism," Keith Whittington explores the distinction between constitutional interpretation and constitutional construction and exploits it to provide a bridge between originalism and other forms of constitutional argumentation. The interpretation/construction distinction is crucial, he argues, for creating "avenues for originalist theory to identify what role originalism itself can play within constitutional practice and how it can be effectively integrated into a broader theory of constitutional maintenance and elaboration."[9] Whittington defends originalism against the charge that it is closed to all alternative modes of constitutional interpretation, arguing that various forms of constitutional argumentation may be acceptable provided that they are designed to discover and implement the original meaning of the constitution. As he puts it, the key point of difference between originalists and non-originalists lies in their conceptions of the legitimate scope of judicial authority, and "is fundamentally a disagreement over the necessary warrants for judges to disregard legislation."[10]

II

New originalism represents only one stream of contemporary originalist thought – one member of the family of originalist theories.[11] Others who agree with the new originalists about the importance of what Solum describes as the "fixation thesis" – the idea that the semantic meaning of a constitutional text is fixed at the moment of its enactment – nevertheless disagree with them about the appropriate methodology for determining that meaning. "Old" originalists maintain that the meaning of a constitutional text is fixed by the original intentions of its authors. In his contribution to Part II,

[8] 65. [9] 76.
[10] 86.
[11] Solum, Goldsworthy, and Whittington represent only one stream of new originalist thought. Consider also the "original methods" originalism of John O. McGinnis & Michael B. Rappaport, "Original Interpretive Principles as the Core of Originalism," 24 Const. Comment: 371 (2007).

"Interpretation and Intention," Larry Alexander argues in "Simple-Minded Originalism" that although intention-based originalism is "considered heretical among most legal academics . . . it is so orthodox among ordinary folks as to escape notice."[12] Alexander defends the use of author's intended meaning to interpret constitutional texts against critics of originalism, particularly Berman. He also defends intended meaning against concerns about the practical obstacles to determining original intentions, while attacking the concept of "original public meaning" deployed by the new originalists as artificial and highly manipulable.

Stanley Fish's contribution, "The Intentionalist Thesis Once More," similarly carries the intentionalist brief against its interlocutors, and in particular Berman. Fish rejects the contributions of the new originalists as "scholastic, a dizzying structure of cycles and epicycles built on a mistake,"[13] and, like Alexander, holds that there is only one correct answer to the question, "what is the meaning of a text?" As he puts it, "a text means what its author or authors intend."[14] But Fish is skeptical that there is any value in searching for a methodology to interpret constitutional texts. Such a methodology is unavailable, he argues, because interpretation is an empirical rather than a theoretical task. It may, in a particular case, turn out to be impossible to figure out what the intention was. Nevertheless, Fish argues that recovering that meaning is the only job that the interpreter has.

What is at stake between new and old variants of originalism – particularly when it appears that the original intention behind the constitutional text is ignoble – is displayed concretely in Bradley Miller's contribution, "Origin Myth: The *Persons Case*, The Living Tree, and the New Originalism." Miller revisits the case revered in Canada as the font of living constitutionalism (that is, the constitution as a "living tree") and argues that it has been misunderstood and misrepresented in Canadian constitutional law. Properly understood, he argues, the decision of the Judicial Committee of the Privy Council overturning the decision of the Supreme Court of Canada (which had held that women were not "qualified persons" eligible for appointment to the Canadian Senate) reflects the triumph of proto-new originalism over original intentions originalism, rather than the triumph of "living tree" interpretation over originalism *simpliciter*. He argues that Canadian constitutional law, once purged of this misreading, is consistent with originalist forms of argumentation.

[12] 87. [13] 99.
[14] 100.

III

The essays in Part III, "Originalism and Constitutional Settlement, consider the implications of a normative argument often made for originalism (one also identified by Goldsworthy), namely that constitutions are political agreements that settle some matters and preclude change outside their formal amending formulas.

In "Originalism's Constitution," Grégoire Webber asks what originalism assumes about the nature of a constitution and explores the functions that written constitutions perform in an attempt to assess the relevance of originalist theory. Seeking to understand originalism through the model of a constitution, he constructs a fictional constitution (called the "original constitution") that allows for the core commitments of originalism to be satisfied. To this end, Webber identifies three constitutional commitments that are necessary for originalism to guide constitutional interpretation and construction: The original constitution is written at the founding and changed only by its amendment procedure; the original constitution provides rule-like prescriptions; and the original constitution occupies a delimited domain, leaving some sphere of decision making to democratic activity.

Relying on the model of originalism's constitution, Webber argues that originalism is controlling only where interpretation is determinant. Yet, for so many real-world constitutions, interpretation only goes so far. Real-world constitutions leave much to be accomplished through construction; they are in many respects incomplete as statements of law and therefore unable to satisfy the condition precedent for originalist interpretation. Many things were left out of the written constitution and open for later determination, and the task of constitutional authoring that was begun at the moment the constitution was written is, on Webber's account, an ongoing one, guided but not determined by originalism, and participated in by judges and political actors alike.

James Allan and Grant Huscroft both address originalism through the lens of the institutional function of judicial review. In his contribution, "The Curious Concept of the Living Tree (or Non-Locked-In) Constitution," Allan hypothesizes about the process of adopting a written constitution and the intentions that underlie it. He argues that the practice of constitution making makes no sense outside of the intention that the settlement reflected in the constitutional text be honored, and that those deliberating over the meaning of the constitutional text seek to ascertain what this settlement was. For Allan, the settlement function performed by a constitutional text necessitates ascertaining intentions, which entails, he argues, the old originalism articulated by Alexander and others.

Huscroft is sympathetic to Allan's argument but takes a different tack and ventures more deeply into questions of methodology in his contribution, "Vagueness, Finiteness, and the Limits of Interpretation and Construction." He acknowledges the interpretive difficulties caused by the vague and underdeterminate language that characterizes contemporary bills of rights and seems to open up a vast role for judicial review. He argues, however, for the recognition of what he considers the ultimate limit on the interpretation of bills of rights – a limit that originalists and living constitutionalists alike must respect: Bills of rights are supposed to be finite instruments. That is, they protect only the rights they enumerate, and the vagueness of those rights neither invites nor allows courts to provide a rights-based answer to every problem that can conceivably become the subject of litigation.

Originalists need some means of determining the boundaries of legitimate construction when textual meaning runs out, whereas living constitutionalists must make sense of rights having eschewed the idea that they may have some fixed, core meaning. Bills of rights are typically limited in their scope by design, and the absence of some rights that might have been enumerated may reflect a decision to deny constitutional authority to them, despite the strong moral claims they present. In other words, the silence of a bill of rights may have normative significance. Drawing on experience with the *Canadian Charter of Rights and Freedoms*, Huscroft argues that the deliberate silence of a bill of rights limits the scope of legitimate construction for originalists as well as the scope for "growth and expansion" of the bill of rights under a living constitutionalism approach. Some purported constitutional rights, such as economic and social rights, were deliberately excluded from the *Charter*, and courts must give effect to the constitutional settlement this decision reflects rather than take advantage of vaguely worded guarantees to amend in effect, the *Charter*.

IV

Part IV, "Challenges and Critiques," includes criticisms of the originalist project from three very different positions. Stephen D. Smith is a friendly critic, but in "That Old-Time Originalism" he questions the value of the new originalism's increasing analytical sophistication and calls for a return to the old intentions-based originalism of Alexander and Fish. Exchanges between Solum and Berman, he says, "provide a lengthy and dazzling list of conceptual claims, shadings, and distinctions,"[15] and Smith worries about the barriers to

[15] 226.

entry created by a scholasticism of the discipline. More fundamentally, he questions whether originalism is collapsing under the weight of its sophistication "into its long-time nemesis, the idea of the 'living constitution'."[16] He fears that "originalism is no longer available as a distinct approach to further (or at least attempt to further) the worthy purposes . . . for which it was devised – namely constraining courts in history-grounded ways and, even more importantly, serving democracy by enabling democratic institutions to enact constitutional provisions with relatively definite and fixed meanings."[17]

Among the non-originalist critics of originalism, Mitchel Berman is peerless in his ability to engage with originalist scholars on their own ground. In his contribution, "Reflective Equilibrium and Constitutional Method," Berman breaks new ground, articulating a methodology to test the soundness of any normative constitutional theory (originalist or otherwise) based on Rawlsian reflective equilibrium. The test case for his theory is debate over the interpretation of the natural-born citizenship clause of the United States Constitution that occurred in the lead-up to the American presidential election in 2008. Berman argues that the legal outcomes of cases should follow our "strong considered judgments" about the correct legal outcomes, and if a methodology produces judgments at odds with these convictions that is good reason to reject the methodology. Berman sees this requirement as particularly challenging for contemporary originalism.

Berman answers a number of originalist objections and focuses on rebutting the intentionalist thesis offered by Stanley Fish. He argues that the intentionalist thesis conflates the separate issues as to what the speaker meant with what the text he uttered actually means, and that the argument from rationality proffered in support of the intentionalist thesis is not sound. Stanley Fish replies in a postscript to his contribution, insisting that there is no distinction between what the speaker meant and what his text means. Words cannot mean something apart from what their author meant them to mean: "(n)o intention, no text, no meaning, no point to interpretation."

Brian Bix mulls over the contributions of the new originalists and sets out two challenges for originalist theorists to overcome in his contribution, "Constitutions, Originalism, and Meaning." First, he questions the cogency and stability of the new originalist's distinction between assessing the meaning of a text and applying that meaning in an adjudicative or legislative process. Bix cautions that unlike descriptive interpretive contexts where something objective in the world (like "water" or "gold") determines what counts as water and gold, the referent in interpreting legal concepts (like "valid contract") is

[16] 230. [17] 232–3.

far more controversial. He urges the new originalists to engage more fully with those legal philosophers, such as Dworkin and Gadamer, who maintain that the interpretation of a text and its application in any particular instance are not separate actions but a single unitary process.

Bix also questions whether originalists intend for their theories to be understood "as a general or universal theory rather than one dependent on contingent claims about our/one nation's constitutional text, history, and politics."[18] To what extent does the originalist project make sense within a constitutional setting – unlike the United States – in which judicial review is expressly authorized? Why should one mode of constitutional argumentation be applied universally to very different constitutions? Bix suggests that plausible answers could be developed by reference to the normative significance of intentions (an idea clearly resonant with Alexander, Allan, Goldsworthy, Huscroft, and Webber), or through Joseph Raz's service conception of authority.

V

For all of its sophistication, originalism is viewed in some quarters as a protest movement rather than a scholarly endeavor.[19] It has been the subject of parody and deprecation, sometimes by those who understand it least, and it has been ignored by many – including some who otherwise extol the benefits of comparative constitutional law scholarship.[20] Originalism has been all but banished from constitutional discourse in Canada in favor of a "living tree" conception of the constitution,[21] and it finds few proponents in other western countries with written constitutions. When it comes to interpreting bills of rights, proportionality and balancing – concepts that may be antithetical to originalism – appear to be ascendant.

Nevertheless, the key ideas behind originalism – that constitutions reflect commitments that should be honored and that their text necessarily constrains the range of possible interpretation (and construction) – have appeal even for those who purport to reject originalist premises. No court, so far as we are

[18] 299.

[19] E.g., Robert Post and Reva Siegel, "Originalism as a Political Practice: The Right's Living Constitution", 75 Fordham L. Rev. 545 (2006).

[20] E.g., Justice Michael Kirby, "Constitutional Interpretation and Original Intent: A Form of Ancestor Worship?" (2000) 24 Melbourne U. L. Rev. 1.

[21] See Justice Ian Binnie, "Constitutional Interpretation and Original Intent" and Grant Huscroft, "A Constitutional 'Work in Progress'? The Charter and the Limits of Progressive Interpretation", both in Grant Huscroft & Ian Brodie (eds.), *Constitutionalism in the Charter Era* (2004) and Bradley W. Miller, "Beguiled by Metaphors: The Living Tree and Originalist Constitutional Interpretation in Canada" (2009) 22 Can. J.L. & Juris. 331.

aware, considers things like the intentions of the framers, the original meaning of the words they adopted, or even common expectations and understandings about the constitution to be irrelevant to the task of applying the text of the constitution to resolve real disputes. The dispute between originalists and non-originalists centers not on the *relevance* of these things but on the *authority* that they should be accorded.

The "challenge of originalism" refers not only to the challenge that originalist theory poses to the living constitution and other forms of non-originalist theory, but also to the challenge that originalist theory faces from within. As Steven Smith cautions, the developments that offer the promise of reconciling originalism and living constitutionalism raise the prospect that originalism might become subsumed within living constitutionalism and thereby lose its *raison d'etre*. Some scholars are ready to pronounce that originalism has become indistinguishable from non-originalism.[22] This is, of course, a debatable point, but it is clear that originalist scholars face a considerable challenge in articulating an approach to constitutional construction that renders originalism sufficiently flexible to resolve unanticipated claims of right, on one hand, while remaining true to the settlement function of constitutions on the other. Living constitutionalists are justly criticized for paying lip service to the settlement reached in a constitutional text, only to assert that the meaning of the text – especially of rights provisions – is so vague that the possibilities for judicial construction turn out to be almost boundless. Originalists must be wary of any approach to construction that has the similar effect of rendering constitutional meaning largely irrelevant.

Originalist theory has little purchase outside of the United States and it is under pressure within the United States – not only from American critics but also from the prospect of the growing influence of foreign constitutional law in American courts. Because the institution of judicial review is less controversial outside the United States, such concerns about judicial power as exist are more likely to sound in the counsel of judicial restraint – in particular, arguments for deference to the elected branch[23] – rather than in endorsements of theories perceived to be designed to limit judicial power at the outset. Nevertheless, if, as contemporary proponents such as Solum and Barnett argue, originalism is not primarily concerned with limiting judicial review, but is instead a matter

[22] See *e.g.*, Peter J. Smith, "How Different Are Originalism and Non-Originalism" 62 Hastings L. J., 707 (2011).

[23] See *e.g.*, Aileen Kavanagh, "Deference Rather than Defiance: The Limits of the Judicial Role in Constitutional Adjudication" in Grant Huscroft (ed.), *Expounding the Constitution* (2008) 184.

of constructing the most normatively appealing structure for reasoning with a constitution, originalism ought to attract greater international attention.

Whatever the future for originalist theory, engaging with the analytical resources of originalism must be a priority for constitutional scholars of all stripes. Much can be achieved in improving constitutional discourse if scholars abandon a preoccupation with labels and defending empires and focus instead on finding resolution to issues that are of common concern: ascertaining the normative significance of agreements reached through constitutional texts; articulating and refining the methodology of interpreting constitutional texts; and establishing the nature and limits of judicial review granted by constitutional texts. The essays in this volume promise to deepen the reader's understanding of originalism in the multiplicity of its paths and to play a part in the common goal of originalist and non-originalist constitutional scholars alike: reasoning with constitutions and constitutional rights toward the public good.

PART ONE **Exposition and Defense**

1 What Is Originalism? The Evolution of Contemporary Originalist Theory

Lawrence B. Solum

I. INTRODUCTION

Debates over "originalism" have been a central focus of contemporary constitutional theory for three decades. One of the features of this debate has been disagreement about what "originalism" is. More worrisome is the possibility that the arguments between contemporary originalists and their opponents, the "living constitutionalists," are confused – with each side of the debate making erroneous assumptions about the content of their opponent's theories.

The aim of this chapter is to clarify these debates by providing a history of contemporary originalism and then developing an account of the core or focal content of originalist theory. The history reveals that contemporary originalist theory has evolved – the mainstream of originalist theory began with an emphasis on the original intentions of the framers but has gradually moved to the view that the "original meaning" of the constitution is the "original public meaning" of the text. Even today, originalists disagree among themselves about a variety of important questions, including the normative justification for a constitutional practice that adheres to original meaning. Despite evolution and continued disagreement, however, contemporary originalist theory has a core of agreement on two propositions. First, almost all originalists agree that the linguistic meaning of each constitutional provision was fixed at the time that provision was adopted. Second, originalists agree that our constitutional practice both *is* (albeit imperfectly) and *should be* committed to the principle that the original meaning of the Constitution constrains judicial practice. The question whether living constitutionalists actually disagree with these core principles of originalist theory is a complex one – to which we shall return at the end of this chapter.

II. A WORD ABOUT THE WORD: THE ORIGINS OF "ORIGINALISM"

The first appearance of the term "originalism" in Westlaw's database of legal periodicals is found in an article by Paul Brest in 1981,[1] but Brest had used both "originalism" and "originalist" in 1980[2] (in an article that is not included in the database). So far as Brest knows, he coined the word.[3] Here is how Brest defined "originalism":

> By "originalism" I mean the familiar approach to constitutional adjudication that accords binding authority to the text of the Constitution or the intentions of its adopters.[4]

The disjunctive "or" in the last clause of Brest's definition presaged a debate among originalists, but what is most striking about this passage is Brest's assumption that his audience already understood the features of the view he was about to criticize. Brest's neologism caught on, and the words "originalism" and "originalist" appear frequently from 1981 onward.[5]

Whatever the origins of the terms "originalism" and "originalist," scholarly usage of related phrases extends at least as far back as the 1930s. The phrase "original meaning" was used in the constitutional context in a Yale Law Journal article in 1938 discussing the controversy over "substantive due process":

> There would be far greater advantage in restoring the original meaning of the 'privileges and immunities' clause and by the process of inclusion and exclusion letting the country know what are now federal privileges, than in forcing the court to draw upon the fathomless depths of the 'due process' clause to give effect to their personal convictions of economic and social propriety.[6]

It is perhaps no coincidence that the original meaning of the Privileges *or* Immunities Clause continues to hold the constitutional stage seventy years later.

[1] Paul Brest, "The Fundamental Rights Controversy: The Essential Contradictions of Normative Constitutional Scholarship," 90 Yale L.J. 1063 at 1090 (1981).

[2] Paul Brest, "The Misconceived Quest for the Original Understanding," 60 B.U.L. Rev. 204 at 234 (1980) [Brest, "Misconceived Quest"].

[3] Email exchange between Lawrence B. Solum and Paul Brest, December 2, 2009.

[4] Brest, "Misconceived Quest," *supra* note 2 at 204.

[5] For example, a search on Google's Books Ngram Viewer reveals no use of the term before 1980 and a steady increase in use of the word "originalism" in books published after the early 1980s. *See* http://ngrams.googlelabs.com/graph?content=Originalism&year_start=1975&year_end=2008&corpus=0&smoothing=3 (search for "originalism" from 1975 to 2008 in the "English" database on Google Books).

[6] Edwin Borchard, "The Supreme Court and Private Rights," 47 Yale L.J. 1051 at 1063 (1938).

The related phrase "original intentions" appeared in 1938, in a closely related context:

> Wholly apart from Bingham's personal understanding of his phraseology, his original intentions in drafting it, or the relations existing between the Cleveland and Mahoning Railroad and other members of the Joint Committee, it is possible that Reverdy Johnson, in the course of the Committee's deliberations, or perhaps even in private conversation with Conkling, mentioned Justice Grier's decision as among the most recent involving the due process clause, and in this manner precipitated a frank discussion of the entire problem of corporate rights.[7]

And "original understanding" made its first appearance in the Westlaw database in a well-known 1949 article by Charles Fairman.[8]

Judicial usage of the "originalism" and the associated phrases "original meaning," "original intentions," and "original understanding" in a constitutional context seems to post-date academic usage. The first use of the phrase "original meaning" in the text (exclusive of citations) of an opinion by a Supreme Court Justice occurred in Justice Black's dissent in *Harper v. Virginia State Bd. of Elections*[9] in 1966:

> Since the *Breedlove* and *Butler* cases were decided the Federal Constitution has not been amended in the only way it could constitutionally have been, that is, as provided in Article V of the Constitution. I would adhere to the holding of those cases. The Court, however, overrules *Breedlove* in part, but its opinion reveals that it does so not by using its limited power to interpret the original meaning of the Equal Protection Clause, but by giving that clause a new meaning which it believes represents a better governmental policy. From this action I dissent.[10]

The first similar occurrence of "original meaning" in a majority opinion occurs in a footnote in Justice Powell's 1977 opinion for the Court in *Ingraham v. Wright*.[11] "Original understanding" made its first similar appearance in Justice Harlan's 1970 dissent and concurrence in *Oregon v. Mitchell*.[12] The term "original intentions" first occurred in Chief Justice Berger's 1983 dissent in *Solem v.*

[7] Howard Jay Graham, "The 'Conspiracy Theory' of the Fourteenth Amendment," 48 Yale L.J. 171 at 189–90 (1938) (citation omitted).

[8] Charles Fairman, "Does the Fourteenth Amendment Incorporate the Bill of Rights?: The Original Understanding," 2 Stan. L. Rev. 5 at 5 (1949) (exploring the meaning of the Fourteenth Amendment's clauses "at the time the Amendment was adopted").

[9] 383 U.S. 663 at 671 (1966).

[10] *Ibid.* at 671–2.

[11] *Ingraham v. Wright*, 430 U.S. 651 at 670 n. 39 (1977).

[12] 400 U.S. 112 at 165 (1970).

Helm.[13] The term "originalist" first occurred in Justice Scalia's 1995 dissenting opinion in *Roper v. Simmons*,[14] and "originalism" made its first appearance in Justice Stevens' 2005 dissenting opinion in *Van Orden v. Perry*.[15]

The word "originalism" is a neologism – a word that was coined for the purpose of carving up theoretical space. Brest's original usage introduced an ambiguity by referring to "text" or "intentions." In addition, Brest's new word resonated – presumably this was deliberate – with other phrases with long histories of usage in a variety of legal contexts ("original meaning," "original understanding," and "original intention"). Moreover, Brest used the terms "originalism" and "originalist" to refer to a position that he was criticizing. Brest's term caught on, and eventually was adopted by proponents of the views that had affinities with the object of his critique. As a consequence, the words "originalism" and "originalist" are ambiguous – used by scholars, lawyers, judges, and the public in a variety of different ways. It seems likely that as a matter of lexicography, "originalism" is a family resemblance term – with several overlapping senses.

This deep ambiguity in the meaning of originalism is further complicated by the sociology of the legal academy and the politics of judicial interpretation. Legal theorists who self-identify as originalists are likely to strive to police the boundaries of the "originalism," seeking to exclude implausible views and to focus debate on the versions of originalism that they believe are true, correct, or most reasonable. Legal theorists who oppose originalism may have precisely the opposite motivation, seeking to identify originalism with its least defensible variations. Political champions of originalism are likely to focus on simplified "sound bite" versions of the theory that conflate the content of originalist theory with the goals it seeks to achieve: "Originalism is the theory that judges should follow the law and not make it." Likewise, political opponents might define originalism as a view that is obviously unpalatable: "Originalism is anti-woman."

For all these reasons, the road to conceptual clarity in debates about originalism will be rocky. The quest for agreement on a single definition of originalism is likely to prove Quixotic. For this reason, stipulated definitions of originalism should be avoided. Readers of theoretical texts are imperfect, and the stipulated meaning of "originalism" is likely to be ignored or forgotten. A more promising approach should begin with the facts. "Originalism" is an ambiguous theoretical term. There is a family of originalist constitutional theories. To make progress in the debates about "originalism," we will need to map the

[13] 463 U.S. 277 at 310 (1983).
[14] 543 U.S. 551 at 626 (1977).
[15] 545 U.S. 677 at 729 (2005).

theoretical space, identifying the ways in which different versions of originalism vary and the ways in which they resemble one another.

III. A VERY SHORT HISTORY OF CONTEMPORARY ORIGINALIST THEORY

The first step toward an answer to the question "What is originalism?" was an investigation of the origins of the word "originalism." The second step is a history of the theories associated with that word. The history offered here is necessarily brief, partial, and incomplete. A complete version of the story would require a long monograph. The aim of the very short history in this part is to identify the most important theoretical developments, with an emphasis on the developments that are most relevant to the current state of originalist theory.[16]

A. *Original Intentions of the Framers*

Contemporary debates about originalism trace back to the early 1970s. In 1971, Robert Bork wrote "Neutral Principles and Some First Amendment Problems,"[17] an article that is sometimes considered the opening move in the development of contemporary originalist theory. Bork's essay was only loosely "originalist" in the contemporary senses of that term. The following passage is representative:

> There appear to be two proper methods of deriving rights from the Constitution. The first is to take from the document rather specific values that text or history show the framers actually to have intended and which are capable of being translated into principled rules. We may call these specified rights. The second method derives rights from governmental processes established by the Constitution. These are secondary or derived individual rights. This latter category is extraordinarily important. This method of derivation is essential to the interpretation of the first amendment, to voting rights, to criminal procedure and to much else.[18]

The emphasis on "text" and "history" is recognizably originalist, but Bork's notion of "derived rights" is not clearly anchored in original meaning or original intentions.

[16] For a different view from an earlier time, see Daniel A. Farber, "The Originalism Debate: A Guide for the Perplexed," 49 Ohio St. L.J. 1085 at 1085 (1989) (offering a concise "tourist guide" introduction to the "original intent" debate).

[17] Robert H. Bork, "Neutral Principles and Some First Amendment Problems," 47 Ind. L.J. 1 (1971).

[18] *Ibid.* at 17.

In 1976, then-Associate Justice William Rehnquist authored "The Notion of a Living Constitution," which, based on the writings of the Framers, explicitly criticized living constitutionalism and implicitly endorsed originalism.[19] A year later, in 1977, Raoul Berger penned *Government by Judiciary*,[20] which argued that the Supreme Court's interpretations of the Fourteenth Amendment were contrary to the original intentions of its Framers. In 1985, then-Attorney General Edwin Meese put originalism on the political agenda in a well-publicized speech before the American Bar Association.[21] Meese's speech included the following passage:

> In reviewing a term of the Court, it is important to take a moment and reflect upon the proper role of the Supreme Court in our constitutional system. The intended role of the judiciary generally and the Supreme Court in particular was to serve as the "bulwarks of a limited constitution." The judges, the Founders believed, would not fail to regard the Constitution as "fundamental law" and would "regulate their decisions" by it. As the "faithful guardians of the Constitution," the judges were expected to resist any political effort to depart from the literal provisions of the Constitution. The text of the document and the original intention of those who framed it would be the judicial standard in giving effect to the Constitution.[22]

Bork, Rehnquist, Berger, and Meese did not develop anything that approaches a full-blown constitutional theory, but their views suggested something like the theory we now call "original intentions originalism," the view that the original intentions of the Framers should guide constitutional interpretation.

B. The Misconceived Quest and the Original Understanding of Original Intentions

Following Berger's book, but five years before Meese's speech, Paul Brest wrote "The Misconceived Quest for the Original Understanding,"[23] one of the most

[19] William H. Rehnquist, "The Notion of a Living Constitution," 54 Tex. L. Rev. 693 (1976).

[20] Raoul Berger, *Government by Judiciary* (1977).

[21] See Edwin Meese III, "Speech Before the American Bar Association" (July 9, 1985), *reprinted in The Great Debate: Interpreting Our Written Constitution* (Paul G. Cassel ed., 1986), online at http://www.fed-soc.org/resources/id.49/default.asp [Meese, "Speech Before the American Bar Association"]; see also Edwin Meese III, "The Case for Originalism," The Heritage Foundation (June 6, 2005), online at http://www.heritage.org/Press/Commentary/a.cfm>; Lynette Clemetson, "Meese's Influence Looms in Today's Judicial Wars," *New York Times*, Apr. 17, 2005, at A1.

[22] Meese, "Speech Before the American Bar Association," *ibid.*

[23] Brest, "Misconceived Quest," *supra* note 2.

cited and influential contributions to constitutional theory.[24] Brest's article advanced a variety of criticisms of original intentions originalism, including: (1) the difficulty of ascertaining *the* institutional intention of a multimember body in general;[25] (2) the particular problems associated with identifying *the* intention of the members of the Philadelphia Convention and the various state ratifying conventions in the case of the original Constitution and of Congress and the various state legislatures in the case of amendments;[26] (3) the problem of determining the level of generality or specificity of the Framers' and ratifiers' intentions;[27] (4) the problem of inferring intentions from constitutional structure;[28] (5) the difficulty of translating the Framers' and ratifiers' beliefs and values given changes in circumstances over time;[29] (6) the problem of the democratic legitimacy – that is, that the Constitution of 1789 was drafted and ratified without the participation of women and slaves;[30] and (7) the problem of instability, in that an inflexible constitutional order cannot adapt to changing circumstances.[31] Brest had much more to say, and there were many other critics of originalism, but this list is sufficient to illustrate the reception that originalism received from constitutional theorists in the late 1970s and early 1980s.

Brest also raised the problem of the Framers' and ratifiers' interpretive intentions,[32] and his remarks anticipated Jefferson Powell's 1985 article, "The Original Understanding of Original Intent."[33] Powell's article interrogated the assumption that original intentions originalists believed that the Framers themselves expected that the Constitution would be interpreted to conform to their intentions. Although Powell conceded that there were references to "original intention" and "intent of the framers" in the constitutional discourse of the Founding era, he argued that those phrases did not represent an early version of original intentions originalism. Instead, he argued that "[t]he Philadelphia framers' primary expectation regarding constitutional interpretation was that the Constitution, like any other legal document, would be interpreted in accord with its express language."[34] Both the evidence for Powell's thesis

[24] A Westlaw search of the JLR database for the string corresponding to the title yielded 719 hits on November 10, 2008.

[25] Brest, "Misconceived Quest," *supra* note 2 at 214.

[26] *Ibid.* at 214–15.

[27] *Ibid.* at 216–17.

[28] *Ibid.* at 217–18.

[29] *Ibid.* at 219–22.

[30] *Ibid.* at 230.

[31] *Ibid.* at 231.

[32] *Ibid.* at 215–16.

[33] H. Jefferson Powell, "The Original Understanding of Original Intent," 98 Harv. L. Rev. 885 (1985).

[34] *Ibid.* at 903.

and its implications are controversial, but its effect on scholarly opinion was profound. The strongest implication of the article is that original intentions originalism is a self-effacing theory because it requires that the Framers' intentions regarding interpretation be respected, but those intentions require that the Framers' intentions be disregarded.

Brest and Powell were hardly the only critics of original intentions originalism, but their arguments, combined with others, were important in forming the scholarly consensus of the era.[35] Essentially, that consensus accepted the claim that the original intentions of the Framers could not serve as the basis for a viable theory of constitutional interpretation and construction.[36]

C. *Original Understanding of the Ratifiers*

During this period, the originalism debate took a brief detour into a variant of original intentions originalism that emphasized the understandings[37] or intentions of the ratifiers – either the state ratifying conventions understood as corporate bodies or of the individuals who attended the ratifying conventions and voted in favor of ratification.[38]

We need not tarry long over this twist in the debate. The move to ratifiers' understanding or intent is best understood in conjunction with popular sovereignty as a justification for originalism. The ratifiers, rather than the Framers, could plausibly be viewed as expressing the political will of "We the People." However, all of the problems that attended the equation of constitutional meaning with Framers' intent seem to attach to ratifiers' intent.

[35] This is not an intellectual history of the originalism debates, and I am not claiming that either Brest or Powell articulated the first or best version of the claims they made. No string cite can do justice to the literature. There were many influential critics of original intentions originalism; one of the most important was Ronald Dworkin. *See* Ronald Dworkin, "The Forum of Principle," 56 N.Y.U. L. Rev. 469 at 470 (1981).

[36] Randy E. Barnett, "An Originalism for Nonoriginalists," 45 Loy. L. Rev. 611 (1999) ("The received wisdom among law professors is that originalism is dead.") [Barnett, "An Originalism for Nonoriginalists"].

[37] See Richard H. Fallon, Jr., "Judicially Manageable Standards and Constitutional Meaning," 119 Harv. L. Rev. 1275 at 1317 (1996) (defining "originalism" as "the theory that the original understanding of those who wrote and ratified various constitutional provisions determines their current meaning") [Fallon, "Manageable Standards"].

[38] See Charles A. Miller, *The Supreme Court and the Uses of History* (1969) at 157–88 (arguing that originalism should look to the intent of the ratifiers as well as of the Framers); see also Charles A. Lofgren, "The Original Understanding of Original Intent," 5 Const. Comment. 77 at 113 (1988) ("Indeed, it is not too much to say that at least some of the founders saw the ratifiers' historical or subjective intent as a check on constructions which cut loose from the original understandings of the sovereign people.").

Moreover, evidence may be even more difficult to obtain[39] and the problems of group intention – of multiple conventions with multiple members – even more confounding with respect to ratifiers' intent. To the extent that the ratifiers' understanding is rooted in the public meaning, the emphasis on ratifiers is merely a way station on the journey from original intentions to original public meaning.[40]

D. *We the People*

The year before Meese gave his speech to the American Bar Association and Jefferson Powell wrote about the original understanding of original intent, Bruce Ackerman delivered his *Storrs Lectures*, entitled "Discovering the Constitution," at Yale Law School.[41] It was in these lectures that Ackerman's theory of constitutional politics made its first wide impression on the community of constitutional scholars. Ackerman's theory distinguishes ordinary politics – what happens when state legislatures and Congress enact statutes, for example – from constitutional politics. Here is the very first statement of Ackerman's view, *dualism*, in the second lecture:

> [T]he Federalist elaborates a dualistic conception of political life. One form of political action – I shall call it constitutional politics – is characterized by Publian appeals to the common good, ratified by a mobilized mass of American citizens expressing their assent through extraordinary institutional forms. Although constitutional politics is the highest kind of politics, it should be permitted to dominate the nation's life only during rare periods of heightened political consciousness. During the long periods between these constitutional moments, a second form of activity – I shall call it normal politics – prevails. Here, factions try to manipulate the constitutional forms of political life to

[39] See Henry P. Monaghan, "Our Perfect Constitution," 56 N.Y.U. L. Rev. 353 at 375 n.130 (1981) ("Although the intention of the ratifiers, not the Framers, is in principle decisive, the difficulties of ascertaining the intent of the ratifiers leaves little choice but to accept the intent of the Framers as a fair reflection of it.").

[40] Similar points could be made about what might be called "popular meaning," the view that the relevant intentions or understandings should be those of "We the People" or the popular sovereign – the relevant actor for popular constitutionalism. If the relevant intentions are those of each and every citizen, then popular constitutionalism suffers from compounded versions of the ills that afflict intentionalism. If popular constitutionalism points to public meaning, then it is simply another version of original meaning originalism. For discussion of popular constitutionalism, see Larry Kramer, *The People Themselves: Popular Constitutionalism and Judicial Review* (2004); see also Larry Alexander & Lawrence B. Solum, "Popular? Constitutionalism?" 118 Harv. L. Rev. 1594 (2005) (book review).

[41] Bruce A. Ackerman, "The Storrs Lectures: Discovering the Constitution," 93 Yale L.J. 1013 (1984) [Ackerman, "Discovering the Constitution"].

> pursue their own narrow interests. Normal politics must be tolerated in the name of individual liberty; it is, however, democratically *inferior* to the intermittent and irregular politics of public virtue associated with moments of constitutional creation.[42]

Ackerman's theory served as an answer to Alexander Bickel's countermajoritarian difficulty: the problem of democratic legitimacy that attends judicial review by unelected judges.[43] Judges as faithful agents of the "We the People," who legislate in rare constitutional moments – or later "periods" – act more democratically than do legislators, who serve special interests and escape the people's attention during the extended periods of ordinary politics.

As developed in the *Storrs Lectures*, Ackerman's theory focused on three constitutional moments: the Founding (the Constitution of 1789), Reconstruction (the Thirteenth, Fourteenth, and Fifteenth Amendments), and the New Deal. Here is the initial appearance of that idea in the lectures:

> Speaking schematically, this historical story is dominated by three peaks of high importance that tower over valleys full of more particular meanings. The first peak, of course, is the Founding itself: the framing of the original Constitution and the Bill of Rights, *Marbury v. Madison* and *McCulloch v. Maryland*. The second peak is constituted by the legal events surrounding the Civil War: the judicial failure in *Dred Scott* and the constitutional affirmations of the Civil War Amendments. The third peak centers around the legitimation of the activist welfare state: the long Progressive struggle against judicial resistance and the dramatic capitulation by the Old Court before the New Deal in 1937. Time and again, we return to these moments; the lessons we learn from them control the meanings we give to our present constitutional predicaments.[44]

Because Ackerman's theory purported to legitimize progressive New Deal constitutionalism, his view might have been construed as the polar opposite of originalism, but at a deep level, Ackerman's theory seemed to require an account of original meaning. Without employing original meaning, judicial enforcement of the Constitution could not be legitimized by democratic constitutional politics. In other words, a theory of original meaning is required for constitutional content to be determined by "We the People."

[42] *Ibid.* at 1022–3 (citations omitted).

[43] See generally Alexander M. Bickel, *The Least Dangerous Branch: The Supreme Court at the Bar of Politics* (1962); see also Kenneth D. Ward & Cecilia R. Castillo, eds., *The Judiciary and American Democracy: Alexander Bickel, the Countermajoritarian Difficulty and Contemporary Constitutional Theory* (2005).

[44] Ackerman, "Discovering the Constitution," *supra* note 41 at 1051–2.

Ackerman's development of popular sovereignty theory has been extraordinarily influential, and others have contributed important work in this vein,[45] prominently Akhil Reed Amar,[46] Ackerman's colleague at Yale Law School. Cass Sunstein has described Amar's position in the following terms:

> [I]n the law schools the most influential originalist may be Akhil Reed Amar, an ingenious and prolific scholar at Yale Law School. Describing himself as a "textualist" who is interested in history, Amar is methodologically quite close to Scalia. He is intensely interested in the text and in the historical record, and he is generally searching for the original meaning of contested terms. Amar wishes to know what the Constitution "really means," and he puts that question as if it were largely or entirely a matter of excavation.[47]

Although Sunstein's interpretation of Amar is surely plausible, characterizing Ackerman and Amar's theoretical position in originalist terms is problematic, in no small part because they both eschew explicit theorizing about constitutional interpretation. Nevertheless, even if Ackerman and Amar do not describe their views as originalist, it is clear that their approaches to the Constitution, which emphasize popular sovereignty and the constitutional text, have had both direct and indirect influences over contemporary theoretical debates explicitly concerned with originalism.[48]

E. Original Public Meaning and the New Originalisms

This sets the stage for what is sometimes called "the New Originalism"[49] and is also labeled "Original Public Meaning Originalism."[50] Whatever the actual origins of this theory, the conventional story identifies Justice Antonin Scalia as having a key role. As early as 1986, Scalia gave a speech exhorting

45 See, *e.g.*, Kurt T. Lash, "A Textual-Historical Theory of the Ninth Amendment," 60 Stan. L. Rev. 895 (2007) [Lash, "A Textual Historical Theory"]; Kurt T. Lash, "Originalism, Popular Sovereignty, and Reverse Stare Decisis," 93 Va. L. Rev. 1437 (2007) [Lash, "Originalism"].

46 See Akhil Reed Amar, *America's Constitution: A Biography* (2005); Akhil Reed Amar, *The Bill of Rights* (1998).

47 Cass R. Sunstein, "Originalism for Liberals," The New Republic, Sept. 28, 1998, at 31, online at http://home.uchicago.edu/~csunstei/originalism.html (reviewing Amar, *The Bill of Rights*, *ibid*, and Akhil Reed Amar & Alan Hirsch, *For the People* [1998]).

48 Thus, it is no accident that Amar and Ackerman's students describe themselves as originalists. See, *e.g.*, Lash, "A Textual-Historical Theory," *supra* note 45 at 900 ("I will consider the historical record and attempt to identify which of the possible textual meanings are more or less plausible, given historical evidence of original public understanding. In this way, I hope to provide an account of the Ninth Amendment satisfactory in terms of both originalism and textualism.").

49 See, e.g., Keith Whittington, "The New Originalism", 2 Geo. J.L. & Pub. Pol'y 599 (2004).

50 See, *e.g.*, Randy E. Barnett, "An Originalism for Nonoriginalists" *supra* note 36.

originalists to "change the label from the Doctrine of Original Intent to the Doctrine of Original Meaning."[51] The phrase "original public meaning" seems to have entered the contemporary theoretical debates through the work of Gary Lawson,[52] with Steven Calabresi as another "early adopter."[53] The core idea of the revised theory is that the original meaning of the Constitution is the original *public* meaning of the constitutional text.

Randy Barnett[54] and Keith Whittington[55] have played prominent roles in the development of the New Originalism. Both Barnett and Whittington base their theories on a foundation of "original public meaning," but they build on the views of Scalia and Lawson in a variety of interesting ways. For the purposes of this very brief survey, perhaps their most important move is to embrace the distinction between "constitutional interpretation," understood as the enterprise of discerning the semantic content of the Constitution, and "constitutional construction," which we might tentatively define as the activity of determining the legal effect of the constitutional text. One mode of construction involves judicial specification of constitutional doctrine when the text is vague, but construction can take place in the political branches as well.[56] This distinction explicitly acknowledges what we might call *the fact of constitutional underdeterminacy*: The original meaning of the text does not fully determine constitutional doctrine or its application to particular cases.[57]

[51] Antonin Scalia, Address Before the Attorney General's Conference on Economic Liberties in Washington, D.C. (June 14, 1986), *in Original Meaning Jurisprudence*: *A Sourcebook* 101 at 106 (U.S. Dep't of Justice ed., 1987); see also Caleb Nelson, "Originalism and Interpretive Conventions", 70 U. Chi. L. Rev. 519 at 554–55 (2003) (noting that most originalists have accepted Justice Scalia's suggestion).

[52] See Gary Lawson, "Proving the Law", 86 Nw. U. L. Rev. 859 at 875 (1992). For extended discussions of "original public meaning," see Vasan Kesavan & Michael Stokes Paulson, "The Interpretive Force of the Constitution's Secret Drafting History", 91 Geo. L.J. 1113 at 1127 (2003); Samuel T. Morison, "The Crooked Timber of Liberal Democracy", 2005 Mich. St. L. Rev. 461 at 465.

[53] See Steven G. Calabresi & Saikrishna B. Prakash, "The President's Power to Execute the Laws", 104 Yale L.J. 541 at 553 (1994).

[54] See Randy E. Barnett, *Restoring the Lost Constitution* (2004).

[55] See Keith E. Whittington, *Constitutional Construction* (1999); Keith E. Whittington, *Constitutional Interpretation* (1999).

[56] Another important early adopter of this distinction (in the context of constitutional theory) was Robert Clinton. *See* Robert N. Clinton, "Original Understanding, Legal Realism, and the Interpretation of 'This Constitution,'" 72 Iowa L. Rev. 1177 (1987).

[57] See Lawrence B. Solum, "Semantic and Normative Originalism: Comments on Brian Leiter's 'Justifying Originalism'" Legal Theory Blog, Oct. 30, 2007, <http://lsolum.typepad.com/legaltheory/2007/10/semantic-and-no.html> (observing that conventional semantic meaning of a text can underdetermine its application in several ways); *cf.* Lawrence B. Solum, "On the Indeterminacy Crisis: Critiquing Critical Dogma", 54 U. Chi. L. Rev. 462 (1987) (distinguishing determinacy, indeterminacy, and underdeterminacy).

With this turn, original meaning originalists explicitly embrace the idea that when the original public meaning of the text "runs out," application of the linguistic meaning of the constitutional text to a particular dispute must be guided by something other than original meaning.

Once originalist theory (in some important instantiations) had acknowledged that vague constitutional provisions required construction, this step opened the door for reconciliation between originalism and living constitutionalism. The key figure in that reconciliation has been Jack Balkin through his influential 2006 and 2007 essays, "Abortion and Original Meaning"[58] and "Original Meaning and Constitutional Redemption."[59] In these essays, Balkin argued for a reconciliation of original meaning originalism with living constitutionalism according to a theory that might be called "the method of text and principle." The meaning of the "text" provides a constraining framework within which constitutional "principles" operate. One understanding of Balkin's view is that the "text" requires interpretation and the "principles" are matters of constitutional construction.

Predating much of the American work on the New Originalism was Jeffrey Goldsworthy's work, addressing the Australian Constitution but developed with an explicit awareness of the theoretical debates swirling around American constitutionalism. Goldsworthy's first major statement, "Originalism in Constitutional Interpretation,"[60] was published in an Australian law review in 1997. As Goldsworthy's work illustrates, innovations in American constitutional theory may have been anticipated elsewhere, and American theorists have no monopoly on the creation of new (or the resurrection of old) theoretical constructs.

F. *Original Applications and Original Methods*

Two very recent ideas deserve particular mention: "original applications" and "original methods." The phrase "original applications" or "original expected applications" seems to originate with Jack Balkin,[61] but Mark Greenberg and

[58] Jack M. Balkin, "Abortion and Original Meaning", 24 Const. Comment. 291 (2007) [Balkin, "Abortion"].

[59] Jack M. Balkin, "Original Meaning and Constitutional Redemption", 24 Const. Comment. 427 (2007) [Balkin, "Original Meaning"].

[60] Jeffrey Goldsworthy, "Originalism in Constitutional Interpretation", (1997) 25 Fed. L. Rev. 1; and Jeffrey Goldsworthy, "The Case for Originalism" in this volume. See also Lawrence B. Solum, "Goldsworthy on the New Originalism", *Legal Theory Blog*, Nov. 2, 2007, online: <http://lsolum.typepad.com/legaltheory/2007/11/goldsworthy-on-.html>.

[61] See Jack M. Balkin, "Abortion", *supra* note 58 at 293; Jack Balkin, "Original Meaning", *supra* note 59; Jack Balkin, "Alive and Kicking: Why No One Truly Believes in a Dead Constitution",

Harry Litman articulated similar distinctions between "original meaning" and "original practices" and "meaning" and "application" in their important 1998 article, "The Meaning of Original Meaning."[62] Although Greenberg and Litman deserve the credit for the deepest and most thorough discussion of the issues, my account here will focus on Balkin's formulation, which brings the idea of original expected applications into the New Originalism, not as a component but rather by way of exclusion. Greenberg and Litman saw their point primarily as a criticism of originalism; Balkin sees the same issue, but concludes that originalism is strengthened by excluding "original expected applications."[63]

The distinction is a simple one. The linguistic meaning of a text is one thing, and expectations about the application of that meaning to future cases are a different thing. Balkin makes use of the distinction to argue that some originalists have conflated meaning with expected applications:

> Originalists generally assume that if we do not apply the constitutional text in the way it was originally understood at the time of its adoption we are not following what the words mean and so will not be faithful to the Constitution as law. But they have tended to conflate two different ideas – the expected application of constitutional texts, which is not binding law, and the original meaning, which is. Indeed, many originalists who claim to be interested only in original meaning, like Justice Antonin Scalia, have encouraged this conflation of original meaning and original expected application in their practices of argument.[64]

The fact that *original expected applications* are distinct from *original meanings* should not imply that the two are unrelated. Expected applications of a text may offer evidence about its meanings, even if these applications are neither decisive evidence of meaning nor meaning itself.

Of course, some originalists may contest Balkin's move and argue that original expectations originalism is viable. The justification could be that reliance on original expectations is the distinctive characteristic that marks originalist theories as originalist.[65] However, this view appears incorrect given

Slate, Aug. 29, 2005, online: <http://www.slate.com/id/2125226/>; Jack Balkin, "Clarence Thomas's Originalism," *Balkinization*, July 11, 2007, online: <http://balkin.blogspot.com/2007/07/clarence-thomass-originalism.html>.

[62] Mark D. Greenberg & Harry Litman, "The Meaning of Original Meaning," 86 Geo. L.J. 569 (1998).

[63] Balkin, "Original Meaning," *supra* note 59 at 446.

[64] Balkin, "Abortion," *supra* note 58 at 292–3.

[65] *Cf.* Christopher L. Eisgruber, *Constitutional Self-Government* (2001) at 25–6 (characterizing originalism as relying on original expectations).

the history of originalist thought, and it is certainly contrary to the theories of New Originalists like Balkin, Barnett, and Whittington.

Another very recent development is the emergence of what might be called "original methods originalism," the view that the original meaning of the Constitution includes the methods of interpretation that the Framers, ratifiers, and/or public of the Founding era could, would, or should have expected to guide constitutional practice. This view is strongly associated with Michael Rappaport and John McGinnis.[66] They write:

> [T]he focus of originalism should be on how a reasonable person at the time of the Constitution's adoption would have understand (sic) its words and thought they should be interpreted. The Constitution's provisions were based on commonly accepted meanings and the interpretative rules of the time. Some of the provisions had clear meanings. Others may have seemed ambiguous, but the enactors would have believed that their future application would be based [on] the interpretive rules accepted at the time. Thus, their assessment of the meaning and the desirability of the Constitution would depend on the interpretive rules that they thought would apply.[67]

We can call this approach "original methods originalism," reflecting its commitment to the methods of interpretation that characterized the Founding era. Notice that McGinnis and Rappaport's formulation of their idea does not embrace the distinction between *interpretation* and *construction* in the Whittington/Barnett sense.[68]

In a different vein, an important contribution to understanding the implications of the New Originalism appeared in a 2006 article by Richard Fallon, titled "Judicially Manageable Standards and Constitutional Meaning."[69] Fallon does not embrace originalism, but he identified the key distinction

[66] Their view is stated briefly in John O. McGinnis & Michael B. Rappaport, "Original Interpretive Principles as the Core of Originalism," 24 Const. Comment 371 (2007).

[67] *Ibid.* at 374.

[68] To the extent that McGinnis and Rappaport believe that original methods recover the linguistic meaning or semantic content of the constitutional text, their theory faces severe obstacles. The public linguistic meaning of a text cannot be the legal construction that is placed upon that text by legal interpreters. Legal methods operate on the semantic content fixed by linguistic meaning: they do not create it. To think otherwise is to confuse meaning in the semantic sense with meaning in the applicative sense. See Lawrence B. Solum, "Semantic Originalism" (November 22, 2008). Illinois Public Law Research Paper No. 07–24. Available at SSRN: <http://ssrn.com/abstract=1120244>.

[69] Fallon, "Manageable Standards," *supra* note 37; see also Michell N. Berman, "Constitutional Decision Rules," 90 Virginia L. Rev. 1 (2004).

between the meaning of the Constitution (its semantic content) and implementing rules of constitutional law (legal content):

> Despite large apparent differences between originalism and nonoriginalist theories, originalist and nonoriginalist judges converge in their decisions surprisingly often. Given the strident debates among constitutional theorists, one well might wonder how so much agreement could eventuate. The reason, I would suggest, is that what we call constitutional theories or theories of constitutional interpretation are often theories about constitutional meaning that implicitly accept the permissibility of a disparity between constitutional meaning and implementing doctrine. If constitutional theories fix the meaning of the Constitution, but stipulate that implementing doctrines sometimes permissibly diverge from it, then such theories are less complete and thus less practically significant than their proponents suggest.[70]

Fallon's distinction between the semantic content of the Constitution and the legal content of constitutional law put the following question of contribution on the table: How does the semantic content contribute to legal content?

G. *New Critics of the New Originalism*

The New Originalism has sparked a new wave of criticism.[71] The first of the new critics is Stephen Griffin, the author of "Rebooting Originalism,"[72] a powerful critique of the New Originalism. Griffin's critique has thoroughly absorbed the theoretical significance of the shift from original intentions to original public meaning, but it is not clear that he fully appreciates the importance of the Whittington/Barnett distinction between construction and interpretation.[73] Although Griffin has a variety of important and well-argued criticisms of the new originalists, two features of his article are especially important for present purposes. First, Griffin's core argument against the New Originalism is normative: He argues that consistent and exclusive use of originalist methodology would represent a major change in interpretive practice, and that originalists must therefore offer a normative justification for their theory.[74] Second, Griffin's critique does not consider the possibility that

[70] *Ibid.* at 1317–18 (citation omitted).

[71] See, *e.g.*, Mark Tushnet, "Heller and the New Originalism," 69 Ohio St. L.J. 609 (2008).

[72] Stephen M. Griffin, "Rebooting Originalism," 2008 U. Ill. L. Rev. 1185 (2008).

[73] The distinction is never discussed in a theoretical way. The first mention appears on page 34 of his essay. *Ibid.* at 1217.

[74] *Ibid.* at 1196–1205.

original meaning originalism might include a semantic thesis – a non-normative claim about the linguistic meaning of the Constitution.[75]

A second new critic is Mitchell Berman, whose critique of originalism is tendentiously titled "Originalism Is Bunk."[76] Berman's essay is deep and rich, raising some old objections to originalism, providing new foundations for others, and developing new positions. One of the crucial moves in his piece is his argument that the term "Originalism" (when capitalized) should be reserved for the strong claim that original meaning, whatever that might be, should trump other considerations in constitutional practice. He summarizes this claim as follows:

> Originalism proper is strong originalism – the thesis that original meaning either is the *only* proper target of judicial constitutional interpretation or that it has at least lexical priority over any other candidate meanings the text might bear (again, contrary judicial precedents possibly excepted). [FN49] It entails (but is not equivalent to) the thesis that nothing that transpires after ratification of a particular constitutional provision, save a subsequent constitutional amendment, has operative (as opposed to evidential) bearing on what courts ought to identify as constitutional meaning.[77]

Berman's identification of "Originalism" (with a capital "O") with what he calls "strong originalism" is surely mistaken. For example, Justice Scalia's (paradigmatically originalist) opinion in *Heller* did not dismiss precedent as irrelevant; instead, he argued that the only relevant precedent, *United States v. Miller*,[78] was distinguishable.[79]

In 2006, the New Originalist theorist, Randy Barnett, wrote "Scalia's Infidelity: A Critique of Faint-Hearted Originalism," which explicitly disagrees with Justice Antonin Scalia on the question of force, contending that Scalia allows departure from original meaning on the basis of three factors: (1) precedent, (2) justiciability, and (3) settled historical practice.[80] In addition to Scalia, originalists of various stripes have taken the position that original meaning can be trumped by precedent for a variety of reasons and is subject to a variety

[75] No variant of the root word "semantic" appears in Griffin's article. Although the term "meaning" and its variants appear numerous times, there is no indication that Griffin appreciates the possibility that originalism might be a semantic theory.

[76] Mitchell N. Berman, "Originalism Is Bunk," 84 N.Y.U. L. Rev. 1 at 35 (2009) [Berman, "Originalism Is Bunk"]. See also the exchange between Berman and Stanley Fish in their contributions to this volume.

[77] Berman, "Originalism Is Bunk," *ibid.* at 22.

[78] 307 U.S. 174 (1939).

[79] *District of Columbia v. Heller*, 128 S.Ct. 2783 at 2814 (2008) [*Heller*].

[80] Randy E. Barnett, "Scalia's Infidelity: A Critique of 'Faint-Hearted' Originalism," 75 U. Cin. L. Rev. 7 at 13 (2006).

of constraints, as evidenced by the work of Kurt Lash, Lee Strang, and this author.[81]

Confining "Originalism" (in its focal meaning) to the view that original meaning must trump all other considerations is misleading. Moreover, this move has the unfortunate effect of defining the topography of argument in a way that eliminates plausible forms of originalism from the originalist camp, leaving only the most implausible and extreme views in contention. The equivalent move by a critic of non-originalism would be to define "Non-originalism" with a capital "N" as the view that "original meaning" in any form can never be considered in constitutional interpretation or construction. A more productive characterization of the debate might focus on three disagreements between originalists and non-originalists: (1) debates over the question whether the linguistic meaning of the Constitution should be viewed as fixed at the time each provision is framed and ratified; (2) arguments about the relative importance of the original meaning of the text versus other considerations, such as purpose, practice, precedent, and principles; and (3) differences over the extent to which constitutional construction is constrained by the linguistic meaning of the text.

A third source of new criticism is "*Living Originalism*,"[82] jointly authored by Thomas Colby and Peter Smith. They state their argument boldly:

> In fact, just as with nonoriginalism, there is profound internal disagreement on the originalist side of the line. A review of originalists' work reveals originalism to be not a single, coherent, unified theory of constitutional interpretation, but rather a smorgasbord of distinct constitutional theories that share little in common except a misleading reliance on a single label.[83]

The question that Smith and Colby raise is an important one, and we shall return to it in Part IV of this chapter.

[81] See Lash, "Originalism," *supra* note 45 at 1441 (stating that "popular sovereignty-based originalism . . . does not require the complete abandonment of stare decisis" and "[a] theory of stare decisis that takes into account the majoritarian commitment of popular sovereignty may justify upholding an erroneous precedent"); Lawrence B. Solum, "The Supreme Court in Bondage: Constitutional Stare Decisis, Legal Formalism, and the Future Of Unenumerated Rights," 9 U. Pa. J. Const. L. 155 at 159 (2006) (arguing for originalist theory that gives trumping force to precedent); Lee J. Strang, "An Originalist Theory of Precedent: Originalism, Nonoriginalist Precedent, and the Common Good," 36 N.M. L. Rev. 419 at 420 (2006) (offering originalist theory in which "limited respect is due some nonoriginalist constitutional precedent").

[82] Thomas B. Colby & Peter J. Smith, "Living Originalism," 59 Duke L.J. 239 (2009) [Colby and Smith, "Living Originalism"].

[83] *Ibid.* at 244.

H. District of Columbia v. Heller & McDonald v. City of Chicago

Supreme Court decisions that squarely address the fundamental issues of constitutional theory are rare, but *District of Columbia v. Heller*[84] is such a decision. The key passage in the majority opinion is unmistakably originalist:

> In interpreting this text, we are guided by the principle that [t]he Constitution was written to be understood by the voters; its words and phrases were used in their normal and ordinary as distinguished from technical meaning.[85]

The implications of the majority's conclusion that the Second Amendment protects an individual right to possess and carry weapons were disputed by Justice Stevens and Justice Breyer in their dissenting opinions. Justice Stevens, in particular, offered a lengthy dissent, focusing in part on the purposes that animated the Second Amendment and raising a number of arguments relevant to the original intentions of the Framers.[86]

The majority opinion in *Heller* covers a good deal of territory, much of it contested by the dissents, but, for the purpose of completing this brief survey of the contemporary development of originalist theory, the important feature of *Heller* is methodological. The Court examined each of the operative words and phrases in the Second Amendment, examining the semantic content of "the people," "keep," "bear," and "arms." The Court concluded its examination as follows: "Putting all of these textual elements together, we find that they guarantee the individual right to possess and carry weapons in case of confrontation."[87] In examining each of the operative words and phrases, the Court examined evidence of usage from the period the Second Amendment was proposed and ratified. For example:

> Before addressing the verbs "keep" and "bear," we interpret their object: "Arms." The 18th-century meaning is no different from the meaning today. The 1773 edition of Samuel Johnson's dictionary defined "arms" as "weapons of offence, or armour of defence." Timothy Cunningham's important 1771 legal dictionary defined "arms" as "any thing that a man wears for his defence, or takes into his hands, or useth in wrath to cast at or strike another."[88]

Another example:

> The phrase "keep arms" was not prevalent in the written documents of the founding period that we have found, but there are a few examples, all of which favor viewing the right to "keep Arms" as an individual right unconnected

[84] *Heller, supra* note 79.
[85] *Ibid.* at 2788 (citations omitted).
[86] See, *e.g.*, *ibid.* at 2837 n. 28 (Stevens, J., dissenting).
[87] *Ibid.* at 2797 (majority opinion).
[88] *Ibid.* at 2791 (citations omitted).

> with militia service. William Blackstone, for example, wrote that Catholics convicted of not attending service in the Church of England suffered certain penalties, one of which was that they were not permitted to "keep arms in their houses."[89]

Additionally:

> At the time of the founding, as now, to "bear" meant to "carry."[90]

Bracketing the question as to whether *Heller*'s analysis of the linguistic evidence was correct, the methodology of Justice Scalia's majority opinion was clear: The Court focused on the evidence of the original public meaning of the text. Given the inevitable differences between judicial practice and constitutional theory, it is hard to imagine finding a clearer example of original public meaning originalism in an actual judicial decision.

Heller is not the Supreme Court's last word on originalism and the right to bear arms. In *McDonald v. City of Chicago*,[91] the Supreme Court addressed the question whether the Second Amendment right to bear arms applies to the states. This question implicates a long-standing constitutional controversy. Many originalists believe that the application of the Bill of Rights (including the Second Amendment) to the states should be grounded in the Privileges or Immunities Clause of the Fourteenth Amendment, but the Supreme Court's decisions have settled on the Due Process Clause as the basis for what is called "incorporation."[92] Although Justice Alito's plurality opinion contains originalist passages, it relies on the non-originalist approach.[93] Justice Thomas's concurring opinion, which provided the crucial fifth vote, rested incorporation on the Privileges or Immunities Clause instead.[94]

If *Heller* was a clear endorsement of originalism, *McDonald* is a mixed message at best. Prominent originalists, including Randy Barnett, have praised Justice Thomas's concurrence and criticized the majority.[95] But the relationship of *McDonald* to originalism is not a simple one. On the one hand, *McDonald* could be read as compatible with an originalism that makes an exception for deeply entrenched precedent. On the other hand, skeptics might read

[89] *Ibid.* at 2792 (citations omitted).
[90] *Ibid.* at 2793 (citation omitted).
[91] 130 S.Ct. 3020 (2010).
[92] See generally Lawrence B. Solum, "Incorporation and Originalist Theory," 18 J. Contemp. L. Issues 409 at 412 (2009).
[93] 130 S.Ct. at 3030–1 (Alito, J., plurality opinion).
[94] 130 S.Ct. 3059 (Thomas, J., concurring opinion).
[95] See Randy Barnett, The Supreme Court's Gun Showdown, Wall Street Journal, June 29, 2010, http://online.wsj.com/article/SB10001424052748703964104575335060436777670.html.

McDonald as reflecting antipathy (among the plurality justices) for any doctrine that would legitimate unenumerated rights.

IV. WHAT IS ORIGINALISM?

The question "What is originalism?" is itself ambiguous. One version of the question asks, "What is the meaning of the word 'originalism'?" The answer to that question is that the word is now ambiguous – having several different related senses in both scholarly and popular discourse. A second version of the questions is, "What are the necessary and sufficient conditions for content of a constitutional theory to qualify as 'originalist'?" That question should be taken off the table of serious scholarly inquiry. Originalism is not a natural kind; the term "originalism" is not used to point to the single true and correct version of originalist theory. It is simply not the case that the theories that we call "originalist" all share some set of essential characteristics. A third version of the question might be, "Which member of the family of originalist theories should be designated (or stipulated) as 'originalism' (with or without a capital 'O') for the purpose of theoretical discussion among constitutional theorists?" Although it would be possible to pursue the project of reaching agreement on this question, there are substantial obstacles to be overcome. No person or institution has the authority to settle questions of usage in constitutional theory. There are powerful incentives for advocates and opponents of different forms of originalism (both inside and outside the academy) to use the term "originalism" in ways that advance their practical or theoretical agendas. None of these three versions of the what-is-originalism question identifies a fruitful line of inquiry.

Does the fact that originalism is a family of theories that cannot be explicated via a series of necessary and sufficient conditions entail the further conclusion that the question "What is originalism?" should be abandoned altogether? Before we answer that question in the affirmative, we could consider the possibility that the family of originalist theories can be described systematically. We may be able to develop a systematic account of the similarities and differences among the varieties of originalism, and that account might allow us to identify themes or core ideas that most (if not all) originalists share.

For example, different versions of originalism offer different accounts of the determinants of original meaning. A rigorously developed typology would require a systematic investigation of all the relevant texts, but an informal survey suggests that the following versions of originalism would figure prominently: (1) original intentions originalism (the view that the meaning of the text is determined by the intentions of its authors), with subvariants for: (a) framers' intentions, (b) ratifiers' intentions, and (c) framers' and ratifiers' intentions; (2) original public meaning originalism (the view that the meaning of the text is determined by the conventional semantic meaning of the words and phrases at the time each provision was framed and ratified); (3) original methods originalism (the view that the original meaning is the meaning that would have been derived given the methods of interpretation (and possibly also construction) that were employed at the time each provision was framed and ratified). Doubtless, there are further variations, both within these three clusters and outside them.

The diversity of theories about the determinants of original meaning does not entail the further conclusion that there is no agreement among originalists. Originalists disagree about the question as to *what* determines original meaning (intentions, public meanings, methods), but all or almost all of the originalist writing with which I am familiar agrees on the question as to *when* meaning is fixed. Original intentions originalists agree that the relevant intentions are those of the framers or ratifiers of each provision of the Constitution: Thus, the original meaning of the Constitution of 1789 was fixed by facts about intentions from the period that starts with the opening of the Philadelphia Convention and ends when the ratification process was completed. Original public meaning originalists agree that the conventional semantic meaning of the words and phrases should also be determined by linguistic facts at the time each constitutional provision was framed and ratified. And a similar conclusion holds of original methods originalists.

This pattern of agreement suggests that most or almost all originalists agree that original meaning was *fixed* or determined at the time each provision of the constitution was framed and ratified. We might call this idea *the fixation thesis*. It is no surprise that originalists agree on the fixation thesis. The term "originalism" was coined to describe a family of textualist and intentionalist approaches to constitutional interpretation and construction that were associated with phrases like "original intentions," "original meaning," and "original understanding." These phrases and the word "originalist" share the root word "origin." The idea that meaning is fixed at the time of origination for each constitutional provision serves as the common denominator for all of these expressions. Thus, *the fixation thesis* might be described as a core idea around which all or almost all originalist theories organize themselves.

Almost all originalist theories are theories of constitutional practice – they have something to say about how officials (especially judges and paradigmatically Justices of the United States Supreme Court) should interpret and construe the Constitution. Although it would be theoretically possible for an originalist theory to limit itself to the purely linguistic claim that the semantic content of the Constitution is fixed at the time of origin of each provision, almost all self-identified originalists make further claims about the implications of that fact for constitutional practice.

The variations among originalists in this second dimension can be clarified by marking a distinction between semantic content and legal content. The semantic content of the constitutional text is the linguistic meaning of the document. But the term "meaning" is itself ambiguous. The constitutional text has a linguistic meaning, but that meaning is distinct from the legal implications of the text. Because we sometimes use the word "meaning" to describe such implications, the "meaning of the Constitution" can refer to a set of legal rules (the body of constitutional doctrine) that mediates between the text and the decision of particular cases. The legal content of the constitutional doctrine is simply the set of rules developed by courts (and other officials) for the application of the text to particular cases.

Although originalists agree that the semantic content of the Constitution was fixed at the time each provision was framed and ratified, they disagree about the role that semantic content plays in determining legal content. In other words, different originalists have different views about the constraining force of original meaning. At one end of the spectrum, an originalist might believe that each and every rule of constitutional law must be identical to the original meaning of some provision of the Constitution. On that view, much of the content of contemporary constitutional doctrine would be illegitimate, because it seems clear that wide swaths of constitutional law are judicial creations. A more moderate (but still quite strong) version of originalism might adopt the view that constitutional doctrine cannot contradict the original meaning but allow for the development of supplementary rules (for example, in the case of constitutional provisions that are vague). Further along the spectrum, some originalists might adopt the position that the original meaning should constrain constitutional doctrine but allow for circumstances in which exceptions are legitimate. One such exception might focus on the role of precedent: Some originalists may believe that the Supreme Court can legitimately adhere to precedents that are at variation with the original meaning of the text, where the restoration of the original meaning would be disruptive, upset justifiable reliance, and so forth. An even more modest version of originalism might take the position that the original meaning should govern in cases of first impression, but sanction departures from original meaning whenever a question of legal doctrine has been settled. A very weak version of originalism might require officials (such as judges) to consider the original meaning as one important factor in the determination of constitutional doctrine, but allow the original meaning to be balanced with a variety of other considerations, including precedent, contemporary social interests and values, and so forth. At this end of the spectrum, originalism will begin to merge with forms of living constitutionalism that acknowledge that text and original intentions are relevant factors in determining constitutional applications.

Although the originalists may disagree about the constraining force of original meaning, all or almost all originalists agree that original meaning ought to play an important and substantial role in the determination of constitutional doctrine. Characteristically, originalists believe that the role of original meaning should be constraining – that is, that absent exceptional circumstances (or very weighty reasons), constitutional doctrines that contradict or contravene the semantic content of the Constitution (as fixed at the time of origin) are illegitimate. This pattern of agreement and variation suggests a second idea that forms the core around which originalist theories are organized. All or almost all originalists agree that the original meaning of the Constitution should make a substantial contribution to the content of constitutional doctrine: We might call this idea *the contribution thesis*. Most originalists agree on a fairly strong version of the contribution thesis, which we might call *the constraint principle* (constitutional doctrine must be consistent with original meaning absent very weighty reasons). The contribution thesis forms a second core idea around which different versions of originalism cluster. The constraint principle identifies an important nexus in that cluster – the mainstream of contemporary originalist theory.

Originalists differ in yet another important respect. Different versions of originalist theory provide different justifications for the constraining force of original meaning. Some originalists emphasize the rule of law. Others focus on the idea of popular sovereignty. Yet others emphasize the notion that the conventions of legal practice do not permit judges to deliberately overrule the linguistic meaning of the constitutional text. And still others may make the claim that adherence to original meaning is justified because it will produce better decisions in the long run than the alternative methods of constitutional interpretation and construction. It seems likely that many originalists will rely on some combination of these arguments, and others as well.

Of course these variations in the justifications for originalism are important, but the existence of variations at the level of normative foundation is to be expected, given the pluralism that characterizes the public culture of the American polity in general and the academy in particular. Disagreement at the level of ultimate normative foundations is perfectly consistent with agreement on core originalist principles as an operative judicial philosophy.

What is originalism? Within the domain of constitutional theory, originalism is a family of views that cluster around two central ideas: the fixation thesis and the contribution thesis. All or almost all originalists agree that the original meaning of the Constitution was fixed at the time each provision was framed and ratified. Almost all originalists agree that original meaning must make an important contribution to the content of constitutional doctrine: Most originalists agree that courts should view themselves as constrained by original meaning and that very good reasons are required for legitimate departures from that constraint.

What then should we make of Colby and Smith's claim that originalism is "a smorgasbord of distinct constitutional theories that share little in common except a misleading reliance on a single label"?[96] Colby and Smith are certainly correct that the term "originalism" is not used to describe a single theoretical position characterized by strong agreement among its proponents on all the important constituent elements. But this does not entail the conclusion that the only thing that unifies most (or even almost all) originalist theories is "misleading reliance on a single label." The two ideas that provide the focal point of agreement among almost all originalist theories – the fixation thesis and the contribution thesis – are directly and transparently related to the label, "originalism," and the cognate notions of "original meaning" or "original understanding." Originalists agree that the "meaning" (the semantic content or linguistic meaning) of the constitutional text was fixed at the time that each provision of the constitution was framed and ratified. The fixation thesis expresses the idea that the "origin" or "time of origination" of each constitutional provision fixes its meaning, which originalists call the "original meaning." There is nothing misleading about the use of the term "originalism" as the label for this view. Moreover, the family of originalist theories is organized around another central idea: the fixation thesis and its strong variant, the constraint principle. Almost all originalists agree that the original meaning ought to make a substantial and important contribution to constitutional doctrine, and most originalists make the stronger claim that this contribution ought to constrain constitutional doctrine (absent very good reasons for departure from the original meaning).

What about the important differences that remain? Does the fact that originalists disagree about important matters somehow ground an argument against the validity of the best versions of originalist theory? Initially, it is difficult to see how this argument might go. Colby and Smith are certainly correct to the extent that they argue that originalism cannot claim strong theoretical unity as a virtue – to the extent that originalists have made that claim, they are simply incorrect. Originalism is a family of theories that cluster around the fixation

[96] Colby & Smith, "Living Originalism," *supra* note 82 at 244.

thesis and the contribution thesis – not a single theory whose proponents agree on all the important details.

But from the fact that originalists almost all agree about two core ideas but disagree about much else, it does not follow that no version of originalism is correct. Consider the analogous situation that holds in the natural sciences. Suppose that at one stage in the development of the theory of evolution, there were competing accounts of the mechanism by which natural selection actually occurred. (Until the discovery of DNA, the actual mechanism was uncertain.) From this fact, it would surely not follow that no version of the theory of evolution could be true or that competing versions of the theory were united only by a "misleading label." The more sensible response to theoretical disagreement is to ask the question, "Which version of the theory is right, correct, or best?" The argument that evolution must be wrong because evolutionary biologists disagree about important questions is simply a subtle variation on the genetic fallacy (no pun intended).

The originalist family of theories is actually relatively immature as academic theories go. One might read the progression from original intentions of the framers to the understandings of the ratifiers to the original public meaning of the text as a story of increasing fracture and degeneration, but the same narrative may eventually come to be seen as a story of progress and increasing sophistication.

Perhaps the most worrisome and most persistent disagreement among originalists is the one tacitly identified by Brest when he coined the term "originalism" – originalists continue to disagree about the role of "original intentions" and "original public meaning." Colby and Smith emphasize this worry:

> [O]riginalists' specific claims that their approach alone properly treats the Constitution as a form of law and properly limits the judiciary to its appropriate role in a democratic society . . . start from the premise that originalism (and only originalism) treats the Constitution as having a fixed and determinate meaning. Yet the meaning that a committed originalist judge would find obviously turns on the particular brand of originalism that the judge applies. And over the last thirty-five years, that meaning has been anything but fixed. A judge committed to the originalist enterprise would once have invoked original intent, and would today have the freedom to choose from a smorgasbord that includes original intent and many other originalist approaches.[97]

Colby and Smith exaggerate to the extent that they claim that theoretical divergence among originalists would give judges discretion to pick and choose among originalist theories – each judge would be bound across cases to employ

[97] *Ibid.* at 283.

the theory she believed was correct, but the essence of their point is correct: There are real and substantial differences between the competing versions of originalist theory.

But the importance of the disagreement between intentionalist and public meaning originalists should not be exaggerated. The form of intentionalism that has emerged in recent years emphasizes the semantic intentions of the authors of the constitutional text – best understood as a complex combination of the framers and ratifiers. The view is that the linguistic meaning of the text is a function of the intentions (or mental states) of its authors. Public meaning originalism takes the view that the linguistic meaning of the constitutional text is a function of its conventional semantic meaning – which is determined by patterns of usage among the relevant linguistic community.

It is possible for intended meaning and public meaning to diverge, but in the case of a legal text, such divergence will be rare in practice. The authors of the constitutional text knew that those who would read and interpret the text would have limited access to information about idiosyncratic semantic intentions: For example, the records of the Philadelphia Convention and the ratifying conventions were not publicly available in the era that immediately followed ratification. For this reason, the semantic intentions of the ratifiers are likely to closely track original public meaning – a point that is recognized by sophisticated originalists of both the intentionalist and public-meaning varieties. And it is no surprise that this divide in originalist theory is accompanied by agreement (in principle) in application. Originalist theory must account for linguistic facts on the ground – and this means that such theories must converge to adequately account for the relevant evidence.

V. ORIGINALISM AND LIVING CONSTITUTIONALISM

The chief aim of this chapter is a modest one: to lay a foundation that can help clarify and sharpen debates about originalist constitutional theory. The strategy has been to address the question "What is originalism?" in the context of the evolution or development of originalist theory. In this penultimate section of the chapter, these efforts will be applied to the debate between originalists and living constitutionalists.

The first and perhaps the most important point is that it is misleading to characterize controversies between originalists and living constitutionalists as a single debate. There are several versions of originalism, and it seems likely that there are many versions of "living constitutionalism." The first best approach to that fact would involve an investigation of "living constitutionalism" that parallels the exploration of originalism undertaken in this chapter, but on this occasion, we must settle for the second-best approach by relying on a representative example of living constitutionalism as a starting point. Justice William Brennan of the United States Supreme Court offered an influential formulation of living constitutionalism:

> To remain faithful to the content of the Constitution, therefore, an approach to interpreting the text must account for the existence of the substantive value choices and must accept the ambiguity inherent in the effort to apply them to modern circumstances. The Framers discerned fundamental principles through struggles against particular malefactions of the Crown: the struggle shapes the particular contours of the articulated principles. But our acceptance of the fundamental principles has not and should not bind us to those precise, at times anachronistic, contours.[98]

Brennan's formulation allows us to identify two ideas that are associated with living constitutionalism. The first idea is that constitutional principles must be adapted to changing circumstances. The freedoms of speech and of the press at the time of the framing and ratification of the First Amendment had "particular contours" adapted to the communications technologies of the late eighteenth century. These principles will take on different contours when applied to the early twenty-first-century world of the Internet. The second idea is somewhat different and might be at odds with Brennan's formulation. One might believe that constitutional practice should reflect changing values as well as changing circumstances. On this view, the set of "fundamental principles" might grow and change while the constitutional text remains the same.

Are living constitutionalism and originalism competing theories? That question can and should be reformulated as a series of inquiries. Are some versions of originalism consistent with living constitutionalism? Are other versions incompatible? Once the question is reformulated in this way, it becomes clear that there are both compatibilist and incompatibilist stories to tell about the relationship between living constitutionalism and originalism.

The compatibilist story about the relationship between living constitutionalism and originalism can be articulated via the distinction between constitutional interpretation and constitutional construction that is associated with the New Originalism. Compatibilism could be the view that originalism and living constitutionalism have separate domains. Originalism has constitutional interpretation as its domain: The linguistic meaning of the Constitution is fixed. Living constitutionalism has constitutional construction as its domain: The vague provisions of the constitution can be given constructions that change

[98] William J. Brennan, Jr., "The Constitution of the United States: Contemporary Ratification," 27 S. Tex. L. Rev. 433 at 437 (1986).

over time to adapt to changing values and circumstances. A fully specified living constitutionalism would have to provide a theory of constitutional construction that satisfies this description, and we can imagine that there could be a variety of such theories.

If living constitutionalism accepts the fixation thesis, some theory of semantic content, and some version of the contribution thesis, then living constitutionalism is committed to the idea that the constitutional text provides constitutional law a *hard core*. Originalists and some living constitutionalists could agree that the hard core of determinant constitutional meaning should not yield to changing circumstances and values and agree that in the "construction zone" created by the abstract, vague, and general provisions of the text, constitutional doctrine can "live" and "grow" in response to changing circumstances and values.

But some living constitutionalists may deny that there is a hard core. They might believe that even the core of constitutional law is malleable and subject to manipulation. That is, they might assert that the living constitution has a *soft core*. What then about incompatibilism?

There are at least two different ways in which living constitutionalism could make assertions that are inconsistent with originalism. One possibility is that living constitutionalism is a theory of linguistic meaning. That is, living constitutionalists could be understood as denying the fixation thesis and asserting that the semantic meaning of a given constitutional provision changes in response to changing circumstances. But there is another version of living constitutionalism that would result in incompatibilism. Some living constitutionalists may deny what I have called *the constraint principle*. This version of living constitutionalism could accept the claims made by the most modest versions of originalism (for example, that original meaning should be an important factor in the determination of constitutional doctrine) but deny the claim that original meaning should strongly constrain judicial interpretation and construction of the Constitution. This view can be stated somewhat tendentiously to bring out the feature that creates the incompatibility. Some living constitutionalists may believe that courts should have the power to amend the Constitution in order to eliminate what Justice Brennan might have called the "anachronistic contours" of the constitutional text. Proponents of this view are not likely to use the word "amendment" to describe this power, but that word seems an accurate characterization of the implications of their position.

Of course, this account of compatibilist and incompatibilist stories about originalism and living constitutionalism is only a sketch. Filling it out would require a careful reconstruction of the actual positions held by various participants in contemporary debates about constitutional theory. The sketch was offered to illustrate the importance of clarity in these debates. If we begin with the assumption that originalism must be incompatible with living constitutionalism, that assumption may well obscure the most important issues. Originalists and living constitutionalists may find common ground on the very issues they believe to be the heart of the controversy. Once these misconceptions are cleared away, the new ground for contestation may look a bit different and new issues may take center stage.

VI. CONCLUSION

One of the goals of this chapter has been to motivate a reorientation of the debates about originalism in constitutional theory. Constitutional theory can be practiced as politics by other means. Originalism can be viewed as the "conservative" theory, and living constitutionalism as the "liberal theory," but that picture is oversimplified at best. There is an alternative to the politicization of constitutional theory. Originalism and living constitutionalism can be debated on the intellectual merits, but that will only occur if participants in the debates view these theories in their best light and apply the principle of charity to the arguments of their opponents.

"Originalism" is an ambiguous term. The family of contemporary originalist constitutional theories contains substantial diversity, and there may be no single thesis on which all self-described originalists agree. Despite the variety of originalist theories, there are two central ideas that serve as the focal point or core of contemporary originalism. Almost all originalists agree that the original meaning of the Constitution was fixed at the time each provision was framed and ratified. Most originalists agree that the original meaning of the Constitution should strongly constrain the content of constitutional doctrine.

2 The Case for Originalism

Jeffrey Goldsworthy

I. THE BEST ARGUMENT FOR ORIGINALISM

The best argument for originalism is simple, straightforward, and powerful[1]:

1. A constitution, like any other law, necessarily has a meaning that preexists judicial interpretation of it.
2. The meaning of a law is part (perhaps all) of what it is; therefore, to change the meaning of a law is to change the law.
3. The original meaning of a constitution is neither its original literal meaning (called "sentence meaning" by philosophers) nor its originally intended meaning ("speaker's meaning"); it is, instead, its "utterance meaning," which is determined by a restricted range of evidence, extratextual as well as textual, of what its founders intended it to mean.
4. When a constitution itself requires that it be changed only by some special democratic procedure, this binds judges as well as other officials. The judges must not change the constitution – or, by inference from Proposition 2, its meaning – by purporting to "interpret" it.
5. Any judge who violated that requirement would flout the constitution itself, the rule of law, the principle of democracy, and (in many federal systems) the principle of federalism.
6. When interpreting such a constitution, the judges' primary duty is to reveal and clarify its pre-existing meaning. When that meaning is

[1] Much of the material in this chapter is derived from my earlier work, especially "Originalism in Constitutional Interpretation" (1997) 25 Fed. L. Rev. 1 (Goldsworthy, "Originalism"); "Interpreting the *Constitution* in Its Second Century" (2000) 24 Melbourne U.L. Rev. 677 (Goldsworthy, "Interpreting the Constitution"); "Raz on Constitutional Interpretation" (2003) 22 Law & Phil. 167 (Goldsworthy, "Raz on Constitutional Interpretation"); "Questioning the Migration of Constitutional Ideas: Rights, Constitutionalism and the Limits of Convergence," in Sujit Choudhry (ed.), *The Migration of Constitutional Ideas* (2006) 115; and "Constitutional Interpretation: Originalism" (2009) 4 Philosophy Compass 682.

insufficiently determinate to resolve the case at hand, their secondary duty is to act creatively and supplement it. To supplement the meaning of the constitution is not to change it.

Two additional propositions respond to popular but misguided non-originalist criticisms:

7. Although judges must not deliberately change the constitution, there are at least four ways in which constitutional law can and does legitimately evolve over time. To that considerable extent, originalism is perfectly consistent with "common law constitutionalism" and "living constitutionalism."
8. Consistent application of any constitutional theory, including originalism, might lead to grave injustice in a particular case. Judges might then be morally bound to disobey the constitution while pretending to obey it. But a theory justifying occasional "noble lies" about what the constitution means is not a theory about what it really means.

In what follows, these propositions will be referred to as Propositions 1–8. Each one requires elaboration, qualification, and defense, which are provided in the next section.

To illustrate the argument, I use an example from the Australian Constitution, which does not include a Bill or Charter of Rights that limits legislative power. Section 51 empowers the Australian Parliament to make laws for the "peace, order, and good government of the Commonwealth" with respect to thirty-one enumerated subject matters. Read literally, in ignorance of its original, intended meaning, this phrase might seem to limit the Parliament's powers by authorizing judges to invalidate legislation that, in their opinion, is inimical to the peace, order, and good government of the Commonwealth. But when the Constitution was enacted in 1900, the phrase was well understood by lawyers to have the opposite meaning.[2] It had previously been held by the Privy Council that it did not impose judicially enforceable limits to the legislative powers it granted: It was a stock phrase that the Imperial Parliament routinely used in colonial constitutions to confer plenary power – power not inherently limited, although possibly subject to extraneous limits – with respect to enumerated subject matters.[3] But are judges today obligated to hold that the phrase still has what is well known to be its original, intended

[2] *D'Emden v Pedder* (1904) 1 C.L.R. 91 at 110–11 (per Griffith CJ); *Union Steamship Co of Australia Pty Ltd v King* (1988) 166 C.L.R. 1 at 9–10.

[3] *R v Burah* (1878) 3 A.C. 889; *Hodge v The Queen* (1883) 9 A.C. 117; *Powell v Apollo Candle Co. Ltd* (1885) 10 A.C. 282; *Riel v The Queen; ex parte Riel* (1885) 10 A.C. 675 (P.C.).

meaning? Or can the judges rely on its literal meaning to justify subjecting the Parliament's powers to previously unrecognized limits amounting, in effect, to a judicially crafted Bill of Rights? I return to these questions in the Conclusion.

II. ELABORATION, QUALIFICATION, AND DEFENSE

Proposition 1: A constitution, like any other law, necessarily has a meaning that pre-exists judicial interpretation of it.

A law necessarily means something – nothing meaningless can be a law – and its meaning is part of what it is.[4] Its meaning (or, if it is ambiguous, meanings) must pre-exist judicial interpretation. Otherwise it could not guide behavior until judges interpreted it. Indeed, it could not *be law* until they interpreted it. If meaningful laws could only exist after and as a result of judicial interpretation of texts, then the judges would be the only real lawmakers. Law would be like a baseball pitch as seen by the umpire who supposedly said, "It ain't nothin' 'til I call it."

The most radical kind of non-originalism would deny Proposition 1 and hold that a constitution has no legal meaning until it is judicially interpreted. This view might be adopted by someone who denies that sentences in a natural language have any meaning before they are "interpreted," but given that any interpretation would also be expressed in a natural language (and therefore, *ex hypothesi*, meaningless), that would be too silly to warrant consideration.

A more sophisticated position is defended by Mitchell Berman. He comes close to denying Proposition 1 when he rejects "the idea that a legal norm pre-exists argumentation about it" and maintains that "legal norms are constituted by actual arguing practice, that is, by the reasoning of participants in the practice," "argumentation that frequently culminates in, but is not reducible to, judicial resolution."[5] For him, law does not pre-exist the argumentative activity of lawyers: It emerges from it.[6] On this view, legal texts such as statutes and constitutions "ain't nothin' 'til the legal profession calls 'em," after putting them through its battery of argumentation. But this entails that legislatures cannot really make law or have genuine authority to make law: They can merely provide raw material to be turned into law by the legal profession, after subjecting it to complex argumentative processes that can bend, stretch,

[4] Goldsworthy, "Originalism," *supra* note 1 at 10.

[5] M.N. Berman, "Constitutional Theory and the Rule of Recognition, Toward a Fourth Theory of Law," in M.D. Adler and K.E. Himma, eds, *The Rule of Recognition and the U.S. Constitution* (2009) 269, 286, 288 note 54, and 286 note 49, respectively.

[6] *Ibid.* at 290.

shrink, or expand it. This comes close to denying that such texts are laws at all – because a law, by definition, is something with a meaning – until they are processed by the legal profession. I find this highly implausible. As I see it, the argumentative norms of the profession when applied to such texts are, to a large extent, aimed at revealing and clarifying a meaning that is assumed to pre-exist them, which communicates the authoritative decisions of the lawmaker, even if they sometimes justify supplementing or (within strict limits) repairing that meaning.

A version of what is sometimes called "pluralism" might also come close to denying Proposition 1. Pluralists maintain that in interpreting a constitution, judges always are and should be guided by many diverse considerations, such as text, structure, history, precedent, prudence, and justice.[7] Pluralists do not distinguish between interpretation (a) as a process of revealing or clarifying pre-existing meaning; (b) as a process of supplementing that meaning to resolve indeterminacies;[8] and (c) as a process of changing that meaning to improve the constitution.[9]

Insofar as judges are engaged in either the second or third process, pluralism seems inescapable. In deciding how to supplement or change the meaning of a constitution, a broad range of considerations is necessarily relevant. But insofar as judges are engaged in revealing or clarifying the pre-existing meaning of a constitution, pluralism is dubious. It might come close to denying Proposition 1, by asserting that a constitution always has multiple meanings from which judges must choose. Admittedly, a constitution has more than one meaning when it is ambiguous. But pluralists would make a much more radical claim if they were to assert that judges can always choose between many different meanings: This would come very close to holding that it has no meaning until they have given it one.

In discussing Proposition 3, different kinds of original meaning will be identified: literal or sentence meaning, intended or speaker's meaning, and utterance meaning.[10] It is also possible to distinguish these from current sentence meaning (which might differ from the original sentence meaning) and current conventional meaning (which might be based on a popular but mistaken belief about the utterance meaning). A pluralist might argue that any constitutional provision necessarily has several if not all of these meanings,

[7] Mitchell N. Berman, "Originalism Is Bunk" (2009) 84 N.Y.U. L. Rev. 1 at 73 (Berman, "Originalism Is Bunk"); Ethan J. Leib, "The Perpetual Anxiety of Living Constitutionalism" (2007) 24 Const. Comment. 353 at 360–1 (Leib, "The Perpetual Anxiety").

[8] See Proposition 7.

[9] See Proposition 4.

[10] See also Berman, "Originalism Is Bunk," *supra* note 7 at 43.

and that judges are therefore forced to choose among them.[11] As we will see, however, this is false. The meaning of a constitutional provision is its utterance meaning. Sentence meaning and speaker's meaning are not alternative meanings; rather, both contribute to utterance meaning.

The "multiple meanings" hypothesis disaggregates and dissipates meaning. Because this version of pluralism would come close to an implausible denial of Proposition 1, some other version – such as one asserting that judges have (limited) authority to supplement or change the meaning of a constitution – is preferable. This is considered in relation to Proposition 4.

Proposition 2: The meaning of a law is part (perhaps all) of what it is; therefore, to change the meaning of a law is to change the law.

This seems obvious and indisputable.

Proposition 3: The original meaning of a constitution is neither its original literal meaning (called "sentence meaning" by philosophers) nor its originally intended meaning ("speaker's meaning"); it is, instead, its "utterance meaning," which is determined by a restricted range of evidence, extra-textual as well as textual, of what its founders intended it to mean.

What is the nature of the meaning that necessarily pre-exists judicial interpretation? It cannot be the original literal meaning (which philosophers call the "sentence meaning") of the constitutional text. "Literalism" in legal interpretation has long been condemned, for very good reasons. It is a byword for a narrow, formalistic, and obstructionist approach to interpretation. The authors of legal documents, whether contracts, wills, statutes, or constitutions, inevitably fail to express themselves with perfect clarity and comprehensiveness. To limit the meaning of their document to the literal meanings of its words maximizes indeterminacy, absurdity, and the frustration of their intentions or purposes. It maximizes indeterminacy because it ignores evidence of authorial intention or purpose that can often resolve problems caused by

[11] Berman, *ibid.*, could possibly be interpreted as making this argument. He says he is concerned with "the initial . . . step of deriving legal meaning" from the constitutional text, rather than the subsequent step of creatively resolving indeterminacies (*ibid.*, at 39, note 100); he distinguishes among various different kinds of meanings that an utterance might have (*ibid.* at 43); and he later says that in interpreting constitutional provisions, judges can select between originalist and non-originalist interpretations on a case-by-case basis (*ibid.* at 77, 82–3). On the other hand, he sometimes assumes that a constitutional provision might have a clear "original meaning," while denying that it is binding on judges today: *e.g.*, *ibid.* at 24, 82.

ambiguity, vagueness, incompleteness, or inconsistency. It maximizes absurdity because the proper understanding of any utterance depends on understanding unexpressed assumptions; if they are ignored, the result will often be nonsensical.[12] Orthodox principles of interpretation can avoid such a result by presuming that it could not have been intended and is therefore excluded by implication. Literalism cannot recognize implications (other than those of logical entailment), because they depend on evidence of authorial intention in addition to the literal meanings of the words used. That would be a disaster for legal interpretation. The meaning of a statute or constitution depends just as much on tacit assumptions as that of other texts.[13] As Felix Frankfurter remarked, the most fundamental question in legal interpretation is: "What is below the surface of the words and yet fairly a part of them?"[14] The literalist's implausible reply must be: "nothing."

The original meaning of a constitution also cannot be identical to whatever its founders intended it to mean (which philosophers call its "speaker's meaning"). The claim that the meaning of any communication is identical to its speaker's meaning seems plainly false. It is a commonplace that the meaning people intend to express or imply can differ from the meaning they in fact express or imply. People can intend to say or imply something but fail to do so, and conversely, they can say or imply something they did not intend. If we are told that we have misunderstood someone's utterance, we often defend ourselves by replying "I now realize what she meant to say, but that's not what she did say," or "He may not have intended to imply that, but he did."[15] Defending a speaker's meaning account, Stanley Fish replies that "having your meaning misunderstood doesn't mean that your meaning is something other than what you have determined it to be."[16] That is true, but it misses the point, which is that when your utterance fails to communicate your meaning to your intended audience (through your fault, not theirs), but conveys some other meaning to them instead, that other meaning – and not your meaning – will generally be the meaning of your utterance.[17]

[12] Jeffrey Goldsworthy, "Implications in Language, Law and the Constitution," in Geoffrey Lindell (ed.), *Future Directions in Australian Constitutional Law* (1994) 150 at 157–9 (Goldsworthy, "Implications").

[13] *Ibid*; Jeffrey Goldsworthy, "Marmor on Meaning, Interpretation and Legislative Intention" (1995) 1 Legal Theory 439 (Goldsworthy, "Marmor on Meaning and Interpretation").

[14] Felix Frankfurter, "Some Reflections on the Reading of Statutes" (1947) 47 Colum. L. Rev. 527 at 533.

[15] Jeffrey Goldsworthy, "Moderate versus Strong Intentionalism: Knapp and Michaels Revisited" (2005) 42 San Diego L. Rev. 669 at 677 (Goldsworthy, "Moderate versus Strong"). See also Berman, "Originalism is Bunk," *supra* note 7 at 44–6 and 52.

[16] Stanley Fish, "The Intentionalist Thesis Once More," in this volume at 101.

[17] For a fuller account, see Goldsworthy, "Moderate versus Strong," *supra* note 15.

In law, as in everyday life, the meaning of a communication is what we might call its "utterance meaning," as distinct from both its sentence meaning and its speaker's meaning. Utterance meaning is the full meaning of an utterance, implied as well as expressed, and it depends on what the speaker's meaning appears to be, given evidence that is readily available to his or her intended audience, including the sentence meaning of the utterance and other clues such as its context.[18] What the speaker's meaning appears to be, given this evidence, may be different from the actual speaker's meaning.

This thesis is based mainly on two propositions. First, the meaning of a communication cannot be something hidden within the speaker's mind and inaccessible to its intended recipient, such as an intended meaning that is confided only to the speaker's spouse or written in a private diary.[19] In particular, the meaning of a communication, such as a law, that is addressed to all or part of the general public, must be publicly accessible, not private. Secondly, in the case of law, the irrelevance of esoteric legislative intentions also follows from the rule of law. The law can only provide a practicable framework for social interaction if its meaning is public, or at least publicly ascertainable, and imposing penalties or costs for a failure to comply with hidden intentions is obviously unfair.

Sentence meaning, speaker's meaning, and utterance meaning are not alternative meanings from which interpreters are free to choose. Instead, sentence meaning and speaker's meaning both contribute to utterance meaning. In everyday life, we do not regard ourselves as free to prefer a literal meaning to an obviously intended meaning just because we have a moral preference for the consequences of doing so. Suppose that Bill Green tells me to "give this money to Susan," and I know that he means his daughter Susan Green (and I also know that he knows that I know, and relies on my knowing it). I have the ability to give the money to Susan Black instead, on the ground that her need is greater. I cannot plausibly justify doing so by maintaining that: (a) Bill's instruction had multiple meanings from which I had to choose and (b) I was justified in choosing its literal meaning rather than its obviously intended meaning and then resolving the consequential indeterminacy (the literal meaning does not identity "Susan") myself because that enabled me to achieve a morally preferable outcome. That would flout common sense about

[18] See, *e.g.*, *ibid.* at 670–1; Goldsworthy, "Implications," *supra* note 12 at 150–2; Goldsworthy, "Marmor on Meaning and Interpretation," *supra* note 13 at 442.

[19] See Goldsworthy, "Marmor on Meaning and Interpretation," *supra* note 13; William E. Tolhurst, "On What a Text Is and How It Means" (1979) 19 British Journal of Aesthetics 3; Jerrold Levinson, "Intention and Interpretation: A Last Look", in Gary Iseminger, ed., *Intention and Interpretation* (1995) 221.

the meaning of Bill's instruction. It would also be blatantly opportunistic. There might be an even stronger moral reason to give the money to a homeless man, yet I would be attempting to rationalize my action by appealing to the wholly fortuitous circumstance that Susan Black happens to share the same first name as Bill's daughter. The same is true of law. The literal meaning and intended meaning of the phrase "peace, order, and good government" are not alternative meanings from which the judges are free to choose in order to achieve the morally best result. The meaning of the phrase is its utterance meaning, which is its established legal meaning – well known to the founders and intended by them – at the time the constitution was enacted.[20]

Recognizing that utterance meaning is in principle distinct from both speaker's meaning and sentence meaning has various advantages. Instead of the meaning of an utterance sometimes being speaker's meaning, sometimes sentence meaning, and sometimes something in between – such as sentence meaning "with modifications" (as in the case of Lawrence Solum's account of "clause meaning") – the meaning of an utterance is always its utterance meaning.[21] When the meaning of an utterance appears to be its sentence meaning, the reason is usually that its sentence meaning is the only evidence of the speaker's meaning that is readily available to the intended audience. Other apparent exceptions – such as when, in a supermarket, I seek my wife's intended meaning when interpreting a shopping list she wrote – are not examples of the speaker's meaning *being* the meaning of the utterance in question, but instead of the interpreter being more interested in the speaker's meaning than the meaning of the utterance as such, and using the latter only as evidence of the former. If, for example, my daughter happened by chance to be with me in the supermarket, and convinced me that my wife had intended an item on the list to mean x rather than y, I would buy x even if the item as written indicated that she had intended y. The fact that in interpreting utterances we may be seeking speaker's meanings does not show that utterance meanings and speaker's meanings are one and the same thing.[22] In any particular case, utterance meaning may be similar or even identical to sentence meaning, or to speaker's meaning, or to both. It all depends on how much contextual evidence of speaker's meaning is or was readily available to the intended audience, and how far speaker's meaning goes beyond sentence meaning.

[20] See *supra* note 2.

[21] Lawrence B. Solum, "Semantic Originalism" (November 22, 2008). Illinois Public Law Research Paper No. 07–24. Available at SSRN: <http://ssrn.com/abstract=1120244> at 52–5.

[22] *Cf.* Berman, "Originalism is Bunk," *supra* note 7 at 53.

For such reasons, instead of talking of "original intentions," leading originalists now talk of "original public meaning," which depends on what was in some sense publicly known of the founders' intended meaning.[23] The term "original public meaning" itself has several possible meanings, one being "original conventional semantic meaning."[24] But this pays insufficient attention to the phenomenon of implication. Most implications cannot be inferred just from the text of the law in question; they can only be inferred from the text understood in the light of information about the intentions or purposes of the lawmaker that is (or was) readily available to the lawmaker's intended audience. Many implications are presuppositions or implicit assumptions, and our ability to identify these and most other kinds of implications depends on pragmatics (concerning the contexts in which utterances are made) as well as semantics.[25] The theoretical shift from original intentions to original public meaning therefore cannot be complete, because public meaning depends partly on public knowledge of what the lawmakers intended, in addition to knowledge of conventional semantic content. Any evidence of a speaker's intention that is readily available to the speaker's intended audience is "public" in the relevant sense. Even if "legislative history," such as convention debates, is excluded, other contemporaneous public knowledge may still be relevant: for example, knowledge of beliefs, values, and purposes that were widely shared among the founding generation.

Another complication is that, as courts have always acknowledged, constitutional provisions may have technical legal meanings. Examples in the United States Constitution include the *ex post facto* clause and the due process clause.[26] The phrase "peace, order and good government" in the Australian Constitution is another example. Technical legal meanings are known to lawyers, and the courts have often treated lawyers as the lawmakers' "intended audience," or at least laypeople only through the medium of professional legal advice. "Public meaning" should be understood accordingly.

Sensible originalists also maintain that evidence of only certain kinds of speaker's intentions is relevant. It is now common to distinguish between the founders' "semantic" intentions, which concern the meaning of what the constitution provides, and their "expectation" or "application" intentions, which

[23] E.g., Lawrence B. Solum, "What Is Originalism? The Evolution of Contemporary Originalist Theory," in this volume at 23.

[24] Lawrence B. Solum, "Originalism and the Natural Born Citizen Clause" (2008) 107 Mich. L. Rev. First Impressions 22 at 24.

[25] Goldsworthy, "Implications," *supra* note 12.

[26] Mark Tushnet, "The United States: Eclecticism in the Service of Pragmatism," in Jeffrey Goldsworthy (ed.), *Interpreting Constitutions, A Comparative Study* (2006) 7 at 28–9.

concern the effects of what it provides – such as how it should be applied in particular cases.[27] These two kinds of intentions differ partly because people may hold erroneous beliefs about the proper application or other effects of what they say. It has become widely agreed that "expectation" or "application" intentions are only indirectly relevant to constitutional interpretation, as evidence of semantic intentions.[28] The objective is to reveal and clarify the meaning of the norms that the founders enacted, and not to discover their beliefs about how those norms ought to be applied. Those beliefs are not part of the constitution and have no legal status. Our systems of government are based on the principle of the separation of powers, including the independence of the judiciary: Lawmakers enact the law and judges apply it according to its true meaning, regardless of the lawmakers' opinions or preferences. In addition, the lawmakers' beliefs about how their law ought to be applied may be erroneous: They are not infallible authorities when it comes to interpreting and applying their own laws. Like the rest of us, they sometimes fail to choose the right words to achieve their application intentions. When they do so, evidence of their application intentions cannot displace their semantic intentions.[29]

Proposition 4: When a constitution itself requires that it be changed only by some special democratic procedure, this binds judges as well as other officials. The judges must not change the constitution – or, by inference from Proposition 2, its meaning – by purporting to "interpret" it.

Modern constitutions usually include a special, democratic procedure for their own amendment, and either expressly provide or imply that they may be changed only through that procedure. For example, Article V of the U.S. Constitution seems to imply that it prescribes the exclusive means of constitutional amendment, which binds even the sovereign people, and evidence of original intent corroborates that impression.[30] Section 128 of Australia's

[27] Ronald Dworkin, "Comment," in Antonin Scalia, A *Matter of Interpretation*, Amy Gutmann (ed.), (1997) 115, 116 and 119 [Dworkin, "Comment"]. The term "enactment intention" would be better than "semantic intention," because the relevant intention might concern content that is implied rather than expressed.

[28] See Berman, "Originalism is Bunk," *supra* note 7 at 28.

[29] For example, they may clarify what would otherwise be an ambiguity, make it obvious that a word or phrase was used in a non-literal or special sense, or justify holding general terms to be subject to an implied qualification, by revealing that the lawmakers expressed themselves ineptly or took something for granted: See Goldsworthy, "Originalism," *supra* note 1 at 31.

[30] This has been generally accepted: see, *e.g.*, Henry P. Monaghan, "We the People[s], Original Understanding, and Constitutional Amendment," 96 Colum. L. Rev. 12 (1996); David R. Dow,

Constitution is more explicit, stating that "This Constitution shall not be altered except in the following manner," which involves a referendum. There is no apparent reason why judges, but not other officials, should hold themselves to be exempt from the prohibition of constitutional change by other means. To change the meaning of a law is to change the law.[31] It would seem to follow that, when the utterance meaning of the constitution is discoverable, judges should adhere to it.

There are several ways by which non-originalists might attempt to escape this conclusion. One is to argue that the meaning of a constitution can evolve without the judges (or anyone else) deliberately changing it. On this view, the meaning of a constitution depends partly on the context in which it operates, and therefore evolves in response to external social and political developments. The judges can recognize that the meaning has changed, without causing it to change. As an Australian judge put it, "discerning growth is not the same thing as making changes."[32] But this is a very odd view. It is true that the conventional meaning of words that appear in the constitution can shift over time. But it does not follow that their meaning within the constitution automatically shifts as a consequence. The conventional meanings of many words that appear in Shakespeare's plays have shifted over the last four centuries, but it does not follow that their meanings within his plays have shifted. The words as used in his plays continue to mean what they meant when he first used them. It is notable that the "spontaneous evolution" thesis is sometimes repudiated even by those who might have been expected to promote it. For example, Ronald Dworkin contemptuously rejects the notion that constitutional provisions "are chameleons which change their meaning to conform to the needs and spirit of new times" as "hardly even intelligible."[33] And Lawrence Tribe, another well-known critic of originalism, also emphatically denies that he regards the constitution "as something that 'grows and changes' by some mystical kind of organic, morphing process."[34] The odd idea that the meaning of the Constitution can spontaneously mutate is at best a fig leaf for the quite

"When Words Mean What We Believe They Say: The Case of Article V," 76 Iowa L. Rev. 1 (1990); John R. Vile, "Legally Amending the United States Constitution: The Exclusivity of Article V's Mechanisms," 21 Cumberland L. Rev. 271 (1990–91).

[31] See Proposition 2.

[32] Sir Victor Windeyer, *Some Aspects of Australian Constitutional Law* (J. A. Weir Memorial Lecture, Edmonton, March 13–14, 1972) at 38.

[33] Dworkin, "Comment," *supra* note 27 at 122. Whether or not this coheres with Dworkin's rejection of originalism is debatable: For an argument that he is really a kind of originalist, see Jeffrey Goldsworthy, "Dworkin as an Originalist" (2000) 17 Const. Comment. 49.

[34] Lawrence H. Tribe, "Comment," in *A Matter of Interpretation*, *supra* note 27 at 73.

different idea that the judges are entitled to act creatively, and give it a new, more "up-to-date" meaning.

A second way of escaping the conclusion would be to construe the constitution's amendment procedures as governing only changes made to the text of the constitution, and not changes made to the meaning of the text, or at least not changes wrought by judicial interpretation.[35] But that would surely be an odd construction. As we have seen, to change the meaning of a law is to change the law. What would be the point of forbidding changes to the constitution made by textual amendment, except by a special democratic procedure, but permitting changes to it made by textual "interpretation"? It would, of course, be possible for a constitution explicitly or implicitly to exempt judges from its prohibition of change other than by the procedures it prescribes. Evidence of original intent could, conceivably, reveal that the founders intended this. But it is surely unlikely that they would have deliberately permitted judges to change a constitution that ordinary democratic procedures are forbidden to change. Such an institutional arrangement, if it exists anywhere, would be a very unusual exception to the argument put forward here.[36]

In response to this argument, Mitchell Berman says that it is "obvious" that "the grant of an exclusive power to change the constitutional text is logically compatible with a practice in which the text's meaning can change over time."[37] This is not at all obvious to me, although it may depend on what he means by "logically compatible"[38] If changing the meaning of a law amounts to changing the law, then democratic institutions cannot possess a truly exclusive power to change a constitution if the judges have power to change its meaning. The judges' power necessarily constitutes an exception to a purportedly exclusive power vested in democratic institutions. Of course, in a looser, practical sense of "logical," it might not be illogical to confer

[35] For an argument that judges generally have authority to change the meaning of a constitution, see Joseph Raz, "On the Authority and Interpretation of Constitutions: Some Preliminaries," in Larry Alexander (ed.), *Constitutionalism; Philosophical Foundations* (1999) 152 (Raz, "On the Authority and Interpretation of Constitutions"), criticized in Goldsworthy, "Raz on Constitutional Interpretation," *supra* note 1. Raz repeats his arguments in his *Between Authority and Interpretation: On the Theory of Law and Practical Reason* (2009), with no reference to my criticisms.

[36] Goldsworthy, "Raz on Constitutional Interpretation," *supra* note 1 at 170–71.

[37] Berman, "Originalism Is Bunk," *supra* note 7 at 65.

[38] Berman mistakenly attributes to me the argument that non-originalist judges would exercise an unlimited amending power tantamount to that which the constitution bestows on other institutions: see Berman, *ibid.* That was never my argument: see Goldsworthy, "Interpreting the Constitution" (the article that Berman cites), *supra* note 1 at 684–85, and the text at notes 40–42 *infra*.

an otherwise exclusive power on democratic institutions that is subject to such an exception. It might arguably make sense to vest an exclusive power to formally amend a constitution in democratic institutions, but then carve out an exception by vesting a limited and sporadic power to change the constitution's meaning in the judiciary. Indeed, Berman sketches just such an argument. He says that a system in which, after much time has gone by, interpreters can "assign" new meanings to words "might prove attractive" because it might sensibly realize a good balance of stability and flexibility. Allowing a second and changing group to assign meaning (not just *any* meaning, mind you) to the text furthers flexibility, which means that it promotes the likelihood of interpretations that make for substantively good law. But putting the second group in the position of interpreters of a previously written text and not of text writers constrains that latter group's range of possible choices, thereby promoting stability and predictability.[39]

Originalists would reply that their theory strikes the optimum balance between stability and change. As Proposition 7 asserts, originalism is consistent with at least four ways that constitutional law can legitimately evolve over time in addition to the process of formal amendment.[40] Moreover, to authorize judges to change the meanings of the constitution's words would be to establish a haphazard and opportunistic method of change. The judges would not be able to change the constitution whenever this would facilitate just outcomes. They could only substitute one meaning that a word or phrase can conventionally bear for another, and they could do so only occasionally, when permitted by the vagaries of linguistic mutation and ambiguity.[41] The opportunity to smuggle a new meaning into the constitution would arise only if the literal meaning of its words were fortuitously pliable, as in the previous example of my "creative interpretation" of Bill's direction to give his money to Susan.[42] This would amount to a very limited and sporadic power of quasi-amendment depending on chance.

No historically plausible case can be made for attributing such a design to those who founded either the Australian or American constitution.[43] Berman must argue that this institutional division of labor has been established by

[39] *Ibid.* at 68.

[40] See Proposition 7.

[41] *Ibid.* at 68.

[42] See elaboration of Proposition 3.

[43] For Australia, see Greg Craven, "Heresy as Orthodoxy: Were the Founders Progressivists?" (2003) 31 Fed. L. Rev. 87; for the United States, Caleb Nelson, "Originalism and Interpretive Conventions" (2003) 70 U. Chicago L. Rev. 519; Robert G. Natelson, "The Founders' Hermeneutic: The Real Original Understanding of Original Intent" (2007) 68 Ohio St. L.J. 1239. Jefferson Powell's well-known argument to the contrary is deeply flawed: see, *e.g.*, Goldsworthy, "Originalism," *supra* note 1 at 10 note 54.

subsequent official acquiescence in a judicial practice of changing the constitution while purporting to interpret it. This is a third possible way that non-originalists might attempt to refute Proposition 4 – by arguing that, regardless of the original meaning of the constitution's own amendment clause, the rule of recognition constituted by subsequent consensus among legal officials allows judges to change the constitution.

But this is dubious. For a start, it seems unlikely that either the executive or legislative branches of government would condone the judicial branch engaging in de facto constitutional amendment. Admittedly, the United States may differ from Australia in this regard. I am confident that most Australian politicians would be outraged by the prospect of judges bringing about substantive constitutional change disguised by the weasel word "interpretation." On the other hand, one possible reading of the Senate's rejection in 1987 of Robert Bork as a Justice of the Supreme Court is that Democrats approve of judges creating new constitutional rights (as long as they are the right kind of rights). But the preferences of Democrats hardly constitute the widespread consensus among officials that is needed to constitute a rule of recognition. Moreover, the nature of those preferences is uncertain: Perhaps the Democrats merely feared a judicial reversal of previously created rights, contrary to the doctrine of *stare decisis*. Or perhaps they were persuaded by scholarly notions of "living constitutionalism" that are, in fact, consistent with originalism.[44] After all, there is scant support even in the academic literature for the proposition that judges have lawful authority to change the constitution when it has a determinate meaning. Many American theorists who are commonly regarded as non-originalists, such as Ronald Dworkin, are more accurately classified as moderate originalists. Dworkin himself has said: "The important choice judges and other interpreters of the Constitution must make . . . is not between the original understanding and some other method of interpretation but between reductive and abstract versions of the original understanding."[45]

Even more tellingly, appellate court judges themselves do not openly claim to possess legal authority to change their nation's constitution. In *Marbury v Madison*, Marshall CJ famously based the power of judicial review partly on this premise: "It is emphatically the province and duty of the judicial department to say what the law is."[46] From this premise it follows that it is the province of the judges to say what the constitution is and to enforce it

[44] See Proposition 7.

[45] Ronald Dworkin, "Jurisprudence and Constitutional Law", in Leonard W. Levy, Kenneth L. Karst, and John G. West Jr., eds., *The Encyclopedia of the American Constitution Supplement I* (1992) 288 at 291.

[46] 5 U.S. (1 Cranch) 137 at 177.

accordingly. Interpretation is within their province insofar as it is necessary to clarify what the constitution is when its meaning is unclear. This reasoning provides no foothold for judicial authority to say what the constitution ought to be and to change it accordingly.

Non-originalists might reply that judicial rhetoric of this kind is outdated and no longer represents judicial opinion, and that in any event we should focus on what judges actually do, not what they say they do.[47] Admittedly, many cases could be cited in which judges appear to have changed the constitution. Even some originalists admit this. Justice Antonin Scalia has gone so far as to concede that:

> it would be foolish to pretend that . . . [originalism] has become (as it once was) the dominant mode of interpretation in the courts. . . . The interpretive philosophy of the "living Constitution" – a document whose meaning changes to suit the times, as the Supreme Court sees the times – continues to predominate in the courts, and in the law schools. Indeed, it even predominates in the perception of the ordinary citizen, who has come to believe that what he violently abhors must be unconstitutional.[48]

But Scalia's concession may be premature. First, one must be very careful in interpreting what judges do. Constitutional law in countries such as the United States and Australia obviously does change over time, sometimes quite dramatically. But there are many reasons for change other than judges deliberately engaging in "amending interpretation," which are summarized in the elaboration of Proposition 7. Secondly, even in cases where it seems clear to observers that the judges are changing the constitution, they do not claim to be doing so. They do not say, for example: "although the constitution currently means *x*, we believe that morally it ought to mean *y*, and therefore we have decided to change it." Instead, they take great pains to demonstrate that their interpretation is faithful to the constitution as it is. This is true, for example, of the most controversial decisions of the United States Supreme Court, in cases such as *Lochner v New York*,[49] *Brown v Board of Education*,[50] and *Roe v Wade*.[51] Even when judges purport to enforce unenumerated, supposedly implied principles, they invariably claim to have discovered those principles in the constitution, not added them to it. This surely indicates that they know they lack lawful authority deliberately to change the constitution. If there is a discrepancy between what they say they do and what on occasions they

[47] Raz, "On the Authority and Interpretation of Constitutions," *supra* note 35 at 177.
[48] Justice A. Scalia, "Foreword" (2008) 31 Harv. J.L. & Pub. Pol'y 871 at 871.
[49] 198 U.S. 45 (1905).
[50] 347 U.S. 483 (1954) [*Brown*].
[51] 410 U.S. 113 (1973).

actually do, the former is much better evidence of the scope of their lawful authority than the latter. Any claim about the lawful scope of judicial authority must be able to pass the test of public candor: If that claim is not and cannot be candidly asserted in public by the judges themselves, it is almost certainly false.

Proposition 5: Any judge who violated that requirement would flout the constitution itself, the rule of law, the principle of democracy, and (in many federal systems) the principle of federalism.

A constitution that included no procedure for amendment – one that purported to be eternally immutable – or whose amendment procedure was prohibitively difficult to use would be vulnerable to the objection that later generations should not be controlled by the "dead hand of the past." But if it includes an amendment procedure that is reasonably democratic and practicable, today's generation is not restricted by the dead hand of the past in any invidious sense. Those who are restricted by the exclusivity of that procedure are government officials, legislative, executive, and judicial, who might otherwise have had power to alter the constitution themselves. The strongest normative argument for originalism therefore appeals, not to the authority of the dead hand of the past, but to the authority of the living hand of the present: "The people" today, or their representatives, who have exclusive legal authority to change their own constitution. The most powerful objection to non-originalism is that it usurps their power to change their constitution.

Originalism is motivated by respect for the requirements of the constitution itself, and therefore of the rule of law: The prescribed amending procedure should not be evaded by lawyers and judges disguising substantive constitutional change as interpretation. It is also motivated by the principle of democracy or popular sovereignty: If the constitution is to be changed, the consent of the electors or their representatives should first be obtained directly and expressly, and not taken for granted by a presumptuous elite purporting to read their minds and speak on their behalf. In addition, it may be motivated by the principle of federalism: Amending procedures often include supermajority requirements designed to protect regional interests, which would be all too easily bypassed by judges presuming to divine the "contemporary needs and values" of the nation as a whole.

All this, of course, presupposes that the constitution, including its amendment procedure, has sufficient moral authority that it generally ought to be obeyed. What is the source of its authority? Although some American originalists think otherwise, it cannot be the "will" or "sovereignty" of "the people" who supposedly first created it. First, it is too difficult to make sense of "the people" as a real but extra-legal (natural) corporate entity; also, those who in past centuries claimed the mantle of "the people" were usually a small, privileged elite. Secondly, it is very hard to understand how people today could be subject to the authority of "the people" of one or two centuries ago. As Sydney Smith quipped, it is not plausible that dead legislators have authority over those "who toss their remains about with spades, and use the relics of these legislators, to give breadth to broccoli."[52] People can, of course, be bound by laws (and constitutions) made in the distant past; it is, after all, of the essence of law that decisions are governed by norms laid down in the past. Although the "dead hand" of the past may have no authority over the living, its handiwork certainly does. But this must be for reasons other than the original lawmakers' now defunct authority. Thirdly, some constitutions, such as Canada's, are plainly just as authoritative as that of the United States, although they were not made by "the people" in any real sense. The Canadian Constitution was a statute of the British (and Imperial) Parliament, passed in 1867 in the exercise of its lawful (indeed, legally sovereign) lawmaking authority.[53] But that is not the reason for that Constitution's continuing authority today, partly because the British Parliament no longer has any authority (moral or legal) over Canadians or Canadian law[54] – just as (although for a different reason) those who created the United States Constitution no longer have any authority over Americans or American law.

Fourthly, "the people" cannot possess genuine sovereignty – if that means unlimited lawmaking authority – anyway. A legally constituted corporate entity such as the British Parliament can have lawful authority to make laws that is not subject to any legal limits – this is called "sovereignty" in British constitutional law – but it cannot plausibly claim to have moral authority to make laws that is not subject to any moral limits. Morally unlimited authority cannot exist: No one can have moral authority to make laws (or constitutions) that violate fundamental principles of morality. Yet "the sovereignty of the people," when it is claimed to have been used to make a constitution independently of or even contrary to pre-existing law, must refer to moral, not legal, sovereignty. Moreover, it is moral and not legal authority that is needed here, to ground a moral obligation to obey the constitution. It might be suggested that the term "sovereignty" is an unfortunate exaggeration, and that it is sufficient that "the people" possess moral authority to make a constitution that is subject to moral

[52] Sydney Smith, "Review of *The Book of Fallacies: from Unfinished Papers of Jeremy Bentham,*" (1825) 42 Edinburgh Review 367 at 371.

[53] The *British North America Act, 1867,* 30 & 31 Victoria, c. 3 (U.K.).

[54] Since passage of the *Canada Act, 1982* c. 11 (U.K.).

limits. But the authority of a constitution could not then rest simply on the will of the people: It would also depend on its complying with the moral principles that limit their authority.

A working constitution that is generally accepted as morally authoritative is indeed morally authoritative because it is essential to decent, civilized life – provided that it does not include moral flaws so egregious that they outweigh that benefit. This is because it provides the community with the incalculable benefits of an established and accepted set of procedures for making collective decisions binding on all its members; in other words, because the only realistic alternative is usually some form of grievous civil strife, such as anarchy or civil war.[55] The constitution protects and empowers, as well as restricts, subsequent generations, and these benefits are inseparable from the restrictions: They are two sides of the same coin. If some attempt to evade the restrictions by acting unconstitutionally, others may be tempted to follow suit, putting the constitution itself at risk along with the protection and empowerment it provides. The procedures that a constitution prescribes for its own amendment exemplify this coincidence of empowerment and restriction. Although every constitution is flawed, as long as it provides reasonably practicable and democratic procedures for its own amendment, those procedures are authoritative because any attempt to evade them – even if successful – might set a perilous precedent. If judges, for example, were openly to change the constitution contrary to the prescribed amendment procedure, other legal officials might be tempted to follow suit (which is why, when judges occasionally do so, they pretend not to). Judges have no more warrant than the other branches of government, or the citizen, for disobeying a law that they deem inconvenient. Indeed they have less, especially when that law is the most fundamental norm of the legal system, which guarantees democratic control over constitutional change. Some working constitutions, of course, may be so unjust and intractable to lawful amendment that they lack authority and may legitimately be evaded, unlawfully changed (perhaps surreptitiously by judges: see Proposition 8), or even overthrown. But the tragic consequences of many revolutions show how cautious people should be before deciding that they are in that predicament.

Some non-originalists argue that judges may on occasion deliberately depart from the constitution's original meaning to enhance the constitution's moral legitimacy and fortify its claim to moral authority. They say that the present generation cannot be expected to respect or even obey a constitution that has fallen too far behind the progress of conventional morality.[56] But this seems

[55] S. Holmes, *Passions and Constraint: On the Theory of Liberal Democracy* (1997).

[56] Leib, "The Perpetual Anxiety," *supra* note 7; Mitchell N. Berman, "Originalism and Its Discontents" (2007) 24 Const. Comment. 383 at 401.

implausible when the constitution includes a democratic procedure for its own amendment. The main function of such a procedure is to enable the community to prevent the constitution from becoming so out of touch with the community's needs and values that its legitimacy and authority might be imperiled. Why would the voters, and their representatives, fail to make use of the procedure if faced with such a threat? Even an amendment procedure as difficult to use as Article V of the Unites States Constitution would surely be galvanized into action to avoid a collapse of constitutional authority. Admittedly, it is possible that the community at large might be blind or indifferent to the unjust operation of a constitutional provision on a minority group. That possibility is discussed under Proposition 8, later in the chapter.

Proposition 6: When interpreting such a constitution, the judges' primary duty is to reveal and clarify its pre-existing meaning. When that meaning is insufficiently determinate to resolve the case at hand, their secondary duty is to act creatively and supplement it. To supplement the meaning of the constitution is not to change it.

The word "interpretation" is used in law to denote two different processes. One involves *revealing or clarifying* the meaning of a legal text, a meaning that, despite being previously obscured, was possessed by the text all along. The other process involves *constructing* the meaning of a text by adding to it meaning that it did not previously possess.[57] To mark this distinction, the second, creative process has recently been called "construction" rather than "interpretation."[58] But, given that popular use of the term "interpretation" encompasses both processes, it might be better to distinguish between "clarifying" and "creative" interpretation. The controversy over constitutional interpretation is concerned mainly with clarifying interpretation. The central question is not how judges should decide constitutional disputes when the constitution itself proves insufficiently determinate to provide a solution, but how they should ascertain whether or not it does provide a solution and, if so, what that solution is.

Clarifying interpretation is frequently unable to resolve interpretive problems raised by constitutions that, like other laws, are often ambiguous, vague, contradictory, insufficiently explicit, or even silent as to disputes that judges must decide. Sensible originalists concede that even resort to the founders'

[57] F. Reed Dickerson, *The Interpretation and Application of Statutes* (1975) at 2–5 and ch. 3. See also Lawrence B. Solum's contribution to this volume, "What Is Originalism? The Evolution of Contemporary Originalist Theory."

[58] Keith E. Whittington, *Constitutional Interpretation: Textual Meaning, Original Intent and Judicial Review* (1999) at 5–9.

intentions cannot answer all, or probably even most, interpretative disputes of the kind that appellate courts are required to resolve. They hold that interpretation begins with an examination of all admissible evidence of the lawmakers' intentions, but not that, in difficult cases, it very often ends there.[59] If admissible evidence of those intentions does not resolve a dispute, then judges may be forced to act creatively and, after considering matters such as consistency with general legal doctrines and principles, public policy, and justice, stipulate what the disputed provision should thenceforth be taken to mean. They must settle the dispute: They cannot wash their hands of it and leave the parties to fight it out in the street. Furthermore, when judges act creatively in this way, they are free to take into account contemporary values. "Pluralism" is an attractive – indeed, the obviously correct – theory of how creative, rather than clarifying, interpretation should be conducted.[60]

There should be little controversy about this, because it would make no sense for originalists to deny it. But it does not follow that judges may legitimately change a constitution when it has a determinate meaning, in order to improve or update it. Before any need for creativity has been established, when the judges are engaged in clarifying interpretation, attempting to ascertain what the constitution does in fact mean, they must be guided by admissible evidence of the founders' intentions. As explained under Proposition 1, any constitutional theory must acknowledge that a constitution has *some* meaning that pre-exists judicial interpretation and should offer an account of the nature of that meaning. If the meaning of a constitution is not its original meaning, then non-originalists should tell us what it is. It is hard to see how pluralism could be a viable response, except insofar as a variety of considerations may constitute evidence of the founders' intentions. This includes justice, because it is usually reasonable to presume that lawmakers did not intend injustice.

Proposition 7: Although judges must not deliberately change the constitution, there are at least four ways in which constitutional law can and does legitimately evolve over time. To that considerable extent, originalism is perfectly consistent with "common law constitutionalism" and "living constitutionalism."

It is often said that all legal instruments, but especially constitutions, need to be interpreted flexibly so they can adapt to changing circumstances and community values. Originalism is often criticized for being unable to accommodate

[59] For the meaning of "admissible," see the explanation of "utterance meaning," under Proposition 3.

[60] See Keith Whittington's contribution to this volume, "On Pluralism within Originalism."

this need. But there are many ways in which constitutions can be flexibly interpreted, in the light of contemporary circumstances or values, which are consistent with public meaning versions of originalism.

The first way is through creative interpretation, which is often needed to supplement constitutional provisions that are ambiguous, vague, inconsistent or otherwise partly indeterminate.[61] A large part of what is properly called "constitutional law" consists of general doctrines, methodological principles, and interpretations of specific provisions that are consistent with, but not mandated by, either the bare text of the constitution or what is reliably known of its founders' intentions and purposes. This law is the legitimate creation of the judges, who may continue to develop it in the interests of good government, subject to the legal principle of *stare decisis* and to the underlying constitution insofar as its meaning is determinate.

The second way is through the operation of the principle of *stare decisis*. Judicial mistakes in the interpretation or application of constitutional provisions may be perpetuated because of that principle, but they can also be subsequently repudiated and overruled notwithstanding it. The possibility of judgments being mistaken or, at least, perceived by later judges to have been mistaken is particularly strong when constitutional provisions embodying abstract moral principles are in question. *Brown v Board of Education*,[62] which overruled the decision in *Plessy v Ferguson*,[63] can be justified on this basis. The principle of *stare decisis* should probably be extended to mistakes in the interpretation of the constitution originally made by the non-judicial branches of government. Just like erroneous judicial rulings, they may – in Robert Bork's words – "have become so embedded in the life of the nation, so accepted by the society, so fundamental to the private and public expectations of individuals and institutions, that [they] should not be changed now."[64]

The third way in which constitutions can be interpreted flexibly arises from the occasional need for judges to depart from the literal meaning of a constitutional provision to fulfill its original purpose. Sometimes the language used in an old constitution proves inadequate to achieve its purpose in the modern world because of social or technological developments that its founders did not anticipate. An uncontroversial example is the provision in the United States Constitution vesting exclusive power in Congress to raise and maintain "Armies" and "a Navy" and to regulate "the land and naval Forces."[65] When

[61] See Proposition 6.

[62] *Supra* note 50.

[63] 163 U.S. 537 (1896).

[64] Robert H. Bork, *The Tempting of America; The Political Seduction of the Law* (1990) at 158 (Bork, *The Tempting of America*).

[65] *The Constitution of the United States of America* (1787), Article I, Section 8.

aircraft were developed, it would have defeated the provision's obvious purpose if Congress had been denied the power to raise and maintain an air force. Most lawyers would agree that the courts may stray from the literal meaning of such a provision without violating the constitution's amendment procedure, provided they do so only in an incremental fashion that is necessary to achieve the provision's obvious, original purpose. This can be consistent with the original public meaning of the provision because that is not the same as its original literal meaning.

The fourth way is entailed by the long-established distinction between the meaning of a constitution and its application.[66] Courts have frequently affirmed that, although the meaning of the constitution cannot change except by formal amendment, its application can legitimately change as a result of changes in the circumstances to which it is applied. The High Court of Australia borrowed John Stuart Mill's terminology of "connotation" and "denotation" to draw the same distinction (today, more philosophically sophisticated concepts such as sense and reference, and intension and extension, could be used for the same purpose).[67] The application, denotation, reference, or extension of a term is comprised of all the things in the world (or all possible worlds) that it denotes or refers to; its meaning, connotation, sense, or intension consists of the criteria or the function that determine its denotation.

This distinction can explain quite dramatic changes in the operation of a constitution. For example, the Australian Parliament has the power to legislate with respect to external affairs, a term whose original meaning probably included the power to implement international treaties that the executive government has ratified.[68] Early in the twentieth century, the treaty-implementing power was very modest because the number of treaties ratified was small, and the kinds of subject matters they dealt with were also very limited in number and scope. Because of a massive increase in all these respects, the power now has a much greater ambit and practical impact than when the constitution was first enacted. As a result, the shape of Australian federalism has changed dramatically without the meaning of the constitution having been altered.

[66] *Home Building & Loan Assoc. v Blaisdell* (1934) 290 U.S. 398 at 451 (per Sutherland J); *Village of Euclid v Ambler Realty Co* (1926) 272 U.S. 365 at 367; *South Carolina v United States* 199 U.S. 437 at 448 (per Brewer J). See also Mark D. Greenberg and Harry Litman, "The Meaning of Original Meaning" (1998) 86 Geo. L.J. 569; Berman, "Originalism Is Bunk," *supra* note 7 at 28.

[67] See Christopher R. Green, "Originalism and the Sense-Reference Distinction" (2006) 50 Saint Louis U. L.J. 555.

[68] *Victoria v Commonwealth* (1996) 138 A.L.R. 129.

A consequential distinction between *intended* meaning and *intended* application is also important. If the meaning of a constitutional provision is its original public meaning, it may depend partly on original public knowledge of what the founders intended it to mean. But it need not depend on original public knowledge of how they intended the provision to be applied in particular cases. As previously mentioned, it may depend partly on original public knowledge of their semantic intentions but not of their expectation or application intentions.[69] The rule of law and the separation of powers require that judges decide for themselves how it should be applied, according to its true meaning, rather than slavishly deferring to whatever applications the lawmakers may have expected or desired. Because that decision may depend on judgments of fact or value – depending on the terms of the provision – and because in making these judgments judges are properly guided by the beliefs and values of their own time and place, there is legitimate scope for temporal variation in the application of constitutional provisions. For example, to properly apply a provision incorporating a moral principle, judges must decide what the principle requires rather than what the lawmakers may have believed it required. The United States Constitution arguably includes many moral principles, such as the "equal protection" clause of the Fourteenth Amendment. To properly apply them, judges today must make moral judgments, not factual judgments about the founders' beliefs. This is why the Supreme Court's decision in *Brown*, that racially segregated education violated the equal protection clause, was not wrong just because it was inconsistent with the expectation or application intentions of a majority of those who adopted the clause. Most originalists say it was right, because the original public meaning of the relevant clauses of the Fourteenth Amendment included a general moral principle of equality.[70] Even Ronald Dworkin, widely but dubiously regarded as a non-originalist, now accepts that this assessment of *Brown* depends on the founders' semantic intentions in enacting those clauses.[71]

For all these reasons, public meaning versions of originalism are consistent with both the content and application of constitutional law having considerable flexibility and capacity to be adapted by the judiciary to contemporary needs and values. Continuing judicial development of the very large, judge-made body of constitutional law can sensibly be called "common law constitutional interpretation," and is perfectly consistent with public meaning

[69] This is a restatement of the distinction between semantic and expectation intentions: See the final paragraph under Proposition 3.

[70] See, *e.g.*, Bork, *The Tempting of America*, *supra* note 57 at 82; Michael J. Perry, *We the People; the Fourteenth Amendment and the Supreme Court* (1999) ch. 3.

[71] Ronald Dworkin, *Justice in Robes* (2006) at 123; see also text to notes 33 and 45 to this chapter.

versions of originalism.[72] Indeed, sensible originalism is compatible with the non-originalist metaphor of constitutions as "living trees" that grow and change in response to social developments. For example, all the ways in which constitutional law can legitimately evolve, according to Aileen Kavanagh's detailed account of "living constitutionalism," seem to be consistent with originalism so conceived.[73] On this view – recently defended by the prominent former non-originalist, Jack Balkin – a properly refined, and therefore moderate, version of originalism turns out to be equivalent to the most persuasive version of non-originalism.[74] As both theories are purged of their weaknesses, they are moderated and eventually merge. Originalists wonder what more, by way of flexibility and capacity for "evolution," non-originalists could possibly want.

Proposition 8: Consistent application of any constitutional theory, including originalism, might lead to grave injustice in a particular case. Judges might then be morally bound to disobey the constitution, while pretending to obey it. But a theory justifying occasional "noble lies" about what the constitution means is not a theory about what it really means.

It is possible for a constitutional provision, given its original public meaning, to be extremely unjust. This is often supposed to embarrass originalists. In the United States, the decision about slavery in *Dred Scott v Sandford*,[75] which purported to be based on original meaning, has been pressed as an example. Whether or not the Supreme Court correctly understood the original meaning of the provisions bearing on that case has been a subject of debate. But either way, originalists must concede that injustice might occasionally result from the strict application of their theory. It would be a dangerous folly to imagine that any constitution is flawless, a "perfect constitution" that is guaranteed never to embody or authorize injustice.[76]

On the other hand, injustice might also result from non-originalist interpretation. There is no guarantee that interpreting a constitution according to contemporary values and beliefs, rather than those of the founders, must produce morally superior outcomes. This is because there is no guarantee that

[72] Originalists are therefore able to accept many of the arguments made in David A. Strauss, "Common Law Constitutional Interpretation" (1996) 63 U. Chicago L. Rev. 877.

[73] Aileen Kavanagh, "The Idea of a Living Constitution" (2003) 16 Can. J. Law and Juris. 55.

[74] Jack M. Balkin, "Abortion and Original Meaning" (2007) 24 Const. Comment. 101, and "Original Meaning and Constitutional Redemption" (2007) 24 Const. Comment. 427, relying especially on the distinction between intended meanings and expected applications.

[75] 60 U.S. 393 at 426 (1856).

[76] Henry P. Monaghan, "Our Perfect Constitution" (1981) 56 N.Y.U. L. Rev. 353.

contemporary values will always be superior to those of the past. Justice Scalia has remarked on "the wide eyed, youthful meliorism" displayed by some non-originalists: "Every day, in every way, we get better and better. Societies always *mature*, they never *rot*."[77]

Even if originalism did lead to more injustices than non-originalism, it might still be preferable on the ground that strict fidelity to the prescribed amendment procedure is more faithful to the principles mentioned previously – the rule of law, democracy, federalism, and so on. In law, no individual decision, considered in isolation, can be so self-evidently meritorious that it should be reached regardless of its consistency with general principles applied in other cases. The discipline of law is the discipline of general principles: It is inherently opposed to ad hoc decision making.

In any event, the possibility of judges being placed in the dilemma of being legally bound to apply morally repugnant laws is hardly confined to constitutional law. Moral obligation trumps legal obligation, so perhaps in some cases judges should lie about the law by pretending that it means something they know it does not mean. If judges openly flouted the constitution, they would set an extremely dangerous precedent that the other branches of government might be tempted to follow. Consequently, in those rare cases in which judges might be morally justified in changing the constitution to mitigate extreme injustice, it would usually be morally incumbent on them to do so surreptitiously, by pretending to interpret it in a legally orthodox manner – in short, to lie. But a theory that justifies occasional noble lies about what the constitution means, in order to avoid extreme injustice, is not a theory about what the constitution means. It is a theory about pretended – rather than genuine – constitutional interpretation.

Supposedly sophisticated, tough-minded "realists" or "pragmatists" sometimes portray constitutional adjudication as far-sighted statesmanship, a branch of High Politics rather than humdrum law, in which legal requirements must be weighed against other important considerations, and the constitution boldly reshaped if justice or good government so demands. The statesman (or woman) must take legal formalities, including the allocation of institutional authority to change the constitution, into account. But the statesman is not bound by them, even if, as a matter of prudence, he must often pretend to be.

This is not the occasion to take on the pragmatists. I merely submit that in countries whose constitutions (including their amendment procedures) are democratic and tolerably just, the collective weight of the many moral

[77] Justice A. Scalia, "The Role of a Constitutional Court in a Democratic Society" (1995) 2 The Judicial Review 141 at 145.

reasons against judges changing a constitution, contrary to the prescribed amendment procedure, is so heavy that it can be outweighed only by extremely powerful considerations likely to arise only in exceptional circumstances. In such countries, there should be a presumption that the constitution and its amendment procedure ought morally to be obeyed, especially by judges whose sworn duty is to uphold it.

CONCLUSION

To highlight the differences between originalist and non-originalist interpretation, consider again the phrase "peace, order, and good government," used in the Australian Constitution in granting legislative powers to the national Parliament. The phrase has a well-known original meaning – a technical legal meaning very different from its literal one – which originalists insist that judges must continue to accept. The phrase is well known to have been intended to grant plenary power with respect to the subject matters enumerated.[78] If judges today were to adopt its literal meaning, they would change the constitution in a radical way, in effect adding to it an indeterminate number of new, judicially enforceable limits to legislative power. The Constitution does not include anything like a Bill or Charter of Rights granting the judges broad authority to invalidate legislation that (in their opinion) violates human rights or other unspecified principles of good government.[79] Given the referendum procedure that section 128 requires for amendments, one would surely expect that before the judges could acquire such authority, the Constitution would have to be amended formally by referendum. The Constitution itself, and therefore the rule of law, as well as the principles of democracy and federalism, require that such a major constitutional change first be approved by the electors.[80]

But not so, the non-originalist says – or logically should say. The founders included the words "for the peace, order and good government of the Commonwealth" in section 51 of the Constitution. They may have intended those words to grant plenary power, but that intention is not decisive. The literal meaning of the words is – fortuitously – capable of bearing the opposite meaning. The judges are therefore free to interpret them as conferring on the judges

[78] See *supra* note 2.

[79] The Constitution does include some express limits to legislative power that are obviously intended to protect important principles of good government. But as indicated by the maxim *expressio unius est exclusio alterius*, this merely emphasizes the absence of other limits, and especially the absence of a broad Bill of Rights.

[80] See Proposition 5.

precisely that broad authority to invalidate legislation on human rights or other grounds that the founders intended to withhold. The original, intended meaning of the words is not binding, so the judges are free to choose which of the alternative interpretations best serves what they take to be the values of contemporary Australia. So there is no need for any referendum. The words can legitimately be held to have a new meaning – the opposite of their original, intended meaning – without the words themselves having to be changed.

A non-originalist such as Mitchell Berman might reply that he, too, would disapprove of judges using interpretation to bring about such a radical change to the Australian Constitution. Non-originalists, he points out, accept that judges operate under constraints imposed by the "argumentative norms of a culture and of a practice."[81] One such norm requires that original meanings, although not binding, be given considerable weight.[82] Another norm is that judges should seek public acceptance of their interpretations, which requires consideration of "evolving popular understandings."[83] This is inapplicable to the Australian example, because there is no popular understanding of the phrase in question. On the other hand, a further argumentative norm is that judges should weigh up the substantive merits of alternative interpretations, according to "widely accepted values like welfare, preference-satisfaction, security, liberty, equality, and justice."[84] The preferable interpretation, says Berman, is guided by our reasons for engaging in the activity of interpreting, and constitutions "might be understood and valued – in part to secure good outcomes within broad constraints."[85] It follows that a non-originalist judge who believes that justice would be best served by the existence of judicially enforceable rights would have a good reason to interpret the phrase literally, as imposing previously unrecognized limits on Parliament's legislative powers. The question would then be whether that reason outweighs whatever reasons non-originalists have to abide by original meaning.[86] Berman does not spell out these reasons, but given that he rejects my argument that changes to the meaning of the constitutional text violate the exclusivity of the amendment clause, they presumably do not include the principles I have emphasized.[87] It is therefore far from clear that non-originalist judges should resist the temptation to adopt the proposed radical new "interpretation" of the phrase in question. Everything depends on the relative weights they attribute to all the competing factors they take to be relevant, of which fidelity to the original meaning is

[81] Berman, "Originalism Is Bunk," *supra* note 7 at 65–66.
[82] *Ibid.* at 68, 74 and 81–83.
[83] *Ibid.* at 56–57 and 73.
[84] *Ibid.* at 79.
[85] *Ibid.* at 55.
[86] See *ibid.* at 82–83.
[87] See the text accompanying notes 37–39, *supra*.

only one. Berman rejects the demand that non-originalists should develop a "theory" to guide the reasoning of non-originalist judges.[88] His reassurance that judges operate under constraints is therefore far from comforting. In the end, it amounts to saying: "Trust the judges to do the right thing."

As my final conclusion, I would reiterate Propositions 1–8 set out in the first part of the chapter.

[88] Berman, "Originalism Is Bunk," *supra* note 7 at 85.

3 On Pluralism within Originalism

Keith E. Whittington

A lot of thought and debate goes into the drafting of a constitution. Fundamental interests of society are affected by the choices made about constitutional design and constitutional language. Political opportunities are created or foreclosed by constitutional choices. Values, interests, and groups are recognized, valorized, neglected, or worse. Whether the process of creating a constitution is relatively open and participatory or relatively closed and elitist, the stakes are high and the process of constitution making is a deliberate one.

But after constitutions are drafted, they must be put into practice. No matter how carefully and thoughtfully crafted at their origins, constitutions must still be interpreted and implemented over time to remain effective and relevant. Disputes over constitutional meaning quickly arise under every constitution, and new problems emerge that challenge the ingenuity of those who seek to adhere to pre-existing constitutional commitments and to operate within an established constitutional framework. The constitutional project does not end with a moment of founding. A successful constitutional enterprise requires ongoing efforts at constitutional maintenance, and sometimes significant revision.

It is no surprise that the process of implementing constitutions is controversial. The stakes remain large when it comes time to making choices about how best to interpret and effectuate constitutional requirements. Agreement over how best to elaborate the constitutional text has tended to break down. To complicate matters further, disagreements over the substance of political disputes have tended to infect ideas about how constitutions ought to be interpreted. Repeated efforts have been made in the United States to make constitutional interpretation a bit more orderly, but success has been limited.

There is a variety of common forms of constitutional argumentation in the United States. Appeals to the original meaning of the Constitution or the historical intentions of those who drafted and ratified the constitutional text are among the common sets of arguments that lawyers and judges use when attempting to construe and apply the meaning of the Constitution, but these are not the only forms of constitutional arguments that legal and political actors offer in support of their positions. Explicit originalist arguments exist in an environment of "pluralism in constitutional interpretation."[1]

This chapter will briefly state the position that I have defended elsewhere, that originalism is the best approach to interpreting a written constitution, and discuss the important distinction between the interpretation and construction of constitutional meaning. The central goal of the chapter is to examine the relationship between originalism and other approaches to constitutional interpretation. It is often argued that originalism is particularly hostile to the use of the full variety of the forms of constitutional argumentation, to "pluralism." But originalism need not imply the irrelevance of other forms of constitutional argumentation, and the existence of a pluralistic discourse in constitutional interpretation does not by itself suggest that originalism is radically at odds with current practice. Originalists should, in principle, be open to the use of various forms of argumentation so long as such arguments are disciplined to the overarching goal of discovering and implementing the original meaning of the Constitution. What they must resist is the appeal to alternative modes of constitutional arguments as possible trumps to known original meaning. This consideration of the uses and limits of pluralism within originalism also helps clarify the continuing differences between originalists and their critics.

I. INTERPRETATION, CONSTRUCTION, AND DEMOCRATIC AUTHORITY

Originalism, as it is most commonly defended as a mode of constitutional interpretation, emphasizes the public meaning of the constitutional text at the time of its adoption. The effort to interpret the Constitution is the process of trying to grasp that meaning.[2]

This is sometimes known as "public meaning" or "original understandings" originalism, as distinct from "original intentions" originalism. The public meaning form (or originalism simply) has become the more common form of originalism, and the preference for it has both theoretical and practical roots. It urges interpreters to look to the text and what a competent reader of the text

[1] Stephen M. Griffin, "Pluralism in Constitutional Interpretation," 72 Texas L. Rev. 1753 (1994) [Griffin, "Pluralism"].

[2] See also, Lawrence B. Solum, "Constitutional Texting," 44 U. San Diego L. Rev. 123 (2007); Keith E. Whittington, "The New Originalism," 2 Geo. J.L. & Pub. Pol'y 599 (2004) [Whittington, "New Originalism"].

at the time would have understood it to mean (which may be informed by the broader historical context, purpose, and structure of the document, as well as common linguistic usages of the period). The intentionalist form focuses more on the specific intentions of the author or "authors" of a given textual provision to assess what they might have intended that provision to mean. To the extent that the U.S. Constitution, at least, gained its force through popular ratification, we might think that it is its public meaning that carries the most authoritative weight. To the extent that it is hard as a practical matter to identify the coherent intentions of a collective author (potentially across multiple ratification conventions) on many aspects of the text, it may be more fruitful to consider what given constitutional terms or phrases or provisions could be commonly understood to mean in their historical context. A range of evidence may be useful to uncovering the public meaning of the text, including convention debates, but James Madison may not have privileged insight into the meaning of the U.S. Constitution in the same way for an originalist that he might have for an intentionalist.[3]

There is a variety of rationales for adopting an originalist approach to constitutional interpretation. When originalist arguments were first being developed in their modern form in the United States in the 1970s and 1980s, the primary justificatory arguments were negative and aimed at correcting what critics thought had gone wrong in American constitutional jurisprudence in the postwar period.[4] An originalist approach to constitutional interpretation might be a way of imposing some self-discipline on judges. Such arguments in favor of originalism are tied to ideas of "judicial restraint." In one version, judges are restrained by originalism from behaving willfully and imposing their own subjective moral values and policy preferences through constitutional adjudication. Interpreting the terms of the Constitution in light of historical evidence would rein in the tendencies of judges to reach results that seem personally appealing when exercising the power of judicial review. In a second version of judicial restraint, originalism is linked to Thayerian deference to political majorities. If the originalist constitution imposes few substantive constraints on the legislative majorities, and if judges adopt a strong presumption that statutes are constitutional, then judicial review will generally result

[3] I would emphasize "in the same way" here. As a particularly insightful and well-informed contemporary constitutional commentator, Madison is no doubt useful. But Madison *qua* founder has less of a role to play in public meaning originalism than in original intent originalism.

[4] See, e.g., Whittington, "New Originalism," *supra* note 2; Johnathan G. O'Neill, *Originalism in American Law and Politics* (2007); Gregory Bassham, *Original Intent and the Constitution* (1992).

in upholding statutes against constitutional challenges. Still others have more recently justified originalism in terms of the substantive values that it might promote. Whether because the U.S. Constitution, as originally understood, happens to include substantively desirable provisions or because a constitution created through a drafting and ratification of the sort incorporated into the provisions of the U.S. Constitution is relatively likely to be substantively desirable, originalism has been justified by way of the results of that it might produce.[5] Originalism, according to such arguments, preserves substantively attractive constitutional commitments that would otherwise be eroded or transformed.

I have rested my own case for originalism on a different set of arguments. It is widely accepted that the power to set aside laws as unconstitutional is a judicial duty closely connected to the authority of the courts to interpret the terms of the Constitution. If a constitution provides a law that is superior to statute, then judges have a duty to interpret the Constitution and apply it, even when the directives of statutes conflict with the directives of the Constitution. It remains a challenge, of course, to determine what constitutes faithful interpretation of a written constitutional text. I will not attempt to rehearse the controversies over the proper understanding of interpretation here. It will suffice to say that I take the constitutional text to be a purposeful communication, and that the goal of interpretation is to recover the meaning that was being communicated through the text. Faithfully identifying the constitutional rule transmitted through the text provides the starting point for exercising the power of judicial review.[6]

This vision of interpretation and judicial review can be further rooted in a conception of democratic self-governance. We expect judges to interpret *this* text and to regard it as a purposeful communication, not merely as a found object, because it emerged from a duly authorized lawmaker. The Constitution contains rules drafted and ratified by those democratically selected to do so, and it can be changed by duly authorized constitutional legislators. Constitutional interpreters are necessarily cast in the subordinate role of determining the will of that lawgiver as it is expressed through the text. From the originalist perspective, the court, in exercising judicial review, is charged with preserving the constitutional choices that have been deliberately made by specified and democratic procedures. If the court allows government officials to violate the terms of the constitutional text, or the text as originally understood, then it has

[5] See, *e.g.*, Randy Barnett, *Restoring the Lost Constitution* (2005); John O. McGinnis and Michael B. Rappaport, "Originalism and Supermajoritarism: Defending the Nexus," 101 Nw. U.L. Rev. 1919 (2007).

[6] See also, Keith E. Whittington, *Constitutional Interpretation* (1999) [Whittington, *Constitutional Interpretation*]; Keith E. Whittington, "Dworkin's Originalism: The Role of Intentions in Constitutional Interpretation," 62 Review of Politics 5 (2000).

failed to preserve the decisions made by the duly authorized constitutional lawgivers. If the court itself alters the constitutional requirements, departing from the meaning of the Constitution as it was originally understood, then it has likewise failed to preserve the decisions made by the duly authorized constitutional lawgivers. Whatever rules or understandings are substituted in their place may be substantively attractive and may be endorsed by legislative or judicial majorities, but they no longer derive from processes that were authorized to create the Constitution in the first place. Originalism places a particular premium on democratic constitutional lawmaking, as a normative ideal and as a practical reality. The moment of lawmaking may have occurred over two centuries ago or it may be of relatively recent vintage, but what should be normatively important for originalism is not that constitutions are old but that they are drafted and ratified.[7]

But there are many caveats that should be noted even in this brief rendition of the originalist project. The normative desirability of originalism assumes that the Constitution in question is itself worth preserving. If the Constitution itself is so morally flawed that it throws the regime into question, then there are more complicated questions to be raised about whether the Constitution should be interpreted at all and whether the power of judicial review could be constructed on some other foundation. Similarly, this assumes that judicial review is primarily concerned with and authorized by the effort to interpret fundamental rules laid down by a constituent legislative power. It is possible that courts should perform other tasks either in addition to or instead of this function.[8] Future progress in identifying the disagreements between originalists and their critics and working through those disagreements may well come in thinking about what authorizes courts to exercise judicial review in the first place and what range of tasks we want courts to perform in a constitutional democracy and how those might best be characterized and justified.

Given that the first priority of originalism is faithful adherence to the original meaning of the Constitution, the implications for the practice of judicial review are necessarily contingent on the specific text and its history. Originalism, as elaborated here, is concerned with the meaning conveyed through the text. It is not concerned with the expected applications of that text, the expected

[7] See also, Whittington, *Constitutional Interpretation*, *supra* note 6; Keith E. Whittington, "It's Alive: The Persistence of the Constitution," 11 The Good Society 8 (2002); Keith E. Whittington, "Let's Call the Whole Thing Off?" 22 Const. Comment. 101 (2005).

[8] See, *e.g.*, Rogers Smith, "The Inherent Deceptiveness of Constitutional Discourse: A Diagnosis and Prescription," in Ian Shapiro and Robert Adams, eds., *NOMOS XL* (1998); Mitchell N. Berman, "Originalism is Bunk," 84 N.Y.U. L. Rev. 1 (2009); Richard A. Primus, "When Should Original Meanings Matter?" 107 Mich. L. Rev. 165 (2008).

consequences of constitutional provisions, or the particular motivations for adopting a given textual provision. An originalist interpreter is concerned with discovering the constitutional rule or standard or principle that was being adopted, but not with how anyone at the time necessarily expected the rule to be applied or what motivated them to advocate for the inclusion of the rule. Such information may well provide helpful evidence about what the rule itself was commonly understood to be, but the purpose of the historical inquiry for the interpreter is to identify the meaning of the text, not its expected applications or its political purposes. But the content of the rule necessarily depends on the text and its historical context. Whether a given constitutional provision is expansive or constricting and whether the available historical materials help pin down textual meaning or not are empirical questions. Originalism as such does not call on the courts to be particularly deferential to legislatures, nor does it assume that constitutional provisions are necessarily clear or designed to limit the discretion of courts. A given constitutional provision, informed by evidence of original meaning, might well require a judge to strike down a given piece of legislation, or it might well delegate extensive discretionary authority to the courts. The judicial duty is to faithfully interpret the Constitution as it was written and understood, not to artificially confine its meaning.

Constitutional interpretation will never be sufficient. No matter how careful the draftsman or diligent the interpreter, discoverable constitutional meaning will run out. Some provisions may remain vague or ambiguous, either in general or in the context of particular applications of immediate interest. Crucial indeterminacies will remain that will have to be resolved for the Constitution to be effectuated. In other instances, the constitutional text may overlook, fail to resolve, or fail to address (either explicitly or implicitly) constitutional subjects that later become salient.

Constitutional construction is the process of elaborating constitutional meaning to supplement constitutional interpretation.[9] Through construction, contemporary actors resolve indeterminacies and fill gaps in constitutional meaning. So long as the discoverable meaning of the Constitution is not violated, the process of construction works to extend the salience of the Constitution to political life and to help implement the Constitution and carry it into practice. Although a construction of the Constitution is an effort to elaborate and give effect to the Constitution, it cannot claim to be a uniquely faithful rendering of constitutional meaning. It necessarily approaches the Constitution creatively, politically, in order to resolve indeterminacies. For its

[9] See also, Keith E. Whittington, *Constitutional Construction* (1999) [Whittington, *Constitutional Construction*].

success, a construction appeals to its attractiveness and utility to the contemporary context rather than to its historical fidelity. A constitutional construction is contestable not so much on the empirical grounds that it has misconstrued the discoverable meaning of the pre-existing constitution, but on normative and pragmatic grounds that it does not adequately advance the constitutional project that we now want.

The distinction between interpretation and construction does not depend on accepting originalism as the appropriate approach to interpretation. Recognizing the distinction does carry advantages for originalist theory, however. Originalism is often criticized for leaving the Constitution stuck in the past and unable to adapt to changing circumstances, political pressures, and values. Originalist theory has traditionally downplayed the uncertainty or indeterminacy in historical materials and constitutional meaning while emphasizing the static quality of constitutional requirements, which is not surprising given an exclusive focus on interpretation. Originalist theory should instead admit the possibility of indeterminacy in constitutional meaning and be open to examining the ways in which the changing constitutional practices relate to the historical constitution. Recognizing the role of construction in the process of construing and implementing the Constitution, and the ways in which the process of constitutional construction supplements constitutional interpretation, creates avenues for originalist theory to identify what role originalism itself can play within constitutional practice and how it can be effectively integrated into a broader theory of constitutional maintenance and elaboration. Originalism is critically important for thinking about constitutional interpretation and judicial review, but an adequate constitutional theory should do more than understand constitutional interpretation.

II. PLURALISM IN CONSTITUTIONAL INTERPRETATION

Scholars, lawyers, and judges routinely make use of a variety of forms of argument when discussing the meaning of the Constitution and how the power of judicial review should be exercised. Arguments about original meaning are usually characterized as one among many that interpreters might reasonably employ. Many theories of constitutional interpretation, including originalism, can then be characterized as attempting to elevate one common mode of constitutional argumentation above the others, to reduce the pluralism of current interpretive practice to a single method. As a result, any theory that proposes a single method of constitutional interpretation would seem to carry a heavy burden because it asks us to alter our current practice and artificially reduce the scope of available argument and evidence that we otherwise would accept as legitimate and helpful to the interpretive project.

There is no single best way to characterize the common forms of constitutional arguments, but some general categories can be readily recognized. Richard Fallon points to several common forms of constitutional argument, including the use of text, framers' intent, precedent, values, and "constitutional theory" ("an account of the values, purposes, and political theory in light of which the Constitution or certain elements of its language or structure are most intelligible").[10] Philip Bobbitt offers a prominent "typology of constitutional arguments" that includes historical, textual, doctrinal, prudential, structural, and ethical arguments.[11] Walter Murphy and his co-authors take note of several "interpretive approaches," including textualism, originalism, doctrinalism, developmentalism, philosophical approaches, structuralism, purposive approaches, and prudential approaches.[12] Drawing in part on other works, Stephen Griffin suggests a "consensus about the bases for constitutional interpretation" that includes the text, founding intent, precedent, constitutional structure, and national ethos or tradition.[13] Such accounts could be multiplied, with at least a common core of approaches to constitutional interpretation reappearing on such lists.

As Bobbitt observes, such categories make up the "grammar" of our constitutional argumentation.[14] They define the conventionally recognized legitimate moves in the game of constitutional interpretation. Other types of arguments are not conventionally recognized as legitimate and available within the legal discourse about the meaning of the Constitution. Appeals to religious revelation, for example, are out of bounds. Is current public opinion or are foreign court decisions relevant for elucidating the meaning of a constitutional provision? The rules of the game are subject to change, and political actors struggle to include or exclude new forms of argument about the Constitution. Constitutional discourse may also be affected by its institutional context, with some forms of argument being legitimate within some venues but less viable within others.[15] Appeals to electoral mandates and consequences may be fair game in constitutional debate in the political arena but not in the judicial arena, and

[10] Richard H. Fallon, Jr., "A Constructivist Coherence Theory of Constitutional Interpretation," 100 Harv. L. Rev. 1189 at 1200 (1987) [Fallon, "Constructivist Coherence"].

[11] Philip Bobbitt, *Constitutional Fate* (1982) 7 [Bobbitt, *Constitutional Fate*].

[12] Walter F. Murphy *et al.*, *American Constitutional Interpretation*, 3rd Edition (2003) at 389–429.

[13] Griffin, "Pluralism," *supra* note 1 at 1764.

[14] Bobbitt, *Constitutional Fate*, *supra* note 11 at 6.

[15] Whittington, *Constitutional Construction*, *supra* note 9.

scholars may try out forms of arguments in scholarship that would not (yet) be regarded as appropriate in courtroom.

Originalist arguments are regularly included within these broader lists. But such arguments constitute one type among many. Although explicit arguments about the historical meaning of the constitutional text are familiar and among the legitimate moves in the interpretive game, they are not the predominant moves. Arguments from the text and from doctrine are commonplace. Other types of argument may be less frequent but they certainly recur with some regularity. What are the implications of this pluralism?

III. ORIGINALISM WITHIN A PLURALIST ENVIRONMENT

There are potentially two distinct problems that pluralists pose to originalism. The appeal to pluralism may be another way of raising a familiar conundrum for both originalists and their opponents: Must "the Constitution mean what it always meant?"[16] The availability of multiple modalities of constitutional argumentation may become a way for pluralists to depart from or trump the original meaning whenever the results seem dissatisfying or do not line up adequately with some other criteria. Pluralism, in this mode, becomes a way of dispensing with the known meaning of the Constitution while still claiming to interpret the Constitution. Originalists necessarily have to oppose this cafeteria-style approach to constitutional interpretation. Pluralism may raise a second, less radical challenge to originalism. Pluralists might simply note the fact that contemporary constitutional practice is characterized by multiple forms of constitutional argumentation. Originalism does not monopolize, or even predominate, the legal, judicial, or popular constitutional landscape, and so originalists have a heavy burden to bear in trying to unseat that status quo and justify reducing the diversity of the constitutional ecology. It is here that originalists can make a more modulated response.

Against this pluralism, originalism is often taken to be a single-method theory of constitutional interpretation. It would seem to take one of the currently available methods of constitutional argumentation and hold it up as the single correct method. As such, originalism might be seen as advocating the delegitimation of alternative constitutional "modalities" in favor of the exclusive reliance on "historical" arguments regarding framing intent and constitutional

[16] Stephen R. Munzer and James W. Nickel, "Does the Constitution Mean What it Always Meant?" 77 Colum. L. Rev. 1029 (1977).

meaning.[17] At the very least, originalists might be thought to prefer making historical arguments to other forms of argument and to be more responsive to explicitly historical arguments than to other forms of argument.[18]

I think this takes an overly narrow view of how constitutional argumentation should be expected to work within an originalist framework. The common typology with several available argumentative forms that includes originalism within that pluralistic set suggests that an originalist theory would simply select out one of these argumentative forms and dispense with the rest. Explicitly originalist scholarship is likely to focus on historical arguments and evidence of constitutional meaning to elucidate some constitutional provision or problem, but even advocates and judges who are sympathetic to originalism are likely to take advantage of a wider array of argumentative forms. Is this simply evidence of inconsistency or a problematic gap between a single-method theory and a pluralistic practice? Not necessarily. There is a place for pluralism within originalism, but originalist theory would argue that such a wide array of arguments should be carefully disciplined by the overarching interpretive enterprise.

The originalist enterprise is committed to uncovering to the degree possible the meaning of the rule or principle that those who were authorized to create the Constitution meant to communicate, not to making use of any particular form of constitutional argument. Arguments marshaling historical evidence about framing intent and original meaning and drawing on sources such as ratification convention debates or early constitutional commentary are the obvious form that originalist arguments are expected to take. They provide the cleanest examples of the originalist modality for creating and illustrating typologies of constitutional argumentation, and they provide the most direct basis for considering the acceptability and authoritativeness of referencing original meaning to resolve current constitutional disputes.

The goal of the interpretive enterprise, for originalists, is to discover the meaning that the author of the text was attempting to convey through the text. The originalist should not have pre-commitments regarding what type of evidence might be helpful for discovering and understanding that meaning. Originalists are committed to an interpretive effort, not an argumentative form. When available and illuminating, classically historical arguments should be given great weight. But historical materials as such are likely to tell only part of the story. Relevant materials may not be particularly probative of the

[17] Philip Bobbitt, *Constitutional Interpretation* (1991) at 12.

[18] See John B. Gates and Glenn A. Phelps, "Intentionalism in Constitutional Opinions," 49 Political Research Quarterly 245 (1996); Robert M. Howard and Jeffrey A. Segal, "An Original Look at Originalism," 36 Law & Society Rev. 113 (2002).

particular issues that are of concern to us or may in themselves leave substantial indeterminacies to be resolved as to what the constitutional meaning might be.

Other modalities of constitutional argumentation are relevant to the originalist enterprise, and we should expect to see them deployed within an originalist framework. The text of the Constitution is quite appropriately the first piece of evidence that an originalist would consult in interpreting the document. Antonin Scalia frequently refers to his own approach to the task of interpretation as a kind of "textualism" and Akhil Amar's is simultaneously regarded as something of an originalist and as an advocate of a version of textualism.[19] A close textual analysis of the words and phrases that were actually chosen for inclusion in the Constitution, the relationships among them, and their relationship to other texts is a ready starting point for originalist analysis. An originalist might well expect that the words in the text have a "plain meaning" that is readily accessible, and would certainly expect that the words in the text convey meaning and are comprehensible to appropriate audiences even without extrinsic interpretive aids (such as access to the convention debates). The move within originalist theory toward "original meaning" originalism rather than "original intent" originalism puts even greater emphasis on the text as an independent bearer of original meaning.[20] An argument from text may not be decisive, but would be part of the originalist repertoire.

For similar reasons, arguments grounded in structures or values implicit in or embedded in the constitutional scheme or language are likewise fair game for originalists. Unlike some American state constitutions, the U.S. Constitution does not have a general statement of principle recognizing the separation of powers. The Tenth Amendment, and occasionally some other provisions, provides a general textual hook for discussing fundamental principles of federalism. Originalist arguments need not be clause-bound. Arguments drawn from the design of the Constitution or the background assumptions of the Constitution or even the "ethos" or traditions of the people may well be appropriate from an originalist standpoint, so long as the aim is to illuminate the meaning of the constitutional rules put in the place by those who created the Constitution. Examining the constitutional design for clues about original constitutional meaning is, in principle, as useful as examining the constitutional text.[21]

[19] Antonin Scalia, A *Matter of Interpretation*, Amy Gutmann ed. (1997). Akhil Reed Amar, "Intratextualism," 112 Harv. L. Rev. 747 (1999).

[20] Whittington, "New Originalism," *supra* note 2.

[21] For one exploration of related issues, see Randy E. Barnett, "The Misconceived Assumption about Constitutional Assumptions," 103 Nw. U.L. Rev. 615 (2009).

Doctrinal arguments are perhaps the most common form of constitutional argument in contemporary legal and judicial practice. Arguments from text or history or structure take less space in judicial opinions and seemingly carry less weight in judicial decisions than arguments from precedent. There are some good reasons why this should be the case. Precedent provides intellectual shortcuts for thinking about the meaning of a law and how it might be applied to a range of common problems. A case of first impression may require examining the full range of messy arguments relating to constitutional meaning, but over time precedent should have distilled those arguments down to a set of more reliable, accepted, and easy-to-digest conclusions. For the Supreme Court justices, as much as for the lower court judges or executive branch administrators, doctrine provides an easier-to-follow and more detailed constitutional rulebook that does not require mastering and synthesizing a wide array of materials and arguments for every case or problem that might arise. Precedent translates the Constitution into agreed-on, easy-to-administer constitutional rules, and most constitutional cases are really disputes about routine administration of those agreed-on rules, of our baseline constitutional understandings. Once we have gone through the hard work of reaching "agreement" on the meaning of the commerce clause or the equal protection clause and produced *Wickard v. Filburn*[22] or *Brown v. Board of Education*,[23] then for a large class of disputes that are likely to arise relating to those provisions of the Constitution we do not need to return to first principles and reconsider what the Constitution itself means – we simply need to apply what we have learned. Argument from precedent is an effort to create a paint-by-numbers constitution, and in the realm of ordinary politics and governance that is a useful thing to have. Most of what we take to be constitutional interpretation is actually constitutional administration and is not in truth deeply concerned with the task of getting the meaning of the Constitution right.

IV. FOUR CONCERNS

There are four concerns, from an originalist perspective, with operating within this pluralistic argumentative environment. The first concern can be addressed quite briefly. It is possible for the meaning of the constitutional text to be indeterminate, especially in regard to the particular problem that a legal or political actor may be trying to resolve. The interpreter must always take care not to assert greater determinacy of meaning than can be borne by the available evidence. An originalist may well want to turn to additional argumentative forms

[22] 317 U.S. 111 (1942).

[23] 347 U.S. 483 (1954).

and types of evidence in order to supplement traditional historical arguments and evidence and clarify the meaning of the Constitution, but the task (for an originalist) remains one of interpreting the original meaning of the text not to simply create a rule to settle a case. There is, to be sure, often reasonable disagreement over the proper conclusions to be drawn from historical materials. Some other forms of arguments, such as arguments from structure or values, can be even more contestable. The question of how confident a judge must be in his or her interpretation of a constitutional provision in order to act on that interpretation and refuse to apply a conflicting statute is separate from originalism itself (originalism does not itself imply a Thayerian stance on the part of judges), but there is a line to be drawn.

Once we move beyond the realm of interpretation, then other forms of constitutional argumentation may be given relatively free rein. Various modes of constitutional argument and evidence may be useful for an originalist interpreter, but only when and to the extent that they are disciplined by and harnessed to the overarching goal of determining the original meaning being communicated through the text. Once that task has been exhausted, and discoverable meaning has run out, various forms of constitutional argument may still be relevant and useful in the realm of constitutional construction as political actors continue to struggle over and make decisions about what the polity should do.[24]

The other concerns are perhaps more particular to this topic. A second type of concern is that if originalists think that they can marshal all the various modalities of constitutional argumentation, then they simply are not doing it right. In one version of this concern, advocates of "pluralist theories of constitutional interpretation" have suggested that arguments about constitutional meaning can and should be constructed internal to each argumentative form, and then the interpreter should see how well these various arguments align with one another. Rather than yoking text and structure to the common enterprise of explicating original meaning, textualist and structuralist arguments should be allowed to develop on their own terms without reference to other types of arguments or evidence. Only after the best textualist argument about the meaning of a constitutional rule has been constructed should it be laid beside the best structuralist argument to see if they point in the same direction. Although we certainly want to fully evaluate the available arguments and triangulate across argumentative forms, there is little point in regarding each constitutional form as hermetically sealed off from the others. Our

[24] Whittington, *Constitutional Interpretation, supra* note 6; Whittington, *Constitutional Construction, supra* note 9.

understanding of constitutional meaning must ultimately grapple with and be developed in light of the full range of relevant evidence and arguments. At the same time, if the point of the interpretive enterprise is to understand the meaning being conveyed by the author through the text, then the construction of elaborate arguments within the various available modalities undisciplined by a concern with the available historical evidence about historical meaning is unlikely to be fruitful. Developing arguments internal to each modality and then tallying across their results will not produce a meaningful scorecard unless each of those arguments is attempting to reach the same goal. The point is not that arguments from history always trump other forms of argument. Historical evidence may be indeterminate or hard to gather or unnecessary or contestable. Appeals to other argumentative forms may be either necessary or sufficient for resolving a dispute about constitutional meaning in a particular case, but they should take place within an originalist framework. Originalism is less about method or form of argument than about interpretive purpose.

This brings us to the second version of this concern, which is that what I have described is in fact a perversion of these argumentative types. Perhaps an argumentative form "disciplined" by originalism is no longer an independent argumentative form. When Bobbitt describes textualist arguments, for example, he does so in a very particular way. With Hugo Black as his reference point, Bobbitt describes textual arguments as arguments that ascribe "contemporary meanings" to the terms of the document. The use of an "eighteenth-century dictionary" to identify the meaning of a word is specifically ruled out of bounds.[25] This is indeed one common understanding of textualism as a school of thought in constitutional decision making. As a legitimate modality of constitutional interpretation, the strong form that Bobbitt describes would seem to be in serious retreat. Even Ronald Dworkin admits that as interpreters, we are bound to the "semantic intention" of those who drafted the text, and would need to consult the appropriate historical dictionary, not common contemporary usage, to tell "a hawk from a handsaw."[26] We will return to this broader point in a moment. The more immediate point that needs to be made is that not everyone defines the typologies as narrowly as Bobbitt does. Griffin, for example, simply observes that textualism as a form of argument emphasizes the specific words of the constitutional text, and Fallon observes that both historical-meaning and contemporary-meaning varieties of arguments from

[25] Bobbitt, *Constitutional Fate*, *supra* note 11 at 26.

[26] Ronald Dworkin, "The Arduous Virtue of Fidelity: Originalism, Scalia, Tribe, and Nerve," 65 Fordham L. Rev. 1249 at 1251 (1997) [Dworkin "Arduous Virtue"].

the text exist within American constitutional discourse.[27] Pluralism within an originalist framework constrains the range of available arguments *within* the argumentative forms, but the variety of constitutional modalities remains. It would not be surprising to see a committed originalist judge writing opinions that draw on textualist, structuralist, doctrinalist, as well as historical arguments, for example. A non-originalist judge might well do it rather differently, but the styles of argument are unlikely to diverge as radically as critics suggest.

A final concern is that it might be thought that different argumentative forms presuppose conflicting theoretical commitments. Perhaps the originalist invites the subversion of the originalist project and her own normative commitments by deploying anything other than historical arguments about constitutional meaning. Robert Post offers the most direct analysis of this theme. As Post elaborates, different theories of interpretation may rest on different conceptions of constitutional authority. Although it may be equally legitimate within American constitutional practice to appeal to doctrinalism or to originalism, for example, the two sorts of appeals may "invoke and depend upon" distinct claims about the authority of the Constitution generally and the authority of the courts to ignore otherwise valid laws more particularly.[28] Doctrinalist arguments may gain their normative force by drawing from "the authority of law," or by appealing to the value of stability and consistency. By contrast, the normative attraction of originalist arguments may lie in their appeal to "the authority of consent" and the principle that judges should enforce what the lawmaker had ordained and not something else.[29]

It is certainly the case that some of the currently accepted constitutional modalities draw on their own normative theories to establish their legitimacy. There are normative theories available that would help explain why judges might reasonably refuse to apply a statute in the name of contemporary moral values.[30] A judge working within a single argumentative form may implicitly or explicitly be relying on that underlying structure of authority to support an exercise of judicial review. A judge who made purely textualist arguments focusing on the ordinary contemporary meaning of words in the Constitution to support striking down a law implicitly relies on a theory of constitutional and judicial authority that would support such an action.

[27] Stephen M. Griffin, *American Constitutionalism* (1998) at 148; Fallon, "Constructivist Coherence, *supra* note 10 at 1197–98.

[28] Robert Post, "Theories of Constitutional Interpretation," in Robert Post, ed., *Law and the Order of Culture* (1991) at 19.

[29] *Ibid.* at 19–23.

[30] See *ibid.* at 23–26; Bobbitt, *Constitutional Fate*, *supra* note 11 at 26–27; Dworkin, "Arduous Virtue," *supra* note 26; and W.J. Waluchow, *A Common Law Theory of Judicial Review* (2006).

Once the various modalities of constitutional argument are tethered to the originalist enterprise, it is true that they will be constrained by the goal of discovering the original meaning of the text. The full range of argumentative moves that might be regarded as legitimate within those various modalities may no longer be available or appropriate to reaching that goal. The existence of a text with suitably sweeping language would not be sufficient to authorize a judge to launch a "moral reading of the Constitution" driven by contemporary philosophical theories.[31] This does pose some complexities of a type that has already been encountered by originalists. If doctrinal arguments can operate within their own normative system (one emphasizing consistency and stability of law, for example), then originalists who recognize the value and legitimacy of doctrinal arguments will have to confront instances of precedents that conflict with and obscure original meaning rather than help illuminate and apply it. The solution is not to abandon argument from precedent per se or to dismiss the value that precedent can serve within the judicial process. But the value that precedent can serve as an intellectual shortcut and as a stabilizing force within the law can be overwhelmed if the discrepancy between precedent and otherwise recognizable original meaning becomes too great. From an originalist perspective, precedent is a useful tool, but if it ceases to be useful for implementing original meaning then it no longer serves its legitimate function.

Originalists can make use of the plurality of forms of constitutional argumentation, but there remain important differences between originalists and those who would approach the task of judicial review from the perspective of other constitutional modalities. Where originalists are centrally concerned with ascertaining the constitutional rule laid down by the lawmaker authorized to create those rules, others are concerned with using constitutional argument to achieve other ends. When discoverable constitutional meaning is indeterminate, when the possibility of interpretation runs out, then an originalist should be open to the possibility of turning not merely to other constitutional modalities but to a different constitutional task. Political actors may well seek to construct a workable set of constitutional values, practices, and institutions to guide government behavior in the absence of persuasive interpretations of constitutional meaning. But in the presence of discoverable original meaning, an originalist would insist both that the interpretive task is to try to discover what the author sought to convey through the text and that the judicial task is to enforce that meaning. Others might expand the judicial mission. They may find adequate authority to justify judicial review grounded in the consistency

[31] *Cf.*, Ronald Dworkin, *Freedom's Law* (1997).

of doctrinalism or the "contemporary ratification" of modern popular values or the moral justice of philosophical theory. Other constitutional modalities might help provide the legitimating rationale for such uses of judicial power.

The critical point of difference between originalists and others is not the advocacy of a single method of constitutional argumentation. Originalists can accept a pluralism of forms of constitutional argument within an originalist framework. The critical point of difference between originalists and others is over what judges can appropriately do with the constitutional text. A doctrinalist or an advocate of a moral reading of the Constitution may ground the authority of judicial review in something other than the interpretation and application of law laid down by the constitutional lawmaker, but an originalist is likely to be skeptical that judicial review can be justified under such circumstances. The disagreement between originalists and the supporters of other approaches to judicial review is fundamentally a disagreement over the necessary warrants for judges to disregard legislation.

PART TWO **Interpretation and Intention**

4 Simple-Minded Originalism

Larry Alexander*

I. 'TIS A GIFT TO BE SIMPLE[1]

I confess. (Actually, I boast.) I'm a simple-minded originalist. I believe that given what we accept as legally authoritative, the proper way to interpret the Constitution (and statutes, regulations, and judicial orders as well) is to seek its authors' intended meanings – the same thing we do when we read a letter from Mom, a shopping list from our spouse, or instructions for how to assemble a child's toy made in China. Interpreting the Constitution and interpreting a toy's assembly instructions are two tokens of the same type, namely a search for the authors' intended meaning.

Because simple-minded originalism is considered heretical among most legal academics – even if it is so orthodox among ordinary folks as to escape notice – I shall attempt to defend it. But that defense will not be lengthy. The defense of simple-minded originalism is, well, simple.

Suppose someone shows you a piece of paper with marks on it and tells you that the paper contains normative propositions (instructions, do's and don'ts). He asks you to tell him what those normative propositions are (they are to govern him, not you). What would you do?

First of all, you would not think of paper and marks as by themselves constituting normative propositions. If you knew that the paper fell off a paper truck, and that the marks were made by blowing dirt and bird droppings – that is, that no *author communicating norms* had been involved in its production – then you would tell your interlocutor that no normative propositions were to be found on the paper. No author communicating, no norms. (God would count

*Thanks to Alon Harel, Sai Prakash, and Steve Smith. Thanks also to Mitch Berman, who has often served as an intelligent and recalcitrant opponent.

[1] Old Shaker hymn.

as a possible author if one thought he might be attempting to communicate through the blowing dirt and bird droppings.)

On the other hand, if you believed that the marks were in fact made by some person or persons – possibly including God – intending to communicate norms, then you would naturally ask the following: Who were the authors, in what circumstances and with what purposes were they communicating the norms, and what language were they using to do so – English, Esperanto, some idiosyncratic idiolect, a code, and so on?

That is what a simple-minded originalist would do. If it is an author or authors who are communicating norms through marks on paper, then to discover those norms we seek the authors' intended meanings. And their circumstances, purposes, linguistic habits, and so on are all evidence of those intended meanings. (The standard meaning of a phrase in a natural language is evidence – but only evidence – of what meaning the speaker intended to convey in employing it; the speaker may not have had perfect command of the language, may have misspoken, may have been speaking ironically, may have been speaking in an idiolect or code, and so forth.)

Now at this point, someone will surely point out to the simple-minded originalist – that would be me – that there are other "meanings" of a text's meaning besides the intended meaning of its author. There is its meaning in, say, standard English (its Gricean "utterance meaning"[2]). There is its "original public meaning."[3] And so on.

Well, yes and no. Yes, in that I do not deny one can intelligibly speak of utterance meanings in a given language or of original public meanings. But no, in that in doing so, one has not so much departed from the original, authorially intended meaning as merely substituted hypothetical authors for the real ones.

Take, for example, the so-called textualist, who eschews seeking authorially intended meanings in favor of looking to standard utterance meanings. The textualist is hypothesizing authors who speak in a given language (as of a

[2] Jerrold Levinson calls what I have labeled "utterance meaning" "word-sequence meaning." What he calls "utterance meaning" is more context-sensitive and even takes into account the identity of the speaker, though it does not collapse into the speaker's intended meaning. *See* Jerrold Levinson, "Intention and Interpretation: A last Look," in Gary Iseminger ed., *Intention and Interpretation* (1992) 221 at 222–3.

[3] See Lawrence B. Solum's contribution to this volume, "What Is Originalism? The Evolution of Contemporary Originalist Theory," and Lawrence B. Solum, Semantic Originalism (November 22, 2008). Illinois Public Law Research Paper No. 07–24. Available at SSRN: http://ssrn.com/abstract=1120244.

particular date and perhaps a particular place[4]) – how would we know what standard meanings to look to if we did not know the language our authors were using? – and who speak it perfectly. (We would also have to hypothesize that when there is more than one definition of a word, the hypothesized authors always choose, say, the first definition given – which might also entail that we hypothesize their dictionary of choice when there are warring dictionaries.) Moreover, a really pure textualist would never look to the circumstances and purposes of the actual authors in resolving ambiguities, for that would be deferring to authorially intended meanings and thus raise the question: Why not defer to them entirely?

The proponents of interpreting by reference to original public meaning seek some middle ground between the simple-minded originalists like me and the textualists and their hypothetical authors.[5] The proponent of original public meaning – hereinafter OPM – assumes hypothetical authors of the text; those hypothetical authors' intended meaning is the meaning that some hypothetical member of the public who is a contemporary of the actual authors would have believed was the actual authors' intended meaning. So if the choice is between what we now believe is the intended meaning of the actual authors and what this hypothetical member of the public would have (erroneously) believed was their intended meaning, the OPM proponent says choose the latter.

Leaving aside the arbitrariness of constructing this hypothetical member of the public – what did he or she know about the authors and their context, how fluent was he or she, where did he or she live, how generally informed about public affairs was he or she, and so on?[6] – what motivates the proponent of OPM to choose a hypothetical author's intended meaning (the meaning the

[4] Compare English word and phrase meanings in, say, the United States with the meanings of the same words and phrases in England, South Africa, and Australia. Indeed, word and phrase meanings sometimes differ from region to region within the United States.

[5] There are as many stripes of textualism as there are different hypothetical authors who speak a language perfectly but differ in terms of which of multiple definitions they would choose, how much inquiry into context is allowed, and so on.

[6] This is a very deep but almost never noted difficulty with OPM methodology. For suppose we could ask every member of the public in 1791 what he or she believed, say, "freedom of speech" meant. Each member of the public would differ, even if only slightly, in terms of their linguistic facility, their understanding of the general purposes motivating the language of the First Amendment, their familiarity with the debates in Congress and in the state ratifying conventions over the Bill of Rights, and so on. There is no such thing as an "average" of what the members of the public believed the ratifiers meant by "freedom of speech." Nor is there a "median" of such meanings. So one would have to look for the meaning attributed to "freedom of speech" by some "representative" member of the public. But what linguistic facility, familiarity with current events, geographical location, and so on make one a representative member of the public? I do not see any non-arbitrary way of choosing.

hypothetical member of the public would erroneously assume was intended by the actual authors) over the actual authors' intended meaning? As far as I know, there are three problems that the OPM proponent attributes to simple-minded originalism that he believes OPM inquiry avoids.

First, there is a worry that the actual authors might have had secret intended meanings that were different from the meaning they expected their audience to receive. This, however, is a complete red herring. It is incoherent for one to say, "When I said A, I intended meaning X, but I intended that my audience believe that I intended meaning Y." An intended meaning of an utterance is the uptake the speaker intends in his audience. Secret meanings of the type the OPM proponent fears do not exist.[7]

Second, the OPM proponent is worried about the possible unfairness of being governed by norms the true meaning of which might only become apparent at some later date. But this, too, is a red herring. For suppose the authors of the Constitution in saying A intended meaning X, but the hypothetical contemporary member of the public would have taken them to have intended meaning Y. It is only later that we come to believe they intended X by A. Was the public in the interim treated unfairly in assuming Y rather than X? It is hard to see how. Obviously, if the hypothetical member of the public were *ratifying* the Constitution, the meaning he was assuming would be important to him. *But if he assumed it was* Y, *it would be* Y, because as a ratifier, he is the author and is intending Y as the meaning. If he is not a ratifier, then he has to show that he has been somehow harmed by mistakenly believing the actual authors meant Y rather than X. Although misinterpretations – especially authoritative ones, such as Supreme Court decisions – can induce detrimental reliance, *so can misinterpretations of OPM*.[8] Detrimental reliance

[7] As an objection to making interpretation a search for the author's intended meaning, I occasionally encounter the argument that we cannot know others' mental states. This is clearly untrue, however. Although we have no direct access to another's thoughts, we have no difficulty ascertaining them in most instances. I know what my spouse intends for me to buy at the grocery store when I read the list she made even though I have no direct access to her thoughts. The same holds for innumerable conversations and communications that occur daily in our lives. We rely on circumstantial evidence of intended meanings, and in most cases we correctly decipher the author's intended meaning – just as in the criminal law, we routinely prove beyond a reasonable doubt the defendant's *mens rea*.

[8] Given the arbitrariness involved in describing the hypothetical member of the public who is to serve as the touchstone of OPM – see note 6 *supra* – the debates over who that is, and thus over OPM, cannot but be just as fraught with the possibility of error as those over the originally intended meaning. In any event, any interpretive stance that posits a meaning that is independent of the interpreter's beliefs about that meaning will entail the possibility that the interpreter will err. And that in turn entails the possibility that the interpreter will rely on the erroneous interpretation in ways that would be costly if his interpretation were overturned. If

on erroneous interpretations is a problem, but it is not solved by denying that erroneous interpretations are erroneous.

The third problem with simple-minded originalism that OPM proponents hope to avoid is, unlike the first two, a real problem. However, it is not a problem that OPM methodology can avoid. The problem is that of collective authorship and the possibility that the various authors' intended meanings were different and conflicting, entailing the absence of *a single* authorially intended meaning. The OPM methodology cannot avoid this problem *because the hypothetical member of the public might have been aware that the actual authors had these conflicting intended meanings.*[9] If so, then OPM methodology cannot deliver a principled solution to the problem.

The proponents of textualism and OPM methodology substitute hypothetical authors' intended meanings for those of the actual authors.[10] But so long as we can ignore the actual authors and substitute hypothetical ones as the authors of the norms, we have the blessing (or curse?) of fecundity. For we can hypothesize an indefinite number of authors of the norms we seek. We can imagine that the marks on the paper are not in English but in Esperanto or in any number of idiolects or codes.[11] Or perhaps it is the spaces between

the Constitution, properly interpreted, forbids the use of paper money, reverting to its proper interpretation would be catastrophic. But that in itself is not a reason to deny that its proper interpretation is its proper interpretation. It is, rather, a reason to treat the Constitution as other than the supreme law of the land in some cases.

[9] See, *e.g.*, Thomas Colby, "The Federal Marriage Amendment and the False Promise of Originalism," 108 Colum. L. Rev. 529 (2008).

[10] The OPM proponent's hypothetical author is the author whose intended meaning the touchstone member of the public would have believed was the intended meaning of the actual authors.

[11] Marks or sounds do not and cannot declare themselves to be in any particular language, nor can they even reveal whether it is they and not the spaces or silences that are the intended symbolic bearers of meaning.

A text in any language is a code for communicating meaning from the text's author(s) to its intended audience. Deciphered, it produces the intended meaning of its author(s). The Constitution, a statute, and a grocery list are in reality no different from an unintelligible string of letters – *e.g.*, xbrzal – or some other set of mysterious marks – *e.g.*, Δ ¥ ≡ + – which we need the authors' key to decipher. No text can by itself declare the language, idiolect, or code in which it is written or even that it *is* a text.

This point is almost always overlooked by those who believe that even if we jettison the quest for the authors' intended meaning, we will not then be free to impose any meaning we would like the document to convey but will somehow be constrained by its *words*. But severed from their authors' intended meaning, the words will not themselves constrain. How will we know what language they are in? Is the Constitution in English? (How do we know if we disregard its authors?) If in English, is it the standard English of 1789 or that of 2011? Is it in American, British, Australian, Canadian, South African, or Jamaican English? (Again, no fair looking to its authors!) Is it really in English, or is it in Esperanto or in some language unknown to us? Perhaps it is in code (which is what all languages are – what we call codes are just non-standard

the marks and not the marks that are the communicative symbols, perhaps produced by space aliens.[12]

And if we are hypothesizing authors, why do we not hypothesize them in such a way that the intended meanings of their norms are what we would like those norms to mean? (Ronald Dworkin appears to hypothesize authors of the Constitution who mean what Ronald Dworkin would have wanted them to mean; in other words, his hypothetical author of the Constitution is Ronald Dworkin.[13] In the 1970s, David A. J. Richards similarly anachronistically wrote as if John Rawls, whose norms Richards endorsed, had written the Constitution.[14])

Suppose one were to reply: "This just shows that the piece of paper you are imagining can bear an indefinite number of meanings. So let a thousand flowers bloom!"

Well, in the sense that one can hypothesize an indefinite number of authors of the marks (and spaces) with an indefinite number of intended meanings, that is true. Note, however, that if we are not constrained to look for the norms

languages). Perhaps it is the spaces between the marks that are the symbols for conveying meaning. Perhaps it is in Martian.

And how do we tell – again, without looking to the authors – whether the text is a misspeaking of standard English or is the proper use of a nonstandard idiolect? The line between a standard language and an idiolect appears to me to be arbitrary and always shifting. Consider that today, one frequently hears the expression "begs the question" where the speaker clearly intends "raises the question." Is that misspeaking (I say "yes") or just the development of a second meaning of "begs the question"? And if the words themselves can constrain, what meaning do they constrain us to assign to "begs the question," and why?

Finally, some suggest that the constraints we seek are those necessary to make the text produce the best set of rules. *But producing the best set of rules is the task we assigned to the text's authors!* If we are now to ignore their intended meaning, why did we assign them that task?

[12] In asserting the indefinite number of meanings that marks (or spaces, or sounds, or silences) can bear, can I not be accused of the Humpty Dumpty fallacy? Lewis Carroll's Humpty Dumpty, you may recall, asserted that "When *I* use a word, it means just what I choose it to mean – neither more nor less." Lewis Carroll, *Through the Looking Glass* 70 (1872, 1986 edn). And Carroll meant his portrayal of Humpty Dumpty to be derisive.

But there are two ways that one might try to make a word mean whatever one chooses, and only one of these is subject to ridicule. If a word is thought of as an item in a dictionary, one that comes with a standard meaning attached to it, then one cannot will that meaning to be otherwise. However, if a word is thought of as a certain combinations of marks or sounds, then Humpty Dumpty was correct: The word *can* mean whatever its user wishes – though to be successful as a vehicle for communicating that intended meaning, the audience must understand that the author means by, say, "bad" what an English dictionary would give as the meaning of "good."

[13] See, *e.g.*, Ronald Dworkin, *Freedom's Law: The Moral Reading of the American Constitution* (1996).

[14] See, *e.g.*, David A. J. Richards, *The Moral Criticism of Law* (1977) 44–56.

the actual authors intended, what makes the selection of one hypothetical author over another "correct"? When you argue for *your* hypothetical author, and I argue for *mine*, what determines who is correct?

Note also that in a very real sense, each hypothetical author stands for a different document. For what makes the Constitution as it appears in the back of my casebook the same Constitution as the parchment in the National Archives? They are different in all sorts of ways. What makes them the same is that they have the same semantic meaning. But they only have that if they have the same authors and authorially intended meanings.

To see this more clearly perhaps, imagine a French translation of the U.S. Constitution. Suppose a term in the Constitution has no counterpart in French. And suppose the simple-minded originalist, the OPM proponent, the textualist, the Dworkinian, the Rawlsian, and so on would interpret the term differently from one another. Finally, suppose that there were a separate French word for each of these separate interpretations of the term. In that case, the simple-minded originalist's French translation of the Constitution would be worded differently from the OPM proponent's French translation, which would in turn be worded differently from the textualist's, and so on. In that sense, there would be not one Constitution, but as many as there are possible hypothetical authors along with the actual ones.

Finally, consider that legal academics who reject simple-minded originalism for documents they regard as legally authoritative – the Constitution, statutes, and so forth – revert to it when they interpret other normative documents. I mean by that, not only that they become simple-minded originalists when reading their spouse's shopping list or the instructions for assembling a toy, but also that they do so when they read documents that once were legally authoritative or that are legally authoritative for others but are not legally authoritative for the reader in question. Those who reject simple-minded originalism in U.S. constitutional law automatically adopt it if asked to interpret legally dead documents such as the Articles of Confederation or the Constitution of the Confederate States of America, or extra-jurisdictional documents such as foreign laws.[15]

I have to this point attempted to make the case that if we are to attend to the normative propositions in the Constitution, we should seek the intended meanings of its actual authors (the ratifiers), not the intended meanings of any of an indefinite number of possible hypothetical authors. Why otherwise

[15] I always find it amusing that judges and academics who reject originalism in constitutional and statutory interpretation expect *their* judicial opinions and articles to be read in accord with their intended meanings.

would we care about that particular document? It is decidedly odd to care about a document the markings on which were produced by actual people intending to communicate thereby some instructions to others if one is going to disregard *those* instructions in favor of seeing what the instructions would be had they been issued by hypothetical persons of various descriptions. It is not that one cannot do the latter. But nonetheless, it is an enterprise the justification of which escapes me.[16]

But should we care about the norms intended by the actual authors of the Constitution? Even if I am right that caring about the document in the National Archives only makes sense if we care about the intended meaning of its actual authors, that does not itself establish that we *should* care about that document any more than we do care about the Articles of Confederation, the Constitution of the Confederate States of America, or Justinian's Code. Of course, the Constitution, in Article VI, declares itself to be the supreme law of the land,[17] which, if true, would be a good reason to care about it and its originally intended meaning. But merely declaring itself to be the supreme law, which was what its authors intended it to be, cannot make it true that it *is* the supreme law.

Nonetheless, although I will not make the case in this chapter, I believe both that we do accept the Constitution as supreme law and that we should so accept it. And if I'm correct, the Constitution we both do and should accept is the document in the National Archives, the meaning of which is the meaning intended by its actual authors. That is all I will say here in defense of that meaning's status as supreme law.

Some, however, deny that what we accept as supreme law is the Constitution as I have described it. The Constitution as supreme law, they argue, is not the document in the National Archives and its authorially intended meaning. Rather, it is our *practice* of arguing about the supreme law, which we designate by "the Constitution," that itself constitutes the supreme law. The supreme law is constituted by our practice of arguing about it.

[16] Imagine that we delegate to some group the task of coming up with instructions for how to build a government. They convey those instructions in a text. A particular word or phrase they use has, as it turns out, two different standard meanings in the dictionaries of the language they are employing. (But see note 10 *supra* for difficulties in individuating languages, idiolects, etc.) We know from all sorts of circumstantial evidence which of those two meanings they intended. On the other hand, we actually prefer as policy the meaning they did not intend. Would it not be odd, having given *them* the task of coming up with the instructions, to ignore those instructions in favor of instructions they did not intend? *See also* Larry Alexander, "Telepathic Law," 26 Const. Comment. 139 (2010) [Alexander, "Telepathic Law"].

[17] U.S. Constitution, art. VI: "This Constitution . . . shall be the supreme Law of the Land . . . "

I find this view mysterious. Either our arguments about supreme law have an external object, or they do not. If the latter – if they are self-referential – then they are also self-undermining. For we cannot sensibly be arguing about whether we are arguing.

The view that the Constitution is an "argumentative practice" and that cites as proof the undeniable fact that constitutional lawyers argue about what normative propositions the Constitution contains seems to me to represent a category mistake. It substitutes an external point of view that an observer of constitutional arguments might hold – "Constitutional law appears to me to be a never ending series of arguments" – for the internal point of view of those engaged in the arguments. For argument over the Constitution's content does not show that the content itself is an argumentative practice. It would be as if the fact that theoretical physicists argue about how many dimensions the universe contains or about the nature of elementary particles showed that dimensions of the universe and elementary particles are themselves argumentative practices.

If, on the other hand, constitutional arguments have an external object, what is it? "The Constitution," proponents of this view will likely reply, but the reply is unhelpful. It does not tell us *which* Constitution: that of the original authors or that of any of the indefinite number of hypothetical authors. I suspect what the proponents of this view would answer is that the argument over supreme law is really an argument about *whose* Constitution – the original authors' or the various hypothetical authors' – *should be* supreme law. And one surely can argue about *that* – though, as I have said, it is hard to make the case that one should be governed by norms that are the product of marks on parchment made by one set of persons but the intended meanings of which are supplied by imagining that they were produced by another, hypothetical person or set of persons.

And although we surely can argue about whose Constitution – that is, *which* Constitution – should be our supreme law, our actual constitutional practice is one in which the arguments are always about the meaning of *the* Constitution.[18] The participants in our constitutional practice invariably assume they are arguing about *the* Constitution's meaning and not about *which* Constitution should be legally authoritative.

[18] I'm eliding the issue of *stare decisis* – the status of Supreme Court decisions that are regarded as erroneous interpretations of the Constitution; one does encounter arguments in our constitutional practice about whether the Constitution or Supreme Court misinterpretations of it should be supreme law.

Mitchell Berman is an opponent of originalism and a proponent of the "argumentative practice" view of constitutional law. (In his terms, my simple-minded originalism is "hard";[19] if we accept the authority of the framers and ratifiers to tell us how to constitute our government, then the Constitution as their communication of those instructions means whatever meaning they intended to convey thereby.) In his contribution to this volume, Berman offers the method of reflective equilibrium as a theory of constitutional meaning that he believes is superior to originalism.[20] I am not sure how Berman's reflective equilibrium theory fits with his view that the Constitution is an argumentative practice. When reflective equilibrium is reached, argument should cease, or so I would have thought. In any event, the reflective equilibrium theory is no more successful than the "argumentative practice" view, although it fails for quite different reasons.

Berman describes reflective equilibrium methodology quite conventionally:

> The method of reflective equilibrium maintains that our beliefs in a range of domains will be better justified if we seek coherence among different sorts of considered judgments, or considered judgments about different sorts of claims or propositions. In ethics, for example, the method instructs that we should work back and forth among our considered judgments about the rightness or wrongness of particular actions in particular contexts, the general articulable principles that govern our conduct, and the yet more abstract theoretical considerations that shape or determine the principles. Crucially, none of these different types of judgments is uniquely epistemically privileged; in principle, all judgments are revisable in light of all others.[21]

He then describes how reflective equilibrium methodology would apply to constitutional law:

> If this model applies to the constitutional domain, then the direction of argument between constitutional theory and constitutional case holdings ought not to be wholly unidirectional. While the correct outcomes in constitutional cases will often simply follow from application of the correct constitutional theory, the constitutional theory we deploy should itself be answerable to whatever strong considered judgments we may have about the correct outcomes in particular cases – judgments about their *legal* correctness, mind you, not (merely) of their *moral* correctness.[22]

[19] Mitchell N. Berman, "Originalism Is Bunk," 84 N.Y.U. L. Rev. 1 at 35 (2009).

[20] See Mitchell N. Berman, "Reflective Equilibrium and Constitutional Method: The Case of John McCain and the Natural Born Citizenship Clause," in this volume.

[21] *Ibid.* at 247.

[22] *Ibid.* (emphasis in original).

As Berman anticipates, one objection to his theory would be that reflective equilibrium is not a viable method for reasoning about constitutional law, and another would be to deny that we have the kind of case-specific constitutional intuitions on which the methodology depends. I, indeed, agree with both objections.

With respect to reflective equilibrium, which I agree is an appropriate methodology for determining one's moral views, that method is completely inappropriate when it comes to the content of specific posited stuff and to other specific facts. Did or did not the framers put the specific language regarding "natural born Citizen" in Article II? That question – to which the answer is "yes"[23] – is not resolved by reflective equilibrium any more than is the question how high in feet is New Zealand's Mt. Cook. Or if reflective equilibrium does apply to these questions because we must achieve coherence among all of our empirical beliefs – our beliefs about whether there is a natural born citizen clause in the Constitution and the height of Mt. Cook must cohere with our beliefs about the trustworthiness of our eyesight, of geographers' measuring devices, of those who print legal materials, of encyclopedias' renditions of others' reports, and so on – then the objection to applying reflective equilibrium as Berman does devolves into a denial that we have case-specific constitutional or, more generally, legal intuitions of the type on which Berman relies.

Berman asserts that without knowing the intended meaning of "natural born Citizen" in Article II, we can have confident intuitions that John McCain was constitutionally eligible to be President, despite his birth in the Panama Canal Zone to U.S. citizens, and that President Warren Harding was likewise constitutionally eligible, despite his having been born by Caesarian section. I deny, however, that one does or can have constitutional or legal intuitions that pre-exist and provide the grist for building our theory of legal interpretation. Take away the texts of posited law, which, as I have said, are nothing other than the media by which legal authorities' intended meanings are conveyed, and we have no case-specific legal intuitions at all. Of course, we might have some general sense of what reasonable and just laws would look like, and we might assume that *most* laws – in western democracies at least, if not in North Korea – would be relatively reasonable and just. Thus, we might, in the absence of the texts, have decent surmises about the general content of the laws. But I doubt that we have any case-specific intuitions about whether "titles of nobility" are constitutionally outlawed;[24] whether states can issue "letters of marque and

[23] See U.S. Constitution, art. II, sect. I, ¶ 5.
[24] They are. See U.S. Constitution, art I, sect. 10, ¶ 1.

reprisal;"[25] the date on which presidential elections must be held;[26] whether one state can split into two or more;[27] when recess appointments expire;[28] or countless other matters that the constitutional authors address – much less the length of the statute of limitations for fraud in Alabama.[29]

Reflective equilibrium is not a coherent method of constitutional interpretation. Or if it is, it is entirely parasitic on some more fundamental theory of constitutional interpretation, which I have argued must be originalism of the simple-minded variety.

* * *

That is my defense of simple-minded originalism. As promised, it is short, and it is simple – as befits its thesis.

[25] They cannot. See *ibid.*

[26] This is determined by Congress. See U.S. Constitution, art II, sect. 1, ¶ 4.

[27] This is unclear because of the punctuation of the relevant text. See U.S. Constitution, art. IV, sect. 3, ¶ 1. See also Vasan Kesavan and Michael Stokes Paulsen, "Is West Virginia Unconstitutional?" 90 Cal. L. Rev. 291 (2002).

[28] At the end of the next senatorial session. See U.S. Constitution, art. II, sect. 2, ¶ 3.

[29] Which is two years from its discovery by the plaintiff. See Ala. Code 1975 § 6-2-3. *See also* Alexander, "Telepathic Law," *supra* note 16 at 147–50.

5 The Intentionalist Thesis Once More

Stanley Fish

I. CLEARING THE GROUND FOR THE INTENTIONALIST THESIS

The first thing I want to say is that originalism, at least of the intentionalist variety, is not a theory of interpretation. Indeed I would contend that there is no such thing as a theory of interpretation because interpretation is an empirical, not a theoretical, task. That is, it is not carried out under the direction of a set of general instructions or a governing algorithm in a way that promises or guarantees a correct result. Another way of putting this is to say that there is no such thing as a *method* of interpretation, no sequence of steps that, if adhered to, generates a legitimated conclusion. Given that methodology is what parties to the originalist debates are typically in search of, I must confess that I find most of the contributions to those debates uninteresting. What the theorists of interpretation are after they will never find, and although the energy and ingenuity they display are considerable, their efforts, as Steven Smith says in "That Old-Time Originalism,"[1] have become scholastic, a dizzying structure of cycles and epicycles built on a mistake. The aggressive philosophizing about originalism has produced, Smith observes, something so "cumbersome" that it provides neither light nor guidance. My argument shall be that we have the light already in the interpretive acts we perform in ordinary daily life, and that the guidance will not be forthcoming because, to repeat, interpretation is not the kind of thing there is a theory of.

There is, however, such a thing as a theory of what interpretation *is*, an answer to the question, "What is the meaning of a text?' That is a theoretical question because of the level of generality at which it is posed. Not "What does this particular text mean?" but "What does *any* text mean?" or, to rephrase in operational terms, "What does it mean to seek – try to figure out – the

[1] Steven D. Smith, "That Old-Time Originalism," in this volume [Smith, "Old Time Originalism"].

meaning of any text?" An answer to that question will not tell you how to interpret what procedures to follow, but it will tell you what you are doing when you interpret; therefore, it will also tell you what you cannot do and still claim to be interpreting.

My answer to the question "What is the meaning of a text?" is simple and categorical: A text means what its author or authors intend. In one sense, this definition – not theory – of interpretation is modest in its claims and ambitions: It does not help you identify who the author is; nor does it direct you to the evidence of what he, she, it, or they mean. In fact, it does not do anything much except identify the arena of interpretation's practice. And because the claim of the interpretive thesis is that it is the right answer to an old question and not an interpretive guide or method, some of the objections to it – it is not helpful; it does not tell you what to do; it does not guarantee or even promise results; it is hard to pinpoint intentions – are merely reformulations of it.

I will have more to say about these matters later; but first I want to take up one of the most persistent objections to the intentionalist thesis: that even if an author's intention is sometimes relevant to the task of interpretation, it cannot be the whole of interpretation because the meaning of texts is at least partly a function of what its words – understood in the light of public mark-meaning correlations that are independent of the specification of anyone's intention – mean. This objection presupposes a distinction familiar in the philosophy of language between sentence meaning and utterer's meaning. It is the possibility of identifying the first, the argument goes, that makes it unnecessary to fix on the second. Given that at least some of the time you can look at an utterance and assign a meaning to it without concerning yourself with the intention of the author, it cannot be the case that a text means only what its author intends. The fact that we do this all the time, says Mitchell Berman, shows "first that a text could sustain or contain some coherent form of meaning other than the authorially intended one; and, second, that to attribute such an alternative meaning to the text plausibly counts as interpreting it."[2]

Berman begins his elaboration of this double thesis by claiming that sentence meaning is a necessary prerequisite for the forming of an intention and therefore is prior to utterer's meaning:

> [W]ords must have meaning prior to their deployment by a particular speaker in a particular context, because the speaker must have a reason to select

[2] Mitchell N. Berman, "Originalism Is Bunk." Online: http://papers.ssrn.com/sol3/papers.cfm?abstract_id=1078933, at 37. The paper has since been published: 84 N.Y.U. L. Rev. 1 at 39 (2009) [Berman, "Originalism Is Bunk"]. Subsequent references are to the published version except where indicated.

> particular words (or signs or marks), rather than others, as the vehicle for conveying his intended meaning . . . [3]

But Berman confuses and conflates two things that should be distinguished: (1) the formation of meaning and (2) its communication. Assume that what you want to do is communicate something to a public audience. In such a circumstance you would be well advised to deploy sign-meaning correlations that are standard in the culture; not the culture of your trade, or your neighborhood, or your private club, but the mainstream culture of establishment newspapers and institutions (corporations, universities, legislatures, courts). In so doing, you would not be ruled or constrained by the repertoire of public meanings; rather you would be deploying it as a resource; it would be a matter of choice, and of intentional choice, not necessity.

But suppose you were addressing a more private audience, or writing *Finnegan's Wake*, or speaking in dialect, or conversing with your oldest friend, or talking to yourself in the shower; the words you uttered would still be correlated with meanings, but the word-meaning correlations would not be those of standard English; they would be part and parcel of some other code, the elaborate code of an experimental novel or the code you and your friends have fashioned over the years to shut others out, or the code fashioned by you in your private reveries where you split yourself into two. *Pace* Berman, words do not "have meaning prior to their deployment"[4] in the sense that the meaning they have belongs to them naturally. Words have meaning in the context of a code and no code, including the code of standard English (itself always in the process of changing), has a natural – as opposed to a statistical or a sociological – precedence over any other.[5] The choice of code belongs to the speaker; it is he or she who determines what sign goes with what meaning.

Of course, the speaker who deploys a code not known to his audience will be in communicative trouble; like the with-it hipster who says "man, you're so bad" to a suburban square, he will be misunderstood. But having your meaning misunderstood does not mean that your meaning is something other than what you have determined it to be. The square who believes he has been "dissed" (he would not put it that way) is mistaken; he did not get it, and that is a pity all around; and you might even be guilty of a mistake in communicative calculation; you paid insufficient attention to your audience; but what you

[3] *Ibid.* at 44. Berman adds "(aside, of course, from cases in which the speaker self-consciously coins new words)."

[4] *Ibid.*

[5] See Stanley Fish, "Intention Is All There Is: A Critical Analysis of Aharon Barak's Purposive Interpretation in Law" 29 Cardozo L. Rev 1109 at 1125–6 (2008) [Fish, "Intention Is All There Is"].

meant by the sounds you uttered is what you meant, no matter what happened to those words when they entered the circuit of communication.

It follows (and this is the crux of the matter) that if you want to know what the words someone utters mean, you have to know what code or language he is using. As Larry Alexander says, "how would we know what standard meanings to look to if we did not know the language our authors were using?"[6] The words will not tell you. If someone says "you're bad" and means it as an indication of approval, you will not know that unless you know the language within which he is proceeding, the language he presupposes as the conveyor of his intention. In short, intentions are prior to meaning, not, as Berman would have it, the other way around. It is true that for the act of predication to occur, there must be a sign-meaning correlation in place; but just what that correlation is will be a matter for the utterer to specify. The system of meanings belongs to him, not to something called a language. The distinction is not between sentence meaning and utterance meaning, but between the meaning words have within the assumption of an intention to employ standard meanings and the meanings words have within the assumption of an intention to employ some other dialect.

It is in the light of the distinction between one assumed intention and another that Berman's main example should be understood:

> [I]f, wanting the whitish mineral that enhances a food's flavor, I know to ask you to "please pass the salt" and not to "please pass the gas" . . . that's because "salt" means the thing I have in mind antecedent to my choice to use it in this context, and "gas" doesn't. Likewise, you know that my utterance of the word "salt" in this context is evidence of my wanting salt because of the meaning conventionally assigned to the word prior to my usage.[7]

Wrong. What you know when you utter the sound "salt" (it is not a word apart from some system of signification) is that in the present company there is a conventional correlation between that sound and an object (also conventionally constituted, but that is another paper). "Salt" means "the whitish mineral that enhances a food's flavor" in one dialect. It does not mean it by virtue of some essential relationship between the sound and the concept. Because the relationship is (in a non-pejorative sense) "artificial" (Thomas Hobbes's favorite honorific), nothing binds you to it but custom (that is what conventional means); and you can depart from it whenever you choose to and for whatever reason. (Remember, however, that what you will be departing *to* is another conventional, artificial system or code.) "Salt" means the thing Berman "has

[6] Larry Alexander, "Simple-Minded Originalism," in this volume at 89.
[7] Berman, "Originalism Is Bunk," *supra* note 2 at 44.

in mind" only in one conventional system; and while *in that system* "salt" has the meaning he specifies in advance of his choice, in some other system – equally artificial and conventional – some other sound will have that meaning. Berman's knowledge of what he should say to produce a desired result is not linguistic but social. It is entirely possible that in some other social context, the sound he uttered would be "gas" (just as in some contexts the word for what we call coffee is fuel); it all depends on the conventional setting in which he is operating. He of course can flout that setting (and thus minimize the likelihood of communicating), but normally – again a statistical, not a normative, adverb – he will not. If you are at lunch with members of a firm you hope to join, you will say, "please pass the salt," and mean by it what Berman says you will mean. Although public or standard language is just another code, it is the default code, and prudence – not something inherent in an independent entity called "the language" – dictates that, all things being equal, one has recourse to it, both as a producer and interpreter of meanings. But when the assumption that the person you are hearing or reading is employing the default code called public language does not pan out (it just does not make sense), you try something else; and what you are trying are different possible accounts of what the utterer had in mind, not different meanings his words in some sense *have*. That is, you're trying out different accounts of his intention in the hope that one of them will give the words a plausible and coherent meaning.

Berman has a perfect analysis of how that process unfolds, although he does not see it that way:

> If your friend sends you an email proposing that you "meet at 12:00 a.m.," the dictionary meaning is that you should meet at midnight. But if you have reason to believe that he meant noon (perhaps because you have caught him in that error on past occasions or because the email also contained a reference to "lunch," or because you know that he aims to catch an evening flight out of town), then . . . you should interpret his utterance to mean noon, not midnight. But that's a consequence of your goals – your wanting to meet him not to miss him – not something inherent in the nature of meaning or of interpretation.[8]

Wrong again. The "you" in this example reaches the conclusion that her friend meant noon rather than midnight independently of any goal she might have. She would have reasoned the same way if she had been given the example as an academic exercise, if a teacher had said to her, "Let's say that you got this message and knew these things about the sender; what would you conclude about what he meant?" She would have worked out her answer by figuring

[8] Berman, "Originalism Is Bunk," SSRN draft, *supra* note 2 at 46.

out what a person with this history (mixing up A.M. and P.M.) and that plan (catching an evening flight) was trying to convey by these words. Whether she wanted to meet him, or wanted to stand him up, or did not care one way or the other would have been beside the interpretive point. Her performance would have had nothing to do with these or any other "goals" and everything to do with something "inherent" in the nature of interpretation.

I'm not saying that interpretation operates independently of goals; one often engages in the act in the hope that it will further some agenda or redress some wrong or advance the cause of justice. But the goals should not drive interpretation, for if they do, the effort to specify a truth – what it is exactly that these words mean – is compromised by the desire for an outcome. Berman courts and even embraces this danger when he declares:

> Interpretation might be understood as an effort to attribute to a text the meaning that would best serve a hypothetical reasonable interpreter's reasons for engaging in the activity of interpretation or would best serve her . . . criteria for success.[9]

But there is no end of reasons to which the interpretive task can be bent, and once reasons are accorded a place of privilege, interpretation dances to their tune, and meanings are specified because they accord with the interpreter's vision of how things should be, with "her criteria for success." Again, Berman embraces this fate when he writes approvingly of the judge who has the good judgment to "deploy her tools with sensitivity to variations in issue and context." (He calls this exercise of judgment "reflective equilibrium" or "pluralism," as opposed to the monism he associates with "hard" intentionalism.)

> Sometimes she might play a stabilizing or constraining function by tethering her interpretation of constitutional meaning to original understandings; sometimes she should act in accordance with what she deems compelling demands of political justice; sometimes she should, as would a good sports referee, just let the contending forces "play on" by deferring to whatever meaning comes to achieve widespread and stable popular acceptance.[10]

Or, in other words, sometimes she actually interprets; sometimes she legislates; sometimes she takes a poll.

I know that my insistence that being tethered to original understandings is the definition of interpretation – not an "approach" to it; whenever the word "approach" appears coupled to intention as in "the intentional approach," something has gone very wrong – and that other activities, however noble

[9] Berman, "Originalism Is Bunk," *supra* note 2 at 54.
[10] *Ibid.* at 63.

or sensible, are departures from it can sound like a stipulation without an argument. It certainly sounds that way to Berman. Who is to say that these other activities – turning the text's words to present purposes, preferring meanings that advance the cause of justice and equality to the meanings originally intended, taking care not to destabilize views that have long been accepted – cannot fall under the general rubric of interpretation? After all, have I not acknowledged (and argued) that language is conventional and that word-meaning correlations are not found or fixed in nature?

Well, if it is the denotation of a word we are talking about then of course I have no right to restrict the range of activities that might be thought to be instances of it. So let us forget about the word, and just say that there is a difference between asking "what was he or she getting at?" or "what's the message here?" and asking "what can we make of this ?" (the answer is anything we like) or "how can we massage it so that it will serve our needs ?" The first set of questions belongs to an inquiry guided by the desire and determination to get something right. The second set of questions belongs to an inquiry guided only by desires, even if they are called "goals" and "reasons." I'm just saying that when it comes to marks and signs produced by fellow purposive beings, I opt for the first set and therefore I opt for intentionalism.

II. THE INTENTIONALIST THESIS

With the word "purposive" we come directly to the intentionalist thesis which is, as I have already said, that the answer to the question "what is the meaning of a text?" is "A text means what its author or authors intend." Another – not so simple, but in fact prior – way to put it is to say that things that have meaning in the relevant sense – things like texts, utterances, paintings, gestures, facial expressions – are things that have been *created* by a purposive agent. They are not just found in nature; they have been designed, and if you want to know what they mean you have to figure out what the designer had in mind.

There are of course meanings just found in nature, what philosophers from Augustine to H.P. Grice call "natural meanings"; as in "if there's smoke, that means there's a fire" or "tracks with a certain shape mean there's a bear in the vicinity." These signs and others like them are signs of physical processes; they are not signs that some agent is trying to communicate something to you. Signs understood by you to be efforts at communication or expression – signs whose meanings are not fixed in advance by the laws of physics – are not natural, but artificial; that is, they are made and made for a purpose. If years of erosion produce a rock configuration that from a certain angle resembles a face, we do not ask what the sculptor was trying to convey. There is no sculptor, just the accidents of natural processes. Now of course you might decide that the sculptor was God, in which case you could ask what He was trying to convey by the rock formation, but only because you were no longer regarding it as natural. That is, the rock formation would now be a sign of a meaning and you might appropriately try to figure out what it is. If the face in question were one on Mt. Rushmore, you would know immediately that it was designed and, again, you could appropriately inquire into what the designer was trying to convey. You could also resolve to restore it in the event of damage from wind and rain, a resolve that would make no sense if the face were accidentally produced. (It would also make no sense to restore it if you believed that God had sculpted it because you would then presume that he had destroyed it too.)

Now when I say that meanings of the relevant kind are designed, made on purpose, I'm not presupposing a psychological process that I am then committed to describing and/or arguing for. There is no psychology at all being assumed in the argument that what a text means is what its author intends; no claim to be able to look inside peoples' heads. The argument is rational, not empirical; it can be neither confirmed nor disconfirmed by empirical evidence or by the absence of empirical evidence. It just says that to be moved to interpret something, we must believe that the something in question was purposively produced. Just what the mechanism of that purposive production might be – does it involve certain mental states or neurological events? – is not something I address. Nor is it something I need address, for whatever mechanism is posited, it will be the vehicle and crucible of purpose, and purpose, not the particular mechanism of its fashioning, is all the intentional thesis requires and presupposes. Were human beings incapable of formulating purposes, the intentional thesis would be without a ground; but no one, to my knowledge, is pushing that argument.[11]

If the intentional thesis is rational, not empirical, the objections to it must be rational or conceptual too, and take the form of alternative answers to the question, "what is the meaning of a text?" So what are the alternative answers? The most obvious one is the one I have already discussed in my analysis of Berman's arguments. It is the textualist answer: What a text means is determined in large part by the text itself, by the meanings it contains. Berman is not, strictly speaking, a textualist; he describes himself as a pluralist as distinguished from someone like Justice Scalia who believes that texts signal

[11] For an elaboration of this point, see Fish, "Intention Is All There Is," *supra* note 4 at 1123–31. See also Stanley Fish, "There Is No Textualist Position," 42 San Diego L. Rev. 629 at 646–7 (2005).

their own meanings and that these meanings can be decoded by reference to well-established and commonly shared dictionary definitions as they were in place at the time of the text's production. Basically, as we have seen, this is an account of meaning resting on the notion of convention. Although no one any longer believes that the words we use to refer to things belong naturally to those things – an idea satirized in Plato's *Cratylus* – many, like Scalia, do believe that the conventional meanings of words limit what speakers and writers can intend to say and thereby serve as a more or less objective basis for determining what an utterance means.[12] In this view, bothering about intention is both superfluous and dangerous; superfluous because if we have the text we do not need anything else, especially something else not physically visible; and dangerous because if we trade the physical presence and stability of the text for the ghostly presence of an intention, we will be led into the bogs and quicksands of subjectivity and relativism.

There is something to this, but not much. There are of course standard dictionary meanings of words and, I have already said, it is for the most part a default assumption that those who speak and write to us have them in mind when composing. But a default assumption is all it is. It is not a constraint on a speaker's intentional behavior, on what he can mean by deploying this or that sound or mark. To be sure, a speaker or writer can resolve to respect the meanings words conventionally have in ordinary usage; but that resolve is a part of his intention, not a constraint on it; or if it is a constraint, it is one he or she chooses, intentionally.[13] Moreover – and this is the crucial point – the words themselves will not tell you whether or not he or she has chosen it, whether the intentional act that produced the words had as a component the resolve to obey current linguistic conventions. It might in fact become a disputed matter; one party to an interpretive controversy might assert that the poet or the author of a statute or the signator to a contract intended the word meanings found in Webster's *Third*, while the other might contend that, no, the writer was coining new words, or reversing the standard meanings, or assuming the jargon of the trade (a conventional jargon, but not one recognized or listed by Webster). What this hypothetical – not so hypothetical as many will know – shows is, first, that the intention to deploy the standard definitions of words is as special (that is, non-normative) as the intention not to and, second, that it is an intention one has to argue for because the words themselves do not specify it.

[12] Antonin Scalia, *A Matter of Interpretation*, Amy Gutmann ed. (1997).

[13] See Fish, "Intention Is All There Is," *supra* note 4 at 1223–7.

Here is an example I shall now perform. I now assure you that I am speaking to you within a resolve, an intention, to respect ordinary usage; but my assurance might be offered in an ironic or mendacious spirit; and whether or not it is will, again, not be something you can derive directly from my words, even if they included the meta-assurance that I was not being ironic or mendacious; for that meta-assurance might itself have been produced within an intention it did not declare. Infinite regress cannot be defeated theoretically, although of course it is in most cases defeated by the world. (It is only when language is imagined as a system apart from any use that the problem of infinite regress arises.) Reliance on the conventional definitions of words as a guide to a speaker's or writer's intention is the key to interpretation only if it has first been determined that the speaker or writer intends that reliance, and that determination cannot be made by resting in the text. In those instances – and there are many – when reliance on conventional definitions does in fact get you where you want to go – to the meaning – it will not be because you have restricted yourself to the text alone, but because you are reading or hearing it within the right, as opposed to the wrong, intention. Even when it seems that you are just reading the meanings directly off the text, you will be in fact reading them within the assumption – again, not present in them – that the author intended you to so read them.

This is a point Matt Yglesias misses when he claims to refute the intentionalist thesis with this example (a close relative of Berman's example of the person who writes 12 A.M. and means noon by it):

> I write "I went to the store to buy sex toys." What I meant to say was that I bought six toys. Nevertheless I wrote "sex toys" which means something else. There are two kinds of meaning here – the meaning I had in my head and the meaning of the sentence . . . the whole idea that typos . . . and other mistakes are possible depends on the idea that written and spoken words have objective (or at least intersubjective) meanings, public meanings that are distinct from the intentions of the speaker/writer.[14]

I have stipulated that there are public meanings; you can find them in a standard dictionary. But the fact of public meanings does not tell you what any particular utterance means, for a speaker/writer is not obliged to deploy them and in the absence of evidence that he or she intends such an obligation they have no necessary relevance. In other words, while there are public meanings, they are of no interpretive help without an additional step – the step of forming an intention – they cannot supply. It is precisely wrong then to say that public

[14] Matt Yglesias, "Fish on Intentionality." Online: http://tpmcafe.talkingpointsmemo.com/2005/07/20/fish_on_intentionality.

meanings are "distinct from the intentions of the speaker/writer;" their force (should they have a force) will be entirely dependent on the intentions of the speaker/writer. If the intention of a speaker/writer to bind himself to public meanings has not been established, public meanings are nothing more than a list of possible usages that has not yet been narrowed down and does not yet point anywhere. Public meanings are not textual meanings with a special authority; they are just items in a dictionary, with no necessary interpretive implications.

Now to the example. Matt Yglesias intends to communicate the number of toys he bought, but he writes "sex toys." What does "sex toys" mean? How will it be understood by a reader? Yglesias assumes that it will be understood in the light of the standard dictionary definitions, and no doubt that would be the case if his reader knew nothing about him and just fell into the default assumption that standard dictionary meanings were what he was deploying. When a reader knows only that he is dealing with someone who speaks English, standard meanings, as Jeffrey Goldsworthy points out in "The Case for Originalism," will be "the only evidence of the speaker's meaning that is readily available."[15] That is to say, when there is nothing else to go on, an inference from dictionary definitions to the meaning of an utterance is reasonable and prudent. And even when there is something more to go on – when you know the writer's history, temperament, proclivities, biases – dictionary definitions can be looked at as evidence of what a writer means; they just cannot be identified with it, except in those special instances when you are persuaded that the writer intended to be bound by them. In either case – when the utterance's meaning flows from dictionary definitions or when it does not – the words will not be controlling; what will be controlling is the determination of the intention or purpose from which they issue. Goldsworthy gets it just right when he declares that "inanimate entities such as words do not have purposes – only the people who use them";[16] and so when we attribute a purpose or a meaning to words "we must really be attributing it . . . to the people who enacted the provision" or made the announcement or wrote "I bought sex toys."

So how do we determine Yglesias's purpose? Well, he tells us, does he not? "What I meant to say was that I bought six toys." If we take him at his word – that is, if we assume his intention to deploy standard meanings – "sex" is a typo, and he says that the very notion of a typo or a mistake "depends on the idea that written and spoken words have objective . . . public meanings." No, it is

[15] Jeffrey Goldsworthy, "The Case for Originalism," in this volume, at 49.

[16] Jeffrey Goldsworthy, "Interpreting the Constitution in its Second Century," 24 Melbourne U.L. Rev. 677 at 689.

because we begin with the presumed intentions of the speaker/writer that we are able to recognize, or at least suspect, a typo. I cannot count the times I've sent an e-mail reading "I hope hat you are well." (As I type this little message, my computer does not signal a mistake because "hat" is a standard English word.) In most cases, my addressee will not wonder what the word "hat" is doing in the sentence; he will just correct it in the light of the intention he assumes me to have – the intention to issue a pro forma polite greeting – and will read "hat" as "that" without even thinking about it. Unless, that is, he assigns me another intention based on a history between us that includes my having lent him a favorite hat that he has failed to return. Given that history, he might well hear me ironically addressing my purloined chapeau and wishing it well in its new home: "I hope hat you are well."

So the typo appears and disappears depending on what the speaker/writer is thought to be doing. Typos do not announce themselves as such for the same reason that meanings do not announce themselves as such; they come into being (or do not) once an intention has structured a sequence of marks or sounds into words. Is "I bought sex toys" a typo? It depends on what we know or do not know about Yglesias and the intentions we ascribe to him by virtue of our knowledge or ignorance. If we know nothing about him, if he is just a voice coming out of nowhere, we will likely ascribe to him the intentions of a public man, of a newsreader on TV or radio, and, accordingly, we will hear or read what he says in the context of standard dictionary definitions. We will hear or read him saying "I bought dildos and vibrators." (Again we will not be hearing or reading him independently of any intention he might have for we will have posited an intention for him by giving him a personal, or in this case non-personal, profile.)

But suppose we know that he has been out buying toys for his children or that he is prone to mixing up vowels or that he likes to play around with words or that he is obsessed with sex. Then we might conclude either that "sex" is just a mistake of the kind Yglesias often makes in which case "sex" means "six" (just as A.M. means noon in Berman's example); or that Yglesais is just fooling around, like a minor-league James Joyce, in which case "sex" also means "six"; or that Yglesias's unconscious was telling us something about him he does not consciously know, in which case "sex" would mean both "sex" and "six" (it would be a double communication: I bought this number of toys *and* I cannot help thinking about sex). But does Yglesias not announce what he means? Yes, he does, but we are not obliged to rest in his announcement any more than we are obligated to rest in the announcement of a spouse who says she does not want to go to a family gathering because she is tired and, when pressed by skeptical questions, insists, "That's all I mean." Indeed, Yglesias might very well re-read his own sentence and decide that what it means is not as clear as he had thought. He might, that is, decide that his intention was other than he had assumed and declared it to be.

I could produce even more turns on this interpretive screw (no sexual pun intended; do you believe me?), but the point, I trust, has been made. The fact that the word you set down has a standard dictionary definition does not mean that you or your addressee can answer the question "what does it mean?" by consulting the dictionary. You answer the question by inquiring into the intention within which the word was produced, and depending on where the inquiry comes to rest, you might conclude that "sex toys" means dildos and vibrators, or that "sex toys" means a number of toys larger than five and smaller than seven, or that "sex toys" is a mistake in relation to a conscious intention but not in relation to an unconscious one. The one thing you could not conclude is that Yglesias's example proves what he claims it proves – that there is such a thing as sentence meaning "distinct from the intentions of the speaker/writer." Sentence meaning and speaker meaning do not come apart as Yglesias, Berman, and other textualists assert. Indeed there is no such thing as sentence meaning if by the phrase you mean a meaning sentences have as a property; and if this is so, the distinction between sentence meaning and speaker's meaning cannot be the rock on which an account of interpretation is built. No one who calls himself an originalist should subscribe to the distinction, which, as Steven Smith observes, "misleads us, and . . . introduces not light but rather darkness at the heart of originalism."[17]

III. THE INTENTIONALIST THESIS AND ITS DISCONTENTS

Two conclusions follow, both distressing to many. (1) Apart from the assumption or positing of intention, there is no such thing as a text, and therefore the text in and of itself – a non-existent entity – cannot be a candidate for the repository of meaning. (2) Speakers and writers are free to mean anything they like by the words they deploy – yes can mean no, good can mean bad – for meaning is an intentional, not a linguistic, fact (although linguistic facts can be evidence of it). This freedom is not without its costs, and one obvious cost would be a failure to communicate, especially if you employ words with an intention that takes little or no notice of conventional usage. But as I have already argued, communication and meaning are two different things. Communication is about the delivery of meanings; the formation of meanings is an internal matter and has no necessary conventional constraints. I may

[17] Smith, "That Old-Time Originalism," *supra* note 1 at 235.

have no interest in communication and just care about expressing meanings, perhaps only to myself. And I could certainly have no interest in being readily understood by those who confine themselves to the conventions of ordinary usage. I might regard such persons as hopelessly vulgar and commonplace and I might direct my words at an audience of a higher tone, one whose members would be willing to look far afield for my intention and therefore for my meaning. In short, I might be a modern poet, someone of whom it is known in advance that he or she is employing a special, intended, language that it is the reader's obligation to figure out. But one must always remember that the language of ordinary usage is special too – it is historically produced, contingent, artificial, and at most a report on usage, not a necessary constraint on it – and that speaker and writers who bind themselves to that language (by an act of intentional constraint) are no more producing texts that can read themselves than are the most abstruse of modern poets. The so-called straightforward text and the difficult poetic text are what they are and mean what they mean by virtue of the intention with which they are produced.

I say "so-called" because I want to flag (and forestall) another mistake participants in these debates sometime make. It is the mistake of thinking that there are two kinds of texts, straightforward and ambiguous (sometimes called vague), and that the question of intention kicks in only with respect to the latter. Straightforwardness and ambiguity are the properties not of language, but of intentions. Like typos, straightforwardness and ambiguity can appear and disappear when one assumption of intention gives way to another. Recently my wife and I got off a plane at 11:30 in the evening and were greeted by this sign: "Hot pannini sandwiches now being served in the Euro Cafe." What did it mean? One of two things: either, you can go right now to the café and you will find hot sandwiches waiting for you, or, we have now added hot sandwiches to our menu. For a moment we hesitated between these two meanings, but quickly settled on the second because we knew that no restaurant in the airport stayed open that late. Is the sign then ambiguous? No. Once we determined that the intention of those who installed it was to boast about additions to the café's offerings the sign became as straightforward as one might wish, and "now" was understood to mean "as opposed to what had previously been the case" rather than "at this minute." The ambiguity shimmered there before us only so long as we hesitated between two intentions; when the hesitation went away, so did the ambiguity because it was not intended. But suppose it was? Suppose either that the person who wrote the sign wanted to cause a moment of confusion or that "Hot pannini sandwiches now being served in the Euro Café" was written on a classroom blackboard with no additional information provided. In those instances, ambiguity would be produced, not by the language but by the intentional context within which it was encountered. It is no paradox to say that those ambiguities (like the ambiguities of modern poetry) would be perfectly straightforward; they would capture what the text precisely means. As Steven Smith observes, "legislators may sometimes choose to be deliberately ambiguous or vague, but they will communicate their favored ambiguity as precisely as possible," for "they will want the courts and the public to have the blessing and burden of *their* preferred ambiguity, not somebody else's ambiguity."[18] I dwell on this point because attaching the labels "straightforward" or "ambiguous" to language implies that language, considered in and of itself, *has* properties, and to assert that is to reinflate textualism and with it the (false) proposition that the question "what is the meaning of a text?" is to be answered by examining the text itself.

There is another answer to the question that is neither textualist nor intentionalist. It asserts that a text means what its interpreters and ratifiers say it means. It is not authors and their intentions, or texts and their properties, but interpreters and their activities that determine meaning. Sometimes this thesis grows out of a post-structuralist account of meaning as always other than itself, always being grafted and then regrafted onto new contexts where it takes on ever new forms. Meaning, it is said, often by followers of Derrida, cannot be controlled by the intention of any author and is always being abandoned to an "essential drift"[19] that renders it forever indeterminate. But this is an account of the career of communication, not of meaning. The meaning remains what it is, even if determinations of what it is proliferate. But, someone might object, how can you say that meaning remains the same even if determinations of it are always proliferating in a spiral that cannot be stopped? The answer is that when one specification of meaning gives way to another, it is because the second has been judged (by some measure or other) to be more adequate or more correct than the first; and one must ask, more adequate or correct in relation to what? The only answer to *that* question is in relation to something prior to and independent of the efforts to capture it. Only if there is such a something that remains what it is no matter what has been said about it can the history of interpretation be a serious one, be more than a history of creativity or frivolity. There has to be something you are trying to get right, for if there is not, the game of interpretation is unconstrained and moves in it can neither be praised for hitting the target nor faulted for missing it.

[18] *Ibid.* at 236.
[19] Jacques Derrida, "Signature Event Context," *Glyph* 1 (1977).

But what if getting it right is not a priority for you? What if you are just trying, in Richard Rorty's words, to beat the text into a shape useful to your purposes?[20] You do not care what the author meant by the text; you just want to make it mean what you need it to mean. That is what President Bush was trying to do when he appended "signing statements " to the bills he signed. He was saying, this is what I want it to mean, and therefore, this is what it means. One understands the strategy and the desire behind it; but the strategy is political, not interpretive. It is a strategy of rewriting. Rewriting is always what is being done when the interpreter's desire for an outcome takes precedence over the search for meaning. Rewriting is what is authorized by those who say that interpreters determine what a text means. Rewriting is what is urged by those who say that the Constitution is a living document or a living tree and should be read in the light of present goals. Even if the goals are arguably laudable, the moment you prefer their achievement to the task of specifying the author's intention, you have ceased to be an interpreter and have become instead an agent of power.

It follows then that the answer to the question "what is the meaning of a text?" cannot be "whatever its interpreters say it is" because that would amount to saying that the text has as many meanings as there are interpreters of it, which is the same as saying that it has no meaning at all. But what about the old saw that the meaning of the constitution is what the members of the Supreme Court say it is? This is certainly true as a matter of institutional fact, but all it means is that among those who are trying to figure what the framers meant, the members of the Supreme Court have the last word, at least until they are moved to reconsider at which point they will have the last word again. They are not exercising power in the suspect sense – although some feel that they did that in *Bush v. Gore*[21] – they are fulfilling the obligation given them by the law (at least since *Marbury v. Madison*[22]) to identify and enforce the intentions of the author.

IV. THE LIMITS OF THE INTENTIONALIST THESIS

So we come again to the only answer to the question "what is the meaning of a text?" that makes sense: A text means what its author or authors intend. But although I believe this answer to be absolutely and uniquely right, I also believe that it is of no help at all when you sit down and try to figure out what some particular text means. First of all, knowing that a text means what its

[20] Richard Rorty, *Consequences of Pragmatism* (1982) 151.
[21] 531 U.S. 98 (2000).
[22] 5 U.S. (1 Cranch) 137 (1803).

author intends does not even tell you who or what the author is. That is, again, an empirical, not a theoretical, question, and there are no *a priori* limits as to what answer it will receive. St. Paul declares "not me, but my master in me"; that is, I am a mouthpiece for the intention of another. Freud tells us that it is the unconscious that speaks, in dreams and in our compulsive repetitions, and that it speaks in fractured and non-linear ways that can be uncovered only by an analysis that may prove interminable. Some historians argue that it is the spirit of the age, the *zeitgeist*, that speaks, filling and structuring the minds of politicians, preachers, poets, and the proverbial man in the street. Wordsworth believes in a great spirit that rolls through all things including, one presumes, the cortical things with which intentions are formed. And you do not need some fancy theory to complicate the question of the intender's identity. How many husbands and wives have said to their spouses, "That's not you, that's your mother talking"? So which is it? Who or what is the intending agent? Dick and Jane, God, the zeitgeist, the great spirit, Dick's or Jane's mother? There is no independently perspicuous answer, and the answer you would prefer is one that you must argue for by marshaling evidence, and your conviction that a text means what its author intends will not itself be a piece of that evidence; it just sends you in search of it.

Where will you find it? Again the intentionalist thesis is of no help. Evidence can be found anywhere – in texts, in historical archives, in statistical profiles, in psychoanalytic analysis, in the Bible, in the stars. The task is to organize some body of evidence in a way that points to an intending agent and to his or her or its intention. There is no formula for prosecuting either task.

You just have to sit down and do it, every time.

In short, while the truth that a text means what its author intends tells you what you are doing, necessarily, when you are interpreting, it does not tell you how to do it. It is not a methodology, just the answer to a theoretical question. Because interpretation is an empirical, not a theoretical, task, having the right answer to that question will not give you a leg up in the interpretive task; and having the wrong answer will not impair you as you set about to perform it. The intentionalist thesis has no implications or lessons at all for the act of interpreting, except negative ones. It tells you that if you are not looking for intention, you are not interpreting. It tells you that looking for intention is not one among many possible modes of interpretation; it is the only one. It tells you that textualism could not possibly be a mode of interpretation because it has no stable, independent object. It tells you that one can neither be praised for being a strict constructionist nor faulted for not being one because strict constructionism – sticking with the text and only the text – is not a program anyone could possibly enact or fall away from. It tells you that no one and everyone is guilty of judicial activism if by judicial activism you mean departing from the literal text; there is no literal text to depart from, just in-place stipulations of intention; and when you depart from those, you are not committing a crime; you are offering an alternative stipulation and initiating an argument (this not that is what they meant.) It tells you that "the-interpreter's-decide-on-the-basis-of-what-is-best" account of interpretation is the true judicial activism because by attaching interpretation to political hopes and sundering it from authorial intention, it sets interpreters free from any constraints (what I or you think best is not a constraint) and encourages them to make it up as they go along.

And, in a somewhat different vein, the intentionalist thesis tells you that the difficulties attendant upon the attempt to specify intention do not undermine it. Yes, it is often the case, as many have pointed out, that intention is obscure and hard to discern, either because the evidence of it is wanting or contradictory, or because the intending agent is a committee or a congress, or because the intending agent has been dead for 300 years, or because the intending agent is mentally ill or a multiple personality. All of these speak to the fact that in many cases and for many reasons it may prove impossible to figure out what the intention is, but that does not change the prior fact that figuring out what the intention is is the interpreter's job, irrespective of whether or not he or she succeeds in doing it. Getting the right answer to the question "what is the meaning of a text?" is no guarantee that you will be able to do what the answer directs you to do. Identifying the intention and thereby the meaning may, in some instances, prove to be an ever elusive goal. In practical terms, then, the intentionalist thesis – a text means what its author or authors intend – is of no use whatsoever. All it has going for it is that it is true.

Postscript

In a response to this essay, Mitchell Berman charges that I conflate "the questions of what the speaker or author meant and what the text he utters means." Yes, I do, because my thesis is that the distinction Berman thinks I am blurring does not exist. Or rather it could exist only if there could be a text – as opposed to a pattern of marks – apart from the prior assignment of an intention. Using different examples, Larry Alexander, Sai Prakash, Steven Smith, Walter Michaels, and Steven Knapp have explained that when a physical configuration that appeared to be meaningful is shown to have been accidentally produced rather than being designed by a purposive agent it no longer makes sense to interpret it because it is no longer a text, something bearing a message. Textuality, rather than being a repository of meaning independently of intention, is a condition achieved only when intention is assumed and is the object of the interpreter's efforts. No intention, no text, no meaning, no point to interpretation.

Resistance to this argument almost always takes the form of plunking down a piece of language and saying, "See, it's all there, and you don't need to have recourse to intention; just work from the words themselves which carry with them the standard meanings they have in the language." In effect this amounts to displaying some words, declaring their meaning to be obvious, and asking, "What else could they mean?"

The assertion is that the apparently perspicuous meaning has been produced by the stand-alone text. But the text does not stand alone; it has been produced by the assumption of an intention on the part of the writer or speaker, the intention to deploy standard dictionary meanings. That is the default assumption within which we routinely hear and read and it does not seem that we are *actively* making it at all; what we experience is the immediacy of a clear meaning. But if evidence is brought forward indicating that the author spoke or wrote within a different (non-standard) system of mark-meaning correlations, the previously clear meaning would disappear and another clear meaning will have taken its place.

That is why textualism – the idea that words mean something apart from what any author meant – will not work. You cannot see words *as* words without already having assumed that they issue from a particular language, and the words alone (a phrase that is finally incoherent) will not tell you which one it is. Only the speaker can specify what language is being spoken (or written) and therefore only the speaker can specify what the words he utters mean, no matter what standard dictionaries say and no matter what inferences a hearer or reader might make. Humpty Dumpty was right. And Bill Clinton was telling the truth when he said, "I did not have sexual relations with that woman."

Berman tests – and, he thinks, defeats – this reasoning by an example. He imagines me as a vegetarian (God forbid!) who has entered a restaurant where this sign is displayed: "All our sandwiches are now vegetarian." I order one, bite into it, and find myself eating swiss cheese and ham. I protest and the manager explains to me that what the sign says is, "We now only use meat from animals fed on a strictly vegetarian diet." He explains what "vegetarian" means in the language he employed.

Berman then imagines me turning non-intentionalist on the spot and pointing out to the manager that "a 'vegetarian sandwich' does not mean a sandwich consisting of vegetarians, but a sandwich consisting of no meat or meat products." I would be saying, Berman argues, that "the manager is mistaken *about what the sign means*" (emphasis Berman's).

No. If I said anything to the manager it would be something like, "I understand now what you meant by the sign and I understand too that given the language you were deploying, that's what the sign means; but while you are free to depart from standard definitions, you should know that your customers will expect you to honor and use them, and if you want to stay in business, you had better conform yourself to your customers' expectations." Berman thinks you cannot write "vegetarian" and mean by it "the meat of animals fed on a vegetarian diet." Of course you can (and you could even write "vegetarian" and mean by it "Milton scholars eat free"). But if "vegetarian" means something else for your target audience, exercising your right to nominate your own meanings will be self-defeating. Things would go badly, but it would still be the case that your words meant what you intended them to mean. In the scenario Berman conjures up, the disagreement between the manager and me is a disagreement about what words mean. In fact it is a disagreement about the wisdom of speaking within the code we call standard language (a statistical not a normative concept) as opposed to speaking within another, more restricted code.

The issues raised by Berman's example are reminiscent of the issues raised in the famous *Frigaliment* case[23] in which the key question, posed by Judge Friendly, is "what is chicken?" There the dispute is between the ordinary man-in-the-street definition of chicken and the definition of "chicken" prevalent in the industry. It is also a dispute about what each party was entitled to assume about the language being used by the other. It was a dispute, in short, about intention and code and a recognition that the question of what something means is always and necessarily a question of intention.

Berman complains that my insistence that speakers are in control of what their words means (as opposed to the lack of control they have over how their words are taken) amounts to saying that "anything goes"; interpretation, he insists, "is answerable to, and therefore, constrained by, reason." Although I certainly agree that interpretation is constrained, the constraint is to be found not in reason or "the norms of reasoned argument" but in the imperative to specify an intention. And even though there are no rules or recipes for determining what the intention is, the fact that specifying it is your task is constraint enough and prevents you from just doing whatever you like. Anything does go in the act of intending, but the act of figuring the intention out is severely, if imprecisely, circumscribed. If a meaning you propose cannot be plausibly linked to what an author had in mind, you have to give it up, at least if you claim to be interpreting.

[23] *Frigaliment Importing Co. v. B.N.S. International Sales Corp.*, 190 F.Supp. 116 (S.D.N.Y. 1960).

Finally, Berman maintains that "texts often possess, carry or bear more than one type of meaning and that a meaning other than the authorially intended one can sometime be the proper target of interpretation." "Possess" and "carry" are one thing; "bear" is quite another. The meaning a text possesses or carries is the meaning that was put into it by a purposive agent; the meanings a text can bear are infinite. If you are not concerned with the meaning a speaker or writer put into a text, nothing bars you from finding in it whatever you like, perhaps by imagining the text as spoken by someone other than the author (what would Mark Twain or Elvis have meant by these words?), perhaps by treating the text as something produced by a dictionary, perhaps by declaring that you are going to assign the text the meaning a "reasonable man" would have intended. The danger of irresponsibly subjective interpretation – the danger of permitting anything to go – is courted the moment you depart from the constraint of authorial intention and make something else, arbitrarily chosen, your target.

6 Origin Myth: The Persons Case, the Living Tree, and the New Originalism

Bradley W. Miller*

I. INTRODUCTION

Originalism in Canada – to put it charitably – has "never gained much judicial or scholarly support,"[1] and *Edwards v. AG Canada*[2] has been cast as its *bête-noir.*[3] In the *Persons Case*, five women successfully challenged the Canadian federal government's interpretation of section 24 of the *British North America Act, 1867*[4] as blocking the appointment of women to the Senate. Like *Brown v. Board of Education*[5] in the United States, the *Persons Case* has become

*I have benefitted from discussions with Grant Huscroft and Lawrence Solum and from helpful comments on earlier drafts from James Allan and Grégoire Webber.

[1] Ian Binnie, "Constitutional Interpretation and Original Intent" in Grant Huscroft and Ian Brodie (eds.), *Cosntitutionalism in the Charter Era* (2004) 345 at 348 [Binnie, "Original Intent"]. Even though Justice Binnie's observation is formally restricted to "original intentions" originalism, it is a fair statement about all schools of originalism. Originalism in Canada tends to be erroneously equated with original intentions, and Binnie himself – having once set out the distinctions between various schools of originalism – flouts them throughout the rest of his article. For a survey of the attitudes toward originalism held by the Canadian legal academy and judiciary, see Bradley W. Miller, "Beguiled by Metaphors: The 'Living Tree' and Originalist Constitutional Interpretation in Canada" (2009) 22 Can. J.L. & Jur. 331 [Miller, "Beguiled by Metaphors"].

[2] *Edwards v. Attorney-General for Canada*, [1930] A.C. 124 (P.C.) [more commonly known as the *Persons Case*].

[3] See, for example, Justice Binnie's characterization of the *Persons Case* as a "standing rebuke to an overly deferential attitude to originalism." Binnie, "Original Intent," *supra* note 1 at 366.

[4] The *British North America Act, 1867*, 30 & 31 Victoria, c. 3 (U.K.) – since 1982 entitled the *Constitution Act, 1867* – is an act of the UK Parliament constituting part of the written constitution of Canada. Section 24 provides:

> The Governor General shall from Time to Time, in the Queen's Name, by Instrument under the Great Seal of Canada, summon qualified Persons to the Senate; and, subject to the Provisions of this Act, every Person so summoned shall become and be a Member of the Senate and a Senator.

[5] 347 U.S. 483 (1954).

powerfully symbolic of how judicial review under the constitution can be used to attack social injustice.[6] Since the early 1980s, it has also been identified by the Supreme Court of Canada as the fount of non-originalist constitutional interpretation in Canada, the constitutional bedrock on which the methodology of contemporary "living tree" *Charter* interpretation is founded.[7] These two aspects of the case are related: The possibility of judicially led social progress is often said to depend on the availability of non-originalist interpretative methodology.[8] The account of the *Persons Case* as rejecting originalism and establishing the "living tree" methodology of constitutional interpretation in Canada is the focus of this chapter.

The *Persons Case* is often read as having delivered the death blow to originalist constitutional interpretation in Canada, providing two objections to any proposal to engage with originalist constitutional interpretation. At the level of doctrine, the rejection of originalism in the *Persons Case* has, over seventy-five years, been firmly established as a matter of Canadian constitutional bedrock. As a matter of principle, the *Persons Case* demonstrates that originalist interpretation risks binding political communities to the injustices of the past. These two objections have a ready appeal. In the *Persons Case*, the Privy Council not only overturned the Supreme Court of Canada, but rebuked it for deferring to

[6] See, *e.g.*, the editorial of Canadian newspaper proprietor David Asper on the occasion of Persons Day, "A Day to Remember the Famous Five" Editorial, *National Post* (18 October 2006):

> Judicial activism is part of the great history and tradition of Canada, and it has provided much justice to our citizens. We may not always agree with our judges' decisions, but on Persons Day we should at least acknowledge that many of the rights we enjoy today exist because five determined women convinced five lords in England to fix a problem in the law. And the judges had the nerve to do it.

In addition to Persons Day, in 1979, the federal government instituted the Governor General's Awards in Commemoration of the *Persons Case*, on the fiftieth anniversary of the Privy Council decision; the "famous five" are commemorated on the back of the Canadian 50-dollar bill; the Women's Legal Education and Action Fund hosts annual Persons Day breakfasts, etc.

[7] *Hunter et al. v. Southam Inc.*, [1984] 2 S.C.R. 145; *Re B.C. Motor Vehicle Act*, [1985] 2 S.C.R. 486. There was little serious debate over constitutional interpretive methodology in Canada prior to 1982. In 1982, however, the enactment of the *Charter of Rights and Freedoms* necessitated a revisiting of constitutional interpretation. The vague, open-ended nature of the *Charter's* rights guarantees posed an interpretive challenge to the Canadian courts, and the Supreme Court of Canada quickly retrieved from the *Persons Case* the metaphor of the living tree and constructed an interpretive methodology around it. Consensus was quickly achieved on the Court and in the academy. See David M. Brown, "Tradition and Change in Constitutional Interpretation: Do Living Trees Have Roots?" 19 N.J.C.L. (2005) 33. For an exposition of the central commitments of the "living tree" constitutional interpretation in Canada, see Miller, "Beguiled by Metaphors," *supra* note 1.

[8] W. J. Waluchow, *A Common Law Theory of Judicial Review: The Living Tree* (2007).

the intentions of the framers when interpreting the *British North America Act, 1867* (*BNA Act*) as not allowing women to be appointed to the Senate. The Privy Council derided the Supreme Court's "appeal to history"[9] and "narrow and technical"[10] methodology, preferring instead a "large and liberal" style of interpretation that conceived of the constitution as "a living tree capable of growth and expansion within it natural limits."[11] The Privy Council saw itself as faced with two options: (1) joining the Supreme Court in following the path of constitutional originalism to a morally repugnant result, or (2) establishing a non-originalist methodology that would enable courts to respond justly to changing social needs. The Privy Council, on this reading, chose the latter.

The Privy Council's interpretive methodology diverged significantly from the originalism of the Supreme Court. However, I have considerable doubt about the extent to which the Privy Council's reasons can be fairly characterized as following a "living tree" methodology. In what follows, I will offer a close reading of the reasons for judgment in the *Persons Case* both at the Supreme Court and Privy Council, and consider the possibility that the methodology on display in the Privy Council's decision is in fact more closely aligned with originalism; not the originalism of the Supreme Court, but rather the New Originalism that has received significant scholarly attention over the past twenty years. The surprising conclusion that I reach is that this bedrock of Canadian constitutional law is fully consistent with the New Originalism and at odds with the current jurisprudence of the Supreme Court of Canada. Finally, I will provide a brief argument as to why embracing this form of originalism would not, as is often asserted, condemn a political community to constitutional injustice.

II. THE PERSONS CASE: AT THE SUPREME COURT OF CANADA

In 1919, Emily Murphy began advocating for women to be appointed to the Senate of Canada, and shortly thereafter openly sought her own appointment.[12] She received several nominations for a seat in the Senate but was denied appointment by three successive Prime Ministers. Each took the position (supported by legal opinions from the Department of Justice) that a constitutional amendment would be required before women could be appointed to the Senate.[13] Nothing in the *BNA Act* expressly stated that women were

[9] *Person Case*, *supra* note 2 at 134.
[10] *Ibid*. at 136.
[11] *Ibid*. at 136.
[12] Robert J. Sharpe & Patricia I. McMahon, *The Persons Case: The Origins and Legacy of the Fight For Legal Personhood* (2007) 74–103 [Sharpe & McMahon, *The Persons Case*].
[13] *Ibid*. at 75.

ineligible for appointment to the Senate, or public office more generally. The barrier to a Senate appointment, as interpreted by the Department of Justice, was the absence of an express intention to overturn a common law rule. In a series of cases relied on by the Department of Justice, Canadian and English courts had maintained a common law rule that women were ineligible to vote and to hold public office. The rule could only be overturned by explicit legislation to the contrary, as had happened, for example, when women obtained legal voting rights in Canada. Universal adult suffrage, though not realized in all of Canada, had been achieved through legislative reform in most provinces at that time.[14] Unlike these legislative acts, section 24 of the *BNA Act*, according to the Department of Justice opinions, did not manifest a clear intention on the part of the framers to overturn this settled precedent and allow women to be appointed to the Senate.[15]

Murphy eventually became resigned to the fact that there was no prospect of political success and instead turned to the courts, joining with four other women (Henrietta Muir Edwards, Nellie McClung, Louise McKinney, and Irene Palby) in 1927 to petition[16] the federal government to use its reference power to seek advice from the Supreme Court of Canada on the question of whether "the word 'Persons' in section 24 of the *British North America Act, 1867* include[s] female persons?"[17] On October 19, 1927, the Governor General issued an Order in Council to the Supreme Court setting out both the question – whether "the word 'Persons in s. 24 of the *British North America Act, 1867*, include[s] female persons?" – and the government's position:

> The Minister states that the law officers of the Crown who have considered this question on more than one occasion have expressed the view that male persons only may be summoned to the Senate under the provisions of the British North America Act in that behalf.[18]

The Supreme Court of Canada considered itself bound by the existing common law precedents on the incapacity of women to serve in public office. The only way that the case could be resolved in favor of the petitioners, according to the Court, would be if the legislation in question – section 24 of the *BNA*

[14] *Ibid.* at 44. Universal adult suffrage came to Canada piecemeal through a combination of provincial and federal legislation (the federal *Elections Act* incorporated the voters' lists of the provinces), with the western provinces first out of the gate in 1916. All provinces but Quebec had granted women the vote by 1922, with Quebec finally following in 1940.

[15] *Ibid.* at 74–92.

[16] The constitutional provision that permitted five or more interested persons to petition the court has since been repealed.

[17] For a history of the case, see Sharpe & McMahon, *The Persons Case*, *supra* note 12.

[18] *Edwards v. Canada (Attorney General)*, [1928] S.C.R. 276 at 288 [*Edwards*].

Act – evidenced the framers' express intention to overturn that precedent. The Court explained that its task was purely a matter of statutory interpretation:

> [W]e are, of course, in no wise concerned with the desirability or the undesirability of the presence of women in the Senate, nor with any political aspect of the question submitted. Our whole duty is to construe, to the best of our ability, the relevant provisions of the B.N.A. Act, 1867, and upon that construction to base our answer.[19]

A key aspect of the Court's interpretive methodology is that the meaning of a statute is *fixed* at the time that it was enacted:

> Passed in the year 1867, the various provisions of the B.N.A. Act... bear to-day the same construction which courts would, if then required to pass upon them, have given to them when they were first enacted. If the phrase "qualified persons" in s.24 includes women to-day, it has so included them since 1867.[20]

This passage indicates that the meaning of the provision is fixed (or, in the contemporary Canadian idiom, "frozen") at the time the statute was enacted. What "persons" meant in a statute enacted in 1867 is what it must mean in that same statute when interpreted in 1929 or 2011. On this methodology, the word "persons" can never bear a meaning *inconsistent* with (or, more stringently, different from) the meaning fixed in 1867. How is the court to determine what this meaning is? What are the relevant sources that it can canvass? The Supreme Court described its methodology as follows:

> [W]e have to construe not merely the words of the Act of Parliament but the intent of the Legislature as collected, from the cause and necessity of the Act being made, from a comparison of its several parts and from foreign (meaning extraneous) circumstances so far as they can be justly considered to throw light upon the subject.[21]

That is, to ascertain this fixed, original meaning, the Court will direct itself in the first instance to the ordinary meaning of the words used.[22] This is with the expectation that the framers intended the words to bear their ordinary semantic meaning, and that the framers' intentions are therefore evident from the words chosen. But because the semantic meaning is given within a particular context, the Court must consider the whole of the statutory context ("from a comparison of its several parts") and the purpose of the legislation ("the cause and necessity

[19] *Ibid.* at 281–2.
[20] *Ibid.* at 282.
[21] *Ibid.* at 282, citing *Hawkins v. Gathercole*, 6 DeG. M. & G., 1 [*Hawkins*].
[22] "[T]he ordinary and popular sense" *Edwards*, *ibid.* at 282, citing *Chorlton v. Lings* (1868) L.R. 4 C.P. 374 at 298.

of the Act being made") to determine the meaning. The Court contemplates that the semantic meaning of the words of a text, when taken out of context, can in fact be contrary to the framers' intended meaning. In such a case, they approvingly cite *Stradling v. Morgan*[23] as authority or giving priority to the original intent over the literal meaning: "[t]he Sages of the Law heretofore have construed Statutes quite contrary to the Letter in some appearance . . . "[24] What is to control the interpretation is thus the intention of the framers, and the contextual factors are to help in ascertaining what that intention was. So the relevant meaning sought is the meaning that the framers' intended, and the evidence that the court will use to determine this meaning is the ordinary meaning in the context of the whole of the legislation, informed by the purpose of the act and (unspecified) extraneous circumstances. This approach has much in common with the school of constitutional interpretation, which is sometimes referred to as "old" or "original intentions" originalism.[25]

Consider how this methodology was deployed by the Court when it interpreted "persons." First, the Court noted that the ordinary semantic meaning of "persons" in 1867 was ambiguous. It was capable of designating male or female persons or both: "[t]here can be no doubt that the word 'persons' when standing alone *prima facie* includes women."[26] The ambiguity was to be resolved, according to the Court, by giving effect to the intentions of the framers. Not surprisingly (particularly given that the Court at that time was reluctant to admit transcripts of legislative debates into evidence), there is little evidence as to what the framers intended, so the Court made a subtle change of course. While it maintained its focus on framers' intent, the inquiry shifted away from ascertaining the actual intentions of any particular individual or group and toward constructing intentions that could be plausibly attributed to them.

Furthermore, the object of the inquiry was not the framers' intentions with respect to the *semantic* meaning of "persons," but rather their intentions about *application* meaning;[27] that is, how *would* they have answered the concrete question "does section 24 of the *BNA Act* permit women to be appointed to the Senate?" To answer this question about expected application, the Court followed two lines of inquiry. First, it considered the past practice of Canadian

[23] 1 Plowd. 203.

[24] *Edwards*, *ibid*. at 282.

[25] For an overview of original intentions originalism, see Larry Alexander, "Simple-Minded Originalism"; Stanley Fish, "The Intentionalist Thesis Once More"; and Lawrence B. Solum, "What Is Originalism? The Evolution of Contemporary Originalist Theory" in this volume.

[26] *Edwards*, *supra* note 18 at 285.

[27] For the distinction between semantic meaning and application meaning, see Lawrence B. Solum, "Semantic Originalism" (November 22, 2008). Illinois Public Law Research Paper No. 07–24. Available at SSRN: http://ssrn.com/abstract=1120244 [Solum, "Semantic Originalism"].

governments. The evidence was that no Canadian prime minister from 1867 to date had ever sought to appoint a woman to the Senate, and this was taken as evidence that the original understanding (or, equivalently, the original public meaning) of section 24 – an understanding that has been confirmed by every subsequent government – was that section 24 precludes the appointment of women.[28] Second, the Court employed a common law rule of interpretation, adopting the interpretive presumption that legislators are aware of the common law and intend for legislation to be interpreted in a manner consistent with the existing common law, unless express language in the legislation overrides the common law. In this case, the relevant common law rule that was operative in 1867 was that women were under a legal incapacity to hold public office. This was a rebuttable presumption, and to rebut it, the petitioners were required to demonstrate that the framers intended to overturn the common law rule. The Court found no evidence of such an intention.

The Court's reasoning can be summarized as follows:

1. The *BNA Act*, section 24 provides that "qualified persons" may be summoned to sit in the Senate.[29]
2. In interpreting "persons," the word is to be given the ordinary meaning that it would have had in context in 1867.[30]
3. The meaning of the word "persons" in ordinary use in 1867 was ambiguous between male and female persons.[31]
4. Given this ambiguity, the Court is to give effect to how the framers intended that section 24 be *applied*; that is, whether the framers believed that section 24 authorized the appointment of women.[32]
5. The framers of section 24, *had they turned their mind to the question*, would not have understood themselves to have authorized the appointment of women to the Senate.[33]
6. This application meaning of section 24 is evidenced by the fact that no Canadian government since 1867 had appointed a woman to the Senate, which is evidence of a continuing belief that women were not eligible.[34]
7. This application meaning is further supported by a common law interpretive presumption:
   a. That the legislature is aware of the common law and that its statutes should only be interpreted as abridging the common law when the legislature does so using express language.

[28] *Edwards, supra* note 18 at 284–5.
[29] *Ibid. at* 282.
[30] *Ibid.*
[31] *Ibid.* at 286.
[32] *Ibid.* at 285.
[33] *Ibid.*
[34] *Ibid.* at 284–5.

   b. Women were, by a common law rule, legally incapable of holding public office in 1867.
   c. There was no express language used in section 24 of the *BNA Act* to indicate an intention to overturn the common law rule.[35]
8. Therefore, when section 24 is interpreted in a manner consistent with its original application meaning, it means that women in Canada are not among the "qualified persons" who the Governor General may appoint to the Senate.

What qualifies this as an originalist argument? Because there are so many variants of originalist arguments, it is important to grasp firmly which originalist commitments the Supreme Court of Canada held.

Recall that the Supreme Court's first step in its analysis is textualist; it is concerned with understanding the semantic meaning of the word "person" by giving it the ordinary meaning that it had in context in 1867. So the meaning of "person," on this methodology, is fixed (or frozen) as of 1867. This is the holding for which the judgment is best known, and which is now used by contemporary commentators as the point of contrast with not only the Privy Council's decision, but also with the contemporary methodology of the Canadian courts: the "living tree" doctrine.[36]

We know that the meaning of "person" is fixed as of 1867, but what is it that (according to the Supreme Court) "fixes" the meaning? The most plausible answer is the intentions of the framers, formulated as the subjective intent of the people who either drafted or voted for the section (perhaps as delegates to a convention or as members of Parliament). The intention of the framers is usually sought in the ordinary semantic meaning of the words in context.[37] But where the semantic meaning is vague or ambiguous, the interpreter must move to resolve the vagueness or ambiguity by ascertaining the framers' intentions about how the text was to be applied to the concrete case at hand; that is, the interpreter must ascertain the original expected application of the text.

So in the case at bar, the ambiguity about whether "person" indicated men or men and women was to be resolved by a determination of the framers' intentions about how section 24 was to be applied. As previously noted, there is no evidence that the Supreme Court sought, as a question of fact, to ascertain the *actual* intentions of anyone involved in either drafting section 24 or voting for it. It did not, for example, consult the transcripts of any of the debates

[35] *Ibid.*
[36] Miller, "Beguiled by Metaphors," *supra* note 1.
[37] *Edwards*, *supra* note 18 at 282, citing passages from *Stradling v. Morgan*, 1 Plowd. 203 and *Hawkins*, *supra* note 21.

surrounding the adoption of the *BNA Act*,[38] or look at any other personal or other contemporaneous writings of individuals involved. The only historical fact that the Court found relevant with respect to interpreting section 24 was the past practice of the prime ministers who nominated persons for appointment to the Senate pursuant to section 24. That is, the Court took the interpretations of section 24 made by governments over the preceding sixty years and used this as evidence of what "person" meant in 1867. The reasoning seems to have been that (1) each prime minister since 1867 had the authority and duty to interpret the *BNA Act*; (2) each had apparently interpreted it in the exact same way (the evidence being the brute fact that no prime minister had ever nominated a woman for appointment to the Senate); (3) this unanimity was a good reason to believe that "person" in section 24 was intended by the framers to refer to men only.

So the originalism on display is a form of original intentions originalism: The semantic meaning of the words used is taken as evidence of the intentions of the framers, to be supplemented (or even corrected) by any evidence of how the framers intended the provision to be applied. The Court turned to original expected application to resolve the ambiguity in semantic meaning. It then finessed the absence of good evidence about how the framers would have applied section 24, first by holding that the practice of successive governments since 1867 was some evidence of the original intention of the framers, and second, by *attributing* an intention to the framers by the operation of a common law interpretive principle: Parliament is presumed to have been aware of a common law incapacity preventing women from holding public office, and is presumed not to overturn such a rule absent express language.

III. THE PRIVY COUNCIL'S LIVING TREE

The Privy Council overturned the decision of the Supreme Court of Canada and held that "the word 'persons' in section 24 includes members both of the male and female sex, and that, therefore . . . women are eligible to be summoned to and become members of the Senate of Canada."[39] A striking feature of the Privy Council's methodology is that, like the Supreme Court of Canada, it is thoroughly textualist. The Privy Council is concerned with construing the constitutional meaning of section 24 by first ascertaining the semantic meaning of "person." It does not articulate or follow what might be

[38] It does not appear that such evidence was put before it (or that it would have been accepted into evidence if it were).

[39] *Persons Case*, *supra* note 2 at 143.

called a "purposive" methodology; that is, it does not set out to find an interpretation of section 24 that will achieve what the Privy Council understands to be section 24's underlying purpose or policy objective. The advancement of purposes or principles or policy objectives (e.g. to provide for good governance of Canada, to increase the likelihood that those appointed to the Senate will possess requisite ability, to subordinate women, to emancipate women, to promote equality, etc.) are not, on the method on display, used as interpretive criteria. The textualism of the Privy Council is evident throughout the reasons for judgment given by Lord Sankey, and the following passage is exemplary:

> No doubt in any code where women were *expressly* excluded from public office the problem would present no difficulty, but where instead of such exclusion those entitled to be summoned to or placed in public office are described under the word "person" different considerations arise.[40]

That is, on the Privy Council's methodology, the interpretive challenge is not in ensuring that a constitutional rule squares with the objective of a provision, and so the possibility that interpretation will reveal a morally objectionable provision is simply not an interpretive problem.[41] The difficulty the Privy Council faced in interpreting section 24 was the need to resolve an ambiguity in language. Like the Supreme Court of Canada, it was searching for a linguistic fact:[42] the "original meaning" of the word "person."[43]

Before going any further into the Privy Council's technique for ascertaining the meaning of "person," it is important to take note of a critical (yet unarticulated) methodological postulate that infuses the whole of the Privy Council's reasons for judgment. It is a postulate that is fully consistent with a tenet of originalism expressly articulated and followed by the Supreme Court of Canada: that the meaning of a constitutional text is *fixed* at a particular point

[40] *Ibid.* at 133–4 (emphasis added).

[41] That is not to say that a morally objectionable constitutional text creates no problem at all. It creates an enormous problem for all persons (and not just judges) who must consider whether, in whatever deliberations they are engaged in (to return a judgment, to enact legislation, to engage or withhold from some course of conduct), the text provides them with a sufficient reason for action. But deliberations over what course of action to take plays no role at all in the prior and more technical task of ascertaining the semantic meaning of a written text.

[42] On "linguistic facts," see Solum, "Semantic Originalism," *supra* note 27 at 37.

[43] *Persons Case*, *supra* note 2 at 134. It should be emphasized that the Privy Council understood itself as interpreting a text as to the eligibility to sit in the Senate, and not deciding the metaphysical question of whether women are persons. On this point, see Frederick Vaughn, *Viscount Haldane: 'The Wicked Stepfather of the Canadian Constitution'* (2010) 214, noting that "(n)o judicial decision has been more inaccurately reported or more willfully distorted than the decision in the *Edwards* case to exclude women from the Senate."

in time.[44] In the *Persons Case*, the time of fixation is taken as being the time of enactment of the *BNA Act, 1867*. And so, the Privy Council (together with the Supreme Court) was engaged with ascertaining the meaning of "person" as of 1867. The Privy Council was of course aware that the semantic meaning of words can change over time (and can bear different meanings in different contexts and societies). And so it expressly rejected the argument of the AG Canada that the interpretation of "person" be governed by judicial interpretation of statutes that pre-existed the *BNA Act* by several hundred years.[45] Tacitly, the Privy Council accepted that "person" might have meant "men" in a seventeenth- or eighteenth-century statute (to say nothing of what it meant in the first century), but the job of the court was to determine what "person" meant in 1867.

Neither did the Privy Council accept that semantic changes that might have occurred post-1867 could be relevant. The Privy Council did not marshal any evidence of change in the semantic meaning of "person" since 1867, nor is there anything in the reasons for judgment that suggest that the court believed that any such change had occurred. The analysis is complicated by the fact that there is no suggestion in the judgment that the meaning of "person" had changed from 1867 to 1929, but all the evidence suggests that the Privy Council did not accept that any subsequent changes in linguistic usage should influence interpretation. To the contrary, the one external text cited as instructive of the meaning of "person" – a legislative amendment moved by J.S. Mill before a parliamentary committee – was *contemporaneous* to the passage of the *BNA Act* in 1867:

> Neither is it without interest to record that when upon May 20, 1867, the Representation of the People Bill came before a Committee of the House of Commons, John Stuart Mill moved an amendment to secure women's suffrage, and the amendment proposed was to leave out the word "man" in order to insert the word "person" instead thereof: see Hansard, 3r series, vol. Clxxxvii., col. 817.[46]

Interestingly, Sharpe and McMahon also cite (but attach no significance to) newspaper coverage of the oral hearings before the Privy Council that

[44] See the similar observation with respect to the interpretive methodologies of the U.S. Supreme Court in Lawrence Solum, "District of Columbia v. Heller and Originalism," 103 Nw. U. L. Rev. 923 (2009); [Solum, *Heller*].

[45] ". . . their Lordships do not think it right to apply rigidly to Canada of to-day the decisions and the reasons therefore which commended themselves, probably rightly, to those who had to apply the law in different circumstances, in different centuries, to countries in different stages of development." *Persons Case, supra* note 2 at 134–5.

[46] *Ibid.* at 143.

record the judges' preoccupation with original semantic meaning. Unnamed judges are recorded in newspaper accounts as having asked counsel questions indicating "that they believe themselves concerned entirely with the meaning of the word 'persons' used in the *BNA Act* 62 years ago, and the meaning then attached to the word by the imperial Parliament."[47] And when counsel for Edwards et al. argued that "[w]ords may change over the course of a century," Lord Tomlin is recorded as having replied, "[w]e must interpret the words in their meaning at the time the Act was passed."[48] So there is nothing within the reasons for judgment to suggest that the Privy Council believed that changes to a word's meaning subsequent to the enactment of a constitutional text could change the meaning of the constitutional text. All of the evidence is to the contrary: The Privy Council believed that semantic meaning is fixed (or frozen) as of 1867. The methodologies of the Privy Council, the Supreme Court of Canada, and originalist constitutional scholars are, on this point, aligned.

This reading seems to be at odds with Canadian constitutional bedrock: What of the "living tree"? Did the Privy Council not state that the *BNA Act* is "a living tree capable of growth and expansion within its natural limits"? Is this not a clear repudiation of fixed semantic meaning? Did the Privy Council not reject the proposal that it read the word "persons" as though it were fixed in 1867 and instead choose a new meaning that was better adapted to the changed circumstances of twentieth-century political culture? This reading of the *Persons Case* – that it repudiated fixed meaning – simply cannot be maintained. But given the centrality of this misreading to contemporary Canadian constitutional scholarship and doctrine, I must go further in setting out the methodology of the Privy Council, paying close attention to the place of the "living tree" metaphor within it.

Recall that the methodology of the Privy Council in interpreting section 24 was first to search for the semantic meaning of "person," relying on (1) "external evidence derived from extraneous circumstances such as previous legislation and decided cases," and (2) "internal evidence derived from the Act itself."[49] It is in a prologue to the discussion of "internal evidence" and after the discussion of "external evidence" that the Privy Council abruptly makes its famous utterance: "[t]he British North America Act planted in Canada a living tree capable of growth and expansion within its natural limits."[50] The prologue

[47] "Privy Council Is Puzzled Whether Women 'Persons'" *Toronto Daily Star* (25 July 1929), quoted in Sharpe & McMahon, *The Persons Case*, *supra* note 12 at 175.

[48] "Women and the Senate" *Daily Telegraph* (26 July 1929), as quoted in Sharpe & McMahon, *The Persons* Case, *supra* note 12 at 176.

[49] *Persons Case*, *supra* note 2 at 127.

[50] *Ibid*. at 136.

addresses "the circumstances which led up to the passing of the Act"[51] and stresses the differences among the various political communities within the Commonwealth, such that the "customs and traditions" of one country ought not to be used to interpret the legislation of another.[52] In setting forth the history of the Canadian debates and the voting of the delegates in connection with the drafting of the *BNA Act* (and in praising "the political genius of Canadian statesmen") the Privy Council is clearly attempting to minimize the controlling effect of English common law ("so that the Dominion . . . may be mistress in her own house").[53] It is as part of this justification for minimizing the significance of English precedent that the "living tree" metaphor is employed.

It is important to note that the Privy Council did not state that the *BNA Act is* a living tree, but rather that the *BNA Act planted* a living tree. The structure of the metaphor draws a distinction between the *BNA Act* itself and the thing it planted. What the *BNA Act* planted (through the enumerated provisions (including section 129's continuation of existing law) and the preamble's stated aspiration of "a Constitution similar in Principle to that of the United Kingdom") was the Canadian Constitution in its entirety – written and unwritten, convention and law. What the *BNA Act* planted in Canada – what is "living" – is the Constitution, of which the *BNA Act* is only part. The Constitution, according to the Privy Council, includes not only the *BNA Act* (and, we can now add, other statutes such as the *Constitution Act, 1982*) but also "usage and convention"[54] (and, we should make explicit, constitutional doctrine – the principles and rules derived from the written constitution). It is the Constitution as a whole, made up of the totality of its sources, that is characterized by the Privy Council as a living tree capable of growth and expansion within its natural limits, and *not* the specific textual provisions of the *BNA Act*. The task of textual interpretation is always focused on recovering the fixed, semantic meaning of the text.

But constitutional interpretation is not the whole of judicial reasoning with a constitution; that is, it is not the whole of constitutional law. A constitution is not self-executing. There remain gaps to fill, ambiguities to resolve, vague expressions to construe, and contested concepts to specify. None of these is the task of interpretation as practiced by the Privy Council in the *Persons Case* (and, latterly, as defined by the New Originalists). The "living tree" metaphor, I will argue, is only addressed to, and only bears on, this latter stage of analysis that has been usefully termed constitutional construction.

[51] *Ibid.* at 135.

[52] *Ibid.*

[53] *Ibid.* at 136.

[54] *Ibid.*

The Privy Council sought, from the beginning, to ascertain the semantic meaning of "person," and in so doing noted the same ambiguity as the Supreme Court of Canada: "[t]he word is ambiguous, and in its original meaning would undoubtedly embrace members of either sex."[55] How was it to resolve the ambiguity? The extrinsic evidence (which was canvassed over six pages) consisted of armchair history,[56] nineteenth-century case law maintaining a common law rule that women were legally incapable of holding public office[57] and eighteenth-century statutes in which women were denied voting rights in the provinces of Canada, Nova Scotia, and New Brunswick.[58] But the Privy Council held that such history was not a useful aid to interpreting the meaning of "person" as it was used in 1867,[59] and ruled that these "extraneous circumstances" did not constitute a common law interpretive presumption precluding women "from participating in the working of the institutions set up by the Act."[60] Thus, a key point of disagreement with the Supreme Court of Canada emerged: The Privy Council denied the existence of a common law presumption in Canada (without expressing an opinion over whether such a presumption existed in other common law jurisdictions such as England) that women were ineligible to serve in public office.

Unconvinced of the usefulness of the external evidence, the Privy Council moved to consider the "internal evidence," that is, the features of the *BNA Act* as a whole that can assist in the interpretation of "persons" and section 24.[61] It was at this point, before beginning the technical legal analysis of the statute as a whole, that the Privy Council briefly detoured for its meditation on interpretive methodology, including the excursion into the "living tree" metaphor. At this juncture, the Privy Council observed that it had an obligation not to interpret "legislation meant to apply to one community by a rigid adherence to the customs and traditions of another."[62] With this move it neatly sidestepped the potentially troublesome (primarily) English precedent interpreting "person" in other statutory contexts. The Privy Council then recorded the history of deliberation in the provincial assemblies and the drafting of resolutions and their revisions, before praising the revised resolutions, which were said

[55] *Ibid.* at 134.

[56] *E.g.* "Such exclusion [of women from deliberative assemblies] is probably due to the fact that the deliberative assemblies of the early tribes were attended by men under arms, and women did not bear arms." *Ibid.* at 128.

[57] *Ibid.* at 128–30.

[58] *Ibid.* at 131–3.

[59] ". . . their Lordships think that the appeal to Roman law and to early English decisions is not of itself a secure foundation on which to build the interpretation of the British North America Act, 1867." *Ibid.* at 135.

[60] *Ibid.*

[61] *Ibid.*

[62] *Ibid.*

to be "based upon a consideration of the rights of others... expressed in a compromise which will remain a lasting monument to the political genius of Canadian statesmen."[63]

Importantly, the Privy Council noted that the relevant resolutions used to draft the *BNA Act* "do not shed any light on the subject under discussion."[64] Even though the Privy Council noted that such evidence would likely be inadmissible in any event,[65] the search of early proceedings in order to resolve the ambiguity (coming, as it does, immediately on the heels of the Privy Council's account of the deliberative process from which the *BNA Act* emerged, and its praise for the genius of the framers) is suggestive that the Privy Council was searching the resolutions for statements that could help resolve the ambiguity of the meaning of "person" in 1867. Nevertheless, the Privy Council cautioned that its method is not to search for statements of framers' intent: "[T]he question is not what may be supposed to have been intended, but what has been said."[66]

Here, then, emerges a clear difference between the methodology of the Privy Council and that of the Supreme Court of Canada: The Privy Council indicated that it believed that the semantic meaning of section 24 was fixed by the *plain meaning of the text*, whereas the Supreme Court of Canada believed that the semantic meaning was fixed by the *intentions of the framers*. The Supreme Court of Canada thus followed the form of originalist methodology dominant in the United States until the 1980s, and the Privy Council anticipated the subsequent move to original public meaning by jurists such as Justice Scalia.[67] The difference between the two courts in the determination of *how* meaning is fixed (intentions versus original public meaning) is of secondary importance. What is critical to note is the interpretive commitment common to both courts: The semantic meaning of the constitutional text is fixed as of 1867.

After this brief discourse on methodology, the Privy Council began a clause-by-clause search of the *BNA Act* for provisions mentioning "person" or related terms. Buried in the middle of this catalog of constitutional provisions is

[63] *Ibid.* at 136.

[64] Referring, as they did, "generally to the "Members" of the Legislative Council." *Ibid.* at 136.

[65] *Ibid.*

[66] *Ibid.* at 137, citing *Brophy v. A-G Manitoba*, [1895] A.C. 202, 216.

[67] Antonin Scalia, A *Matter of Interpretation*, Amy Gutmann (ed.), (1997). The move to original meaning is discussed in Lawrence B. Solum, "What Is Orignalism? The Evolution of Contemporary Originalist Theory," in this volume.

the abrupt announcement of a rule of constitutional interpretation that Lord Sankey did not attempt to ground in the common law or otherwise justify:

> The word "person" . . . may include members of both sexes, and to those who ask why the word [person] should include females the obvious answer is why should it not? In these circumstances the burden is upon those who deny that the word includes women to make out their case.[68]

So the burden was thus placed on the government to adduce the necessary evidence to resolve the ambiguity. If there was insufficient evidence to safely ground a conclusion one way or the other, the adopted rule meant that the ambiguity would be resolved in favor of the inclusive reading of "person." It was the adoption of this rule of construction in place of the English common law presumption relied on by the Supreme Court of Canada that raised the ire of early commentators on the decision.[69]

At this point, having sidelined English common law and having announced the interpretive presumption in favor of "person" including both male and female, the Privy Council turned to consider the "internal evidence" from the *BNA Act* of the meaning of "person." It was on the basis of this evidence gleaned from the other sections of the *BNA Act* (as well as a passing reference to the *Interpretation Act, 1889*)[70] that the Privy Council formally concluded that "person" in section 24 indicated both male and female persons. The internal evidence included the fact that other sections of the *BNA Act*, such as ss. 11 and 133, use "person" to denote male and female persons.[71] The Privy Council also noted that, some of the time, when what is intended is to denote "male person," the *BNA Act* uses an express limitation such as "male

[68] *Persons Case*, *supra* note 2 at 138.

[69] George F. Henderson, "Eligibility of Women for the Senate" (1929) 7 Can. Bar Rev. 617 [Henderson, "Eligibility of Women"]; W.P.M. Kennedy, "The Judicial Interpretation of the Canadian Constitution" (1930) 8 Can. Bar Rev. 703; Vincent C. MacDonald, "Judicial Interpretation of the Canadian Constitution" (1936) 1 U.T.L.J. 260; W. Ivor Jennings, "The Statute of Westminster and Appeals to the Privy Council" (1936) 52 L.Q.R. 173; W. Ivor Jennings, "Constitutional Interpretation: The Experience of Canada" (1937) 51 Harv. L. Rev. 1 [Jennings, "The Experience of Canada"]; W.P.M. Kennedy, "The British North America Act: Past and Future" (1937) 15 Can. Bar Rev. 393; and Vincent C. MacDonald, "Constitutional Interpretation and Extrinsic Evidence" (1939) 17 Can. Bar Rev. 77. It is telling that none of these commentaries, except Macdonald (1936), even mention the "living tree" metaphor.

[70] That "provides that words importing the masculine gender shall include females." This reference was provided to counter the argument that the use of the masculine pronoun in s. 23, which set out the qualifications of a Senator, was determinative that Senators must be male. The *Interpretation Act* itself was not held to have any direct application in determining the meaning of "person."

[71] *Persons Case*, *supra* note 2 at 140–1.

person" or "male British subject," as in ss. 41 and 84.[72] The Privy Council presumed that the qualifications for senators set out in section 23 of the *BNA Act* (age, citizenship, property ownership, wealth, and residence) constituted a complete list, and noted that being male was not listed as a qualification.[73] Finally, the Privy Council concluded with a restatement of the onus that it placed on the government: "[i]f Parliament had intended to limit the word 'persons' in section 24 to male persons it would surely have manifested such intention by an express limitation."[74] On the strength of this internal evidence, the Privy Council concluded that "person" in section 24 indicates male and female persons.

We can question whether, absent the interpretive presumption adopted, the internal evidence was sufficiently strong to permit the conclusion that "person" in section 24 indicates male and female persons. The fact that "person" is used in other sections of the same statute to indicate male and female persons is hardly conclusive that it was similarly used in section 24. Likewise, the application of the *Interpretation Act, 1889* – referenced only once (and obliquely) in the main body of the reasons,[75] carrying none of the burden of the argument and thrown belatedly at the foot of a summary of considerations on the last page of the judgment – is neither obvious nor beyond debate.

But it is clear that the Privy Council believed that the interpretation of the frozen text, aided by a supplementary rule of construction, was dispositive of the issue before it on appeal. The standard narrative about the Privy Council's methodology as expressed by Sharpe and McMahon (to take one example), that it was born of "the idea that the constitution was a timeless document capable of adapting over time to meet the changing needs of Canadian society,"[76] contains some truth but is entirely mistaken in a vital respect. Canadian constitutional law has adapted to changing circumstances, such as unanticipated technological changes like the telephone and atomic energy, as well as social changes such as the full participation of women in the workforce.[77] This continual adaptation is born of the doctrine that the powers granted in the *BNA Act* "cover the whole area of self-government within the whole area of Canada,"[78] and is a matter of specification, or gap-filling, of the *eiusdem generis* variety.

[72] *Ibid.* at 141. Although, in fact, the phrase "male person" does not appear in these sections, or any other section of the *BNA Act*.

[73] *Ibid.* at 141–2.

[74] *Ibid.* at 141.

[75] *Ibid.* at 139–40.

[76] Sharpe & McMahon, *The Persons* Case, *supra* note 12 at 202.

[77] Examples of how Canadian constitutional law has responded to these and other changes are set out in Miller, "Beguiled by Metaphors," *supra* note 1 at 333–9.

[78] A-G *(Ontario)* v. A.G *(Canada)*, [1912] A.C. 571 (P.C.) [A-G *(Ontario)*] as cited in Jennings, "The Experience of Canada," *supra* note 69 at 20.

It is a sort of progressive interpretation that is equally supported by originalist and non-originalist interpreters.[79] Sharpe and McMahon, however, read the *Persons Case* as going well beyond this sort of modest, common-ground gap filling. In it, they find authority for the astonishing proposition that "that the courts [are] now free, on the basis of changed social circumstances, to permit *what had plainly been forbidden* when the constitution was written."[80] But such a grant of judicial power – to permit what is expressly forbidden – is not entailed by the concept of an organic or living constitution. Neither was it understood in such a way by the Privy Council, holding as it did that if the text had *expressly* provided for the appointment of men only, no interpretive difficulties would have arisen.[81] If the Privy Council had approached the *BNA Act* as though it were a living tree in the sense offered by Sharpe and McMahon, it would have reasoned that: (1) while "person" in section 24 originally meant "male person", (2) new attitudes toward women in Canada meant that Canada had outgrown the concept of personhood reflected in section 24, and that (3) the judiciary was thus authorized to reauthor "person" as inclusive of male and female persons, in spite of the original meaning of 1867. Yet such reasoning is not to be found in the judgment.

It ought to have been no surprise to Sharpe and McMahon that the *ratio* they purport to find – that courts are authorized by changed circumstances to permit what the constitutional text forbids – "did not have an immediate resonance in the Canadian legal community."[82] The reason that the purported *ratio* had no resonance was because it is entirely absent from, and antithetical to, the Privy Council's methodology in the *Persons Case*.[83] Neither should it have been a surprise that "[o]ne finds only passing references to the living

[79] See discussion in Miller, "Beguiled by Metaphors," *supra* note 1 at 337–8.

[80] Sharpe & McMahon, *The Persons Case*, *supra* note 12 at 202 (emphasis added).

[81] In a similar vein, see the Privy Council's reasons for judgment in A-G *Ontario*, *supra* note 78 "in the interpretation of a completely self-governing Constitution founded upon a written organic instrument... if the text is explicit the text is conclusive, alike in what it directs and what if forbids. When the text is ambiguous... recourse must be had to the context and scheme of the Act. Again, if the text says nothing expressly, then it is not to be presumed that the Constitution withholds the power altogether. On the contrary, it is to be taken for granted that the power is bestowed in some quarter unless it be extraneous to the statute itself (as, for example, a power to make laws for some part of His Majesty's dominions outside of Canada) or otherwise clearly repugnant to sense." Cited in Jennings, "The Experience of Canada," *supra* note 69 at 20.

[82] Sharpe & McMahon, *The Persons Case*, *supra* note 12 at 202.

[83] A review of the scholarly literature on point in the decade after the judgment will disclose almost no references to the living tree. The predominant objection to the Privy Council's decision was that it ought not to have departed from treating the *BNA Act* as an ordinary statute, subject to ordinary rules of statutory interpretation, such as giving effect to original intent of the framers as the Supreme Court of Canada had done. *E.g.*, Henderson, "Eligibility of Women," *supra* note 69.

tree principle in the decisions of the Supreme Court well into the 1970s."[84] When they argue that "the *Persons* case did not come into its own until the dawn of the *Charter* era,"[85] they offer no explanation of how it is that this central holding of the *Persons Case* remained hidden from view for fifty years, and accordingly they gloss over the nature of the revolution in judicial review that occurred on reception of the *Charter*.[86] But the *Persons Case* was, in fact, received fully formed in 1929. What transpired at the "dawn of the *Charter* era" was that a convenient phrase was lifted out of context, emptied of its meaning, and pressed into the service of judges seeking historical validation for a new, expanded methodology of judicial review.

IV. THE PRIVY COUNCIL AND THE NEW ORIGINALISM

When read through the lens of originalist interpretation, however, there remains something unsatisfying about Lord Sankey's judgment. I have argued that the Privy Council approached this case with the assumption that its job was to ascertain the meaning of a text, and that it was thoroughly textualist in its method. I have also argued that the evidence suggests that the Privy Council embraced a position that would later be articulated by originalists (both new and old): that the meaning of a text is fixed (or frozen) at the time of its enactment. I argued that contrary to the reasons of the Supreme Court of Canada (but in keeping with the New Originalists), the Privy Council held that the fixed meaning of the text is not to be determined according to the *intentions* of the framers, but rather according to its original public meaning. And finally, I argued that the Privy Council made a mistake in implementing its own methodology; its conclusion ought to have been that the ambiguity could not be resolved on the evidence before it. There was a failure on the

[84] Sharpe & McMahon, *The Persons Case*, *supra* note 12 at 202. Interestingly, the first reference to the Persons case in the modern era, *Quebec (AG) v. Blaikie*, [1979] 2 S.C.R. 1016, came in the year of the fiftieth anniversary of the *Persons Case*, the same year that the federal government instituted the Governor General's Awards in Commemoration of the Persons case.

[85] Sharpe & McMahon, *The Persons* Case, *supra* note 12 at 202–3.

[86] Sharpe, however, supplies the material to answer this question in the 2003 biography of Brian Dickson that he co-wrote with constitutional scholar Kent Roach, *Brian Dickson: A Judge's Journey* (2003). That book documents the conscription of the *Persons Case* by Justice Dickson fifty years after the fact to provide faux-precedential cover for the jurisprudence of the Dickson court celebrated by Sharpe and others. An account of that book's deficiencies in historical method and theoretical analysis is provided by R. W. Kostal, "Shilling for Judges: Brian Dickson and His Biographers" (2006) 51 McGill L.J. 199. For a powerful argument that the "living tree" doctrine is a child of *Charter*-era judging, see David M. Brown, "Tradition and Change in Constitutional Interpretation: Do Living Trees Have Roots?" 19 N.J.C.L. (2005) 33.

part of the drafters to convey the meaning of the legislation precisely. The evidence was simply not determinative as to what "person" meant. Interpretation, then, understood in the narrower sense used by the New Originalists, did not provide an answer to the constitutional question referred by the government of Canada. The whole of the decision, had it been properly reasoned, would not have turned on the interpretation of "person" (as a matter of recovering an historical fact) but rather on the adoption of the rebuttable presumption (that "person" includes female persons) that Lord Sankey stipulated but nowhere attempted to justify or ground.

A firmer foundation for the result was available. To make that case, I will make an argument for what the Privy Council ought to have done if it had in fact determined that the ambiguity of "person" could not be resolved on the basis of the historical and textual evidence. Sometimes, as in the *Persons Case*, interpretation will not yield a single, determinate answer to a constitutional question, but will reveal ambiguity. And while resolving ambiguity is, in the first instance, a matter of interpretation (a matter of determining a linguistic fact),[87] sometimes interpretation can only leave an ambiguity unresolved. Additionally, interpretation may determine that words are not (or not only) ambiguous, but that they are *vague*, admitting of core cases and borderline cases, with no bright lines to distinguish among them.[88] Or words may refer to concepts that are not vague, but are contested for other reasons (e.g. justice, marriage). In all of these cases, interpretation is exhausted before the answer to a constitutional question can be reached. But judicial reasoning is not exhausted by the more or less technical task of statutory interpretation. One of the strengths of the New Originalism is its attention to aspects of judicial reasoning other than interpretation, in part by its insistence that the clear conceptual distinction be maintained between constitutional *interpretation* (a matter of ascertaining the linguistic facts about words) and constitutional *construction*. The time to engage in constitutional construction only begins when the task of interpretation has been concluded.[89]

On one of Solum's formulations, constitutional *construction* is the "activity of translating the semantic content of a legal text into legal rules, paradigmatically in cases where the meaning of the text is vague."[90] But "translation" does not adequately describe the judicial role here; it carries an unfortunate connotation of direct correspondence between the text and the legal rules derived from the text, and thus fails to capture the creative (yet bounded) nature of

[87] Solum, "Heller," *supra* note 44.
[88] *Ibid.*
[89] See Lawrence B. Solum, "What Is Originalism? The Evolution of Contemporary Originalist Theory," in this volume.
[90] Solum, "Heller," *supra* note 44.

construction that elsewhere Solum tirelessly describes throughout his work. Construction is not a matter of determining the meaning of words, but (again in Solum's words) of creating "subsidiary rules that resolve vagueness"[91] or (we can add) other interpretive indeterminacies. The province of construction is the creation of constitutional rules and principles to fill in gaps where the text is indeterminate with respect to a constitutional question. The bounded nature of construction is apparent if one understands construction to be a *determinatio*, an adoption of specific rules that are not themselves morally required prior to their adoption and could well have been made differently.[92] A norm or rule chosen or selected by a process of *determinatio* is rationally underdetermined in the sense that there are other norms or rules that could have been chosen instead and would equally have been supported by practical reason. But the choice is not entirely open-ended: There are choices that will be ruled out as inconsistent with principles of practical reason, particularly by obligations (in any given legal system) to respect existing commitments about the institutional role of the different branches of government, and "fit" with existing law.[93] Apart from the limits that can be inferred from the interpretation of the text itself (e.g., a construction must never contradict the text),[94] little can be said in the abstract about the considerations that ought to guide and limit construction; the appropriate reach of construction is highly contingent on the needs, circumstances, and previous commitments (including decisions to rule out some constructions and decisions about institutional roles and competencies) of the specific political community whose law is under consideration.

The interpretation of a constitutional text (in the narrow sense of interpretation used by the New Originalists) is largely a matter of technique, of description. It is the search for some fact of the matter. When interpretation is completed and the semantic meaning of the text has been described, the judge must still choose or create the legal rules that are consistent with the meaning of the text, and must apply the rules to the facts at hand. This construction includes the identification and selection of norms, rules, and principles from among other competing norms, rules, and principles as bearing on the judicial decision. To return to the specific example from the case at hand, the

[91] *Ibid.*

[92] See John Finnis, *Aquinas: Moral, Political, and Legal Theory* (1998) at 255–74.

[93] Ronald Dworkin, *Law's Empire* (1986), John Finnis, "Commensuration and Public Reason" in Ruth Chang, (ed.), *Incommensurability, Incomparability, and Practical Reason* (1997) 215 at 230–1.

[94] Such a limit is on view in Justice L'Heureux-Dubé's dissent in *R. v. Prosper*, [1994] 3 S.C.R. 236 at 287.

Privy Council (I have argued) ought to have acknowledged that interpretation could return no determinate answer to the question of whether "person" in section 24 included female persons, and then expressly acknowledged that it was now engaged in the construction of supplementary rules to resolve the controversy. And, of course, the Privy Council did in fact construct just such a supplementary rule: the rebuttable presumption that "person" includes female persons. The Supreme Court of Canada, for its part, was similarly engaged in constitutional construction when it adopted a contrary presumption in favor of restricting the reading of person to "male persons." These two divergent constructions demonstrate how construction contains an element of choice. But the choice is not entirely open-ended. It was not an option, for example, to construct a constitutional rule such that "person" for the purposes of section 24 shall mean person over the age of forty. Such a construction would be ruled out by section 23, which expressly set an age qualification of thirty. And when there are multiple possible constructions, each of which are sufficiently consistent with the text, there may be previous commitments of the political community (such as legal principles) and moral reasons that support one construction over another. In the *Persons Case*, there are legal principles (supported by moral reason) to prefer the construction of the Privy Council over the construction of the Supreme Court of Canada; reasons that, if they had been articulated by Lord Sankey, would have immensely strengthened the reasons for judgment. In Dworkin's language, the Privy Council's reasons had better fit and justification. One such legal principle that bears on the outcome of the *Persons Case* is the basic equality of persons, which was, and is, a principle of the common law.[95] But the obligation is deeper than that: It is not only a matter of following precedent, but of reflecting on law's point, its purpose.[96]

If law exists for the sake of benefitting *persons* generally, and serving the needs of those persons in particular political communities, then there can be no justification for excluding any class of persons from law's protection or concern. Paradigmatic exclusions include those noted by Finnis: the exclusion of black slaves from the possibility of obtaining citizenship in *Dred Scott v. Sandford*,[97] the exclusion of the unborn from recognition under the law in *Roe*

[95] See *e.g.*, the extended argument in T.R.S. Allan, *Constitutional Justice* (2001). This is not, of course, to make the argument that equality has always been respected by the common law in every respect.

[96] John Finnis, "The Priority of Persons" in Jeremy Horder (ed.), *Oxford Essays in Jurisprudence*, 4th series (2000) 1 at 4–5.

[97] *Dred Scott v. Sanford*, 60 U.S. (19 How.) 393 (1857).

v. Wade[98] (and in Canada, *Winnipeg v. G(J)*[99]). An exclusion of an entire class of persons from participating in a deliberative political institution – absent any cogent justification such as that provided by age restrictions – is another example.[100] Absent a justification for why women ought to be excluded from participation in the Senate, a law that makes persons eligible for appointment to the Senate ought to be constructed (to the extent that construction is available) as including women. A reflection on the nature of law's authority, of the reasons that we have for treating law as providing authoritative reasons for action, disclose that its claim to our allegiance depends in large measure on its justice. So it would have been entirely appropriate – and preferable – for Lord Sankey to have reflected on the purpose of the *BNA Act* – to serve the common good of a particular political community – and to have articulated that good as being the good of all members of the community, male and female. To recognize women as equal members in that community would require adopting just the constitutional construction that he did – a rule that presumes that "person," in the context of qualification to serve in the political institutions of a society, must mean male and female.

Even where it results in no difference to the disposition ultimately reached, adherence to the New Originalist methodology is a significant advance over conceiving of the constitutional text as fundamentally malleable. The discipline of the interpretation/construction dichotomy includes a respect for the constitutional text and the judicial role, entailing a frank acknowledgment of limits set by the text, and honesty and transparency about the scope and nature of the judicial creativity being deployed in the generation and application of constitutional rules.

V. THE PROBLEM OF INJUSTICE

It might be objected that I have chosen my example too well; happily, in this case, an adherence to originalist methodology would not (and in fact, did not) return a morally objectionable result. But what if we were to pose a counterfactual section 24 in which the framers had expressly stated that *only male persons* were eligible for appointment to the Senate, and *not* women? Interpretation in such a case, as the Privy Council noted, would be easy. There would be no ambiguity or vagueness. The interpretation would clearly

[98] *Roe v. Wade*, 410 U.S. 113 (1973).

[99] *Winnipeg Child and Family Services (Northwest Area) v. G. (D.F.)*, [1997] 3 S.C.R. 925.

[100] This is not to suggest that there can never be justifications for excluding classes of persons from deliberative political institutions. Justifications are readily at hand for excluding, for example, children and non-citizens.

and straightforwardly reveal that section 24 did not authorize the Governor General to appoint women to the Senate. It would seem, then, that originalist methodology in such a case would require a judge to rule against Edwards et al. This is the specter raised by Binnie J. in describing the *Persons Case* as a "standing rebuke to an overly deferential attitude to originalism."[101]

Of course, such a ruling would not mean that Canadians would forever be held back by the "dead hand of the past" and that women could never be appointed to the Canadian Senate. Courts are not the only engine of legal change and it would be hard to believe that, but for judicial intervention, the Canadian Senate would today remain an all-male preserve. Constitutional amendment always remains a possibility, as does legislative and executive action that is not prompted by the courts. But even remaining focused exclusively on the judicial role, things are not so bleak. Originalists are not committed to a form of legal positivism that places law beyond moral evaluation. As Gerard Bradley argued in 1992, "nothing in a sound account of originalism implies that law, including constitutional law, is beyond normative evaluation, or denies that there are natural and inalienable rights."[102] And nothing in a sound account of the judicial role in Canada insulates the judge from the moral obligations that are binding on all persons, whether they are public officials like judges and legislators or persons without public roles.

It is to be expected in a basically just constitutional order (as I take the Canadian system to be) that interpretation of the constitutional text will not be morally problematic. And it is to be expected that on those occasions when interpretation needs to be supplemented by construction, its constitutional constructions will be available that are both consistent with the demands of morality and consistent with existing law.[103] However, in those rare cases where it is not possible to come up with a plausible interpretation that is morally acceptable, and the text is specific enough that it blocks a remedial constitutional construction (as in the counterfactual that I have posed), we must further consider what it is that a judge is being asked to do, and whether applying or following the law would require a judge to violate a binding moral norm. The question of what a judge should do in such a scenario lies within the domain of legal philosophy. And so the answer one gives will depend largely on one's answers to deep questions about the nature and authority of law.[104]

[101] Binnie, "Original Intent," *supra* note 1 at 366.

[102] Gerard V. Bradley, "The Bill of Rights and Originalism," (1992) U. Ill. L. Rev. 417 at 429.

[103] And, in fact, this is how I characterize the Privy Council's decision in the *Persons Case*.

[104] See John Finnis, *Natural Law and Natural Rights* (1980) [Finnis, *Natural Law*]; Joseph Raz, *The Authority of Law*, 2nd ed., (2009); Leslie Green, *The Authority of the State* (1990). Also see helpful discussion in Timothy Endicott, "Subsidiarity of the Law and the Obligation to

While law is presumptively to be treated as authoritative and to be obeyed, its claims to obedience can nevertheless be defeated in circumstances where a law conflicts sufficiently with the goods that law is meant to secure.[105] That is, it remains a possibility for a law to lose its presumptive obligatory force when it is sufficiently unjust, such as when it commands the violation of moral norm of greater force. To use a stock example, it would allow for a judge to refuse to apply a law that called for the judge to knowingly punish the innocent for the greater good of the community.

Lord Sankey would have been morally justified, if confronted with the counterfactual section 24, in advising the Government of Canada that the counterfactual section 24 was unjust and ought not to be applied. And if Lord Sankey had been presiding over an ordinary appeal rather than a constitutional reference, he would have been justified in refusing to apply the counterfactual section 24 with respect to the ban on women's participation, providing that he stated clearly that even though section 24 was the law, it was too inequitable to be applied. But this obligation not to violate a moral norm does not provide judges with plenary authority to refuse to apply the law simply because they find the law to be suboptimal in some respect. It does not, for example, generate a free-standing power to reauthor laws to optimize resource allocations such as, to use a Canadian example, reading economic and social rights into section 7 of the *Charter*, on the grounds that more just distributions could be achieved if such judicially enforceable rights had been included in the *Charter*.[106]

If a judge decides that he or she should refuse to apply an iniquitous law, the judge must be transparent about the fact that the judge is refusing to apply what he or she judges undoubtedly to be the law. There may be adverse consequences to the judge, which flow from that action: appeal, sanction, or even removal from the bench. A judge who frankly states that a law is so egregiously wrong that it cannot warrant obedience allows for other political actors to assess the judge's decision and to disagree and remedy it where necessary. This is preferable to a judicial reauthoring under the guise of interpretation, which arrogates authority that has not been given by the Constitution of Canada.

Obey," 50 Am. J. Juris. 233 (2005), and response by Gerard V. Bradley, "Response to Endicott: The Case of the Wise Electrician," 50 Am. J. Juris 257 (2005).

[105] See John Finnis, "Natural Law Theories" (5 February 2007), s. 1.5.1, online: Stanford Encyclopedia of Philosophy, http://plato.stanford.edu/entries/natural-law-theories/#LegPriRemDefPosLaw

[106] I do not here attempt to set out the circumstances that would justify, as a matter of political morality, a judge in refusing to apply an unjust law, but see the discussion in Finnis, *Natural Law*, *supra* note 102, c. 12 and Finnis, "Natural Law Theories" (5 February 2007), *ibid.* at s. 3.3.

VI. CONCLUSION

So what if I am right, and "living tree" constitutional interpretation is a Dicksonian invention and its institutional pedigree is a hoax? Is there any point to calling foul after play has carried on for nearly thirty years and arguing that there is support for originalist interpretation in Canadian law? First, there is good reason to question "living tree" methodology, not least because, as it has been articulated and practiced in Canadian law, it has functioned as more of an after-the-fact rationalization for judicial decision making than it does as a guide to judicial decision making.[107] Second, it is not a simple matter to determine the extent to which the central commitments of the "living tree" methodology are inconsistent with originalism. This is partially due to the difficulty in establishing just what the central commitments of the "living tree" methodology are.[108] Many of the commitments of this methodology are in fact consistent the New Originalism, with the partial exception of originalism's insistence on fixed meanings. I say "partial exception" because in most cases, the objection to fixed meanings offered by proponents of "living tree" methodology in Canada are confined to fixation by original intention, not original public meaning. The reading of the *Persons Case* I have provided here suggests that the metaphor of the living tree has genuine application to the stage of constitutional construction, and is in that way consistent with New Originalism. The *Persons Case* demonstrates that two of the central commitments of the New Originalism – fixed meanings and the interpretation/construction divide – have a home in what has been accepted as Canadian constitutional bedrock. Furthermore, although Sharpe and McMahon argue that the *Persons Case* established that courts are now free to permit what the constitution forbids, there is no support in the *Persons Case* or elsewhere in Canadian law for such an extreme version of "living tree" methodology.

So it would not be such a revolutionary thing to openly embrace the New Originalism within Canadian constitutional doctrine. But there remains the objection of principle: Should courts embrace the methodology of the New Originalism? Why not just stick with the old creed? Ultimately, it does not much matter whether one uses the label of living tree or originalism. What matters is the soundness of the ideas adopted. Scholars calling themselves originalists have had some insights that can bear much fruit if incorporated into Canadian constitutional doctrine. Two of the key analytical advances are

[107] See Miller, "Beguiled by Metaphors," *supra* note 1, and Bradley W. Miller, "Review Essay: A *Common Law Theory of Judicial Review* by W.J. Waluchow" 52 Am. J. Juris. 297 (2007).

[108] Miller, "Beguiled by Metaphors," *supra* note 1.

a commitment to fixed meanings and to clearly separating the two tasks of interpretation and construction.

An adoption of this methodology (of fixed meanings and the interpretation/construction distinction) would give the Supreme Court of Canada resources with which to adequately respond to demands currently placed on it to embrace "interpretations" (really, constructions) of the *Charter* that are antithetical to the settlement reached under the *Charter* (specifically with respect to economic and social rights). It is imperative that the Court, in considering these issues, confront the limits of interpreting the constitutional texts and frankly acknowledge what is at stake in undertaking what is really constitutional construction. If judges discipline themselves in such a way, they will have to confront the question of whether they have proper warrant in the Canadian constitutional order to undertake the constructions that they have been urged to make in cases such as *Gosselin v. Québec (Attorney General)*.[109] They would avoid passive and obscuring language ("[o]ne day section 7 may be interpreted to include positive obligations")[110] and own up to their own agency. Construction is much more controversial than interpretation and, for purposes of accountability, courts should lay bare when they have stopped doing the one and have started doing the other.

[109] [2002] 4 S.C.R. 429.

[110] *Ibid*. at para. 82.

PART THREE Originalism and Constitutional Settlement

7 Originalism's Constitution

Grégoire C. N. Webber*

INTRODUCTION

What is originalism? Given the breadth and depth of scholarship on the matter, the question may suffer from an embarrassment of different answers.[1] One might appeal to the "old originalism" with its focus on the intentions of the founders or the "new originalism" with its focus on the public meaning at the founding; in turn, one might review the range of *originalisms* that animate constitutional scholarship since the turn to new originalism.[2] Proceeding in this way would reveal that the answer to our question is not obvious or, rather more accurately, any single answer purporting to identify a single account of originalism would likely be contestable. The contest would be raised not only within the family of originalists, but also over who may be admitted therein, as not all self-proclaimed originalists are recognized by others to be members of

*I wish to thank participants at the *Originalism Colloquium* at the University of Western Ontario for excellent discussions and to colleagues at the London School of Economics and Political Science for the opportunity to present the argument at a Department of Law Staff Seminar Series and for offering probative comments. Warm thanks are also due to Graham Gee, Vicki Jackson, Robert Leckey, and Stéphanie Vig.

[1] Indeed, the question itself suffers from an embarrassment of different meanings. For an overview of these many possibilities, see Lawrence B. Solum, "What Is Originalism? The Evolution of Contemporary Originalist Theory" in this volume [Solum, "What Is Originalism?"]. See also Daniel A. Farber, "The Originalism Debate: A Guide for the Perplexed" 49 Ohio State L.J. 1085 (1989).

[2] An excellent overview of the old and new originalism is provided in Keith E. Whittington, "The New Originalism" 2 Geo. J.L. & Pub. Pol'y 599 (2004) [Whittington, "The New Originalism"]. A critical catalog of different "originalisms" is offered in Mitchell N. Berman, "Originalism is Bunk" 84 N.Y.U. L. Rev. 1 (2009) and Thomas B. Colby and Peter J. Smith, "Living Originalism" 59 Duke L.J. 239 (2009).

the same set.[3] But proceeding with this genre of answer would already assume a prior answer to our question. For before one seeks to identify the commands and commitments of originalism, one must situate originalism within the world of constitutional theory, namely as a *theory of interpretation*.[4]

Originalism, of course, is usually situated alongside other theories of constitutional interpretation. In the United States, it is contrasted with living constitutionalism or, in rather less descriptive and more encompassing terms, with "non-originalism."[5] At other times or in other jurisdictions, competing theories of interpretation may include textualism or intratextualism,[6] purposive or progressive interpretation,[7] moral principles,[8] representation-reinforcing interpretation,[9] structural or unwritten constitutional principles,[10] and living-tree constitutionalism,[11] to name but a few.[12] Much of the debate surrounding originalism has focused on its inherent and comparative merits as a theory of interpretation. Reasons supporting originalism have been first-order (inherent to originalism's methodology) and second-order (comparative to other interpretive approaches and instrumental to pursuing good ends), as well as directed to what the task of interpretation *must* of necessity be and what it *should* be.[13]

[3] See Ethan J. Leib, "The Perpetual Anxiety of Living Constitutionalism" 24 Const. Comment. 353 at 355 (2007): "[M]any originalists will read Balkin to be a living constitutionalist in disguise – and may not let him into their club." See also Steve D. Smith's contribution to this volume: "That Old-Time Originalism."

[4] Even this categorization is contested; see Stanley Fish, "The Intentionalist Thesis Once More" in this volume. I take comfort in the thought that, according to Fish, if this categorization is wrong, it is because of a category mistake: "I would contend that there is no such thing as a theory of interpretation" (at 99).

[5] See Randy E. Barnett, *Restoring the Lost Constitution: The Presumption of Liberty* (2004) 92 [Barnett, *Restoring the Lost Constitution*] and "An Originalism for Nonoriginalists" 45 Loyola L. Rev. 611 at 617 (1999) [Barnett, "An Originalism for Nonoriginalists"]: "It takes a theory to beat a theory and, after a decade of trying, the opponents of originalism have never congealed around an appealing and practical alternative."

[6] See Akhil R. Amar, "Intratextualism" 112 Harv. L. Rev 747 (1999) [Amar, "Intratextualism"].

[7] For Canada, see Peter W. Hogg, "Canada: From Privy Council to Supreme Court" in Jeffrey Goldsworthy (ed.), *Interpreting Constitutions: A Comparative Study* (2006) 55 [Goldsworthy, ed., *Interpreting Constitutions*].

[8] See Ronald Dworkin, *Freedom's Law: The Moral Reading of the American Constitution* (1996).

[9] See John Hart Ely, *Democracy and Distrust: A Theory of Judicial Review* (1980).

[10] See David Dyzenhaus, "The Incoherence of Constitutional Positivism" and Mark D. Walters, "Written Constitutions and Unwritten Constitutionalism," both in Grant Huscroft (ed.), *Expounding the Constitution: Essays in Constitutional Theory* (2008).

[11] See W. J. Waluchow, *A Common Law Theory of Judicial Review: The Living Tree* (2007).

[12] See also Mitchell N. Berman, "Reflective Equilibrium and Constitutional Method" in this volume.

[13] Stanley Fish's contribution to this volume is directed to telling us not "how to interpret" but "what [we] are doing when [we] interpret" (at 100). Similarly, both Larry Alexander and Jeff Goldsworthy suggest in this volume that the case for originalism is, well, "simple."

These debates have contributed in important ways to our understanding of originalism. But just as the focus on originalism as a theory of interpretation has assisted in focusing attention on specific commitments of originalism, it has also privileged one vantage point over others, perhaps keeping from view other related commitments. How might these be brought to light?

In this chapter, I wish to explore originalism as something other than a theory of interpretation. This will doubtless strike some as odd. After all, if originalism is a theory of interpretation, how else might one seek to understand it? Yet, this would not be the first time that we are invited to conceive of originalism as something other than a theory of interpretation. For example, believing that "[n]o approach to constitutional interpretation makes sense in every possible world," Sunstein invites us to view originalism as a *place* or *site*.[14] In Sunstein's world of originalism, the "original public meaning is quite excellent," "the democratic process is also very fair and good," and judges, "unleashed from the original public meaning, would do a great deal of harm, unsettling well-functioning institutions and recognising, as rights, interests that do not deserve that recognition."[15] While one may question Sunstein's characterization of originalism's assumptions, his thought experiment makes explicit how originalism may proceed on certain unstated background assumptions, not all of which are brought into full focus when examining originalism as a theory of interpretation in a situated context. The insight that Sunstein offers is less in his articulation of what the various background commitments of originalism might be than in how the exercise of imagining a theory of interpretation other than as a theory of interpretation may reveal what would otherwise remain beyond our immediate grasp.

Recognizing this potential, I wish to reflect on how originalism can be understood, not as a theory of interpretation, nor (as Sustein has proposed) as a place or site, but rather *as a constitution*. What does originalism assume about a constitution? What sort of constitution does it contemplate? In short, the query I wish to explore is: *What is an original constitution*?

On its face, the question seems ill-posed. After all, if originalism is a theory of interpretation, it cannot provide for the very subject matter that is the object of interpretation. Just as a theory of purposive interpretation cannot provide for the purpose that it seeks to expound, originalism cannot, it would seem, provide an account of an original constitution. Theories of interpretation are dependent on something to interpret; they cannot provide that

[14] Cass R. Sunstein, "Second-Order Perfectionalism" (University of Chicago Law & Economics, Olin Working Paper No. 319, 2006).

[15] *Ibid.* at 2–3.

matter of themselves. Yet, this mode of reasoning can be turned on itself: We can ask whether we ever fully know what *it is* that we are interpreting without already engaging, however tentatively, in the exercise of interpretation. If we accept that we cannot fully grasp "the constitution" without a theory of interpretation in hand, then it becomes possible to say that the subject matter of interpretation cannot so easily be divorced from an interpretive approach. If true, "the constitution" may be a different statement depending on who is speaking and what theory of constitutional interpretation they are appealing to.

There is, of course, a practical activity that we identify as constitutional interpretation, which (we assume) refers to the same "constitution" in undertaking the task of interpretation. Yet, upon examination, we realize that some seek to interpret the intent of the framers, others look to the words in their historical context, and yet others still look to principles or judicial precedent. Whereas students of constitutional interpretation all consider their activity to be one of interpreting "the constitution," "some people use the phrase to refer to one sort of object while others use it to refer to another sort of object."[16] In this way, we see how theories of constitutional interpretation interact with their subject matter of interpretation. While one should avoid exaggerating the point, "the constitution" seems to play the role of a "facilitative modern equivocation"; a sort of *placeholder* that interpreters substitute for the founders' intention, the original public meaning, or moral principles, among the alternatives.[17] In the case of real-world constitutions, theories of interpretation all begin with the written instrument, although few end there.[18] The final destination depends on one's interpretative approach.

On this basis, our query – what is an original constitution? – may seem somewhat less ill-posed. How does originalism understand "the constitution"? What does it substitute for that placeholder? How does it determine the equivocation? What model of a constitution does originalism contemplate? Now, attempting to design a fictitious original constitution may suffer from the same contests facing any account of originalism. Different originalists make different commitments and any attempt to select among them will be vulnerable to criticism. Despite the differences between originalists, I believe that three

[16] Steven D. Smith, "What Does Constitutional Interpretation Interpret?" in Grant Huscroft (ed.), *Expounding the Constitution: Essays in Constitutional Theory* (2008) 38.

[17] *Ibid.* at 36.

[18] In the case of the largely unwritten British constitution, we could say that interpretation beings with legal and political practice, not text. The focus of this essay, as befits the theory of originalism, is on a written constitution.

commitments can be fairly attributed to originalism without raising too much contest. I will argue that an original constitution is written at the founding and changed only by the amendment procedure it sets out, is law insofar as it provides rule-like prescriptions, and occupies a delimited domain, leaving the rest to democracy.[19]

This account of an original constitution may be too obvious or thin for some, or mistaken in orientation or underinclusive for others, but I hope that it will be sufficient for present purposes. I hope to show that when one moves from the fictitious world of an original constitution to real-world constitutions in all their diversity, originalism cannot hope to occupy the entire field of constitutional meaning. The choice is not, as it were, between making a real-world constitution fit the model of an original constitution or a non-original constitution; *that* choice is a false choice. Real-world constitutions lend themselves to originalism in some, perhaps many, but not all respects. I will aim to show that this is neither a fault of real-world constitutions nor of originalism; rather, it is a consequence of interpretation's delimited domain within constitutional meaning.

The following account of an original constitution provides a model of a fictional constitution that satisfies, perhaps to a fault, the key commitments of originalism. It seeks to bring to light the commitments originalism would have of us, and of constitutions. The exercise of divorcing real-world constitutions from the model of an original constitution is important, for too much scholarship on originalism conflates the circumstances of real-world constitutions – and the U.S. Constitution in particular – with the circumstances of originalism. This proximity of theory to practice – although illuminating in many respects – at times obscures both, as when the theorist makes the theory fit the facts (consider the criticism that some originalists doctor the evidence to prevent slavery or the death penalty from being sanctioned by an originalist reading of the U.S. Constitution) or when the lawyer moulds the facts to satisfy the theory (consider the attempt by some to make the U.S. Constitution rule-like through appeals to original expected application). As a consequence, theory and its application seem impossible to divorce. This anchor has helped fashion a markedly practical perspective, but it has also at times skewed the debate surrounding originalism. The following account of *an original constitution* cuts loose the anchor.

[19] My attempt to articulate three core commitments originalists would have of a constitution is similar to, and overlaps with, Larry Solum's attempt in this volume to identify a core of agreement within originalist theory: "What Is Originalism?" *supra* note 1.

I. THE ORIGINAL CONSTITUTION AND THE FOUNDING MOMENT

An original constitution is established at its founding, which serves as the definitive reference point for situating the constitution. Events preceding the founding may explain the impetus for and the content of the original constitution, but – like the events that follow the founding – they are irrelevant for identifying the original constitution.[20] Rather, the authoritative discoverable meaning of the original constitution is settled at the founding, being "the time its language is enacted" such that its "fixed meaning should remain the same until it is properly changed."[21]

The written instrument is the product of a moment, an event; it is not a story. The only story (if it can be so considered) that the original constitution allows for is the story it itself prescribes: constitutional amendments. The original constitution is an end-state, a completed project, a story the narrative of which began only to end. It achieves permanence, stability, and continuity – all of which can be referenced back to the original constitution's founding moment.

The Constitution's Writtenness

The idea of a constitutional founding as a single event rather than as a story draws on the original constitution's *writtenness*.[22] The text of the original constitution provides a constant reference: It was written at a specific historical moment. The written character of the original constitution differs from what is often taken to be Britain's distinctively political constitution, which, despite being in many respects written in Acts of Parliament, is in many other respects a constitution of tradition.[23] Tradition, like the constitutional practices that are a part of it, knows no founding moment. It may know of a defining moment or

[20] This should not be taken to dismiss the original intentions of the framers or ratifiers. For the purposes of this essay, I remain agnostic as between the "original intent" and "original public meaning" camps within the originalist family. But see the conclusion for a qualification.

[21] Randy E. Barnett, "The Misconceived Assumption about Constitutional Assumptions" 103 Nw. U. L. Rev. 615 (2009) and Barnett, *Restoring the Lost Constitution*, *supra* note 5 at 103–9. See also Whittington, "The New Originalism," *supra* note 2 at 599.

[22] For a discussion of the writtenness of a constitution and its relationship to commitments that are carried out over time, see Jed Rubenfeld, *Freedom and Time: A Theory of Constitutional Self-Government* (2001), esp. ch. 3 [Rubenfeld, *Freedom and Time*].

[23] See Graham Gee and Grégoire C.N. Webber, "What Is a Political Constitution?" (2010) 30 O.J.L.S. 273. Note that the more important fact of the British constitution's writtenness may be the codes of conduct and other non-statutory instruments published (but not enacted) by Parliament and Her Majesty's government.

a paradigm case, but the tradition itself cannot be so reduced. In many ways, the defining moment is only so identified after the fact as it is incorporated into the evolving tradition. An original constitution, by contrast, is authoritatively identified at the moment it is founded.

To translate tradition into writing is to change tradition, to settle it at a point in its evolution, to select a moment in history as the end of evolution. An original constitution is not tradition – it does not evolve. The written text of the constitution provides a fixed reference against which actions may be measured. This is not to deny that a tradition may build up (indeed, may *need* to build up) around an original constitution, sustaining its authority. After all, because any act of founding may fail, an original constitution has "continuing force only because of the actions of subsequent generations in according the founders' text as their own."[24] But that is not the same thing as identifying an original constitution as a tradition. Unlike tradition, a historical snapshot of an original constitution will always be accurate, whereas a historical snapshot of tradition (insofar as the exercise is possible) will, with time, become dated and misrepresentative of the tradition.

The fixed reference – the founding – discloses an authoritative choice as to what the constitution shall be. Being committed to writing,[25] an original constitution is evidence of what was determined at the founding. It led those with the authority to adopt it to deliberate and to caution the merits of the constitution's clauses and to channel their actions toward or against enactment.[26] The text was the focus of their ultimate agreement, as they proceeded through disagreements on meaning, amendments, substitutions, additions, and other changes to the text. The decision to select a written instrument over an evolutionary tradition secured the meaning of the constitution. To ascribe to it a meaning that it did not bear at its founding is to undermine and to undo its writtenness and the decision to commit matters to writing. In this way, the meaning of an original constitution is fixed by its writtenness.

To express fidelity to the text of an original constitution is to understand that its meaning is discoverable as a "'social fact', determined by social conventions, including conventions which make certain kinds of evidence of the speaker's

[24] Keith E. Whittington, "Let's Call the Whole Thing Off?" 22 Const. Comment. 365 at 374 (2005). See also Paul Brest, "The Misconceived Quest for the Original Understanding" 60 B.U.L. Rev. 204 at 225 (1980) [Brest, "Misconceived Quest"].

[25] The following is based on Lon L. Fuller, "Consideration and Form" 41 Colum. L. Rev. 799 (1941), 900–1, reviewed in Barnett, *Restoring the Lost Constitution*, *supra* note 5 at 101 and "An Originalism for Nonoriginalists," *supra* note 5 at 630–1.

[26] See Jeremy Waldron "Legislating with Integrity" (2003) 72 Fordham L. Rev. 373 and Jeremy Waldron, *Law and Disagreement* (1999) chs. 4 and 6.

intentions relevant [if at all], as well as others which fix dictionary meanings and rules of grammar."[27] Interpretation, in this way, is said to be akin to a "science."[28] Constitutional meaning exists *before* the interpretive exercise is undertaken; it is contained, somehow, within the constitution, not within the mind of the interpreter. To be faithful to the original constitution is to discover *its* meaning and to abide by it.[29] To change the meaning of the original constitution is to change the original constitution and, in so doing, to challenge its authority as a written instrument adopted at a given moment. That challenge is twofold: It is both directed to the founding moment that created the constitution and subversive of the constitution's prescribed method of change – the amendment formula.

By challenging the authority of an original constitution, one denies the authority of the founding moment. One renders the founding moment temporary and turns the constitution into a story with a fixed beginning and without a definite end. The merits of doing so may well depend on whether one views the original constitution as a "covenant with death and an agreement with Hell,"[30] but in seeking to improve the constitution, one is no longer being faithful to its status as written text. The aim of faithful interpretation must be to discover the original constitution's meaning at the founding, not the "commitments that one or another philosopher thinks . . . should have [been] made" or should now be made.[31] Interpretation is a preserving act, drawing on the commitment that "that law continues in force over time until it is amended or repealed," with the consequence that "[i]f the law states a directive, rule, or norm that continues in force over time, we must preserve the meaning to preserve the directive, rule, or norm that the law states."[32]

An original constitution's founding marks an authoritative beginning. It is of no consequence that the constitution may have been inconsistent with prior

[27] Jeffrey Goldsworthy, "Originalism in Constitutional Interpretation" (1997) 25 Fed. L. Rev. 1 at 8 [Goldsworthy, "Originalism in Constitutional Interpretation"].

[28] Antonin Scalia, *A Matter of Interpretation*, Amy Gutmann (ed.), (1997) at 14–15 [Scalia, *A Matter of Interpretation*]. Contrast Keith E. Whittington, *Constitutional Interpretation: Textual Meaning, Original Intent, and Judicial Review* (1999) 175.

[29] I do not mean to suggest that the meaning of the text inheres somehow in the text itself. Stanley Fish's contribution to this volume persuasively argues against this view.

[30] The expression is William Lloyd Garrison's.

[31] See Bruce Ackerman, "The Living Constitution" 120 Harv. L. Rev. 1737 at 1754 (2007) [Ackerman, "The Living Constitution"]; see also Jack M. Balkin, "Original Meaning and Constitutional Redemption" 24 Constitutional Comment. 427 at 438 (2007) [Balkin, "Constitutional Redemption"].

[32] Balkin, "Constitutional Redemption," *ibid.* at 429–30. Some question whether Balkin holds true to his statement.

constitutional requirements;[33] an original constitution is a new overriding moment, it erases that which comes before and premises all that follows. It is, in short, a revolutionary instrument. It contains "the constitution" in exclusive whole; one need not refer to other instruments or to tradition. An original constitution understands post-founding constitutional development as a tradition of constitutional *compliance*, not constitutional *change*.

Understood in this way, an original constitution is an expression of self-government – of living out a people's commitments over time.[34] The constitution's commitments remain their commitments until *they* choose to change them by the mode *they* prescribe in the constitution. The people speak at the moment of the founding only to retreat from the stage. They exercise their power to create the original constitution only once, and thereafter resign themselves to their constitutional forms: the legislature, the executive, the administration, the court, the citizen. It is only through these constitutional forms that the people now speak. In this way, an original constitution can be understood as both a performative act (by the people) and a declarative act (of who the people are).

The assumption that it is the people who authored the original constitution rests on national myth ("it was We the People who adopted this, our, original constitution") or declared truth ("we few assembled here speak for We the People"). This assumption is important to resist claims that the original constitution represents "the dead hand of the past." There is no doubt that in many instances, the reality of historical progression (including emancipation) reveals that the people then were at best only a subset of the people now. But that need not be determinative. After all, we today quite simply were not them then. Should the people now continue to understand themselves as the people then, then an original constitution provides them with a constant reference to their founding moment. This intertemporal association is largely beyond the control of the original constitution and rests on commitments to political

[33] In the case of the U.S. Constitution, the Framers decided that nine states – not the thirteen prescribed by the Articles of Confederation – would suffice to establish the founding moment.

[34] The idea of a constitution as living out commitments over time is explored in Rubenfeld, *Freedom and Time*, *supra* note 22. For the difficulties of this narrative in former British colonies and the debate whether the former colony or the British Parliament framed the constitution, see Justice Ian Binnie, "Constitutional Interpretation and Original Intent" in Grant Huscroft and Ian Brodie (eds.), *Constitutionalism in the Charter Era* (2004) 375 (Canada) [Binnie, "Constitutional Interpretation and Original Intent"] and Goldsworthy, "Originalism in Constitutional Interpretation," *supra* note 27 at 25 (Australia). For a general critique of the "fiction" of "We the People," see Barnett, *Restoring the Lost Constitution*, *supra* note 5, ch 1.

community that an original constitution cannot prescribe, even if its continuing authority rests on such commitments. Yet, if it is the case that the founding moment was *both* performative *and* declarative, then there is some malleability and fluidity in the constitutional forms of the people, with the consequence that the existing constitutionally prescribed forms are provisional. Other forms can be imagined and, if actualized, will challenge the original constitution's ongoing performative and declarative claims.[35]

But whatever be the call to revisit the constitutional forms prescribed, the original constitution maintains that all changes must be effected through the exclusive mode of constitutional change: the amendment formula.

The Exclusive Mode of Constitutional Change

The amendment formula of an original constitution plays two related roles. First, it confirms for greater certainty what would obtain even in its absence: The constitution means what it meant at the moment it was adopted. Why else would an original constitution prescribe a mode for change but for the fact that the meaning of the constitution is fixed?[36] Second, the amendment formula provides not only a mode of constitutional change, but more fundamentally it provides for the *exclusive* mode of constitutional change. For if it is the case that one must be a "faint-hearted originalist" not to follow the original constitution or if one must adulterate the original constitution in order to follow *stare decisis*,[37] then it follows that the original constitution cannot be changed in these ways. It is fixed, stable, and constant subject only to the amendment procedures it prescribes; and if the original constitution did not prescribe any such procedures, it quite simply could not be changed.[38]

[35] See M. Loughlin and N. Walker, "Introduction" in Martin Loughlin and Neil Walker (eds.), *The Paradox of Constitutionalism: Constituent Power and Constitutional Form* (2007) 1–2. See also Ackerman "The Living Constitution," *supra* note 31, for an account of how the American people no longer see themselves in a state-based conception, thus challenging the logic of state-based constitutional amendment procedures provided for in the U.S. Constitution.

[36] See generally Goldsworthy, "Originalism in Constitutional Interpretation," *supra* note 27.

[37] Antonin Scalia, "Originalism: The Lesser Evil" 57 U. Cin. L. Rev. 849 at 864, 861 (1989) [Scalia, "The Lesser Evil"]. Indeed, Scalia states that "*stare decisis* is not *part* of [his] originalist philosophy; it is a pragmatic *exception* to it": Antonin Scalia, "Response" in Scalia, *A Matter of Interpretation*, *supra* note 28 at 140. See also Randy E. Barnett, "Scalia's Infidelity: A Critique of 'Faint-Hearted' Originalism" 75 U. Cin. L. Rev 7 (2006) [Barnett, "Scalia's Infidelity"].

[38] Some constitutions have "eternity clauses" (see the Basic Law for the Federal Republic of Germany (Art 79(3)) that render "inadmissible" certain amendments. This is quite different from judicially proclaimed basic structures that are beyond amendment, as the Indian Supreme Court has declared.

In keeping with the relationship between writtenness and stability, fixity, and continuity, there is a sense in which amendments to the original constitution should not be lightly undertaken. This may be reflected in the amendment formula itself, which may prescribe a more cumbersome mode of constitutional change than was appealed to when adopting the constitution at the moment of the founding. But irrespective of the conditions precedent for achieving a constitutional amendment, an amendment should not be approached lightly – it should be out of the ordinary and altogether exceptional. To do otherwise would be to lessen the importance of the founding and, with it, the authority of the original constitution.[39] For even if an amendment changes the original constitution, it does not (because it cannot) recreate the founding moment. Because the entire process is channeled through the constitutional forms established by the original constitution, any amendment may only *change*, not *found* the constitution, quite irrespective of the degree of change pursued. The people then spoke directly; the people now speak only through their constitutionally prescribed forms.[40] A constitutional amendment provides no new beginning; rather, there is merely a new chapter in (what now becomes) the story of the original constitution. Moreover, where amendments are targeted rather than encompassing, they differ from the founding moment in another important sense: Whereas an original constitution was adopted as a whole, amendments are partial. In this way, even though amendments may recreate perfectly the original constitution's writtenness, they cannot recreate its "wholeness."[41]

Understood thus, the amendment formula *both* provides access to the founding of an original constitution by allowing for change to what was originally determined *and*, by only allowing change according to the original constitution's own channels, confirms the qualitative difference between the founding and all that follows. Hence, although an original constitution does not prevent change, it necessarily conditions it.

No doubt, extra-constitutional evolution occurs, and legislatures, executives, courts, and citizens may act in places where the original constitution

[39] The U.S. Constitution and its amendments provide a particularly powerful statement of the immutability of the founding: All amendments are positioned at the end of the document and do not change the original wording of the Constitution. Contrast this with the *mélange* of constitutional documents comprising the Constitution of Canada, non-exhaustively cataloged at *Constitution Act, 1982*, s. 52(2) ("The Constitution of Canada includes . . . ").

[40] This, too, is part of national myth or declared truth insofar as the people cannot ever speak without institutions, processes, and rules to constitute their voice.

[41] This point is discussed in Amar, "Intratextualism," *supra* note 6 at 795–6 and Akhil R. Amar, "*America's Constitution* and the Yale School of Constitutional Interpretation" 115 Yale L.J. 1997 at 2004 (2006).

does not venture. So long as there is no contradiction with constitutional prescriptions, an original constitution bears no direct relationship with this *extra*-constitutional development. Yet for this very reason, no amount of extra-constitutional change can affect the original constitution's meaning. The story of the original constitution begins with the founding and continues only if there are amendments; there is no other constitutional story to be told.[42]

To argue that existing constitutional arrangements are not as they should be and that the amendment process is too cumbersome to correct them is simply another way of saying that a proposal for constitutional change is not yet ripe for amendment. An original constitution is fixed and proponents of amendments should be hesitant; the narrative of societies is not only one of progression, but also of decline.[43] What is wrong from your political perspective may be right from mine. A core purpose of an original constitution is to prevent change, to settle select matters, and to remove them from political debate and "ordinary politics." The importance of the founding and the difficulty of achieving amendments testify to the importance of what the original constitution speaks to. Should change be sought, it must rise to a level of similar importance before warranting a place on the stage of the original constitution. One cannot coherently argue for the importance of a difficult amendment procedure so as to maintain stability and immutability while arguing for the necessity of changing the original constitution's meaning by other, simpler means.[44] In the end, "either we believe in the need for a cumbersome amendment process or we do not,"[45] and the original constitution does.

II. THE ORIGINAL CONSTITUTION IS LAW

Today, when students of the constitution speak of *constitutional law*, they may, without embarrassment, enumerate a panoply of matters without including the constitution itself. They may, of course, refer to the written constitution, but likely only in secondary importance to precedent, general doctrines, judicially prescribed tests or factors, and the like. With time and no doubt in the mind

[42] *Cf.* Ackerman, "The Living Constitution," *supra* note 31 at 1750: "[E]very American intuitively recognizes that the modern amendments tell a very, very small part of the big constitutional story of the twentieth century."

[43] See Antonin Scalia, "Common Law Courts in a Civil Law System: The Role of United States Federal Courts in Interpreting the Constitution and Laws" in Scalia, *A Matter of Interpretation*, *supra* note 28 at 40–1. See also Balkin, "Constitutional Redemption," *supra* note 31 at 457–8.

[44] See Grant Huscroft, "A constitutional 'Work in Progress'? The Charter and the Limits of Progressive Interpretation" (2004) 23 S.C.L.R. (2d) 413.

[45] Jeremy Waldron, "A Right-Based Critique of Constitutional Rights" (1993) 13 O.J.L.S. 18 at 42.

of many students of the constitution, the accumulation of judicial precedent will come "to assume more importance than the original text."[46] Not so with an original constitution.

An original constitution is written and it is law. This may be too obvious to state; after all, most constitutions contain a supremacy clause, which states that the constitution is the "supreme *law* of the land." Yet, for an original constitution, much is contained in the idea of law. The only constitutional law prescribed by the original constitution is *the law of the original constitution*. To achieve this, the original constitution is best understood as a set of constitutional rules, and any provision that is not law in this specific sense is akin to an inkblot: It is without meaning.

Constitutional Rules

Some scholars provide accounts of a "thin constitution" comprising only declarations of grand principles and preambles announcing high aspirations,[47] leaving the constitution to be no more than a reference in political debate – perhaps a source of neutral language disclosing or directing an overlapping consensus for public reason. A constitution might also, as did many communist constitutions, provide a vision of a perfect future society.[48] It might, in turn, announce directive principles for government policy.[49] Alternatively, some scholars look to a constitution as "the stage for a kind of common-law jurisprudence,"[50] or as a symbolic public statement about the society's commitment to rights.[51]

An original constitution is altogether different. In keeping with the importance of the founding and the associated commitments to stability, fixity, and continuity, an original constitution is law in the sense that it cannot be changed

[46] Hogg, "Canada: From Privy Council to Supreme Court," *supra* note 7 at 90. See also H. Jefferson Powell, *A Community Built on Words: The Constitution in History and Politics* (2002) 2; and Goldsworthy, "Originalism in Constitutional Interpretation," *supra* note 27 at 29.

[47] See Mark Tushnet, *Taking the Constitution Away from the Courts* (1999), where the thin constitution is identified as the U.S. Declaration of Independence and the U.S. Constitution's preamble.

[48] See Andras Sajó, *Limiting Government: An Introduction to Constitutionalism* (1999) 1.

[49] See the "Directive Principles of State Policy" in the Constitution of India, Part IV and the Constitution of Ireland, s 45.

[50] See W. J. Waluchow, "Constitutions as Living Trees: An Idiot Defends" (2005) 18 Can. J. L. & Jur. 207 at 230 [Waluchow, "Constitutions as Living Trees"] and T.R.S. Allan, *Constitutional Justice: A Liberal Theory of the Rule of Law* (2003).

[51] See Jeremy Waldron, "The Core of the Case Against Judicial Review" 115 Yale L. J. 1346 at 1365 (2006); Waluchow "Constitutions as Living Trees," *supra* note 50 at 234–5.

except through the amendment procedure it itself prescribes. It is a prescriptive and authoritative "act of communication . . . conveying meaning from an author to a reader."[52] It provides propositions for action and compliance, not for debate. An original constitution is, in short, an exclusive reason for action or omission, not a premise in evaluating the merits of acting or not. To achieve this, an original constitution provides in writing what much real-world constitutional law provides in precedent and practice. An original constitution is law specific enough to eliminate the need for elaboration. An original constitution is law specific enough to be determinate. An original constitution is law specific enough for its meaning to be discovered exclusively through interpretation. In short, an original constitution is a set of determinate *rules*.

The idea of an original constitution as a set of constitutional rules is familiar to much originalism. The pursuit of "fixed meaning ascertainable through the usual devices familiar to those learned in the law"[53] seeks to satisfy the original constitution's grounding in a founding moment. Much of the confusion surrounding the relationship between the founder's expected applications – "how would the constitution have been applied at the founding" – and the original meaning of the constitution can be understood, at least in part, as the pursuit of a constitution of rules. Now, there is no doubt that the framers responsible for the original constitution "should be held to what they said rather than what they meant" even if "they fail[ed] to say what they mean[t]."[54] But one can understand how easily those who adhere to either the "old originalism" of original intention or the "new originalism" of original public meaning might be tempted by the framers' expected application of the constitution: All expected applications are specific and determinate.[55] They have the determinacy of rules. And a constitution is most fixed, determinate, and unchanging when it is a set of rules.[56]

The force of rules for the original constitution is disclosed by the fact that all – originalists and non-originalists alike – acknowledge that where the

[52] Whittington, "The New Originalism," *supra* note 2 at 613.

[53] Scalia, "The Lesser Evil," *supra* note 37 at 854.

[54] Aileen Kavanagh, "Original Intention, Enacted Text, and Constitutional Interpretation" 47 Am. J. Juris. 255 at 294 (2002) [Kavanagh, "Original Intention"].

[55] For a criticism of how Scalia claims to adhere to original public meaning but practices original expected application, see Jack M. Balkin, "Abortion and Original Meaning" 24 Const. Comment. 291 at 296 (2007); Kavanagh, "Original Intention," *supra* note 54 at 281; Ronald Dworkin, "Comment" in Scalia, *A Matter of Interpretation*, *supra* note 28.

[56] It bears mentioning that while the pursuit of original expected application seeks to confirm the constitution's determinacy, it subverts that pursuit in part by requiring one to go behind (and beyond) the writtenness of the constitution. See the discussion of the "unexpressed intent thesis" in Kavanagh, "Original Intention," *supra* note 54.

constitution is sufficiently rule-like, its original meaning is controlling. All agree that "if the Constitution supplies a rule, that rule prevails,"[57] and that "if a constitutional provision is clear and unambiguous, it is simply applied according to its terms."[58] The examples that are often cited relate to numerical precision, as when the number of members of a legislative assembly is specified or when the duration of a mandate is stipulated in days, months, or years. Matters are altogether otherwise with open-ended provisions, which stipulate only abstract constitutional commands. For this reason, the original constitution's emphasis on stability and fixity calls on rule-like provisions.

An original constitution's rule-like prescriptions satisfy the idea of *inconsistency* that grounds constitutional supremacy and provides the basis for judicial review.[59] Legislative prescriptions and constitutional rules can be inconsistent; executive orders and constitutional rules can be inconsistent. But neither legislation nor executive orders can be obviously inconsistent with a constitutional standard or principle. The standard and the principle must be made more determinate before the idea of consistency can obtain – each must be specified to a rule before legislation or executive orders can be evaluated for consistency.

But an original constitution need never be made more determinate; to do so would suggest that the founding moment was incomplete. An original constitution is neither indeterminate nor underdeterminate. Its provisions are specific and depend for their application only on facts. A rule-like prescription possesses the necessary "specificity in order to connect it to a given situation"; it is, in this way, a "governing rule" that "serve[s] as law."[60] In all cases, an original constitution itself, aided only by tools of interpretation that discover (not create) meaning, allows for the following constitutional syllogism: The constitution provides the major premise; the facts (legislation, executive order) are the minor premise; with the conclusion following as a matter of deductive logic. This process, for some, is akin to a civil law system where rules are specified in advance, and not to the common law's creation of rules to fit the

[57] Michael Stokes Paulsen, "How to Interpret the Constitution (and How Not To)" 115 Yale L. J. 2037 at 2057 (2006). See also Robert H. Bork, *The Tempting of America: The Political Seduction of the Law* (1990) 170 [Bork, *The Tempting of America*] and Balkin, "Constitutional Redemption," *supra* note 31 at 432–3 on how the debate centers especially on the constitution's open-ended rights provisions.

[58] I. Binnie, "Interpreting the Constitution: The Living Tree vs. Original Meaning" (2007) Policy Options (October) 104 at 108.

[59] This idea is explored and challenged in Grégoire C. N. Webber, "The Unfulfilled Potential of the Court and Legislature Dialogue" (2009) 42 Can. J. Poli. Sci. 443.

[60] Whittington, *Constitutional Interpretation*, *supra* note 28 at 6. See also A Scalia, "Response" in Scalia, *A Matter of Interpretation*, *supra* note 28 at 134.

case.[61] For an original constitution, the judicial task is to apply rules to the facts, not to invent rules to fit the facts.

This understanding of an original constitution confirms its authority as a set of legal rules that deliberately and authoritatively settle the matters to which the constitution is addressed. It might be said that for a constitution "to contain an accurate detail of all the subdivisions of which its great powers will admit, and of all the means by which they may be carried into execution, [it] would partake of the prolixity of a legal code, and could scarcely be embraced by the human mind."[62] That may be true, but the alternative is not to understand the nature of a constitution as requiring "that only its great outlines should be marked, its important objects designated."[63] That is a false alternative. For if a constitution does not itself provide the determinacy needed for its application, that determinacy must come from elsewhere. Outlines and objectives do not decide cases; a legal code must be established. What the original constitution proposes is to contain, within itself, the determinacy required for its application. It is, in this sense, to be understood as public law's civil code where interpretation begins and ends with the constitution's writtenness.

Of Inkblots and Other Nonsense

If a constitution wishes to settle the question of abortion, it will create a rule;[64] it will not provide an open-ended provision on liberty or life that might resolve the question one way or another. If a constitution wishes to settle the question of affirmative action programs, it will create a rule;[65] it will not provide an open-ended provision on equality that might resolve the question one way or the other. An original constitution settles questions. Where it speaks, it speaks determinatively, and where the tools of interpretation fail to resolve a question, the original constitution does not speak. If it is the case that further constitutional specification is required, then the original constitution is effectively silent; it is the *author of the further specification* – for example,

[61] See Scalia "Common-Law Courts in a Civil-Law System" and M. A. Glendon, "Comment" both in Scalia, *A Matter of Interpretation*, *supra* note 28. See also Antonin Scalia, "The Rule of Law as a Law of Rules" 56 University Chicago L. Rev. 1175 (1989); Donald P. Kommers "Germany: Balancing Rights and Duties" in Goldsworthy (ed.), *Interpreting Constitutions*, *supra* note 7.

[62] *McCulloch v Maryland*, 4 U.S. 316 at 407 (1819).

[63] *Ibid.* at 407.

[64] See Constitution of Ireland, Article 40 s.(3)(3) (guaranteeing the right to life of the unborn).

[65] See *Canadian Charter of Rights and Freedoms*, s. 15(2) (specifying that affirmative action programs are not inconsistent with the right to equality).

the court – and not the constitution that then speaks. In undertaking the task of further specification, the author is called on to make choices that are not the choices of the constitution. The constitution provides only the first step in the inquiry and cannot direct its further development. In these circumstances, the constitution cannot be *interpreted*; there is nothing determinate to discover. It cannot satisfy the original constitution's claims to determinacy, fixity, and stability. The determinacy is provided elsewhere, after the fact of the founding and without any of the original constitution's stability and fixity. The result is not of the constitution's authority.

Underdeterminate provisions like preambles, standards, and principles are, as far as an original constitution is concerned, akin to inkblots: They are without sense or meaning as law.[66] For an original constitution, provisions must have sufficient meaning to be constitutional prescriptions. Where one cannot "make out the meaning of a provision," one is in "exactly the same circumstance as a judge who has *no Constitution* to work with."[67] For example: "[I]f you had an amendment that says 'Congress shall make no' and then there is an inkblot and you cannot read the rest of it and that is the only copy you have, I do not think the court can make up what might be under the inkblot if you cannot read it."[68]

For an original constitution, the same reasoning holds for underdeterminate provisions. One should not attempt to "find" meaning where none exists. In failing to determine a constitutional prescription, the founders failed to act. Where the reader cannot, relying on tools of interpretation, discover meaning to resolve a question, the framers simply failed to address it. Where there is underdeterminacy, there is indeterminacy.

An original constitution is committed to the idea that the provisions of the constitution seek to achieve something. Where the provisions cannot do so without relying on another actor to complete their meaning, the constitution has failed. Relying on a distinction between *interpretation* and *construction*, which will be explored later, one might say that for an original constitution, constitutional interpretation (discovery of meaning) never runs out and the time for constitutional construction (supplementing meaning) never obtains.

66 They may have sense or meaning as poetry or prose, but not as determinative prescriptions of what legally ought to obtain.

67 Bork, *Tempting of America*, *supra* note 57 at 166 (emphasis added); Whittington, *Constitutional Interpretation*, *supra* note 28 at 89.

68 Nomination of Robert H. Bork to be Associate Justice of the Supreme Court of the United States: Hearings Before the Senate Committee on the Judiciary, 100th Congress 224 (1987) (statement of Judge Robert H. Bork) cited in Kurt T. Lash, "Of Inkblots and Originalism: Historical Ambiguity and the Case of the Ninth Amendment" 31 Harv. J. L. & Pub. Pol'y 467 at 469 (2008).

What an original constitution covers, it covers without gaps, without inconsistency, and without indeterminacy or underdeterminacy. In short, an original constitution is all interpretation. An original constitution is a *zero-construction* constitution.

III. THE ORIGINAL CONSTITUTION AND DEMOCRATIC ACTIVITY

An original constitution is law, understood as a set of determinate rules that settle that which they address. The task of the interpreter is solely one of discovering the meaning of the original constitution – no specification of meaning is required before a constitutional rule is applied. In this way, the original constitution is fixed, stable, and determinate. The task of judicial review is one of holding the authorities constituted *by* the original constitution *to* the original constitution. Constraining the discretion of judges is often identified as one of the indirect (or instrumental) arguments favoring originalism – the "lesser evil" in the world of judicial review.[69] Whatever the merits of this second-order reason, an original constitution prescribes a role for the judicial function as discovering, not inventing, meaning. This relates to another second-order reason that is said to favor originalism: providing greater freedom for democratic activity. Yet, we will see that these are both contingent questions that depend on what the original constitution prescribes and the progress of the society it regulates. The worlds of the constitution and of democratic activity are separate such that democratic activity complies with or violates or proceeds beyond the reach of the original constitution.

The Judicial Function

"It is emphatically the province and duty of the Judicial Department to say what the law *is*," Chief Justice Marshall declared in *Marbury v Madison*.[70] Much has been written about the significance of the word "is" rather than "ought to be," the central idea being that the constitution's meaning obtains irrespective of what the judicial branch would like it to say.[71] The only mode of constitutional change is the amendment formula; no judicial rewriting masquerading as interpretation is consistent with the judicial oath to *uphold* the constitution.

[69] See Kavanagh, "Original Intention, Enacted Text, and Constitutional Interpretation," *supra* note 54 at 259–60; Scalia, "The Lesser Evil," *supra* note 37.

[70] *Marbury v Madison* 5 U.S. (1 Cranch) 137 at 177 (1803) (emphasis added).

[71] See *e.g.*, Jeffrey Goldsworthy, "Raz on Constitutional Interpretation" (2003) 22 Law & Phil. 167 at 170–1 [Goldsworthy, "Raz on Constitutional Interpretation"] and "Proposition 1" of his contribution to this volume.

For a judge to take the oath and do otherwise is akin to "crossing one's fingers when making a promise."[72] After all, the judicial function is not to do justice *simpliciter*, but rather to do justice *according to law*: that is, according to the law of the original constitution.

In this way, Chief Justice Marshall's statement is somewhat misleading for it suggests that the judicial department is necessarily part of the equation of law's meaning. Yet, for an original constitution, it is neither the province nor the duty of the judicial department to say what the law is; rather, it is the province and duty of the *original constitution* to say what the law is. The judicial function is merely to apply the major premise (the constitutional rule) to the minor premise (a legislative or executive act) and to state the conclusion as unconstitutional or constitutional (and only in this indirect way to saw what the law is). The constitutional syllogism, which depends on the determinacy of constitutional provisions, is what "legitimizes judicial review of constitutionality."[73]

It is often said that the old originalism was "a reactive theory motivated by substantive disagreement" with instances of "judicial activism."[74] While it is true that all that "conserves" the past is in some simple sense conservative, the old originalism was associated with a political movement more conservative than then prevailing judicial attitudes, which accused the judges of making the constitution say what they (the judges) wanted it to say. As a remedy, it was argued that the judicial function should be to defer to the other branches. Otherwise, acting under the cover of the judicial function, courts will act "as legislators and substitut[e] their own substantive political preferences and values for those of the people and their elected representatives."[75] The overriding command of old originalism for the judicial department was one of restraint, exemplified by the refusal to declare acts of the legislature unconstitutional. Irrespective of the major and minor premises of the constitutional syllogism, the conclusion should always be the same: Legislation is constitutional. In this way, the old originalism empowered the democratic process and removed the court (and the constitution) from intervening.

As regards the judicial function, an original constitution is better understood from the perspective of new originalism, which does not depend on the contingent composition of the judicial and legislative departments. It is "grounded more clearly and firmly in an argument about what judges are supposed to be

[72] Barnett, "Scalia's Infidelity," *supra* note 37 at 18.

[73] Scalia, "The Lesser Evil," *supra* note 37 at 854. See also Bork, *The Tempting of America*, *supra* note 57 at 162–3.

[74] Whittington, "The New Originalism," *supra* note 2 at 601.

[75] *Ibid*. at 602.

interpreting and what that implies, rather than an argument about how best to limit judicial discretion."[76] It properly recognizes that originalism is politically conservative (or not) only as a contingent matter, depending both on what the constitution prescribes and on the evolution of the society in which it is authoritative. Under an original constitution, the task of the judge is to uphold the constitution by being faithful to the constitution and by striking down acts that are inconsistent therewith. In this way, the judicial function is understood as being twofold: to do no *more* than interpret the meaning discoverable in the original constitution itself and to do no *less* than uphold that meaning against all affronts, no matter how democratic they are held out to be. Depending on the actions of the constituted authorities, more legislative and executive actions could be found unconstitutional under this understanding of the judicial function than under an approach favoring judicial discretion so feared by old originalists. But this is how it must be for the original constitution, which requires obedience to its prescriptions from those authorities it constitutes. The "primary virtue" of the judicial function under the original constitution is "constitutional fidelity," not "judicial restraint."[77] Under the original constitution, judges must stand tall in the face of unconstitutional action; they must also, however, stand back where the constitution does not determine the issue before the court.

According to the original constitution, the judicial function is a delimited one. It involves no discretion in determining meaning, for all underdeterminate meaning is meaningless so far as the judge is concerned. The personal views of the judge have no place in constitutional adjudication. Judges will, at least on occasion, "vote to uphold laws they deeply disagree with, or to strike down laws they would favor, because the basis for constitutional judging . . . is independent of their own preferences."[78] The original constitution firmly resists any suggestion that it is "a mere thing of wax in the hands of the judiciary which they may twist and shape into any form they please."[79] That approach would deny the original constitution its fixity, determinacy, and stability, in addition to the exclusivity of its amendment procedure.

The authority for judicial review rests on the authority of the original constitution. When a judicial declaration of unconstitutionality is issued, one may

[76] *Ibid.* at 609.

[77] *Ibid.* at 609.

[78] Michael W. McConnell, "Active Liberty: A Progressive Alternative to Textualism and Originalism?" 119 Harv. L. Rev. 2387 at 2415 (2006).

[79] Thomas Jefferson, "Thomas Jefferson to Spencer Roane, 6 September 1819" in *The Works of Thomas Jefferson* (collected and edited by P.L. Ford, 1904–1905), Volume 3, Article 1, Section 8, Clause 18, Document 16 online: http://press-pubs.uchicago.edu/founders/documents/a1_8_18s16.html.

not speak of judicial activitism; one may not blame the judges. Rather, even though the declaration is channeled through the court, it is in truth issued by the original constitution. For this reason, one may not speak of a countermajoritarian difficulty either,[80] for this suggests that the judicial function involves more than interpreting the original constitution's discoverable meaning. For the original constitution, any difficulty is *intertemporal,* not countermajoritarian: It relies on past commitments, enshrined in the constitution, which continue to bind.[81] When a court applies the original constitution, "it appeals to legal enactments that *were* approved" at the founding moment.[82] To the extent that the people now seek to overcome the intertemporal difficulty, the original constitution provides them with an exclusive form of constitutional change. But, save a constitutional amendment, the people must now comply with the original constitution then adopted.

The Separate Worlds of Democracy and the Original Constitution

Where an original constitution specifies constitutional rules, democratic activity may not proceed in contradiction. Where an original constitution is silent, democratic activity may proceed freely. Under an original constitution, there is a sharp divide between the constitutional politics of the founding and the normal politics that follow.[83] The two worlds are separate, which is not to deny that democratic activity is constituted by the constitutional forms (including the design of the legislature and the electoral system) provided for in the original constitution. Yet, beyond these forms, in those areas where no constitutional prescriptions are pertinent, there is no subordination of legislation to the original constitution.

The founding moment represents a choice by the framers as to what should be *removed* from democratic activity. A matter that is regulated by the original constitution is removed from democratic activity; "[t]hat is, after all, the whole purpose of constitutional prohibitions" and prescriptions.[84] The constitution

[80] Alexander M. Bickel, *The Least Dangerous Branch: The Supreme Court at the Bar of Politics* (2nd ed., 1986).

[81] See Bruce A. Ackerman, "Discovering the Constitution" 93 Yale L. J. 1013 at 1045–9 (1984).

[82] Ackerman, *ibid.* at 1046; Whittington, *Constitutional Interpretation, supra* note 28 at 43.

[83] The dualist distinction is employed by Bruce Ackerman, but his understanding of constitutional politics extends beyond the founding and formal amendments to what he terms "constitutional moments." See B. Ackerman, *We the People: Foundations* (1991).

[84] A. Scalia, "Romancing the Constitution: Interpretation as Invention" in Huscroft and Brodie (eds.), *Constitutionalism in the Charter Era, supra* note 34 at 340–1 [A. Scalia, "Romancing the Constitution: Interpretation as Invention"].

represents the closure of normal politics with respect to those issues. But, perhaps as importantly, the founding moment also discloses a choice as to what should *remain* within democratic activity. That choice is disclosed impliedly in the sense that all that is not-prescribed by the original constitution remains free to be regulated as the legislature sees fit. But the choice is also *obliquely* referenced in the original constitutional itself. In providing for the constitutional form of the legislature and for the citizens' associated rights of political participation in democratic activity, the original constitution contemplates that there be democratic activity. Of course it does not direct such activity, which it is not to say that it is wholly silent as to how it is exercised. It may be silent about this activity in the sense of not resolving questions that are not subject to determinate constitutional rules, but it nevertheless impliedly shapes the exercise of democratic activity through the constitutionally prescribed forms of "citizen" and "legislator." In this way, the conduct and character of "normal politics" will be, in part, and perhaps in large part, shaped by the original constitution. We might say that democratic activity occurs in the shadow of the constitution.

Any move to remove *additional* matters from democratic activity without having recourse to the amendment procedure (for example, by way of judicial creation parading as interpretation) injures the division between the separate worlds of democracy and the constitution prescribed by the original constitution and, concomitantly, lessens the rights of democratic participation guaranteed in the constitution. If judges rely on "customary usage; inferences from written constitutional principles; and the norms set out or implied in international legal instruments," or any other source of unwritten constitutional principles,[85] they are undoing the divide between democracy and the constitution stipulated at the founding. After all, the reference to *unwritten* principles is "a frank acknowledgement that the 'principles' are not to be found in the written constitutional text, and cannot be derived from the text by normal processes of interpretation."[86] For the original constitution, everything that is added by the court to the constitution in the pursuit of grand principles is "nothing more than an attempt to block self-government by the representatives

[85] See Beverley McLachlin, Chief Justice of Canada, "Unwritten Constitutional Principles: What Is Going On?" (2006) 4 N.Z.J.P.I.L. 147 at 156.

[86] Hogg, "Canada: From Privy Council to Supreme Court," *supra* note 7 at 90. Rubenfeld's commitmentarian model deems understandings of what the proper scope of a constitutional right or power *did not* include as inconclusive, thereby allowing for change between the frontiers of constitutional and democratic authority: Jeb Rubenfeld, *Revolution by Judiciary: The Structure of American Constitutional Law* (2005).

of living men and women."[87] In this sense, all non-formal amendments to an original constitution "contract" the rights of democratic participation, even if they simultaneously "expand" others – a point often neglected by proponents of "evolving standards."[88]

Even though it is sometimes assumed that originalism leaves more room for democratic activity than do rival theories of interpretation,[89] this is also a contingent question. It is rather more accurate to say that an original constitution allows for democratic activity in those areas that it does not regulate. The scope of those areas depends on the prescriptions outlined in the original constitution. Now, democratic activity unconstrained by constitutional prescriptions is not, of course, unconstrained from all prescriptions. No democratic legislature entitled to do anything does just anything. However, should a legislature transgress the moral limits that apply to it, judicial review would be without authority to offer relief if the measure did not contradict a constitutional rule. Where the original constitution is silent, we are, quite deliberately and by design, "at the mercy of legislative majorities."[90]

IV. THE ORIGINAL CONSTITUTION AND THE DELIMITED DOMAIN OF INTERPRETATION

Where does this leave us? What lessons might be taken from the foregoing fictional account of an original constitution? It might be said that I have provided no more than a caricature of originalism, a constitutional model no real-world constitution can (or should aspire to) match. It might be said that this approach distorts originalism more than it assists in understanding it. I hope this is not so. For it is a commonplace that distorting reality sometimes assists one in seeing what *is* somewhat more clearly. In particular, I hope to show that the idea of an original constitution assists one in concluding that the difficulties in realizing originalism may not lie with this theory of interpretation at all; they may rather lie with real world constitutions. I hope to show that real-world constitutions are best understood as being both part original constitution and part non-original constitution, all because originalism's delimited place within real-world constitutions maps onto the delimited domain of *interpretation* within constitutional meaning.

[87] Bork, *The Tempting of America*, *supra* note 57 at 171.

[88] See Scalia, "The Lesser Evil," *supra* note 37 at 855–6; Scalia, *A Matter of Interpretation*, *supra* note 28 at 42.

[89] See *e.g.*, Bork, *The Tempting of America*, *supra* note 57 at 153.

[90] *Lochner v New York* 198 U.S. 45 at 59 (1905) (per Peckham J) discussed in Robert H. Bork, "Neutral Principles and Some First Amendment Problems" 47 Ind. L. J. 1, 10–11 (1971).

Real-World Constitutions

The preceding account of an original constitution has emphasized how it is written at the time of the founding, composed of rule-like prescriptions, and situated in a world separated from democratic activity. It seems to be a fair conclusion to state that no real-world constitution matches in all respects the model of an original constitution just outlined. But it would be premature to take this conclusion to imply a correlative conclusion, namely that real-world constitutions adhere to non-originalism through and through. Accepting that "what we call 'non-originalism' depends on what we think originalism entails,"[91] it seems false to suppose that real-world constitutions are not written at the time of their founding, are not composed of rule-like prescriptions, and are not situated in a world separated from democratic activity, or at least not in every respect. Rather, it seems that real-world constitutions help us see how originalism and non-originalism are not as opposed as their labels suggest.

What, then, is a real-world constitution if it does not match the fictional models of an original and non-original constitution? In a world infatuated with metaphors of balance and proportionality, it might be tempting to appeal to the comfort of some middle ground – as though all real-world constitutions were situated along some *just milieu* between the models of an original and non-original constitution. Yet, such presumptive appeals should be resisted, for another answer seems true: A real-world constitution is *both* an original constitution *and* a non-original constitution, as it exemplifies some but not all of the commitments of each fictitious constitutional model.

Real-world constitutions have *both* rule-like prescriptions established at the founding *and* preamble-like clauses that do not prescribe anything determinate. Real-world constitutions suffer in at least some respects from the common vices of language, including unforeseen indeterminacy, vagueness, ambiguity, gaps, and inconsistencies.[92] The real-world constitutions with which we are most familiar appear to be, *at one and the same time* – albeit in different ways and through different sections, provisions, and clauses – both original and non-original constitutions.

While there have been repeated claims that the choice between originalism and non-originalism is a "false choice,"[93] that is especially true in the context of real-world constitutions. It should be noted, however, that the choice

[91] Balkin, "Constitutional Redemption," *supra* note 31 at 428 (footnote omitted).

[92] See H. L. A. Hart, *The Concept of Law* (2nd ed., 1994) 124–36.

[93] Most recently, see Balkin, "Abortion and Original Meaning," *supra* note 55 and Balkin, "Constitutional Redemption," *supra* note 31.

between an original constitution and a non-original constitution as an abstract matter is not a false choice: Two different accounts of a constitution are in play. A constitution drafter, consciously driven to fulfill the ideal of an original or non-original constitution, is not presented with a false choice – the task of articulating a real-world constitution can be guided, even if not wholly determined, by these opposing choices. But in the context of real-world constitutions, it seems that where the idea of the original constitution resonates with a real-world constitution, it obtains; and where it does not, it cannot. There may, then, in practice be no *choice* – false or otherwise.

Consider the following: Is one faced with a choice when a real-world constitution prescribes a legislative mandate of no more than five years or prescribes no less than *x* and no more than *y* legislators (where *x* and *y* are real numbers)? Are these provisions not determinate, fixed, and stable legal prescriptions? Would it not be false to suggest that these provisions are otherwise and that their meaning is somehow liable to change with time? Consider, in turn, how answers to the same questions seem less obvious where a real-world constitution prescribes "freedom of expression" for all individuals, the "right to vote" for all citizens, and the right against "cruel and unusual punishment" for all convicted persons. Assuming no further particulars, are these provisions not far from the determinacy, fixity, and stability of the previous examples? Is there a choice here? Can one read them as determinate, fixed, and stable legal prescriptions?

In either example, to question whether there is a choice is to ask the question of the real-world constitution *itself*. The distinction between provisions that are drafted in the image of an original constitution and provisions that are drafted in the image of a non-original constitution is the real-world constitution's itself. And originalism counsels that this distinction is discoverable through interpretation.

Originalism and Interpretation

The idea of "interpretation" has become all too present in constitutional practice. It now serves as a placeholder for *discovering* meaning, *supplementing* meaning, and *changing* meaning and encompasses the entire activity from the first premise that is the constitutional text to the end of the reasoning process in all cases. Determining whether pornography is protected expression under "freedom of expression" is said to be a question of interpretation not different in kind from determining whether "arms" refers to the human body or to weaponry in the American constitutional guarantee "the right to bear arms."

On this view, everything is a matter of interpretation; interpretation *never runs out* – it occupies the entire field.

In addition to occupying the entire field from first premise to conclusion irrespective of the underdeterminacy of the constitution, interpretation has also become the vehicle for changing the constitution. It is sometimes maintained that interpretation involves:

> a combination of reasons for respecting the constitution as it exists and reasons for remaining open to the possibility that it is in need of reform, adjustment, or development in order to remove shortcomings it always had or shortcomings that emerged as the government or the society that it governs changed over time.[94]

On this understanding, interpretation exists in "a dialectical tension" and "lives in spaces where fidelity to an original and openness to novelty mix."[95] There is no doubt that this understanding of interpretation – which is said to "romance" the meaning of a constitution and to parade "innovation as interpretation"[96] – resonates with many scholarly and judicial pronouncements. Yet, originalism counsels that it quite simply cannot be right. Interpretation differs from innovation: The first discovers meaning, the second creates it; the first seeks out what is, the second determines what should be; the first is oriented toward conserving the constitution, the second to changing it. To interpret a constitution is to "work on the assumption that the persons who had the authority to make the constitutional text were trying to achieve something in choosing some words over others," such that the "goal of interpretation is to try to find out what that achievement is."[97] Interpretation turns on "the *techne* rationality of laying down and following a set of positive norms identifiable as far as possible simply by their 'sources' . . . and applied so far as possible according to their publicly stipulated meaning".[98] Interpretation looks to posited law as "fact," as what "is," not as "what it ought to be."[99]

Now, this view of law does not always obtain, for constitutional language can be such that there is no "is" or "fact" to be discovered by interpretation, or at least no "is" or "fact" determinate enough to be applied without further specification. In these circumstances, the task of interpretation becomes

[94] Joseph Raz, "On the Authority and Interpretation of Constitutions: Some Preliminaries" in L. Alexander (ed.), *Constitutionalism: Philosophical Foundations* (1998) 152 at 177.

[95] *Ibid.* at 180.

[96] Antonin Scalia, "Romancing the Constitution: Interpretation as Invention," *supra* note 84.

[97] Balkin, "Constitutional Redemption," *supra* note 31 at 491.

[98] John Finnis, "Natural Law and Legal Reasoning" in Robert P. George (ed.), *Natural Law Theory: Contemporary Essays* (1992) 150.

[99] Goldsworthy, "Raz on Constitutional Interpretation," *supra* note 71 at 190.

exhausted before the process of applying the text of the constitution to factual circumstances is concluded. The major premise of the constitutional syllogism lacks specificity. Whereas the original constitution analogizes these instances of underdeterminacy to meaningless inkblots, real-world constitutions do not. They view lack of specificity as calling for greater specificity, not for the abandonment of constitutional meaning.

This call for greater specificity is satisfied by what may be called *constitutional construction*.[100] Construction is "a necessary feature of constitutionalism" and a "supplementary theory" of constitutional meaning where interpretation proves insufficient.[101] Although the model of an original constitution strived to be an exclusively interpretable constitution and, correspondingly, a zero-construction constitution, real-world constitutions are neither. Their meaning is determined in part by interpretation, in part by construction. Interpretation always comes first: It determines the need, if any, for construction. The degree of specificity or determinacy of a real-world constitution is itself revealed by the interpretive undertaking; it resides in the constitution and its meaning. But in those cases where a real-world constitution provides no meaning (or insufficient meaning) to be interpreted, the meaning must be supplemented with construction. Constitutional construction elaborates constitutional meaning where constitutional interpretation cannot; it "supplements other methods of determining constitutional meaning" by providing "[s]omething external to the text" to allow "the text to have a determinate and controlling meaning within a given governing context."[102] Much of constitutional law – precedents, doctrines, judicially prescribed tests and factors – is *constructed* insofar as it supplements the text of the constitution in order to provide it with determinacy where such determinacy cannot be provided by interpretation.

A real-world constitution does not prohibit such constructions; indeed, the underdeterminacy known to many constitutions "is one of the prices we (or the framers) pay for a writing that uses abstract principles in place of specific rules," although "it is also one of the well-known virtues of this particular writing."[103] Where open-ended formulations are used, the constitution

[100] The distinction between *interpretation* and *construction* is employed by Whittington, *Constitutional Interpretation*, *supra* note 28, and *Constitutional Construction: Divided Powers and Constitutional Meaning* (2001) [Whittington, *Constitutional Construction*], and Barnett *Restoring the Lost Constitution*, *supra* note 5.

[101] Whittington, "The New Originalism," *supra* note 2 at 612; Barnett, *Restoring the Lost Constitution*, *supra* note 5 at 118.

[102] Whittington, *Constitutional Construction*, *supra* note 100 at 3, 6.

[103] Barnett, *Restoring the Lost Constitution*, *supra* note 5 at 120 and "An Originalism for Nonoriginalists," *supra* note 5 at 645. See also W. H. Rehnquist, "The Notion of a Living Constitution"

provides no settlement and leaves the resolution of disputes to be *guided* – not determined – by the constitution. The task of completing the constitutional project is left to later generations. Constructions are completions of the constitutional project without being part of the founding. They pertain to the constitution without being the constitution; they are part of what constitutes without being the product of constitution making. In short, they are part of the activity that completes the architecture and, as activity, may be revisited and reconstructed.[104]

Despite their necessary role, constructions are not "analogous to textual amendments,"[105] both in the sense that they do not change the interpretable meaning of the constitution and in the sense that they do not achieve the same status as constitutional amendments. In this way, the constitution remains that which was established at the founding no matter how "crystallized" particular constructions become. A statute constructing constitutional meaning may acquire the status of "superstatute" just as a judicial precedent constructing constitutional meaning may acquire the status of "superprecedent," but they remain constructions and not part of the original constitution.[106]

For some, the task of constructing constitutional meaning – of completing the unfinished task of providing for constitutional determinacy – is a task for political institutions,[107] whereas for others, it is a judicial undertaking;[108] for some, constructions should be justified by appeal to a theory of justice,[109] whereas for others, the contingent development of constructions rest on "political principle, social interest, or partisan consideration"[110] or on the principles somehow contained within the text of the constitution.[111] Stated otherwise, constitutional construction may appeal to the full range of theories that originalists label "non-originalist." But whatever their individual merits, these

(1976) 54 Texas L. Rev. 693 at 694 [Rehnquist, "The Notion of a Living Constitution"]; Binnie, "Constitutional Interpretation and Original Intent," *supra* note 34 at 346–7.

[104] For the development of this idea with respect to constitutional rights, see Grégoire C. N. Webber, *The Negotiable Constitution: On the Limitation of Rights* (2009).

[105] Whittington, *Constitutional Construction, supra* note 100 at 218; Barnett, "An Originalism for Nonoriginalists," *supra* note 5 at 646.

[106] See *contra* Ackerman, "The Living Constitution," *supra* note 31.

[107] See *e.g.*, Whittington *Constitutional Construction, supra* note 100.

[108] See *e.g.*, Goldsworthy, "The Case for Originalism" in this volume; Goldsworthy, "Raz on Constitutional Interpretation," *supra* note 71 at 177; Goldsworthy, "Originalism in Constitutional Interpretation," *supra* note 27 at 20–1.

[109] Barnett, *Restoring the Lost Constitution, supra* note 5.

[110] Whittington, *Constitutional Construction, supra* note 100 at 6, 209.

[111] See Balkin's method of text-and-principle: "Abortion and Original Meaning," *supra* note 55, and "Constitutional Redemption," *supra* note 31.

different approaches all converge on one point: They make no appeal to originalism for *construction*. Construction is non-original because originalism's contribution to constitutional meaning has been exhausted. Construction calls on discretion and judgment and, because the major premise in the constitutional syllogism must be determined further, constitutional construction calls for *adjudication* (in the sense of deciding).[112] It is, by necessity, not a task oriented to discovering what is already there.

Now, the distinction cannot be carried so far as to suggest that construction bears no relationship to the constitutional text. For in "penetrat[ing] beneath the surface of the text" to construct constitutional meaning, one must in turn "*reemerge through the text*."[113] Construction is possible where interpretation is exhausted; yet, to remain a task of fulfilling and supplanting constitutional meaning, the ultimate measure of a constitutional construction must be its consistency with that which is interpreted. No contradiction between construction and interpretation is permissible. Even if interpretation ceases when confronted with underdeterminacy, it continues to guide and to control construction.

* * *

The idea of constitutional construction confirms that it is no fault of originalism that it can go no further than interpretation itself. Because the ideal of an original constitution is never fully actualized in a real-world constitution, other modes of expounding constitutional meaning must be appealed to. But this does not result in a "tension between the theory of originalism, which holds that the Constitution has fixed meaning that courts are bound to respect, and the reality of the framing, which produced a document rife with indeterminacy."[114] This tension obtains only if one attempts to realize the idea of an original constitution fully in a real-world constitution irrespective of how that real-world constitution is written. When one appreciates that real-world constitutions only partially adhere to the model of an original constitution and that *neither* the theory of originalism *nor* real-world constitutions are the worse for it, then originalism can be situated in its proper place. There, originalism

[112] It is perhaps telling that Brest "Misconceived Quest," *supra* note 24 at 228, note 90 refers "to nonoriginalist strategies of constitutional decision making collectively as *adjudication*" (emphasis added).

[113] Randy E. Barnett, "Underlying Principles" 24 Const. Comment. 405 at 413 (2007) (emphasis added). Barnett makes this point in relation to Balkin's text-and-principle account of originalism, but the idea can be generalized.

[114] P. J. Smith, "The Marshall Court and the Originalist's Dilemma" 90 Minnesota L. Rev. 612 at 623 (2006).

can be controlling where interpretation is possible; elsewhere, originalism cannot determine constitutional meaning.

CONCLUSION

The battle for as well as the battle against originalism both attempt to win by selecting the key words of the debate. The key words animating originalist scholarship include *fidelity* to the constitution, suggesting that alternative approaches preach adultery. In turn, living-tree constitutionalist scholarship argues that it is *breathing life* into a constitution that can only *grow* stronger, suggesting the alternative is a dead constitution of frozen rights.[115] These attempts to win through definition are not uncommon in scholarship or in political movements more generally, but they are unfortunate for the scholar's undertaking that should be devoted to a grappling of ideas with others without sophistry or sleights of hand.[116] Of course all prefer "progressive interpretation to regressive; forward thinking to backward" and good to bad,[117] but this is not the choice one is confronted with in constitutional scholarship.

The real-world constitutions with which we are familiar do not instantiate the theorist's model of an original or non-original constitution. No doubt, they all resemble these models in some, perhaps many, but never all respects. The search, it would seem, is not for a single, overarching, exclusive method for expounding constitutional meaning; rather, the search is for an account of which constitutional model obtains when. In turn, this draws on the distinction between constitutional *interpretation* and *construction*, which envisages different methods for expounding constitutional meaning depending on the task at hand. Originalism speaks only to interpretation that is devoted to discovering meaning latent in the constitution. Where that meaning cannot be determined or exhausted, interpretation ceases and construction begins. Now, discriminating between the end of interpretation and the beginning of construction will not always admit of precision and will depend on discriminating between "determinacy and indeterminacy, purpose used to clarify meaning and purpose used to change it, genuine implications and spurious ones, evidence of intentions that illuminates original meanings and that which does

[115] See Binnie, "Constitutional Interpretation and Original Intent," *supra* note 34 at 347; Rehnquist, "The Notion of a Living Constitution," *supra* note 103 at 693.

[116] See Grégoire C. N. Webber, "Expounding Constitutional Scholarship" 25 Constitutional Comment. 171 (2009).

[117] See G. Huscroft, "The Trouble with Living Tree Interpretation" (2006) 25 U. Queensland L. J. 3 at 5.

not, changes in the application of a provision and changes in its meaning, and so on."[118] Yet, despite this and despite the fact that the world of originalism is a delimited one, within this world it can make its claim to be controlling.

I conclude with a thought on the significance of the model of the original constitution for a real-world constitution *over time*. One of originalism's great merits – exemplified by the model of an original constitution – is to render the constitution accessible to the legislator, judge, executive member, and citizen as fixed, stable, and continuous. Constitutions, like law, *communicate*. Where a constitution provides determinate prescriptions, each constituted actor has a compass in hand, able to be guided by the communicating instrument. Yet, this accessibility, which obtains (when it does) especially at the founding, may wane with the passing of time as the constitution's determinate prescriptions fail to abide to the changing semantic conventions of language.[119]

Take two examples from the U.S. Constitution: The word "commerce" at the founding may have been the equivalent to the modern-day expression "intercourse" or "exchange," and not the narrower concern with trade in goods and services; in turn, "domestic violence" may have signified "civil war" at the founding, whereas it now speaks of an altogether different concern. These simple illustrations highlight the possibility that even if the model of an original constitution were fully realized in a real-world constitution at the time of its founding, that real-world constitution may fail to continue to be realized as an original constitution with the passing of time. The virtues of stability and fixity for an original constitution may weaken over time, as we become less familiar with the linguistic conventions that obtained in the past. Worse still, we may fail to be aware of our decreasing familiarity with the constitution's meaning, assuming modern-day linguistic conventions apply to dated usage. In this way, originalism, perhaps more than any other theory of constitutional interpretation, constantly struggles over the past.[120]

In this way, while citizens today are "linked to the origins" of their constitution, they are "linked by a tradition" that citizens at the founding could

[118] J. Goldsworthy, "Conclusions" in Goldsworthy (ed.), *Interpreting Constitutions*, *supra* note 7 at 324–5; Whittington, *Constitutional Interpretation*, *supra* note 28 at 10–11.

[119] I do not here privilege original public meaning over original intent. Indeed, given the constitution's communicative ends and multiple authors and multiple audiences, I would fully expect original intent and original public meaning to overlap. I share Steven D. Smith's intuition in "That Old-Time Originalism" in this volume at 236.

[120] See Robert W. Gordon, "The Struggle Over the Past" 44 Clev. St. L. Rev. 123 (1996); Whittington, *Constitutional Interpretation*, *supra* note 28 at 210.

not have.[121] Because citizens can never fully understand the constitution "in the same way that the framers and ratifiers understood it," they will always, in understanding the constitution, understand it differently.[122] The difference may be minor and inconsequential, or not. But if it is true when it is true, then even a perfect original constitution cannot forever remain perfectly original.

[121] Lawrence B. Solum, "Originalism as Transformative Politics" 63 Tulane L. Rev. 1599 at 1610 (1989).
[122] *Ibid.* at 1610.

8 The Curious Concept of the "Living Tree" (or Non-Locked-In) Constitution

James Allan*

"Is there any point to which you would wish to draw my attention?"
"To the curious incident of the dog in the night-time."
"The dog did nothing in the night-time."
"That was the curious incident," remarked Sherlock Holmes.[1]

In this chapter, I hope to build up to a defense of originalism as the best (or rather, to be precise, as the least bad) approach to constitutional interpretation in the American and Canadian contexts. But I intend to start in a very un-American place.

As something of an anglophile who spent eleven years teaching at a law school in New Zealand, I thought it would be wise in this paper to play to my strengths, as it were. By that I mean I thought I might approach the question of the desirability (or otherwise) of some form of originalism when it comes to constitutional interpretation from the point of view of one who is perfectly at home with a legally unfettered parliamentary sovereignty and, indeed, no written constitution (properly understood) at all. In fact, I am not just at home with them, I think them positively good ways to organize a democratic state, be it one of 4 million people (a la New Zealand) or one of 65 million people (a la the United Kingdom, either today or certainly a few decades back before the European Union complicated matters).

So my starting point is one where there is little or no fear of a *legally*[2] unfettered parliamentary sovereignty system of democratic government. I will

*The author wishes to thank Grant Huscroft, Richard Kay, and Bradley Miller for their comments.

[1] Sir Arthur Conan Doyle, *Silver Blaze* (1894) 534.

[2] It is fairly trite, but perhaps worth repeating, that although a parliamentary sovereignty leaves the elected legislature *legally* unchecked, there are, of course, all sorts of political and moral constraints on these legislators. These range from the fact that elected legislators bring with them to office their own moral codes through to the various political checks tied to the general

not here argue the strengths and weaknesses of such a system under which each generation (loosely understood) is left free, through its democratically elected representatives, to respond to changing social values and to "keep pace with civilization."[3] I will simply note that New Zealand (with no written constitution and no statutory bill of rights until 1990) was the first country in the world to give women the vote. It gave native Maori men the vote in 1867 (and even reserved four legislative seats for them out of fewer than eighty). On some accounts, New Zealand was the first country in the world to set up a social welfare system. And in the 1980s and 1990s, it completely overhauled its economy away from mercantilist protectionism and in favor of competitive free trade, to the point that today's New Zealand's farmers are the least subsidized (by tariffs or direct payments) in the western world. Indeed New Zealand has never lost a WTO case.

Meanwhile the United Kingdom (with no written constitution and no statutory bill of rights until 2000) seems to me to emerge favorably from any direct comparison with the United States (with its powerful judges and embedded bill of rights) as regards, say, the treatment of possible enemy aliens or citizens in World War II (despite the much, much greater damage being inflicted on the United Kingdom) or of suspected terrorists in the last seven or eight years. And both New Zealand and the United Kingdom do better, in my view, than Canada (with its equally powerful judges to those in the United States) when it comes to free speech concerns related to over-great muzzling of opinions related to religion and gay marriage. Relatedly, it would be a tough argument indeed, in my view, to say that the fairness of criminal law prosecutions and of the trial process generally is worse in the United Kingdom (pre- or post-2000) and in New Zealand (pre- or post-1990) than in the United States with its Bill of Rights.

Those two brief paragraphs are not, of course, meant to persuade those attached to the attractions of a written constitution that they are mistaken, or even to think again. They simply are there for those American or Canadian readers who might be dumbfounded at the mere thought that anyone could seriously think that a parliamentary sovereignty arrangement – with an elected

desire to get reelected, the voting system used, and the usual need to appeal to the political center. In a democratic jurisdiction with a written constitution containing an embedded list of rights, it is of course the case that the top judges are *legally* unconstrained, and that we rely on political and moral constraints on them (to ensure that they will interpret in accord with what they take the Constitution actually to mean, not just to say it means what they want it to mean). In any system, some branch of government will (in a sense) be *legally* unchecked.

[3] *Ministry of Transport v Noort*, [1992] N.Z.L.R. 260 at 274 (per Cooke P.). Note that Cooke P. was implicitly referring to the desirability of unelected judges doing this updating.

legislature that is *legally* unlimited – would be a good way to structure a jurisdiction's affairs.

Clearly, however, anyone who might find himself attracted to parliamentary sovereignty government needs to have a lot of confidence in democracy and the outcomes likely to be produced by "letting the numbers count" or democratic self-government.

Whether that sort of confidence is wise or warranted need not concern us here. Instead, let us just take it as our starting point. Let us imagine that we live in a jurisdiction (call it Allania) that currently operates as a parliamentary sovereignty system. In that system, there is a good deal of confidence in, and support for, democratic decision making to resolve the inevitable social disagreements that flow from differing moral outlooks and political frameworks. Smart, well-informed, even nice people simply can be seen to disagree across a wide range of issues in this jurisdiction. There is obvious moral dissensus. To overcome those disagreements and that dissensus and to arrive at a set of legal rules that applies to everyone, a legally unchecked legislature (or parliamentary sovereignty) has up until now operated.

As I noted, this scenario pre-supposes at least a significant degree of support for democratic decision making and "letting the numbers count" processes to resolve social disagreements, including disagreements over issues related to (or articulated in the language of) rights.

So that is our starting point. And now we are going to leave it. In deference to the tide of post–World War II constitutional history, which might be summed up as the triumph of American constitutionalism or at least as the scramble to adopt a written constitution, Allania is going to jettison its parliamentary sovereignty arrangements in favor of a written constitution.

In the course of Allania's journey that sees it change the main aspect of its Rule of Recognition from whatever the elected legislature enacts to whatever the new written constitution allows (as interpreted by the top judges), there will be some stops along the way where we all need to disembark briefly to clarify why something has happened or what the motivations or intentions were. Then we can restart the journey, one that will conclude when Allania has a written constitution. Once that is the case, the crucial question of how this new constitution ought to be interpreted will arise and will be of great practical importance.

In what follows in this chapter, I want to trace out that hypothetical journey in four stops. Each stop will be given a section of its own. Then, with the journey ended and the new constitution adopted and approved, I want to argue why – at least for Americans and Canadians – originalism is the least bad (or, in that sense, the best) approach to interpreting it. Put the other way round, I want to elaborate on what set of assumptions are needed to make some alternative to originalism seem better or preferable. And at that point, I want to argue that those very assumptions – the ones that would prevent or disincline or deter you from opting for some version or other of originalism from the vantage of a point-of-application interpreter *after* the Constitution's adoption – would have made the journey extremely unlikely had you held them at the time the question of whether to opt for a written constitution was being decided. Had the assumptions of those after-the-fact interpreters favoring "living tree" or "most moral" or "Dworkinian best-fit" or "progressivist" interpretations been made explicit at the start of the journey, few citizens would have favored the move to a written constitution (at least few citizens in Allania). There would have been next to no chance of adopting the new Constitution with these assumptions made explicit and widely publicized.

Whether that matters when it comes to interpreting the new Constitution after the fact of its adoption will also be discussed.

I. STOP ONE

We need to be abundantly clear that the written constitution Allania will have is not being imposed on it from outside. This will not be some African-type situation where the departing colonial power leaves in its wake a written constitution to govern the newly independent country. Likewise, it will not be a Japan-like situation where defeat in a large-scale war is followed by the victorious powers (or at least the Americans) imposing a new written constitution on the losers.

If it be true that the issue of a) *how to interpret a constitution* cannot (or rather should not) be wholly separated from b) *what one takes the purpose of a constitution to be*, then we need first to ask or consider whether anyone post-adoption of that constitution cares much, or in the slightest, what the constitution makers and approvers were trying to do. That is another way of asking whether the constitution to be interpreted has legitimacy (or how much legitimacy). Some might answer issue b) above in terms of an Alexander and Kay-style "locking things in" response[4] – that the very point of adopting a written constitution is to lock in certain divisions of powers, say, of rules related to how members of the legislature (and executive) are to be chosen, or maybe some embedded set of rights. These provisions will be, are meant to be, procedurally

[4] See, for example, Larry Alexander, "Introduction" in Larry Alexander (ed.), *Constitutionalism: Philosophical Foundations* (1998). See too Richard Kay's chapter "American Constitutionalism" in the same book.

harder to alter and change than the regular procedure used to enact statutes. And what motivates that desire to lock in certain provisions is the calculation that society is better off "risking rigidity rather than risking security."[5] Others might answer issue b) above in very different, non-Alexander-Kay terms. Their response would forswear any emphasis on a constitution aiming to "lock things in" in favor of understanding it as "a statement of our most important values and the vehicle through which these values are created and crystallized."[6] Yet neither of these responses to issue b) matters much – or at the very least, neither will perform any constraining function on what post-adoption of the constitution interpreters feel they can and cannot do – unless the way that constitution was adopted is nowadays generally perceived to be legitimate.

As I think one can certainly say that about the written constitutions of Canada and the United States,[7] I want this first stop of ours to make it clear that Allania's new written constitution will be the product of a process overwhelmingly perceived to be legitimate. Let us assume that before the new written constitution is approved and adopted, all the voters (both nationally and, if a federation, then in each state) must approve it in a referendum.[8] Indeed we will stipulate that the voters in these referenda were eligible to vote on the basis of a universal adult franchise (so that Allania's procedures are even less vulnerable to attacks on the basis of legitimacy than those of Canada or the United States).

We leave Stop One, then, knowing that the process used to shift Allania from a parliamentary sovereignty to a jurisdiction with a written constitution (one that judges will need to interpret post-adoption) did not involve outside imposition. It did not follow catastrophic defeat in war or a departing bequest by the former colonial master. It was opted for by a clear majority – indeed some sort of supermajority – of adult Allanians then alive.

II. STOP TWO

Our journey has barely restarted when we need to make another stop. When the journey ends, we will have a written constitution that requires interpreting

[5] Alexander, *ibid.* at 4.

[6] Frederick Schauer, "Judicial Supremacy and the Modest Constitution" (2004) 92 Cal. L. Rev. 1045 at 1045.

[7] I can say this even though I suspect that had I been magically transported back in time to War of Independence America – with all my current sentiments, proclivities, beliefs, and preferences – I would myself have been a Loyalist (Benjamin Franklin's son rather than Benjamin Franklin) and probably been part of the significant numbers of United Empire Loyalists who fled America for Canada.

[8] Not unlike the process used to approve and adopt Australia's Constitution.

at the point of application, most obviously by the top judges in the jurisdiction. But we need to know what will be in that new written constitution that will require interpreting. More specifically, in order to focus on essentials, we need to know if there will be a federalist division of powers between the center and states (or provinces) as well as whether there will be an enumerated list of embedded rights (rights overwhelmingly articulated in vague, amorphous terms laying down what on any account are moral abstractions).

In moving from a parliamentary sovereignty to a jurisdiction with a written constitution, Allania might opt to put a federalist division of powers into that constitution, but forswear any bill of rights. (That is the choice Australia made, copying much from the United States but explicitly rejecting a bill of rights.) Alternatively, Allania might opt for a bill of rights, but not federalism (as France did). Or it could opt for both (as both the United States and Canada have done).

Why do we need to know this? In the context of this work, we need to know because it is possible – both on theoretical grounds and as a matter of empirical outcomes – that our post-adoption top judges might adopt different interpretive approaches as regards heads of powers federalism disputes versus rights-based disputes.

Start with federalism issues. The main interpretive alternatives to some version or other of originalism – and by that I mean "progressivist" or "living Constitution" or "living tree" approaches – are hard to apply to division of powers disputes. At its most basic, this sort of dispute will leave parliamentary sovereignty intact. If some state statute is struck down for being outside its power, then the federal or central legislature will have that power and could enact the same statute, should it so decide. Conversely, if some legislative initiative is held to be outside or beyond the power of the center, then the states could enact it, should they so decide. In a very real sense, as I said, opting for a written constitution that embeds a federalist division of powers but no bill of rights leaves parliamentary sovereignty largely (not completely, but largely once we assume the judges engage in honest interpretation) in place.[9]

So on straight federalism heads of powers disputes, one might expect originalism (any version) to be attractive to some people who would shun it for

[9] See James Allan, "Portia, Bassanio or Dick the Butcher? Constraining Judges in the Twenty-First Century" (2006) 17 King's College L.J. 1 [Allan, Portia, Bassanio or Dick the Butcher"] and "A Defence of the Status Quo" in Campbell, Goldsworthy and Stone, (eds.), *Protecting Human Rights: Instruments and Institutions* (2003) 175. For a less clear-cut view, see Adrienne Stone, "Judicial Review without Rights: Some Problems for the Democratic Legitimacy of Structural Judicial Review" (2008) 28 O.J.L.S. 1, and more specifically my reply to Stone "Not in for a Pound – In for a Penny? Must a Majoritarian Democrat Treat All Constitutional Judicial Review as Equally Egregious?" (2010) 21 King's College L.J. 233.

rights-based disputes. Indeed, that may well be an accurate description of Canada.[10] Consider what your alternative outcomes are in such heads of powers federalism disputes. Neither option (state wins or central government wins) is more progressive or more moral or more in keeping with the demands of changing social values – or rather neither is in and of itself; you need a further prop to your argument, namely some sort of empirical basis for thinking one level of elected legislature is more likely to pass such progressive, or socially aware, legislation. But that is not a "progressivist" or "more moral" or "living tree" interpretation of the words used (for example, "trade and commerce"), so much as an underlying preference for one of the two federal levels of government. (Let us be honest: It would be for the Feds, not the states, when put in these terms.)

My point is that some methods of interpretation that are available for interpreting rights – where a potential outcome is that *no* level of government can legislate in the way desired, not merely that the power to so legislate vests here rather than there – are not easily available in federalism disputes. Indeed some may say it is not even clear what a "progressivist" or "living document" approach means in this context. The same may apply to Dworkinian pseudo-originalism, the directive to interpret the words morally because that was the framers' or approvers' intention. For that to be possible, it is arguable that the words used have to be morally pregnant or morally imbued words. And division of powers provisions (e.g., "navy," "inter-state trade") can make that highly artificial.

A more likely alternative to originalism in heads of powers disputes is some version of textual literalism. This is the approach that has largely been taken by Australia's highest court in a century of division of powers disputes.[11] The effect of that approach, however, where the words of each head of power are read individually and separately and given their widest ambit, has been an ever expanding list of approved fields for legislating for the center and an ever shrinking playing field for the states.[12] Meanwhile interpretation based on framers' intentions, or on the original understandings of those approving the constitution in the various referenda, would have produced outcomes considerably less friendly to the center.[13] More to the point of this work, though, that sort of originalist interpretation would have put more constraints on the point-of-application interpreters; it would have left the judges with

[10] See Justice Ian Binnie, "Constitutional Interpretation and Original Intent" in Grant Huscroft and Ian Brodie (eds.) *Constitutionalism in the Charter Era* (2004) 345.

[11] See James Allan and Nicholas Aroney, "An Uncommon Court: How the High Court of Australia Has Undermined Australian Federalism" (2008) 30 Sydney L. Rev. 245.

[12] *Ibid.*

[13] *Ibid.*

fewer plausible or "penumbra of doubt"[14] options than textual literalism leaves them.[15]

Whether you agree with me on that or not, put it aside. Likewise put aside my claim that originalist interpretation is likely to have more adherents for heads of powers disputes than when it comes to how to interpret guarantees or protections afforded in the language of rights. Instead, here at stop two, consider the decision those in Allania will have to make as regards whether to opt for a federation or a unitary state. One factor that will bear on their decision is the most likely answer to the "how will the new written constitution be interpreted?" question. Of course no one can see into the future and know for sure. But the likely or most plausible answer to this question will affect whether some people support this new constitution.

And that is even more the case, I suspect, as regards whether this new constitution ought to contain a bill of rights.

Hence let us assume Allania is mooting the inclusion of a bill of rights (á la Canada and the United States) in its new written constitution. This will clearly involve a greater inroad, a much greater inroad, into parliamentary sovereignty than does federalism and heads of powers disputes between the center and the states (or provinces). And because that inroad is so much more pronounced, the interpretive issue of how the rights-articulated moral abstractions are likely to be interpreted becomes correspondingly more crucial.

Let me put that point slightly more directly. We can assume that one of the big debates in Allania, as it ponders leaving behind parliamentary sovereignty in favor of written constitutionalism, is just this question of whether to include an enumerated list of embedded rights. There will be opponents. They might prevail, as they did in Australia. Similarly there will be supporters. And they might prevail, as they did in the United States and Canada.

Many opponents will object to the inclusion of a bill of rights on grounds approximating those given by Jeremy Waldron[16] – that how decisions are made, not just the substantive quality of the decisions ultimately made, matters. There is both a "how" factor and a "what" factor. Perhaps that might be defended with the further claim that each individual in Allania (based on a

[14] See H.L.A. Hart, *The Concept of Law* (1961) 119 *inter alia* [Hart, *The Concept of Law*].

[15] And note that it is just this sort of textual literalism that Jeremy Waldron advocates in his *Law and Disagreement* (1999). That, however, sidesteps the issue of whether such textual literalism is as determinate (as far as dictating outcomes) for constitutional interpretation as it is for statutory interpretation. I do not think it is. See my "Constitutional Interpretation v. Statutory Interpretation" (2000) 6 Legal Theory 109 [Allan, "Constitutional Interpretation"].

[16] I discuss this in "Jeremy Waldron and the Philosopher's Stone" (2008) 45 San Diego L. Rev. 133 [Allan, Jeremy Waldron and the Philosopher's Stone"], and list there all the main Waldron writings on the point.

non-consequentialist set of assumptions that sees individuals as autonomous agents) has a right to participate in social decision making – even about rights and how they ought to relate to one another, when they can be justifiably limited, what is their proper scope and range, and more.[17] Indeed this right to participate, some of these opponents will say, stands as a right of rights. And it exists in the context of a world in which disagreement is a fact of social life – disagreement that takes place between reasonable, well-meaning, smart, even nice people and does so regarding questions over which the unelected judiciary has no obviously greater moral perspicacity than anyone else. In such circumstances, this line of thinking will contend, bills of rights and the privileged position they afford the judiciary will be highly suspect because they fail to take seriously this right to participate in social decision making, including about rights.[18]

Of course other opponents of bill of rights, including me,[19] will have a more consequentialist, less Kantian or deontological or natural law starting point. But the merits of that debate within the "opposition to bills of rights" camp can be put aside for the purposes of this work. Even the issue of the most persuasive theoretical basis for supporting a bill of rights can be ignored here, because we are ultimately interested in the question of how best to interpret it, and that requires us to assume one is eventually supported and adopted (for whatever reasons) in Allania.

Actually that is not quite right. Why a bill of rights is adopted might (at least for some later-in-time interpreters) affect their view of how best to interpret it. We already know that it will not be the result of being imposed from without (as was the case with, say, Japan's bill of rights). So it will have impeccable democratic credentials in terms of how it – and the new written constitution as a whole – comes into being. Yet even acknowledging that, why people in the future will be prepared to hold themselves committed to the bill of rights adopted now may not be wholly independent of their understanding then of our understanding now. But let me leave that until our journey is complete.

And here, allow me a slight digression before returning to this crucial point. The digression has to do with the ease with which any supporter of bills of rights can ignore the underlying legitimacy of a particular decision-making

[17] See James Allan, "Bills of Rights and Judicial Power – A Liberal's Quandary" (1996) 16 O.J.L.S. 337 [Allan, "A Liberal's Quandary"].

[18] I set out the pre-suppositions of Jeremy Waldron's anti-bill of rights position more fully in Allan, "Jeremy Waldron and the Philosopher's Stone," *supra* note 16.

[19] See, for example, "A Liberal's Quandary," *supra* note 17 and James Allan, "Meagher's Mis-characterisations of Majoritarianism" (2009) 20 King's College L.J. 115 [Allan, Meagher's Mischaraterisations"].

procedure in order to focus exclusively on the outcomes produced by that and other competing procedures. Ought we to factor in some weighting for the perceived legitimacy of the decision-making procedure itself? Or ought we to prefer a blinkered focus on which procedure produces best outcomes (either in a non-consequentialist moral realist sense or even in a consequentialist sense that excludes the benefits flowing from the use of this procedure itself)?

In terms of Allania's move from parliamentary sovereignty to an entrenched and constitutionalized bill of rights, this issue can be reformulated as asking whether democratic decision making has value independently of the particular outcomes (and the moral quality of those outcomes) it produces. I think it does. Larry Alexander, whose views on interpretation generally I find extremely persuasive, seems to disagree (or at least to sit on the fence):

> For Arneson, whatever decision-making form produces the morally best decisions should be chosen, democratic or not. Democracy is only a means to an end, and if another means is instrumentally better, so much the worse for democracy. I have expressed the same skepticism regarding any non-instrumental value in democracy . . . [20]

Here is a pithy way Alexander voices his objection: Would two thugs have a right to take my property – and would I have no right to resist – merely because they are two and I am but one?[21]

Put that way, it is hard to disagree with Alexander. However, putting the issue in that way finesses a crucial factor, namely the existence in society of reasonable disagreement between smart, well-informed, even nice people. The rights in a bill of rights finesse that disagreement by moving to such a high level of moral abstraction – talking, say, of a right to free speech (which virtually everyone supports) rather than of where to draw the line when it comes to campaign finance rules, defamation regimes, and hate speech provisions (where any choice produces dissensus and disagreement that cannot be attributed to stupidity, wickedness, or the need for re-education). Alexander's example plays the same "hide reasonable disagreement" trick, but in a different way. Of course if a majority of thugs outvoted someone to steal his car, or a majority of psychopaths voted to slaughter someone's blue-eyed baby boy, almost all of us (with the possible exception, but only possible exception, of the thugs and psychopaths) would say that the "letting the numbers count" procedure

[20] Larry Alexander, "What Is the Problem of Judicial Review?" (2006) 31 Australian J. Legal Phil. 1 at 10 [Alexander, "What Is the Problem?"]. The "sitting on the fence" comments come at 10–11.

[21] Alexander, "Introduction," *supra* note 4 at 11.

used here cannot justify the outcome. The trick is simply to choose an example where 99.9 percent of readers' moral sentiments (for non-cognitivists) or moral judgments (for moral realists) all point the same way. Then the issue of reasonable disagreement has been finessed, or at least kept from sight.

Try it, however, with different examples. Two people as educated as I and as nice as I say I cannot carry my handgun into their town. I disagree and think that morally I should be able to do this. They say we should all count equally and vote to decide. Or I think minorities and women ought to get some sort of preferential treatment in schooling and jobs, and my two fellow townspeople disagree. Or I want to put Canadian-style hate speech limits on what people can say about others' religious beliefs, and they think this very unwise. And so on, and so on, and so on (replicating all the sorts of issues that, in fact, will end up before the highest court).[22]

In all these sorts of cases, any appeal straight to the justice of the issue or to what is morally best just produces disagreement and dissensus. Likewise, any second-order appeal to what is the best moral worldview or theoretical framework for deciding these first-order justice and moral issues also produces disagreement and dissensus. (And, in that sense, is in no way the same as disputes about facts and the external, causal world and science.[23]) And once we factor in the consideration that disagreement about these sorts of justice and

[22] Larry Alexander gives a less pithy example in "What Is the Problem," *supra* note 20. There he uses the example of a posse capturing men suspected of stealing cattle and of murdering cowboys. The majority of the posse, after some interrogation of the captured men, wants to hang them, believing them to be guilty. A minority of the posse does not, preferring the option of taking them to the nearest legal authorities many miles away. Again, in my view, the example chosen ensures that the minority position meshes with the moral evaluation of the overwhelming preponderance of likely readers (and just to make sure of this, we are told it is later discovered the hanged men were innocent). However, voting on whether or not to hang what turns out to be innocent men does not, to me, reproduce the dilemma faced in liberal democratic societies – like Allania – where decisions have to be made in the name of the group but any decision opted for will be seen as morally right and just by many, and as morally wrong and unjust by many.

Perhaps if this second Alexander example had left the men's guilt ultimately unknowable but likely (on something more than the preponderance of probabilities but less than proof beyond reasonable doubt), included the fact that articles from the murdered men had been found on the captured men, and posited the further variable that the posse had just come into possession of seemingly reliable information of an imminent attack on their hometown demanding a fast-as-possible dash back there to protect otherwise defenseless women and children – perhaps then the issue would look more like one with no blindingly self-evident answer to most of us. We might still think the minority's wanting to take the captured men to the authorities is the right choice. But we might not. And voting – rather than "pull[ing] their guns on the majority" (*Ibid.* at 10) – does seem (to me) to be a way to decide on this revised hypothetical, one that has independent moral value.

[23] Allan, "Jeremy Waldron and the Philosopher's Stone," *supra* note 16.

moral issues is reasonable – that I, personally, am unlikely to be the single *homo sapien* who, after millions of years of evolution, has been blessed with a pipeline to God vis-à-vis what is most moral and most just on these highly contentious and debatable issues – then the procedure used to decide *these* issues (as distinct from the murdering-blue-eyed-babies issues and the thugs-stealing-my-new-car issues) does seem to me to have independent value. Or more bluntly stated, "letting the numbers count" as a decision-making procedure does have a value or weighting independent of the choice or outcome ultimately reached.

As regards these sorts of disputes, one might say (with me) that "letting the numbers count" has instrumental value or good consequences (though Waldron seems to say it has inherent value). It makes acceptance of the decision by those who disagree more likely. It makes citizens' input to change that outcome more likely. (You can spend your Saturdays campaigning for a political party that will change the abortion rules, say, rather than being totally locked out from doing anything other than crossing your fingers and waiting for a few top judges to retire or change their minds.) It counteracts, in part, voter apathy and the temptation for elected legislators to take irresponsible positions (think flag burning), knowing the unelected judges are standing behind them to overrule them. It reduces, at least partially, the elevated position in society of lawyers (and, for that matter, of legal academics). It lessens the need to focus minutely on how judges are chosen.

All these, and more, are consequential advantages of democratic decision making that are independent of the issue of whether the outcomes produced are the morally best ones. They relate to the "how made" issue, not the "what in the end was decided" issue.

Now, I said this was a slight digression, but perhaps I was wrong. Allania, recall, is a parliamentary sovereignty where there is a good deal of confidence in, and support for, democratic decision making to resolve inevitable social disagreements. This support, we are assuming, will not be enough to prevent the adoption of a new written constitution with an entrenched bill of rights. But by the same token, it is unlikely that there will be some sort of Damascene conversion-type move in Allania over to thinking "letting the numbers count," *as a procedure* for resolving disputes, has no value independent of the moral worth of the decisions it produces. And that means support for this new constitutionalized bill of rights – or rather the ability to attract sufficient support to get it approved, adopted, and entrenched – will be influenced by how people in Allania think, or assume, it will be interpreted by latter-day unelected judges. Indeed, given the far greater inroads into parliamentary sovereignty this bill of rights will make, its likely interpretation may well matter a good deal more than how the federalist heads of powers are likely to be interpreted.

III. STOP THREE

Two short stops remain. Both are largely for clarificatory purposes. At this third stop, we alight briefly to ensure Allania's citizens realize that the rights in their mooted bill of rights are not self-interpreting or self-enforcing. In Australia, where the debate over whether to have a bill of rights is a live one, proponents often seem to argue as though the listed moral abstractions articulated in the language of rights can define themselves when it comes to how they will play out in any specific line-drawing question that will reach the courts. That is to say, these instruments are sometimes sold on the unspoken premise that there will be no need for human judgment in deciding whether, say, the right to free speech or to be free from unreasonable search and seizure does or does not result in some statute of the elected legislature being struck down or read down. The technique here is *not* the earlier-mentioned one of finessing disagreement by focusing on the Olympian heights of moral abstractions rather than down in the quagmire of day-to-day contentious line-drawing exercises; it is not quite even the related ploy of leaving the listener blithely to assume that what those vague, amorphous rights will require in specific cases will correspond in some 1:1 way with his or her own beliefs or sentiments (although both those are used, too).

No, at this third stop, we simply are making sure that Allania's citizens are clear that *some* interpretation will be necessary. And the sort of interpretive approach applied will affect the extent to which any traces of parliamentary sovereignty remain. If the rights are interpreted as a broad and generous grant to later-in-time unelected judges to use *their moral judgments or sentiments*, a grant that has at least some scope to grow and expand in line with the growth of a metaphorical tree (however much growth that might be) or in keeping with a progressive view of changing social values, then there will be virtually nothing left of parliamentary sovereignty. On the other hand, if the rights are interpreted as extending no further than the extent intended by the framers – or the extent understood by those Allanians approving the new constitution – then these bill of rights' rights will serve as a floor-level set of guarantees above which parliamentary sovereignty will remain.[24] Hence, if the original intentions/understandings[25] of the enumerated rights do not extend

[24] See my "Portia, Bassanio and Dick the Butcher," *supra* note 9. Justice Antonin Scalia makes the same point in a far more entertaining way in "Romancing the Constitution: Interpretation as Invention" in Grant Huscroft and Ian Brodie (eds.) *Constitutionalism in the Charter Era* (2004) 337 [Scalia, "Romancing the Constitution"].

[25] I put to one side the intra-originalism debate, though I find my own view oscillates between that expressed in the Alexander and in the Smith contributions to this volume.

to abortion or gay marriage or capital punishment, there is nothing, anywhere, that prevents the elected legislature from enacting statutes to deal with these matters – to raise the floor-level protections or guarantees as high as desired by the majority acting through its elected representatives.

Put more bluntly, not all interpretive approaches will be equal insofar as their effects on parliamentary sovereignty. Of course by opting for a bill of rights – any bill of rights[26] – some inroads will be made. Allania will be putting less faith in its democratically elected legislature and a good deal more in its unelected, point-of-application interpreting judges. But the extent of that abjuring of faith will vary, and vary significantly, depending on the approach to interpreting the bill of rights that is ultimately adopted.

Put even more bluntly still, originalist modes of interpretation impose more constraints on the point-of-application interpreter. Or rather, they do so insofar as one believes that a search for historical or past facts limits the answers some changing-through-time group of judges (with individually differing moral sentiments and beliefs) can honestly give more than does a quest to discover the "most moral" or "most progressive" or "most in keeping with civilization and changing social values" answer those same judges can give.[27] This is true whether the latter approach is tied solely to those rights actually enumerated or is broadened to include any that can be said (plausibly or otherwise) to be further implications from the ones listed.

One can accept this without having to subscribe fully to Justice Antonin Scalia's contention that such "living document" interpretive approaches amount to including the following sort of provision at the end of your bill of rights:

> In addition to the restrictions upon governmental power imposed by the Bill of Rights, the States and the federal government shall be subject to such additional restrictions as are deemed appropriate, from time to time, by a majority of the Judges of the Supreme Court.[28]

But whether one goes that far or not, Justice Scalia's question – "[W]hether the framers and ratifiers of the Constitution (or the Fourteenth Amendment) would conceivably have approved [such] a provision"[29] – is telling

[26] For my arguments that even statutory bills of rights make significant inroads into parliamentary sovereignty, see James Allan, "The Victorian Charter of Rights and Responsibilities: Exegesis and Criticisms" (2006) 30 Melbourne U. L. Rev. 906 and "Meagher's Mischaracterisations," *supra* note 19.

[27] For a similar sentiment, see Alexander, "Introduction," *supra* note 4, especially the last few pages.

[28] Antonin Scalia, "Romancing the Constitution," *supra* note 24 at 341.

[29] *Ibid.*

and especially interesting in the context of Allania's move from parliamentary sovereignty status to having a constitutionalized bill of rights. Meanwhile Scalia's answer to his own question – that "[t]o pose it is to answer it . . . it is absurd"[30] – seems virtually impossible to deny or dispute to me, at least while keeping a straight face.

At an extremely bare minimum then, we can restart our journey confident that before adopting or approving this bill of rights, the framers, approvers, and ratifiers in Allania will care about how it is likely to be interpreted.

IV. STOP FOUR

At this last stop before our new written constitution, with its bill of rights and federal division of powers, comes into force, let us disembark one last time. Here we need to raise the issue of whether the rather indeterminate (and no doubt "essentially contested"[31]) notion of an "implication" is best tied to authorial intentions, or if not then to what (if anything). Take an example from Australia. In Australia, the framers produced a constitution that copied much from the United States (and bits from Switzerland, with the background Westminster institutions also being kept). However, after much debate and discussion, they explicitly rejected a bill of rights, preferring to leave these things to the elected parliament, with checks coming from a genuine upper house of review – an elected Senate (which, because of the voting system used, is noticeably harder for the governing/President's party to control than in the United States) and from federalism. And yet some nine decades after the Australian Constitution came into force, the unelected top judges said there existed an implied right to freedom of political communication. These are known in Australia as the implied rights cases.[32]

Now, for anyone who links the concept of an implication to a speaker's or author's intentions – to the conveying of meaning *not* by explicitly stating something but by insinuating it and suggesting it indirectly – this Australian judicial assertion looks incredibly far-fetched. It is not that in everyday life people shun implying things. Quite the contrary. All of us imply things all the time. Generally little rides on any potential misunderstanding, and anyway in

[30] *Ibid.*

[31] W. B. Gallie, "Essentially Contested Concepts" (1956) 56 Proceedings of the Aristotelian Society 167.

[32] See, for example, *Australian Capital Television Pty Ltd v Commonwealth* (1992) 177 C.L.R. 106; *Nationwide News Pty Ltd v Wills* (1992) 177 C.L.R. 1; later revised in *Lange v Australian Broadcasting Corporation* (1997) 189 C.L.R. 520.

daily life we can ask for clarification if we have any doubts about the inferences we are drawing as regards the implications our friend is making.

When it comes to a country's written constitution, however, the framework by which its institutions will be structured and its government operated, the attractions of implying something – rather than stating it explicitly (if sometimes, nonetheless, in rather vague, amorphous terms) – are noticeably less obvious. So if you were a framer of Australia's Constitution, and you thought some sort of right to freedom of political communication was warranted, would you explicitly state or lay down this right? Or would you cross your fingers and hope that the explicitly laid down provisions for a system of representative democracy (sections 7 and 24, as it happens) implied your intentions and that maybe, just maybe, some nine decades down the road, a majority of top judges might "discover" or "find" this implied meaning of yours – a meaning or insinuation that lay buried in the "text and structure" of the Constitution?

If one seeks to link implications to any real-life person's or group's actually held intentions, then of course the obstacles in the way of heading down this path become more numerous. They get more numerous because we know that the actual Australian framers were well aware of the First Amendment in the United States and that they deliberately chose not to insert any similar sort of bill of rights provision. And we realize that something of this magnitude – affording judges the power to trump the decisions of the democratically elected legislature – might generally warrant an explicit provision. And we know that with section 116 of their Constitution, the Australian framers *did* actually lay down an explicit right 'that the Commonwealth shall not make any law for establishing any religion. . . . " Why bother to do that explicitly, but merely imply a right to freedom of political communication? It seems so unbelievably unlikely. It seems as though Australia's so-called implied rights look an awful lot like judicially made-up rights.

However, this only follows for those who tie the concept of an implication to the actually held intentions of real life human beings. What if the notion of implications could be sensibly or coherently divorced from that of actually held (but not explicitly stated) intentions?

The most obvious approach to take in traveling down that route and attempting this divorce starts by noting that words – and marks on paper – do and can convey meaning against a backdrop of shared conventional meanings. Indeed symbols can conceivably convey meaning even if there is no actual author (such as with the hoary example of random typing by monkeys that, after some huge period of time, reproduces a line or two of a Shakespeare sonnet). More to the point, perhaps, given some shared conventional backdrop, words can convey a meaning regardless of what the author or authors intended them to mean.

Conceding all that, it is of little help to the proponents of Australia's implied rights jurisprudence. To make their case, they need to posit that the words used in the Constitution, as conventionally understood, convey a meaning in opposition to the actually held intentions of the framers. This is conceivably possible. But it seems highly unlikely as regards constitutions generally and even more unlikely or implausible as regards the specific question of whether the words in Australia's Constitution, given their conventional meaning, imply a right to the freedom of political communication.

As Richard Kay notes more generally,[33] such a line of thinking – that conventional or public meaning has somehow diverged from, or, more accurately put here, has taken on the exact opposite sense of, the intended meaning – requires you to posit a giant screw-up on behalf of the authors.

Of course there is an alternative approach available in attempting to divorce the notion of implications from any actually held intentions of any real-life people. (And just to sidestep a host of complications, let us restrict ourselves to implications such as these related to rights-based moral matters rather than to technologically driven factual matters such as whether, once invented, fixed-wing airplanes – and so an air force – fall under an "army and navy" head of power or, by default, a power belonging to the states.) This alternative approach requires you to reject the Alexander and Kay "locking things in" view of written constitutions in favor of the "vehicles for expressing society's fundamental values" view. Conceive of constitutions in that second sense, as loose and open vehicles for transmitting what at least sometimes will be nebulous, indeterminate social values, and it no longer is all that difficult to divorce the concept of an implication from that of authorial intentions (or, for that matter, from a public or conventional meaning that has diverged from authorial intentions due to a giant screw-up). Conceive of constitutions in that second, loose and open sense, and you can certainly rescue the concept of implication as it was used in the Australian implied rights cases.

Such a rescue, however, is purchased at a substantial cost. Traveling down this road not only guts the concept of implication of most, if not all, of the constraints or limits on what it allows a user to do; it also comes exceedingly close to elevating future point-of-application unelected judges into latter-day

[33] See Richard Kay's "Original Intention and Public Meaning in Constitutional Interpretation" (2009) 103 Nw. U. L. Rev. 703 [Kay, "Original Intention"].

redrafters, updaters, and all-purpose fixers (from their perspectives, if not everyone's) of the Constitution – redrafters who cannot be gainsaid by the elected legislature or anyone else (shy of a constitutional amendment).[34]

So at this final stop, we may be wise to enquire how many people in Allania find this an appealing prospect. We might wish, in other words, to determine up front whether future interpretation making use of the concept of implications will, or will not, be tied to authorial intentions (and hence to some version or other of originalism).

V. AT JOURNEY'S END

With our four stops behind us, we can now say Allania's journey has come to an end. It now has a new written constitution with a federal division of powers and an embedded bill of rights. How to interpret that new Constitution will soon become a highly important question, important in the practical sense that it will affect the lives of many, most, or all of Allania's citizens (depending on what you take to be an influence, or to count as an effect, on people's lives).

In the rest of this chapter, I will argue that originalism is the least bad approach to interpreting this new Constitution.

Let me begin this argument, however, by distinguishing statutory interpretation and constitutional interpretation. What follows relates to the latter. I happen to believe there are good grounds for distinguishing the two, grounds I have set out in an earlier paper.[35] At its most basic, my claim in that earlier paper was that a plain, or ordinary, or public-meaning approach (even to the point of denying access to the legislative history) has much to recommend it in the statutory context. The plain meaning of the words used generally (perhaps overwhelmingly) coincides with their intended meaning. Where there is honest ambiguity, this plain meaning approach might, after all, allow recourse to extrinsic aids as to intent. The elected legislature can respond in the ordinary way – without needing to resort to some extremely difficult to invoke supermajoritarian procedure – when the judges' view of the statute's words' plain meaning happens to differ from legislators' actual intentions. Indeed,

[34] This critique of mine would apply, too, to T.R.S. Allan's argument about what can be implied into an unwritten constitution. See his "Constitutional Justice and the Concept of Law" in Grant Huscroft (ed.) *Expounding the Constitution* (2008) 219.

[35] See Allan, "Constitutional Interpretation," *supra* note 15. Of course Larry Alexander and Richard Kay and no doubt a good many others disagree with me on this point.

legislative pre-eminence is best protected, and judicial power limited, by according statutory words their plain and ordinary meaning.[36]

By contrast, I noted, those final two points do not apply to constitutional interpretation. In addition, constitutions require a certain level of generality; in comparison with a tax code, or planning law regime, or almost any decent-sized statute, a written constitution will be short, general rather than specific, and relatively indeterminate. Any embedded bill of rights will be even more vague and amorphous. In sum, interpretation according to original intentions imposes the most constraints and external limits – when honestly applied – on the point-of-application judge interpreting a written constitution. For statutes, though, that may well not be true. There, a plain-meaning approach, over time, may better ensure legislative pre-eminence.[37]

At the heart of the matter, putting aside all refinements and the groundwork provided by the four stops on this hypothetical journey of mine, that same claim about which approach to interpreting a written constitution imposes the most external constraints on the judiciary is the one I am making here. It is originalism[38] – *not* approaches that seek to read the words in a moral way, or in a way that evolves and changes according to contemporary values and contexts, or in some conditional hypothetical way that reflects what enactors' intentions *would be today*, or even in a way that accords the text its plain meaning – that I think imposes the most constraints on the judge.

Of course not everyone will agree with that, and not everyone who does agree will go on to find attractive this goal of constraining judicial power and discretion. So let us return to Allania's hypothetical journey. Let us spell out the assumptions needed to make some alternative to originalism appear more attractive. And let us focus on interpreting the bill of rights, because (to paraphrase the Frank Sinatra song) if you are an originalist there, you are an originalist everywhere when it comes to constitutional interpretation.

A first, and obvious, ground for rejecting originalist interpretation is that the founding events are, from today's vantage point looking back at them, widely or universally seen to be illegitimate. Where a written constitution is imposed from the outside, by a departing colonial master or by a vanquishing military foe, that will very often be the case. But we explicitly ruled that out as regards

[36] *Ibid.* [37] *Ibid.*

[38] And within originalist modes of interpretation, I note again that I oscillate between the Larry Alexander and Richard Kay-type defenses of original intent and a more skeptical Steven D. Smith-style defense of it. See Alexander, "Simple Minded Originalism" and Smith, "That Old-Time Orginalism" in this volume.

Allania, not least because it did not happen in the case of the United States or (in a meaningful way) in Canada.

Even where the written constitution is homegrown, of course, its legitimacy can be questioned or attacked. In our hypothetical, Allania's new Constitution was stipulated to have passed the staunchest of universal suffrage hurdles, although, as the next point makes clear, one need not accept majoritarianism as an indicator of legitimacy. True, most people do as far as one's written Constitution is concerned, even people who in other contexts (perhaps ironically) look far less favorably on full adult franchise majoritarianism. Turning from our hypothetical to the United States and Canada, however, leaves more room to attack the legitimacy of the founding events – think of slavery, no franchise for women, proceeding without the agreement of Quebec (or indeed without any plebiscite or election specifically on point and so with no notice to the electorate). Having mooted those lines of possible attack, my own sense is that in both countries, the founding events are overwhelmingly seen to be legitimate. If so, the most obvious basis for rejecting originalism disappears.

A second ground for rejecting originalism is equally straightforward. Here you just come out of the closet and admit that democratic decision making is not that important to you. And let me be clear what I mean. As noted at stop three of our hypothetical journey, any move to a written constitution will involve a sacrifice of self-government in favor of judicial oversight. Here I am referring to the *extra* sacrifice involved in foregoing originalist interpretation in favor of, say, what is believed to be the most moral reading or the most progressive reading. It is that extra degree of foregone or forsworn self-government that might be accepted with a simple "other things matter to me more" reply.

But not in Allania. Allanians are prepared to move to a written constitution, but not at any cost. They will write a check to the judiciary, but not a blank check. Originalist interpretation of the rights in the bill of rights treats those rights as more or less determinate floor-level guarantees, above which parliamentary sovereignty operates. Other approaches enlarge the range of plausible outcomes, some significantly. Given the posited lack of fear in Allania of a legally unconstrained legislature, the interpretive approach that leaves the greatest residue of parliamentary sovereignty is likely to be most people's preferred approach.

Nor will reciting slogans about originalist interpretive approaches amounting to "ancestor worship" be overly effective in Allania. If citizens there wished not to be locked in by the new constitution, and by the original intentions or understandings of its reach and scope, they could have remained a parliamentary sovereignty. In a straight-out choice where "ancestor worship" is wholly shunned and hence either a) the elected legislators or b) the unelected judges are left free to update and keep pace with civilization according to their particular moral consciences' views of what is best, few Allanians would opt for the judges.

Scalia asserts the same is true of Americans. I agree (though, with much regret, I have to concede that I am not completely confident the same is true of Canadians). Of course this assumes that it is made clear to people – as we stipulated at stop three – that the bill of rights and the rest of the written constitution are not self-interpreting. But make that assumption and it then seems to me that any spelling out in advance of what the effects of non-originalist interpretive approaches will be vis-à-vis judicial power would make it extremely difficult, if not impossible, to get sufficient support to adopt or approve the new constitution at all – if these non-originalist options be the interpretive approaches on offer. (And for what it is worth, I can say that proponents of a bill of rights in Australia never spell this out.)

And notice that the same claim would apply to the underlying assertion of Dworkinian originalism or pseudo-originalism mentioned at stop two, namely the assertion that the framers and approvers and ratifiers intended latter-day judges to interpret the rights in the bill of rights (and maybe other parts of the Constitution) in the way those latter-day judges thought was most moral – subject only to the demands of integrity and a Herculean best-fit theory that justifies what has been decided already. That sort of Dworkinian originalism obviously rests on a factual claim, a claim about what in fact was intended. Richard Kay says it is more or less settled that Dworkin is wrong on this question of historical fact.[39] Kay also notes that there is "something odd about arguing against use of the original intentions by invoking an interpretation based on original intentions,"[40] which is hard to dispute. Yet the point from above that carries over to Dworkinian originalist theories is this: If in fact the constitution makers had the intention Dworkin says they did, they could never have explicitly spelled it out (and the implications it would have vis-à-vis later judicial power) and still have garnered sufficient support to have the bill of rights approved and adopted. Whatever else one might say about Dworkinian theories of constitutional interpretation, they are an acquired taste that for many is never acquired.

A third ground for rejecting originalist interpretation involves a refusal to accept that anything other than the post-adoption perspective matters. What brought the Constitution (and these particular words in this form) into being, in other words, becomes irrelevant. Now in one sense, this is simply to assert

[39] See Kay, "Original Intention," *supra* note 33.
[40] *Ibid.* at 708.

that originalist interpretation is defective or sub-optimal, a sort of tautological claim. But it can be taken in a different way, as suggesting that the text of the Constitution ought to be treated as a brute fact: "Here it is. How it got here should not influence what you interpret it to mean."

For citizens of Allania, this is unlikely to hold much allure, given the highly participatory and democratic input that went into its creation. And in terms of national cohesion and the benefits thought to flow from recognizing a shared history (whether partly based in myth, or not), this is a non-starter.

Worse, the brute-fact approach glosses over a key question for people like Larry Alexander and Richard Kay and others who see constitutions as being about locking things in. If it turns out that a constitution is just going to be treated as a brute fact whose history is irrelevant, and hence one that will be interpreted in some sort of "living document" way, then is that outcome more attractive to the Kays and Alexanders than parliamentary sovereignty? I think some of them would have to admit they would prefer parliamentary sovereignty (as Scalia implies he would). Related to that is the fact that these sorts of interpretive approaches, if spelled out, would likely have made the framers jettison the bill of rights (though perhaps not heads of powers federalism). Does that matter?

A fourth ground for rejecting originalist interpretation takes a quite different tack. Here one goes right back to my earlier claim – that in the context of interpreting a written constitution, originalism imposes more external constraints on the point-of-application judge than any other interpretive approach – and one rejects it. This would involve asserting that the search for historical fact (when honestly pursued) is less (or no more) constraining than the attempt to "find" or "discover" the most moral answer, or the Dworkinian best-fit answer, or the most progressive answer, or some other alternative (when honestly pursued). I have argued before that this is implausible,[41] although I suppose if the historical record happened to be sparse enough, and so the "penumbra of doubt"[42] large enough, this could conceivably be true. In the case of the United States, though, and even more so of Australia, it is not true.

VI. CONCLUSION

I suppose the arguments in this chapter make me what Keith Whittington calls an "old originalist."[43] I value originalist constitutional interpretation for the

[41] See Allan, "Constitutional Interpretation," *supra* note 15.

[42] Hart, *The Concept of Law, supra* note 14 at 119.

[43] Keith Whittington, "The New Originalism" (2004) 2 Geo. J.L. & Pub. Pol'y 599. See too Whittington's contribution to this volume, "On Pluralism within Originalism."

constraints it imposes on latter-day unelected judges, at least when pursued honestly. (And I mean that in a "more constraints than the alternatives" sense only.) I do not value it in the abstract or in all imaginable situations. I value it in the circumstances of Allania, the United States, Canada, and Australia (though the absence of a bill of rights in the latter means we can ignore that jurisdiction in many ways). If we are going to have a written constitution, especially one with a bill of rights, then we Allanians want a locked-in (or comparatively locked-in) notion of what future judges can tell us it means, not least when that meaning might be used to invalidate or strike down the enactments of the democratically elected legislature.

No doubt there is room to point out that originalist constitutional interpretation is not ideal in imposing constraints on what the honest interpreter can say the rights in the bill of rights mean – there are gaps, indeterminacies, uncertainties, and so a need to fill in these gaps in this "penumbra of uncertainty"[44] at the point of application. The live question, however, is whether originalist constitutional interpretation is better on this score – has a smaller penumbra of honest doubt and uncertainty – than any alternative. This question, and the answer one gives, is determinative; or rather, it is for those in Allania who, like me, put an independent value – a "how made" value – on democratic decision making as a good way to resolve at least some of society's contested and debatable moral issues (not just squabbles over tax rates or what percentage of GDP to put toward health care, and not automatically excluding moral issues that have been translated into the language of rights).

Methods of constitutional interpretation that explicitly or implicitly treat the meanings of the terms[45] in the document as capable of growing and expanding and changing shape and circumference in line with some metaphorical "living tree" – or at least with what present-day judges, by a majority vote among themselves, think are the ramifications of such an imagined tree's branches – impose too few constraints on the judicial branch of government.[46]

In cases such as Australia's implied rights cases, or *Roe v Wade*[47] in the United States, or just about any *Charter* case in Canada, where the intentions of the framers, approvers and ratifiers are ignored completely (and indeed,

[44] Hart, *The Concept of Law*, *supra* note 14 at 131.

[45] As noted earlier, I focus on bills of rights and put aside issues of technological change and whether, in heads of powers disputes, say, a term can be read to include new inventions. Firstly, the fact-value distinction is important. Secondly, heads of powers disputes make massively smaller inroads into parliamentary sovereignty.

[46] Membership in this judicial branch (no pun intended) will alter over time, and those who are members at any one time will have a range of differing moral views, judgments, and sentiments.

[47] 410 U.S. 113 (1973).

contradicted), it can seem as though the range of plausible outcomes dictated by the interpretive theory used is virtually unlimited. It can seem as though the Constitution is doing none of the work. At that point, things look very curious indeed, as Sherlock Holmes might remark.

> "Is there any point to which you would wish to draw my attention?"
> "To the curious concept of the 'living tree' constitution."
> "The 'living tree' constitution itself often doesn't do any of the work in arriving at the answer."
> "That is why it is a curious concept," remarked Sherlock Holmes.

9 Vagueness, Finiteness, and the Limits of Interpretation and Construction

Grant Huscroft*

I. INTRODUCTION

The most important questions that arise in judicial review under bills of rights typically involve the most vaguely worded rights. Rights to "equal protection" and "due process" in the *U.S. Bill of Rights* and to "equal protection and equal benefit of the law without discrimination" and "fundamental justice" in the *Canadian Charter of Rights and Freedoms* raise profoundly difficult moral and political questions, and the way in which they are interpreted by the courts has far-reaching consequences in the constitutional order. Given the stakes, concern about the legitimacy of particular approaches to constitutional interpretation is inevitable and it will not do to insist that "[i]t is emphatically the province and duty of the Judicial Department to say what the law is."[1] The question is not *whether* the judiciary must interpret the constitution but *how* it should do it.[2]

"New" originalist theory addresses the challenge posed by vaguely worded rights by emphasizing a distinction between "interpretation" and "construction." Interpretation is concerned with determining the linguistic meaning of the text of the bill of rights and is the first task for a court. Once meaning is ascertained the court turns to the task of construction, developing secondary rules or doctrines to flesh out the content of vaguely worded rights in order to resolve particular disputes.[3]

*Thanks to James Allan, Jeffrey Goldsworthy, Margaret Martin, Bradley Miller, Paul Rishworth, and Grégoire Webber for their comments on earlier drafts.

[1] *Marbury v Madison*, 5 U.S. (1 Cranch) 137 at 177 (1803).

[2] I am assuming that judicial review of some sort is inevitable with a bill of rights.

[3] See generally Keith E. Whittington, *Constitutional Interpretation* (1999) and *Constitutional Construction* (2001); Randy E. Barnett, *Restoring the Lost Constitution* (2004) [Barnett, *Restoring the Lost Constitution*]; and Lawrence B. Solum, "Semantic Originalism," http://ssrn.com/abstract=1120244.

So far, so good. But interpretation may not take us very far at all; linguistic meaning can "run out" very early in the process of judicial review,[4] and when it does, originalist theory faces a considerable challenge. How are secondary rules or doctrines fleshing out the content of vaguely worded rights to be constructed when the meaning of those rights is itself underdetermined?

This is a challenge, to be sure, but it is by no means unique to originalism. Although they reject the premise of fixed linguistic meaning, living constitutionalists do not assert that vaguely worded constitutional rights can bear *any* meaning the Court may choose to ascribe to them. What is it, then, that guides and ultimately limits the enterprise of judicial review? What stops the Court from treating vaguely worded rights as though they are, in effect, radically indeterminate?

The answer, I suggest, is that originalists and living constitutionalists alike approach their tasks – or should approach their tasks – on the understanding that bills of rights are finite instruments. That is, bills of rights protect only the set of rights they enumerate, and although those rights may be very broad they are not so broad as to cover the entire domain of rights that might be protected by a bill of rights.[5] The finite character of a bill of rights as a whole establishes the ultimate limit on the scope of the vaguely worded rights it includes.

Take the Canadian *Charter* as an example. The *Charter* was not adopted in the expectation that the rights it enumerates would – or should – address every problem that might arise. On the contrary, like all bills of rights, the *Charter* is a political agreement; its contents reflect the bargaining and compromise that was required in order to attain the political consent necessary to entrench it in the constitutional order. And like any political agreement,

[4] Lawrence B. Solum "What is Originalism? The Evolution of Contemporary Originalist Theory", in this volume at 23–4.

[5] I am putting to one side Randy Barnett's arguments concerning the Ninth Amendment ("The enumeration in the Constitution, of certain rights, shall not be construed to deny or disparage others retained by the people."). Barnett argues that the Ninth Amendment establishes a "presumption of liberty" and as such protects liberties, and in particular what he describes as natural liberty rights. See Barnett, *Restoring the Lost* Constitution, *supra* note 3, chs. 9–10. The orthodox account of the Ninth Amendment is that it is not a source of constitutionally protected rights. Instead, it precludes the constitutionalization of the enumerated rights from having negative consequences. The *Canadian Charter of Rights and Freedoms* contains an analogous provision (s. 26: "The guarantee in this *Charter* of certain rights and freedoms shall not be construed as denying the existence of any other rights or freedoms that exist in Canada.") that is understood in the same way. See Peter W. Hogg, *Constitutional Law of Canada* (2009) [Hogg, *Constitutional Law of Canada*] (describing s. 26 as a "cautionary provision, included to make clear that the *Charter* is not to be construed as taking away any existing undeclared rights or freedoms," which he describes as rights or freedoms protected by common law or legislation). On this account, s. 26 appears to be redundant, for the *Charter* could not properly be understood to have that effect.

the *Charter* may be considered imperfect by those who did not get everything that they wanted – or got things they did not want at all. Living constitutionalist Wil Waluchow acknowledges as much when he says that bills of rights "entrench prior decisions about which rights deserve constitutional protection . . . [r]easonable people might wish, if we could start with a clean slate, for a slightly different collection of rights from those settled upon."[6]

Waluchow makes the point in passing but it is much more significant than he recognizes, for in making it he concedes the premise of finiteness. Choices *were* made when the *Charter* was adopted – not simply to entrench some rights but, more importantly, to deny constitutional protection to others. Some of these choices are well known – so well known, in fact, that they can be acknowledged in passing. So, for example, Waluchow notes that property rights were omitted from the *Charter*.[7] I suspect that sympathy for this result makes it easier for proponents of living constitutionalism not only to acknowledge the choice but to give effect to it. But the key point is this: To acknowledge the omission of *any* right from the *Charter* is to concede that the *Charter* is *finite*. Once this concession is made, it cannot be assumed that the *Charter* includes *any* particular right, no matter how morally attractive its inclusion may seem.

I want to explore the idea of finiteness and its consequences in this chapter. Although my focus will be on Canadian experience with the *Charter*, in my view the idea of finiteness and its implications are not unique to the *Charter*.

II. THE *CHARTER* AS A "LIVING TREE"

At the outset of the *Charter* era, Chief Justice Dickson of the Supreme Court of Canada saw stark alternatives: The Court would "either breathe life into the *Charter* or reduce it to a hollow promise of things that may have been."[8] The perceived failure of the *Canadian Bill of Rights* – a federal statutory bill of rights thought to have failed as a result of judicial indifference – led him to equate the success of the *Charter* with judicial boldness in interpreting it. "When the occasion cries out for new law, let us dare to make it," he said.

[6] W. J. Waluchow, *A Common Law Theory of Judicial Review: The Living Tree* (2007) at 240 [Waluchow, *The Living Tree*]. Waluchow adds that, despite the existence of "deep disagreement about the contents of the rights protected in Charters, there is seldom serious disagreement over the legitimacy of the rights actually chosen" (*ibid.*). It is revealing that Waluchow does not see anything odd in this situation, because disagreement about the content of the rights chosen suggests that there is no meaningful agreement as to their adoption. Having finessed profound disagreement about the meaning of the rights chosen, it is difficult to see why their legitimacy should be presumed.

[7] *Ibid.* at 240, note 28.

[8] Speech to Provincial Court Judges, quoted in Robert J. Sharpe & Kent. Roach, *Brian Dickson: A Judge's Journey* (2003) at 309 [Sharpe and Roach, *A Judge's Journey*].

"Let us recognize that the law is a living organism, its purpose is to serve life, its vitality is dependent upon renewal."[9]

This was an endorsement not simply of living constitutionalism but an expansive conception of it, and when the opportunity arose to implement his vision in *Hunter v Southam Inc.*,[10] Chief Justice Dickson reached back to a decision of the Judicial Committee of the Privy Council, *Edwards v Canada (Attorney General)*,[11] for support. In that case, Lord Sankey described the task of interpreting the *British North America Act, 1867*[12] (UK legislation then functioning as Canada's Constitution) as follows:

> The British North America Act planted in Canada a living tree capable of growth and expansion within its natural limits. The object of the Act was to grant a Constitution to Canada. . . . Their Lordships do not conceive it to be the duty of this Board – it is certainly not their desire – to cut down the provisions of the Act by a narrow and technical construction, but rather to give it a large and liberal interpretation.

Lord Sankey's remarks were intended to enhance lawmaking authority in Canadian legislatures by encouraging a liberal construction of the Constitution. Applied to the *Charter*, however, his living tree metaphor promotes expansive conceptions of rights, which necessarily limits rather than enhances the scope for lawmaking by the legislature.[13] The living tree metaphor was invoked for this reason: It emphasized the potential of judicial review and so facilitated the bold approach that Chief Justice Dickson favored.[14] To describe

[9] Speech to Dalhousie Law School, quoted *ibid.* at 310. Chief Justice Dickson's zeal to play a leading role under the *Charter* led the Court to decide issues prematurely, sometimes without the benefit of full argument, and often in prescriptive terms that belied the very evolutionary premises on which the decisions were supposed to be based. It is remarkable, for example, that Chief Justice Dickson took it on himself to draft a one-size-fits-all approach to limiting rights under s. 1 in *R v Oakes* without the benefit of full argument from the parties, relying primarily on the research of judicial clerks and the Court's executive legal officer. It is remarkable, too, that he is praised rather than criticized for doing so. The story is told in Sharpe and Roach, who describe the s. 1 methodology set out in *R v Oakes* as "five of the most important pages ever written in Canadian constitutional law" (*ibid.* at 334), but cannot bring themselves to criticize Chief Justice Dickson's presumption. See also Sujit Choudhry, "So What Is the Real Legacy of *Oakes*? Two Decades of Proportionality Analysis under the Canadian Charter's Section 1" (2006) 34 S.C.L.R. (2d) 501 at 521–2.

[10] [1984] 2 S.C.R. 145 at 155 [*Southam*].

[11] [1930] A.C. 124 at 136 (P.C.) [*Edwards*].

[12] 30 & 31 Victoria, c. 3 (U.K.). (*BNA Act*).

[13] See F. L. Morton and Rainer Knopff, "Permanence and Change in a Written Constitution: The 'Living Tree' Doctrine and the Charter of Rights" (1990) S.C.L.R. (2d) 533 [Morton and Knopff, "Permanence and Change"], and Hogg, *Constitutional Law of Canada*, *supra* note 5, ch. 33.7(b).

[14] Not least because of the context in which the metaphor was announced. In *Edwards, supra* note 11, the Privy Council determined that women were "qualified persons" eligible for appointment to the Canadian Senate. *Edwards* is now widely regarded as an equality case,

the *Charter* as a "living tree" was, it seemed, to free it from the confines of its text and history.

No doubt, breathing life into the *Charter* was preferable to reducing it to a hollow promise, but this was not a choice that needed to be made at the outset of the *Charter* era. There was no need to emphasize the possibilities for growth and expansion in so new a constitutional document,[15] but Chief Justice Dickson had his eye on the longer game. He was attempting to set the tone for a new constitutional era by establishing a more expansive role for the Court,[16] and the majority of the Court followed his lead. The focus of the case law has, as a result, been on the potential for the growth and expansion of *Charter* rights. Lord Sankey's explicit caution – that growth and expansion is bounded by the "natural limits" of the constitution – has been all but ignored.

Proponents of living constitutionalism tend to downplay the significance of growth and expansion of the *Charter*. For their part, "dialogue" theorists insist that judicial review matters far less than is supposed, because the *Charter* establishes a "weak" form of judicial review. It is usually possible, they argue, for Canadian legislatures to pass new legislation to achieve a particular purpose following a judicial decision to strike down legislation under the *Charter* – even following the adoption of the most expansive conception of *Charter* rights by the Court.[17] Thus, it is said, the *Charter* impacts mainly on legislative means rather than ends.[18]

emphasizing the potential of judicial review – and living-tree interpretation in particular – to deliver social justice. Cf. Bradley Miller, "Origin Myth: The Persons Case, The Living Tree, and the New Originalism," in this volume.

[15] *Cf. R. v. Prosper* [1994] 3 S.C.R. 236 at 287 [*Prosper*] per L'Heureux-Dubé J., dissenting (internal citations omitted):

> While the "living tree" theory would perhaps let us by-pass the will of the legislature, that theory is usually used to put right an interpretation which is no longer in accordance with the current socio-economic context . . . I doubt it can be used to interpret a constitutional document, such as the *Charter*, which is still in its infancy at a time when the socio-economic context has not evolved.

[16] Chief Justice Dickson's biographers, Kent Roach and Robert Sharpe, lavish praise on him for his approach to the *Charter*, citing with approval his desire to "play a leading role in defining the scope and impact of the *Charter* generally." Dickson's embarrassing self-description as "the John Marshall of Canada" passes without comment. Sharpe and Roach, *A Judge's Journey*, *supra* note 8 at 325.

[17] The seminal article is Peter W. Hogg and Alison A. Bushell, "The *Charter* Dialogue between Courts and Legislatures (Or Perhaps the *Charter of Rights* Isn't Such a Bad Thing After All)," (1997) 35 Osgoode Hall L.J. 75. See also Peter W. Hogg, Alison A. Bushell Thornton, and Wade K. Wright, "*Charter* Dialogue Revisited – Or 'Much Ado About Metaphors'" (2007) 45 Osgoode Hall L. J. 1. Volume 45 of the Osgoode Hall Law Journal includes commentaries by several scholars, including myself, in addition to a reply from Hogg *et al.*

[18] Stephen Gardbaum makes a similar argument, suggesting that balancing or proportionality review by courts "counters the judicial monopoly in constitutional decision-making that

I have criticized dialogue theory extensively and do not propose to revisit the debate here.[19] Suffice it to say that it is misleading to portray *any* system in which the Court can strike down democratically enacted legislation as a "weak" form of judicial review. Dialogue theory is better understood as a rationalization of judicial power rather than a justification for it. No matter how the theory is regarded, however, it has nothing to say about how particular *Charter* rights should be interpreted or constructed and should not distract us from dealing with the question at hand. According to the terms of the living tree metaphor, the *Charter* may grow and expand within its natural limits. If the Court is to be faithful to the metaphor, those limits – the finite character of the *Charter* itself – must be addressed.

III. NATURAL LIMITS IN THE SUPREME COURT OF CANADA

The *Marriage Reference*[20] is one of the few cases in which the concept of natural limits has been considered by the Supreme Court of Canada. Argument over the concept of natural limits in that case arose under the *Constitution Act, 1867* (formerly known as the *BNA Act*) rather than the *Charter*, in the context of an action for a declaration that the common law limitation of marriage to opposite-sex couples was unconstitutional. Section 91(26) of the *Constitution Act, 1867* provides that Parliament has exclusive lawmaking authority in regard to "marriage and divorce," and at trial it was held that the term "marriage" had a core meaning that limited the scope of Parliament's lawmaking ability.[21] That decision was overturned on appeal, but the trial court's argument was raised by one of the interveners in the Supreme Court of Canada. The Court replied to the argument as follows:

> The natural limits argument can succeed only if its proponents can identify an objective core of meaning which defines what is "natural" in relation to marriage. Absent this, the argument is merely tautological. The only objective core which the interveners before us agree is "natural" to marriage is that it is the voluntary union of two people to the exclusion of all others. Beyond this,

typically occurs where rights conclusively determine constitutional outcomes within a system of judicial review; a finality that is rendered highly problematic by the indeterminate nature of many of the relevant rights." See Gardbaum, "A Democratic Defense of Constitutional Balancing" 4 Law & Ethics of Human Rights 78 at 93 (2010).

19 See Grant Huscroft, "Rationalizing Judicial Supremacy: The Mischief of Dialogue Theory" in James Kelly and Christopher Manfredi (eds.), *Contested Constitutionalism: Reflections on the Charter of Rights and Freedoms* (2009) 50; and Grant Huscroft, "Constitutionalism from the Top Down" (2007) 45 Osgoode Hall L. J. 91.

20 *Reference re Same-Sex Marriage*, [2004] 3 S.C.R. 698 [*Marriage Reference*].

21 *EGALE Canada v. Canada (Attorney General)* (2001), 95 B.C.L.R. (3d) 122.

> views diverge. We are faced with competing opinions on what the natural limits of marriage may be.
>
> Lord Sankey L.C.'s reference to "natural limits" did not impose an obligation to determine, in the abstract and absolutely, the core meaning of constitutional terms. Consequently, it is not for the Court to determine, in the abstract, what the natural limits of marriage must be. Rather, the Court's role is to determine whether marriage as defined in the *Proposed Act* falls within the subject matter of s. 91(26).
>
> In determining whether legislation falls within a particular head of power, a progressive interpretation of the head of power must be adopted. The competing submissions before us do not permit us to conclude that "marriage" in s.91(26) of the *Constitution Act, 1867*, read expansively, excludes same-sex marriage.[22]

In this passage the Court equates the idea of natural limits with an "objective core of meaning" about the constitutional provision in question, but does not elaborate on the concept. It sounds like the fixation thesis from new originalism, but the Court is in essence *denying* the existence of such a meaning in regard to marriage and establishing a burden on proponents of natural limits to establish otherwise. Consider the Court's remarks about the positions of the interveners in the *Marriage Reference*. When the case was argued, the exclusivity of opposite-sex marriage was a norm common to legal systems (and religions) around the world. Nevertheless, the Court considered it significant that the numerous interveners in the case had different conceptions of marriage. The only objective core of marriage on which they agreed was that it was natural to limit marriage to two people.[23] Beyond this, the Court noted, "We are faced with competing opinions on what the natural limits of marriage may be."[24]

What is the relevance of competing opinions about the meaning of a constitutional provision? One would suppose that the Court would resolve the difference in opinion by declaring one side or the other to be "right." The Court, however, insisted that "it is not for the Court" to determine the natural limits of the term "marriage"; Lord Sankey's living tree metaphor does not require the Court to determine the core meaning of constitutional terms "in

[22] *Marriage Reference, supra* note 20 at paras. 27–9.

[23] This objective core will be contested in litigation challenging the constitutionality of the *Criminal Code* prohibition of polygamy, pursuant to a reference from the British Columbia government: http://www2.news.gov.bc.ca/news_releases_2009–2013/2009AG0012–000518.htm.

[24] *Marriage Reference, supra* note 20.

the abstract and absolutely." Why not? How can the Court apply the Constitution in a manner that respects its natural limits if it does not determine the core meaning of its provisions? The Court did not explain. Instead, the Court stated that its task was simply to determine whether the proposed legislative definition of marriage falls within the subject matter of the relevant constitutional provision said to authorize it.

Bradley Miller has argued that, on this approach, the Court is unlikely to identify natural limits in any case in the absence of unanimous opinion that allows it to treat that agreement as evidence of an objective meaning.[25] If this is so, then the mere fact of disagreement between self-interested litigants suffices to preclude the Court from recognizing the existence of natural limits. But this is not the only problem evident with the Court's reasoning.

The Court rejected the natural limits argument in the concept of marriage as tautological only to assert another tautology in its place. If progressive interpretation "must be adopted," as the Court asserts, of course it follows that "the competing submissions before us do not permit us to conclude that marriage . . . read expansively, excludes same-sex marriage." But this puts the cart before the horse. The terms of the living tree metaphor contemplate progressive interpretation *subject to* whatever bounds are established by the natural limits of the constitution. The first part of the metaphor is subordinate to the second.

It will not do, then, to ignore the concept of natural limits or to consign the concept to secondary importance. The natural limits of a constitutional provision may remain implicit and unexplored, as, for example, in cases in which the case law is considered well settled. Where it is not, however, and the Court contemplates the adoption of an expansive interpretation of a constitutional provision, it is incumbent on the Court to situate that interpretation within the natural limits of the constitution as a whole, and it is difficult to see how this can occur if the Court refuses to engage with the core of the provision in question.

In the *Marriage Reference*, the Court addressed the concept of natural limits in the context of an argument about lawmaking authority. How would the Court's approach apply in the context of the *Charter*?

The Court might take the same position – that it is under no obligation to determine the core meaning of *Charter* rights in the abstract and absolutely, and that its role is simply to determine whether or not a rights claim comes under the protection of a *Charter* right. But is it possible for the Court to make

[25] Bradley W. Miller, "Beguiled by Metaphors: The Living Tree and Originalist Constitutional Interpretation in Canada" (2009) 22 Can. J. L. & Jur. 331 at 366.

sense of vaguely worded *Charter* rights without having *some* conception of the core meaning of those rights? Living tree proponents typically avoid this question by highlighting – indeed, making a virtue of – the incremental nature of the growth and development likely to occur through the use of common law methodology. In this way, the existence of limits can be acknowledged, but by proceeding incrementally the Court need never confront them. At some point, however, incremental growth and development of individual *Charter* rights can have a profound impact on those rights, tantamount to a change to the *Charter* itself. Is this sort of growth and development legitimate?

IV. GROWTH, DEVELOPMENT, AND CONSTITUTIONAL CHANGE

Plainly, Lord Sankey did not think so. *In Re Regulation and Control of Aeronautics in Canada*,[26] a decision reached following his decision in *Edwards* establishing the living tree metaphor, Lord Sankey made the point this way:

> [T]here is always a danger that in the course of [interpreting an Act of Parliament] the terms of the statute may come to be unduly extended and attention may be diverted from what has been enacted to what has been judicially said about the enactment.
>
> To borrow an analogy; there may be a range of sixty colours, each of which is so little different from its neighbour that it is difficult to make any distinction between the two, and yet at the one end of the range the colour may be white and at the other end of the range black. Great care must therefore be taken to consider each decision in light of the circumstances of the case in view of which it was pronounced, especially in the interpretation of an Act such as the British North America Act, which was a great constitutional charter, and not to allow general phrases to obscure the underlying object of the Act . . . [27]

Although the Supreme Court of Canada has never asserted a power to change the Constitution through its case law, there is no doubt that it has done so.[28]

[26] [1932] A.C. 54.

[27] *Ibid.* at 70. Morton and Knopff noticed this some time ago in "Permanence and Change," *supra* note 13.

[28] For example, the Supreme Court of Canada changed the Canadian Constitution when it invented an obligation to bargain in good faith following a referendum favoring the secession of a province from the Canadian federation in *Reference re Secession of Québec*, [1998] 2 S.C.R. 217. The change here was one of supplementation, with the Court adding a provision to the Constitution in order to address hypothetical political circumstances. *Cf.* Hogg, *Constitutional Law of Canada*, *supra* note 5, ch. 5.7(b) ("there is no historical basis for the proposition that a referendum in the province that desires to secede should impose an obligation of negotiation on the other parties to the amending procedures. However, this is now the law of Canada.").

When the stakes are high enough, courts in most countries may do the same. Are they justified in doing so?

Raz and the Argument for Change

Joseph Raz is one of the few to argue that courts not only can, but sometimes *should*, change a constitution.[29] Raz begins from the premise that judicial decisions interpreting a constitution are justified only if they are morally justified, and on occasion judges must disregard the law of the constitution to reach morally justified decisions. His tolerance (or enthusiasm) for disregarding the law of the constitution is tempered by his acknowledgment of the importance of considerations such as fidelity to the law of the constitution, institutional considerations, and so on. But Raz says that these considerations are but additional moral considerations, and as such they may be outweighed by the need to obtain a morally just result. Raz downplays the radical character of his approach, suggesting that judicially imposed constitutional change will be infrequent: "None of this should be taken to imply that all defects in a constitution can be put right through ingenious interpretation," he says. "All I am saying is that sometimes this is possible."[30]

Raz's argument is noteworthy for what it seems to lack: any concern for political legitimacy. Raz appears to be utterly unconcerned with the people – those who adopted the constitution or those subsequently bound by it. His is a top-down approach to constitutional law in which judges answer all of the moral questions that matter. As Jeffrey Goldsworthy has argued, no judge would dare assert the authority that Raz insists they have. The closest they could come is to mask their true purposes:

> [I]n those rare cases in which judges might be morally justified in changing the constitution to mitigate extreme injustice, it would usually be morally incumbent on them to do so surreptitiously, by pretending to interpret it in a legally permissible, conserving manner. In other words, the judges would be required to lie.[31]

[29] J. Raz, "On the Authority and Interpretation of Constitutions: Some Preliminaries" in L. Alexander (ed.), *Constitutionalism: Philosophical Foundations* (1999) 152 (republished in Raz, *Between Authority and Interpretation* (2009) 323) [Raz, "On the Authority and Interpretation of Constitutions"].

[30] *Ibid.* at 178. It is difficult to know what to make of this. Of course anything is possible in that it *can* happen, but this is far from an argument that it ought to happen, or happen in other than exceptional circumstances in any event.

[31] Jeffrey Goldsworthy, "Raz on Constitutional Interpretation" 22 Law and Phil. 167 (2003) at 185.

Now, most judges would claim to be offended by the idea that they should lie.[32] They are likely to be comfortable, however, if they think that their decisions are contributing to a process of *subtle* change to the constitution, however radical that change may turn out to be. The incremental nature of common law methodology means that no one judge will be held responsible for having changed the constitution; responsibility will be shared by all those who interpreted it before him or her. Raz is sanguine about radical change that is reached gradually,[33] but ultimately the extent of the change he would permit through interpretation is not clear.

The existence of a constitutional amending process should be an embarrassment for Raz, but he has no compunction about ignoring it. Anticipating the objection that the entrenchment of a constitution means that it is undesirable that it be amended by judicial interpretation rather than through its amending procedures, he says simply: "It may mean that this is what their authors intended, but it does not follow that their view is sound."[34]

Hunter v Southam *Revisited*

Raz's position is unattractive, but the Supreme Court of Canada appears to endorse it in the context of its commitment to living tree constitutionalism. Writing for the Court in *Hunter v Southam*,[35] Chief Justice Dickson said as follows:

> The task of expounding a constitution is crucially different from that of construing a statute. A statute defines present rights and obligations. It is easily enacted and as easily repealed. A constitution, by contrast, is drafted with an eye to the future. Its function is to provide a continuing framework for the legitimate exercise of governmental power and, when joined by a *Bill* or a *Charter of Rights*, for the unremitting protection of individual rights and liberties. Once enacted, its provisions cannot easily be repealed or amended. It must, therefore, be capable of growth and development over time to meet

[32] *Cf.* Antonin Scalia, "Romancing the Constitution: Interpretation as Invention" in Grant Huscroft and Ian Brodie (eds.), *Constitutionalism in the Charter Era* (2004) 337 at 337 [Scalia, "Romancing the Constitution"]:

> This is not to say that American judges did not occasionally "update" the Constitution by finding within it various prescriptions and proscriptions it did not originally contain. But they did it the good old-fashioned way: they lied about it. Nowadays it is no longer necessary to lie – which is not a good thing if you believe, as I do, that hypocrisy is the beginning of virtue.

[33] Raz, "On the Authority and Interpretation of Constitutions," *supra* note 29 at 364.

[34] *Ibid.* at 363.

[35] *Southam, supra* note 10.

new social, political and historical realities often unimagined by its framers. The judiciary is the guardian of the constitution and must, in interpreting its provisions, bear these considerations in mind.[36]

Dickson's dictum is treated with considerable reverence in Canadian constitutional law, but no matter how often it is recited it remains problematic.[37] It simply does not follow from the difficulty in amending the *Charter* that the Court should grow and develop *Charter* rights. On the contrary, the difficulty in amending the *Charter* counsels in favor of judicial humility – modesty rather than boldness – in "growing and developing" *Charter* rights. The difficulty in amending the *Charter* cannot at once be a burden for the people and a license for the judiciary.

Chief Justice Dickson never makes clear the extent of the growth and development he has in mind in *Hunter*, but in relying on the difficulties in amending the constitution in arguing in support of progressive interpretation he must be taken to be endorsing the idea that constitutional change by the judiciary may be justified. After all, the difficulty in amending the constitution would be irrelevant if the growth and development contemplated were within the natural limits of the *Charter*.

Viewed in this light, Chief Justice Dickson's dictum is far more radical than has been understood. Perhaps perceived defects in the *Charter* might one day become an acute problem the Court is compelled to rectify, but as Jeffrey Goldsworthy has argued we should expect this sort of situation to be extraordinary. In normal circumstances the judiciary has no business changing the *Charter*, especially to supplement perceived deficiencies. As Justice L'Heureux-Dubé – a *proponent* of the living tree – once insisted, "living tree" interpretation cannot be used to "transform completely a document or add a provision which was specifically rejected at the outset. It would be strange, and even dangerous," she insisted, "if courts could so alter the constitution of a country."[38]

V. TAKING STOCK

To this point I have argued that bills of rights are finite, and that respect for the idea of finiteness must inform any approach to understanding the vaguely

[36] *Ibid.* at 155.

[37] The argument that follows is based on Huscroft, "A Constitutional 'Work in Progress'? The Charter and the Limits of Progressive Interpretation" in G. Huscroft and I. Brodie (eds.), *Constitutionalism in the Charter Era* (2004) 413 [Huscroft, "A Constitutional 'Work in Progress'?"].

[38] *Prosper*, *supra* note 15 at 287.

worded rights they enumerate. The Supreme Court of Canada's commitment to living tree constitutionalism makes clear the importance of finiteness by situating the possibility for growth and expansion of *Charter* rights in the context of the Charter's "natural limits."

But how is finiteness to be determined? Like most bills of rights, the *Charter* enumerates the rights it protects and does not specify the rights it excludes. It does not follow, of course, that because a right is not specifically enumerated that it cannot be subsumed within the protection of one or more of the vaguely worded rights that are enumerated. But as the example of property rights demonstrates, the silence of the *Charter* may have normative significance that ought to be respected. Is there a role for originalism, or considerations inspired by originalism, in determining the significance of constitutional silence?

VI. ORIGINALISM REVISITED

Originalism was dispatched by the Supreme Court of Canada in the *B.C. Motor Vehicle Reference*.[39] In that case, the Court seized on the vagueness of the term "fundamental justice" in section 7 of the *Charter*[40] as a means of expanding the right to embrace substantive content as well as the procedural protection that it had been designed to provide. In doing so, the Court expanded the scope of judicial review under the *Charter* considerably, in the face of evidence not only that this interpretation was not intended but also that the framers had attempted to avoid it. Testimony from the Assistant Deputy Minister, the Deputy Minister, and the Minister of Justice at the Special Joint Committee of the Senate and of the House of Commons on the Constitution made clear that the expression "fundamental justice" was adopted on the understanding that it was synonymous with natural justice, the common law term then understood as providing only procedural protection.[41] It is well known that framers of the *Charter* were keen to avoid the American concept of substantive due process; the historical record was clear in this regard and the Court knew as much. After all, the *B.C. Motor Vehicle Reference* was decided only three years following the adoption of the *Charter*.

[39] *Re B.C. Motor Vehicle Act*, [1985] 2 S.C.R. 486 [*B.C. Motor Vehicle Reference*].

[40] Section 7: Everyone has the right to life, liberty and security of the person and the right not to be deprived thereof except in accordance with the principles of fundamental justice.

[41] See the discussion in Hogg, *Constitutional Law of Canada*, *supra* note 5, ch. 47.10. One consequence of the rejection of originalism is that the Committee's work is now cited only rarely, and few scholars think it significant. The contrast with American scholarship is great: Most American scholars can cite the *Federalist* chapter and verse.

The Court was prepared to consider the evidence of the framers' intentions but was unwilling to accord it any significant weight. Justice Lamer explained as follows:

> If speeches and declarations by prominent figures are inherently unreliable (*per* McIntyre J. in *Reference re Upper Churchill Water Rights Reversion Act, supra*, at p. 319) and "speeches made in the legislature at the time of enactment of the measure are inadmissible as having little evidential weight" (*per* Dickson J. in the reference *Re: Residential Tenancies Act 1979, supra*, at p. 721), the Minutes of the Proceedings of the Special Joint Committee, though admissible, and granted somewhat more weight than speeches should not be given too much weight. The inherent unreliability of such statements and speeches is not altered by the mere fact that they pertain to the *Charter* rather than a statute.
>
> Moreover, the simple fact remains that the *Charter* is not the product of a few individual public servants, however distinguished, but of a multiplicity of individuals who played major roles in the negotiating, drafting and adoption of the *Charter*. How can one say with any confidence that within this enormous multiplicity of actors, without forgetting the role of the provinces, the comments of a few federal civil servants can in any way be determinative?
>
> Were this Court to accord any significant weight to this testimony, it would in effect be assuming a fact which is nearly impossible of proof, *i.e.*, the intention of the legislative bodies which adopted the *Charter*. In view of the indeterminate nature of the data, it would in my view be erroneous to give these materials anything but minimal weight.[42]

Even assuming that evidence suggested a particular interpretation, Justice Lamer expressed concern that *Charter* rights not be "frozen in time." He characterized this concern in terms of the living tree metaphor:

> Another danger with casting the interpretation of s. 7 in terms of the comments made by those heard at the Special Joint Committee Proceedings is that, in so doing, the rights, freedoms and values embodied in the *Charter* in effect become frozen in time to the moment of adoption with little or no possibility of growth, development and adjustment to changing societal needs. Obviously, in the present case, given the proximity in time of the *Charter* debates, such a problem is relatively minor, even though it must be noted that even at this early stage in the life of the *Charter*, a host of issues and questions have been raised which were largely unforeseen at the time of such proceedings. If the newly planted "living tree" which is the *Charter* is to have the possibility of growth and adjustment over time, care must be taken

[42] *B.C. Motor Vehicle Reference, supra* note 39 at paras. 50–52.

to ensure that historical materials, such as the Minutes of Proceedings and Evidence of the Special Joint Committee, do not stunt its growth.[43]

In deprecating the use of "historical materials" in interpreting the *Charter* on the basis that they might "stunt its growth," Justice Lamer begged the question by assuming that growth of the *Charter* through the judicial review *should* occur. But the Supreme Court of Canada's rejection of originalism is not all that it seems. Consider the sorts of concessions invariably made in non-originalist arguments about interpreting bills of rights. In the context of an article entitled "Originalism Is Bunk," Mitchell Berman has no difficulty in acknowledging that the intentions of the framers, the understanding of those who ratified the bill of rights, and the original public meaning of the text of the *U.S. Bill of Rights* are all relevant to "proper constitutional interpretation". Indeed, Berman goes so far as to describe the relevance of these things as "a trivial thesis without dissenters."[44]

Berman's concession is as relevant in Canada as in the United States. The usual question is not *whether* a court may take these sorts of originalist considerations into account but how much weight they will be accorded – in other words, how significant they will turn out to be. The conclusion that property rights are not protected by the *Charter* is largely uncontroversial despite its originalist provenance. Everyone knows, we might say, that property rights are not protected by the *Charter*; everyone is familiar with the history of the *Charter* and the intention of its framers to omit it. One of the most prominent proponents of living tree interpretation, Peter Hogg, considers it uncontroversial to state that the framers "deliberately omitted any reference to property in s. 7" in order to avoid the American due process experience (based on his reading of the history of the drafting of the *Charter*) and to insist that the right to liberty in s. 7 "must be interpreted as not including property"[45] as a result. Hogg makes the same point about the right to "security of the person."[46]

[43] *Ibid.* at para. 53.

[44] 84 N.Y.U.L. Rev. 1 at 21 (2009). Berman distinguishes various commitments to originalism, strong, moderate, and weak, and focuses on the notion that the constitution has a fixed, discoverable meaning that has lexical priority over other possible meanings.

[45] See Hogg, *Constitutional Law of Canada*, *supra* note 5, ch 47.7(b).

[46] *Ibid.* at ch 47.9: "The omission of property from s. 7 was a striking and deliberate departure from the constitutional texts that provided the models for s. 7 . . . The omission of property rights from s. 7 greatly reduces its scope." Lest there be any doubt about the implications of this, Hogg goes on to note that the *Charter* affords no protection against the taking of property, among other things. He adds that the omission of property rights from the *Charter* "requires that [the terms liberty and security of the person in s.7] be interpreted as excluding economic liberty and economic security; otherwise, property having been shut out of the front door, would enter by the back" (*ibid.*).

I suspect that originalist considerations are far less likely to be accorded great weight – if indeed they are acknowledged at all – when they are invoked in support of arguments for natural limits on the *Charter*, and hence limits on the ability of the Court to grow and develop the *Charter* to include rights that are thought to reflect stronger moral claims than property rights.

The finite nature of the *Charter* means that there should be categorical answers to some rights questions, but the Court's commitment to living tree growth and expansion dissuades it from providing those answers. And if categorical answers are not given at the outset, when the nature of the constitutional settlement effected by the adoption of a bill of rights is well understood, it is unlikely that they ever will be: The wise ancestors who adopted a bill of rights will one day come to be perceived as a group of long-dead people who have no business locking their descendants into constitutional commitments that may be considered improvident.

VII. ECONOMIC AND SOCIAL RIGHTS

Economic and social rights are perhaps the best demonstration of the phenomenon in Canada. Does the *Charter* include a right to an adequate standard of living? To housing? To healthcare or education? It is often argued that such rights can properly be inferred from section 7 of the *Charter*, the same provision that has been held not to protect property rights. Section 7 provides as follows:

> Everyone has the right to life, liberty and security of the person and the right not to be deprived thereof except in accordance with the principles of fundamental justice.

Now, I take it to be clear that the *Charter* does not include a right to an adequate standard of living, to housing, to health care, or to education, just as it is clear that it does not include property rights. This is – or should be – an "everyone knows" situation: The same sort of originalist evidence and argument that is relied on in excluding the protection of property rights could be invoked to demonstrate the exclusion of economic and social rights.[47] At the same time, however, it is clear that economic and social rights enjoy considerably greater political support than property rights – especially in the academy – and many

[47] This is simply another way of saying that the *Charter*, like most bills of rights, is a statement of civil and political rights.

scholars advocate that section 7 can and should be understood as including them.[48]

The Supreme Court of Canada has been unable to bring itself to declare that the *Charter* does not protect economic and social rights. It had the chance to do so in the early days of the *Charter*, when the nature of the constitutional settlement was clear and it would have been easy to do so. Chief Justice Dickson was prepared to acknowledge the exclusion of property rights from the *Charter* – an exclusion he describes as intentional – and to treat that exclusion as having a significant effect in regard to property, but he would go no further:

> What is immediately striking about [s. 7] is the inclusion of "security of the person" as opposed to "property". This stands in contrast to the classic liberal formulation, adopted, for example, in the Fifth and Fourteenth Amendments in the American Bill of Rights, which provide that no person shall be deprived "of life, liberty or property, without due process of law". The intentional exclusion of property from s. 7, and the substitution therefor of "security of the person" has, in our estimation, a dual effect. First, it leads to a general inference that economic rights as generally encompassed by the term "property" are not within the perimeters of the s. 7 guarantee. This is not to declare, however, that no right with an economic component can fall within "security of the person". Lower courts have found that the rubric of "economic rights" embraces a broad spectrum of interests, ranging from such rights, included in various international covenants, as rights to social security, equal pay for equal work, adequate food, clothing and shelter, to traditional property – contract rights. *To exclude all of these at this early moment in the history of Charter interpretation seems to us to be precipitous.* We do not, at this moment, choose to pronounce upon whether those economic rights fundamental to human life or survival are to be treated as though they are of the same ilk as corporate-commercial economic rights. In so stating, we find the second effect of the inclusion of "security of the *person*" to be that a *corporation's* economic rights find no constitutional protection in that section.[49]

[48] Advocates include M. Jackman, "The Protection of Welfare Rights under the Charter" (1988) 20 Ottawa L. Rev. 257; D. Wiseman, "The Charter and Poverty: Beyond Injusticiability" (2001) 51 U.T.L.J. 425; M. Young, "Section 7 and the Politics of Social Justice" (2005) 38 U.B.C. L. Rev. 539; M. Jackman and B. Porter, "Socio-Economic Rights under the Canadian Charter" in M. Langford, ed., *Social Rights Jurisprudence: Emerging Trends in International and Comparative Law* (2008) 209; and W. Mackay, "Social and Economic Rights in Canada: What Are They and Who Can Best Protect Them?" (2009) 45 S.C.L.R. 385 at 411 [Mackay, "Social and Economic Rights"].

[49] *Irwin Toy Ltd. v. Quebec (Attorney General)*, [1989] 1 S.C.R. 927 at 1003–4 (emphasis added).

One could be forgiven for thinking that the question "does the *Charter* protect economic and social rights?" should yield a definite answer: Either it does or it does not. But Chief Justice Dickson appears to have regarded the vague concept of "security of the person" as almost radically indeterminate. Not only did he refuse to make a categorical decision about the protection of economic and social rights, but his refusal came after having articulated the idea in dramatically expansive terms. Lower courts, he said, have found that rights to social security, pay equity legislation, adequate food, clothing, and shelter may all be protected, and it would be "precipitous" for the Court to exclude such rights so early in the life of the *Charter*. Notice the move here: Chief Justice Dickson did not consider whether social and economic rights were *included* in the *Charter*. Instead, he asked whether or not they should be *excluded from* the *Charter*, as though the decision were entirely within the Court's discretion.

Fast-forward seventeen years to *Gosselin v Quebec (Attorney General)*,[50] in which the Court was asked to interpret section 7 of the *Charter* as requiring a minimum level of social assistance payments. Two dissenting judges of the Court were prepared to hold that section 7 "readily accommodated" an obligation on government to provide what they described as "basic protection" to citizens. Justices Arbour and L'Heuereux-Dubé acknowledged that the Court had, in previous cases, interpreted section 7 as protecting only legal rights, but this was of no moment. They explained:

> As s. 7 jurisprudence has developed, new kinds of interests, quite apart from those engaged by one's dealings with the justice system and its administration, have been asserted and found to be deserving of s. 7 protection. To now continue to insist upon the restrictive significance of the placement of s. 7 within the "Legal Rights" portion of the *Charter* would be to freeze constitutional interpretation in a manner that is inconsistent with the vision of the Constitution as a "living tree" which has always been part of the Canadian constitutional landscape.[51]

This passage is revealing for a couple of reasons. First, Justices Arbour and L'Heureux-Dubé are careful to describe their concern as with the "interests" protected by section 7. This undersells what they are really doing, which is attempting to add additional rights to section 7 – that is, to change the *Charter*. How much easier to portray an argument for constitutional change as though what is being proposed is a mere accretion to an existing right – an evolution in the *interests* the right is understood to protect. To describe economic rights as mere interests is to diminish the radical character of the change they proposed.

[50] [2002] 4 S.C.R. 429 [*Gosselin*].

[51] *Ibid.* at para. 317.

But even in the context of protecting interests, the breadth of the discretion they assert is remarkable. According to Justices Arbour and L'Heureux-Dubé, it is normal for the Court to interpret section 7 by determining which interests are "deserving" of protection. It is as though the *Charter* says: "[T]he enumerated rights may be supplemented by such additional rights as the Court considers appropriate."[52] There can be no pretence that this is an approach that acknowledges or respects natural limits.[53]

The majority of the Court in *Gosselin* rejected the argument that section 7 includes positive economic rights, but did not do so with any conviction and certainly did not do so categorically. In essence, Chief Justice McLachlin's majority opinion answers the question: "Does the *Charter* include positive economic rights?" by stating: "Maybe, but not yet":

> *One day s. 7 may be interpreted to include positive obligations.* To evoke Lord Sankey's celebrated phrase in *Edwards v. Attorney-General for Canada*, the *Canadian Charter* must be viewed as "a living tree capable of growth and expansion within its natural limits". It would be a mistake to regard s. 7 as frozen, or its content as having been exhaustively defined in previous cases.

[52] Justice Scalia has made a similar point about jurisprudence under the Fourteenth Amendment:

> It seems to me that a sensible way of approaching this question is to ask oneself whether the framers and ratifiers of the Constitution (or of the Fourteenth Amendment) would conceivably have approved a provision that read somewhat as follows:
>
> > In addition to the restrictions upon governmental power imposed by the Bill of Rights, the States and the federal government shall be subject to such additional restrictions as are deemed appropriate, from time to time, by a majority of the Judges of the Supreme Court.
>
> To pose that question is to answer it. And if it is absurd as an express provision, why is it not doubly absurd as a supposed *implication* of the provision that "no person shall be deprived of life, liberty, or property, without due process of law?

See Scalia, "Romancing the Constitution," *supra* note 32 at 341.

[53] Sometimes this is given away by advocates for social and economic rights, who speak openly of "transforming" the *Charter*. See *e.g.*, Martha Jackman, "What's Wrong with Social and Economic Rights?" (2000) 11 N.J.C.L. 235 at 246 (footnote omitted):

> In rejecting the call for judicial recognition and enforcement of social and economic rights through *Charter* review, we sanction the continued violation of the rights that are most significant to those who are most in need of rights protection. And we give up a precious opportunity to transform our constitution into a more faithful reflection of the values and aspirations expressed in the *Universal Declaration* – values and aspirations that most Canadians continue to share.

See also, Mackay, "Social and Economic Rights," *supra* note 48 at 411, describing *Gosselin* as "a missed opportunity for the courts to carve out at least a modest role for themselves in alleviating the plight of the poor."

> I do not believe that there is sufficient evidence in this case to support the proposed interpretation of s. 7. I leave open the possibility that a positive obligation to sustain life, liberty, or security of the person may be made out in special circumstances.[54]

The essential premise of the dissenting opinion – the ability of the Court to change the *Charter* by recognizing new rights *deserving* of protection – appears to be shared by the majority. The only difference is one of timing. The *Charter*, according to the majority, does not protect economic and social rights *today*, but it may do so tomorrow. Chief Justice McLachlin is candid in stating that the *Charter* may, one day, *be interpreted to include* positive obligations. Thus, defeat in *Gosselin* may eventually prove to be no more than a temporary setback for those seeking to obtain economic and social rights from the *Charter*.[55]

VIII. CONCLUSION

Why is the Supreme Court of Canada so unwilling to take the idea of natural limits seriously? If the *Charter* does not include a particular right, why not say so? It is not a romantic conception of the *Charter* to acknowledge that it is finite, but it is a realistic one that respects the political settlement that underlies its adoption.

None of this is to say that it is easy to determine the limits of the *Charter*. But consider the alternative to trying. In the absence of accepted criteria informing the decision as to which additional rights the *Charter* protects, a decision that a particular right deserves *Charter* protection may reflect nothing more than the normative preferences of the Court – a preference, say, for the protection of economic and social rights over property rights.

A decision that the *Charter* does not protect a particular right does *not* deny that a strong moral right may exist. It simply recognizes that the *Charter* does not convert all moral rights into legal rights. Like all bills of rights, the *Charter* leaves much to be addressed in the ordinary democratic processes. In short, the finite character of the *Charter* means that, sometimes, the Court must respond to a claim that the *Charter* protects a particular right by stating simply: No, it does not.

[54] *Gosselin, supra* note 50 at paras. 82–3 (emphasis added).
[55] Huscroft, "A Constitutional 'Work in Progress'?" *supra* note 37.

PART FOUR **Challenges and Critiques**

10 That Old-Time Originalism

Steven D. Smith*

Whether courts should interpret constitutional provisions according to their "original meaning" was a live and much-debated question a generation ago and, perhaps surprisingly, it is a live and much-debated question now. But current debates are not just well-worn reruns of the older ones. The conspicuous change is that the subject has become more theoretically sophisticated than it once was. Contemporary discussions increasingly exhibit the influence of philosophy in an analytical vein.

So, has that influence been beneficial? In this essay, I want to question whether it has been. And I want to attempt a modest and tentative defense of the old-fashioned originalism, not so much against its cultured despisers as against its cultured supporters.

I grant from the outset that I may lack standing to offer this defense – doubly so, given that I am neither an originalist nor a philosopher. But I do consider myself an originalist sympathizer – a fellow traveler, perhaps[1] – and I also browse from time to time in philosophical writing. It may be that only someone with these half-credentials would have the ability – or if not the ability, at least the inclination – to attempt a defense of the kind offered here.

I acknowledge as well the imprudence – and perhaps the impudence? – of offering this sort of defense in an academic setting, where it is likely to provoke suspicions of obscurantism, anti-intellectualism, and yokelism. Doubts about

*I thank Larry Alexander, Michael Perry, Sai Prakash, Mike Rappaport, Mike Ramsey, and Maimon Schwarzschild for helpful comments on an earlier draft. Commentary, discussion, and criticism at the colloquium provided plenty of material for further reflection; for present purposes, however, I have left the essay largely in its original form.

[1] Years ago, I described myself as an "originalist wannabe" (Steven D. Smith, "The Writing of the Constitution and the Writing on the Wall," 19 Harv. J.L. Pub. Pol. 391 at 391 (1996)), but I have since drifted, albeit erratically, in a Burkean direction. See Steven D. Smith, "Separation as a Tradition", 18 J. Law & Politics 215 (2002).

philosophical sophistication are likely to have more resonance in the domain of real-world practice where, as Plato noted a long time ago,[2] philosophy gets little enough respect anyway. Still, I happen to find myself in an academic setting, and it is too late in my case, alas, to avoid the previously noted suspicions. And it is even possible – though I make no promises – that the questions raised here may, in an oblique or perverse way, actually contribute something to clarifying our academic understandings. Hence this defense, or half-defense.

I. NOT YOUR DADDY'S ORIGINALISM

When I was a law student, back in the 1970s, the claim that original meaning should govern constitutional interpretation seemed relatively straightforward, and the debate surrounding the claim was largely innocent of fine-grained conceptual distinctions. I was only a student, of course, and not an especially auspicious or diligent one, and my memory may be inaccurate in any case. No doubt there was more sophistication in the discussions than I recall. But my recollection, basically of discussions in and out of class and of assigned readings,[3] was that although there was plenty of disagreement – about whether original meaning was actually ascertainable, about whether courts should follow that meaning even if it was ascertainable, and of course about what the original meaning of particular constitutional provisions (like the free speech clause, or the due process clause) actually was – people did not seem to think that the notion of an original meaning in itself was especially problematic or complicated. Terms like "original meaning," "original understanding," and "framers' intentions" were tossed about pretty much interchangeably.

There was, to be sure, the occasional debate about who "the framers" were. Were they the "drafters" or the "ratifiers"? For provisions in the United States Constitution, for example, should original meaning be determined by what the delegates to the Philadelphia convention intended or by what people in the ratifying conventions had in mind? *That* issue had been flagged years earlier in the important Charles Fairman article about "incorporation."[4] In addition, Ronald Dworkin had already deployed the "concept/conception" distinction to criticize an originalist approach to constitutional law that he attributed to Richard M. Nixon.[5]

[2] Plato, Republic, Bk. VI, 488–500b.

[3] My constitutional law courses (although it would be only a slight exaggeration to say that *all* classes at Yale were constitutional law courses) were taught by a diverse bunch – Bruce Ackerman, Charles Black, and Robert Bork.

[4] Charles Fairman, "Does the Fourteenth Amendment Incorporate the Bill of Rights?" 2 Stan. L. Rev. 5 (1949).

[5] See, *e.g.*, Ronald Dworkin, *Taking Rights Seriously* (1977) at 131–7 [Dworkin, *Taking Rights Seriously*].

Still, with these exceptions, the live issues seemed mostly historical and normative, not theoretical or conceptual. The question of how to aggregate intentions of multiple authors was occasionally noticed, but it did not bring discussions to a standstill. After all, multimember bodies – legislatures, faculties, professional associations, churches – express themselves all the time, don't they?

In the intervening decades, the situation has changed noticeably. Debates over originalism have become less commonsensical, more conceptually formidable. Two developments in particular deserve notice.

First, the central notion of what "original meaning" is has evolved. Some originalist authors divide the progression into three stages.[6] At stage one, they say, original meaning was thought to refer to a particular set of subjective mental states usually described as "framers' intentions." Robert Bork and Raoul Berger are typically viewed as the leading originalists of this stage in the United States. At stage two, represented most prominently by Justice Antonin Scalia, original meaning acquired a more "objective" sense[7]: The term now referred to something like the "public meaning" of a provision. At stage three, original meaning became more idealized: What matters is not what flesh-and-blood members of the public at the time a provision was enacted actually thought it meant, but rather what it *really* meant, so to speak, or what an idealized audience would have understood it to mean. We look for "something a bit more hypothetical," Gary Lawson explains, "such as the understanding that the general public *would have had* if all relevant information and arguments had been brought to its attention."[8]

Not everyone would join in this particular description, of course. If my recollection is correct, at stage one, proponents of original meaning were not so much committed to "framers' intentions" in conscious *opposition to* "public meaning," for example; rather, they simply failed to notice – or declined to acknowledge – any solid distinction between these. This would explain why someone like Robert Bork, a central figure of stage one, could so easily shift from framers' intentions to public meaning once the latter came to be favored.[9]

[6] I follow here the account given in Vasan Kesavan & Michael Stokes Paulsen, "The Interpretive Force of the Constitution's Secret Drafting History," 91 Geo. L.J. 1113 at 1134–48 (2003) [Kesavan and Paulsen, "The Interpretive Force"].

[7] At least proponents of this type of meaning often describe it as "objective": I am not entirely sure why; I would have thought that the "public" consists of persons – surely "subjects," not "objects"– as much as the "convention" or the "legislature" does.

[8] Gary Lawson, "Delegation and Original Meaning," 88 Va. L. Rev. 327 at 341 n. 51 (2002) (emphasis added), quoted with approval in Kesavan & Paulsen, "The Interpretive Force," *supra* note 6 at 1145.

[9] Robert H. Bork, *The Tempting of America: The Political Seduction of the Law* (1990) at 144 [Bork, *The Tempting of America*].

In addition, even today, some originalists – including some prominent and astute ones – continue to defend the subjective or "intentionalist" version against later innovations.[10] In general, though, the three-stage description probably does capture a general shift in the dominant opinion among self-proclaimed originalists.

A second and related change is that originalist theory has grown more theoretical and sophisticated than it once was. A host of distinctions has been infused into the debate. Thus, as noted, theorists now routinely distinguish between "intentionalism" and "textualism"[11] (and among different versions of each),[12] and they also distinguish between descriptive and normative dimensions of originalism,[13] between "interpretation" and "construction,"[14] between "hard" and "soft" originalism,[15] and among "expected applications" versus "semantic meaning"[16] versus "original methods" originalism.[17] These are only some of the most central and frequent variants. Recent work by a proponent like Larry Solum or a critic like Mitch Berman combines[18] to provide a lengthy and dazzling list of conceptual claims, shadings, and distinctions, explicated

[10] See, *e.g.*, Richard S. Kay, "Original Intention and Public Meaning in Constitutional Interpretation," 103 Nw. U.L. Rev. 703 [Kay "Original Intention and Public Meaning"]; Stanley Fish, "Intention is All There Is: A Critical Analysis of Aharon Barak's Purposive Interpretation in Law," 29 Cardozo L. Rev. 1109 (2008) [Fish, "Intention is All There Is"]; Larry Alexander & Saikrishna Prakash, "'Is That English You're Speaking?': Why Intention Free Interpretation is an Impossibility," 41 San Diego L. Rev. 947 (2004) [Alexander and Prakash, "Is That English"]; Paul F. Campos, "Against Constitutional Theory," in Paul F. Campos *et al.*, *Against the Law* (1996) 116 [Campos, *Against the Law*]. The intentionalist version is represented in this volume in the essays of Larry Alexander and Stanley Fish.

[11] See, *e.g.*, Randy E. Barnett, "An Originalism for Nonoriginalists," 45 Loy. L. Rev. 611 at 617–31 (1999).

[12] Compare John F. Manning, "Textualism and Legislative Intent," 91 Va. L. Rev. 347 (2005) with Caleb Nelson, "A Response to Professor Manning," 91 Va. L. Rev. 451 (2005). Manning and Nelson in these articles are mainly concerned with different versions of textualism as applied to *statutory* interpretation.

[13] See, *e.g.*, Lawrence B. Solum, "Semantic Originalism" (November 22, 2008). Illinois Public Law Research Paper No. 07–24. Available at SSRN: http://ssrn.com/abstract=1120244 at 8–9 (distinguishing between "factual" and "moral" originalist claims) [Solum, "Semantic Originalism"].

[14] Keith E. Whittington, *Constitutional Construction* (1999); see also Solum, *ibid.* at 65–86.

[15] Mitchell N. Berman, "Originalism Is Bunk," 84 N.Y.U. L. Rev. 1 at 6 [Berman, "Originalism Is Bunk"].

[16] See Solum, "Semantic Originalism," *supra* note 13 at 20–1; Mark D. Greenberg & Harry Litman, "The Meaning of Original Meaning," 86 Geo. L.J. 569 (1999) [Greenberg & Litman, "The Meaning of Original Meaning"].

[17] John O. McGinnis & Michael B. Rappaport, "Originalism and Supermajoritarianism: Defending the Nexus," 101 Nw. U. L. Rev. 1919 (2007).

[18] See Solum, "Semantic Originalism," *supra* note 13; Berman, "Originalism Is Bunk," *supra* note 15.

by reference to the thought of philosophers including Austin, Grice, Quine, and Wittgenstein.

In short, the subject has become scholasticized. Older originalist heroes like Bork and Scalia, though they still labor beside us, by now are viewed, even by originalists, with a mixture of filial respect and condescending embarrassment.[19] These venerable figures can look like conceptual neophytes, klutzing around among concepts and distinctions that they do not quite grasp.[20]

It is a melancholy spectacle, maybe – like watching Willie Mays falling down in the outfield while playing for the Mets at the end of his glorious career. But that's how life goes: People who were once the main players get older, get out of date, get left behind. If philosophical sophistication serves to clarify the subject, the change has to be regarded as progress – doesn't it? – even if some of the old champions are unable to keep up.

II. THE COSTS OF SOPHISTICATION

Perhaps. But even the sponsors of the new sophistication might admit that the progress has not been cost-free. Two costs in particular deserve notice. We can describe these costs as exclusion and dissolution.[21]

[19] See, *e.g.*, Kesavan & Paulsen, "The Interpretive Force," *supra* note 6 at 1140:

> [E]ven though Justice Scalia remains the dominant figure in the shift to originalist textualism, his is not always the most refined or consistent version of the theory. In some ways, he is a leader whose followers have bettered the leader's own work. Scholars and judges a half-generation younger than Scalia, who are in some respects his heirs, often appear to be employing more thoroughly and carefully honed versions of originalist textualism.

[20] This is the gist, I think, of Ronald Dworkin's critique of Scalia. See Ronald Dworkin, "Comment," in Antonin Scalia, *A Matter of Interpretation*, Amy Gutmann ed., (1997) 115 [Scalia, *A Matter of Interpretation*], though Dworkin employs diplomatic (or perhaps sarcastic) understatement. *Ibid.* at 121 ("You will now understand my concern about Scalia's consistency."). For a less respectful criticism, see Andrew Koppelman, "Phony Originalism and the Establishment Clause," 103 Nw. U.L. Rev. 727. Koppelman contends that Scalia employs a version of originalism that Koppelman derisively calls "I Have No Idea Originalism." And he concludes that "the 'originalism' that one now finds on the Supreme Court is a phony originalism, opportunistically used to advance substantive positions that the judges find congenial. There are originalists who deserve to be taken seriously, but none of them are Supreme Court justices" (at 749). See also Randy E. Barnett, "Scalia's Infidelity: A Critique of "Faint-Hearted" Originalism," 75 U. Cin. L. Rev. 7 at 13 (2006) (arguing that in view of Scalia's widespread departures from a sound originalism, "Scalia is simply not an originalist.") [Barnett, "Scalia's Infidelity"].

[21] These are not the only costs. Another cost, arguably, is fragmentation: Like Christianity following the Protestant Reformation, originalism is divided into camps and can no longer present a

One cost is that as a subject becomes more conceptually complicated, it may also tend to become the exclusive province of a narrower group of people – namely those who are fluent in the concepts, diction, distinctions, discursive moves, sources, and authorities that have come to dominate or define the field. Many lawyers and scholars may lack the ability to master this discourse – *a fortiori* for citizens generally. Or they may simply lack the incentive. The investment required for full participation becomes inflated while the lag lengthens between the expenditure of time and effort and the payment of actual dividends (if there ever are any). Faced with these barriers to entry, potential originalists may simply decide to redirect their resources elsewhere.

Imagine Sally, who initially is vitally interested not in constitutional theory for its own sake, much less in philosophy; her concern – a more practical and urgent one – is whether the Constitution prohibits the death penalty. (Maybe she is defending a client in a homicide case.) To address the question on "originalist" grounds in a fully respectable way, it seems, Sally would need to master a series of abstruse distinctions and work through a variety of questions about what sort of originalism she favors before getting to the substantive issue she actually cares about. She might not manage to complete this obstacle course at all, but might trip over some conceptual hurdle before ever reaching her destination.

For example, after a bit of study and reflection, Sally might be persuaded by some version of "original methods" originalism. We should construe the Eighth Amendment, she comes to conclude, according to the interpretive methods contemplated by the provision's enactors. But what were those methods, exactly? If there is no agreement today about what *our* interpretive methods are (as seems evident in the debates among originalists, and between originalists and non-originalists), how likely is it that, two centuries later, we can figure out what *their* methods were?[22] Would they not have faced many of the same interpretive alternatives and issues we do? Yet if this is the correct method of originalism, it seems we cannot get on to capital punishment until we have resolved it.[23]

united front or position. The problem is presented – reveled in – in Thomas B. Colby & Peter J. Smith, "Living Originalism," 59 Duke L.J. 239 (2009).

[22] See Caleb Nelson, "Originalism and Interpretive Conventions," 70 U. Chi. L. Rev. 519, (2003) (arguing that interpretive methods were not fixed at the time the U.S. Constitution was adopted).

[23] It might be, of course, that the different originalisms will lead to the same conclusion, so that the choice of versions does not make a practical difference. But that possibility seems *prima facie* unlikely: Why would theorists have spent so much effort elaborating on distinctions that make no difference to any actual conclusions? And in any case, there seems no way to know

Foreseeing all of this, Sally could be excused if she simply decided to forego the effort and avoid the predictable futility. Originalism, it seems, is not a venture for the faint of heart or mind.

How serious a disadvantage this exclusion amounts to is no doubt debatable. It might not be a disadvantage at all. On the contrary: Many subjects – law among them, arguably, and *a fortiori* philosophy – might benefit by being restricted to the professionals. (The certified professionals often think so.) In addition, part of the compensation for pursuing the unglamorous and comparatively unlucrative life of the theorist is no doubt the gratifying sense of superiority one gets to enjoy with respect to the non-specialists. *They* may wield more power and get more of the rewards and recognition, the theorists may tell themselves, but *we* at least have the satisfaction of knowing that we are not guilty of the embarrassing conceptual blunders so conspicuous on every page of their work. In an idle moment, an uncharitable observer might wonder whether some such sentiment influences some of the more derisive academic treatments of Justice Scalia's originalism, for example.

However the case may be for law generally, though, or for philosophy, *for originalism* exclusion has to be counted as a cost, I think – and a significant one. After all, originalism is supposed to be an approach that actual lawyers and judges can employ in deciding actual cases. So if the approach becomes so conceptually cumbersome that only a theoretical elite can fully understand and participate in it, then what good is originalism? It would be as if a new Henry Ford were to design the perfect car, except that it is so complicated that only people with advanced degrees in engineering can actually drive it.

In addition, part of the appeal of originalism, I suspect, has always been its inclusively commonsensical quality, in contrast to fancier hermeneutical approaches associated with the likes of Heidegger and Gadamer. Originalism, it seemed, was not heavy or ponderous. It made interpretation seem much like the sort of communication we all engage in routinely. No need to strive for anything so dauntingly ethereal as "self-transcendence" or a "rising to a higher universality" in a "fusion of horizons"[24] : Just do basically the same

in advance that this will be so, and so Sally seemingly would still need to attempt to figure out which version is preferable and what conclusions follow from the different versions.

[24] See Hans-Georg Gadamer, *Truth and Method* (1999 2d rev. trans) 300–7. See, *e.g.*, *ibid.* at 305:

> Transposing ourselves consists neither in the empathy of one individual for another nor in subordinating another person to our own standards; rather, it always involves rising to a higher universality that overcomes not only our own particularity but also that of the other.

thing you do when you talk with a colleague, or shop from a grocery list,[25] or make dinner from an old recipe for fried chicken.[26] Insofar as sophistication despoils originalism of this commonsensical quality, it deprives the approach of a major part of its reason for being.

Which leads to a second and more serious cost of sophistication: The more contemporary versions and discussions threaten to dissolve originalism as a distinctive position by collapsing it into its long-time nemesis, the idea of the "living Constitution" (or, in Canadian jurisprudence, of the constitution as a "living tree"[27]).

The danger is apparent, or already realized, in the work of originalism's most recent high-profile convert (or infiltrator?) – Jack Balkin.[28] Much like Michael Perry's a generation ago,[29] Balkin's acceptance of originalism may seem surprising, given his general tendencies and preferred conclusions: It is almost as if Richard Dawkins were to announce that he has become a creationist and born-again Christian. In this instance, though, it turns out that Balkin sacrifices little or nothing by the conversion; conversely, in gaining Balkin and like-minded thinkers, originalism loses . . . well, its soul.

Originalism has been proposed and defended for various purposes, but these surely have included (a) constraining courts and preventing them from simply reading current fashions into constitutional law, (b) preserving the ability of democratic institutions – of "We the People" – to make meaningful decisions about their constitutions by enacting provisions with relatively definite and fixed meanings, and c) providing a basis for criticizing "activist" decisions of (or in the spirit of) the Warren Court, such as *Griswold v. Connecticut* and *Roe v. Wade*. Balkin explains, however, that the best version of originalism is not the "expected applications" version but rather the "method of text and principle."[30] We must interpret the text according to the "principles" that . . . what is the correct verb here? . . . that "underlie" it,[31] or that it "points to," or "embodies,"[32]

[25] See Paul F. Campos, "A Text is Just a Text," 19 Harv. J.L. & Pub. Pol'y. 327 at 328, 330 (1996).

[26] Gary Lawson, "On Reading Recipes and Constitutions," 15 Geo. L.J. 1823 at 1825–6 (1997).

[27] See W.J Waluchow, "Constitutions as Living Trees: An Idiot Defends," 18 Can. J.L. & Juris. 207 (2005).

[28] See Jack M. Balkin, "Original Meaning and Constitutional Redemption," 24 Const. Comment. 427 (2007) [Balkin,"Constitutional Redemption"]; Jack M. Balkin, "Abortion and Original Meaning," 24 Const. Comment. 291 (2007) [Balkin, "Abortion"].

[29] See Michael J. Perry, "The Legitimacy of Particular Conceptions of Constitutional Interpretation," 77 Va. L. Rev. 669 (1991).

[30] Balkin, "Abortion," *supra* note 28 at 295.

[31] *Ibid.* at 295, 303.

[32] Balkin, "Redemption," *supra* note 28 at 489; Balkin, Abortion, *supra* note 28 at 305.

or "presumes,"[33] or "adopt[s],"[34] or "enacts,"[35] or "endorses,"[36] or "employs,"[37] or is "connected to,"[38] or (here the seemingly staid constitutional text reveals its more erotic aspect) "attempt[s] to embrace."[39] And these principles are sufficiently supple and broad that they can easily accommodate, if not quite *any* conclusion, then just about any conclusion one might want to reach. So it turns out that *Roe* is entirely consistent with originalism:[40] If they had only known, all of the anguish of people like John Ely[41] was wholly unnecessary. *Brown v. Board of Education* (which originalists have generally liked but fretted over[42] and have struggled to try to justify[43]) turns out to be an easy case and textually overdetermined.[44] And the question of whether the heightened legal protection of the Fourteenth Amendment extends to homosexuals is "easy"[45]: Of course it does!

More generally, the distinction between originalist constitutionalism and its traditional nemesis, the "living Constitution," vanishes.[46] Thus, Balkin reassures Mitch Berman that there is no need to import new principles into the Constitution; "if we are willing to view these aspirations with sympathetic eyes, and in a spirit of magnanimity," the original principles are already ample enough to do whatever work we might reasonably expect the Constitution to do.[47]

In the same vein, it seems that there is no reason why Ronald Dworkin, that long-time Beowulf to originalist Grendels like Scalia and Bork (and, earlier, Richard Nixon), should not now be invited to raise a cup in the mead hall of originalists.[48] Indeed, Balkin's deployment of the distinction between "expected applications" originalism and the "text and principle" variety of originalism is little more than a rechristening of the "concept/conception" analysis offered by Dworkin decades ago, and is used to similar effect.[49] But if Balkin can be an originalist by virtue of favoring interpretation based on the "principles" contained in constitutional provisions rather than "expected

[33] Balkin, "Abortion," *supra* note 28 at 304.

[34] Balkin, "Redemption," *supra* note 28 at 452.

[35] *Ibid.* at 497.

[36] Balkin, "Abortion," *supra* note 28 at 303.

[37] Balkin, "Redemption," *supra* note 28 at 449.

[38] Balkin, "Abortion," *supra* note 28 at 305.

[39] *Ibid.* at 304.

[40] See generally *ibid.*

[41] John Hart Ely, "The Wages of Crying Wolf: A Comment on *Roe v. Wade*," 82 Yale L.J. 920 (1973).

[42] See, e.g., Earl M. Maltz, "A Dissenting Opinion to *Brown*," 20 S. Ill. L. J. 93 (1995).

[43] See, e.g., Bork, *The Tempting of America*, *supra* note 9 at 74–83.

[44] Balkin, "Redemption," *supra* note 28 at 451.

[45] *Ibid.* at 494, 501.

[46] Balkin, "Abortion," *supra* note 28 at 291–5; Balkin, "Redemption," *supra* note 28 at 432–6.

[47] Balkin, "Redemption," *supra* note 28 at 500. See generally *ibid.* at 486–503.

[48] Apologies for reversing sides mid-metaphor.

[49] See *supra* note 5.

applications," there is no apparent reason why Dworkin should not be an originalist by virtue of advocating fidelity to the enactors' "concepts" rather than their "conceptions." Jeffrey Goldsworthy thus demonstrates that Dworkin is indeed a species of originalist.[50]

Old-time originalists might naturally be suspicious of the announced conversions of characters like Balkin (and Randy Barnett, and Michael Perry), and they might try to exclude these would-be converts from the fold.[51] Still, Balkin, Barnett, and Perry seem to be sincere in their professions. More importantly, as noted, these new inductees reach their unorthodox or unsettling conclusions mainly by insisting that constitutional provisions be interpreted in accordance with their supposed "principles." But originalists can hardly object to this stance, given that even the purest among them have themselves typically insisted on the same thing, and have freely used the strategy to fend off attacks (such as the "dead hand" objection).[52] So it seems that originalists have little choice but to welcome their erstwhile predators into the flock.

But is this lying down together of lions and lambs a development to be welcomed? Or a disappointment? It is as if after all these many years, someone were to discover that the Yankees and the Red Sox – or Arsenal and Manchester United – have all along in reality been the same team, engaged in staged intrasquad scrimmages, and somehow no one until now had noticed. Who could be happy over that discovery?

To be clear: The loss here is not simply that a cherished rivalry is lost, or that decades of polemics and intense constitutional theorizing come to look like a massive misexpenditure of time and analytical energy. Those are sunk costs, perhaps, which might be well worth paying anyway as the price of hermeneutical harmony. The real harm, however, is that originalism is no longer available as a distinct approach to further (or at least to attempt to further) the worthy purposes, previously noted, for which it was devised – namely constraining courts in history-grounded ways and, even more importantly, serving democracy by enabling democratic institutions to enact constitutional provisions with

[50] See Jeffrey Goldsworthy, "Dworkin as Originalist," 17 Const. Comment. 49 (2000).

[51] In what might seem an audacious show of upstartism, Barnett acts to pre-empt any such measure by excommunicating the patriarch Justice Scalia! See Barnett, "Scalia's Infidelity," *supra* note 20.

[52] See, *e.g.*, Gerard V. Bradley, "Beguiled: Free Exercise Exemptions and the Siren Song of Liberalism," 20 Hofstra L. Rev. 245 at 249–50 (1991) (arguing that "originalism presents no question of rule by the 'dead hand of the past'" because "[o]riginalists properly seek in the historical materials an intelligible principle capable of guiding contemporary decision") [Bradley, "Beguiled: Free Exercise Exemptions"].

relatively definite and fixed meanings. That seems a regrettable loss (even for those who doubt originalism's ability ultimately to provide what it promises).

In short, theoretical sophistication comes with heavy, even exorbitant costs.

And so we are entitled to ask: Is such sophistication a net blessing? Or even if it is not, is it nonetheless an unavoidable evil? Like the genie who has been let out of the bottle, is the theoretical sophistication that has stripped originalism of its innocence a despot (or philosopher-king?) that, once let at large, we have no choice but to submit to?

Near the end of a recent article on "Semantic Originalism" that amounts to a theoretical *tour de force* of the subject, Larry Solum poses this sort of question. Solum imagines a reader of his article who complains about "the colonization of the legal academy by philosophy," and who objects that this colonization makes originalism less accessible to non-philosophers. In response, Solum points out that various legal fields have drawn profitably on other disciplines: Tort theorists who make use of economics are a conspicuous example. Solum then goes on to observe that

> [w]hether a particular set of theoretical tools illuminates rather than obfuscates is not a question that can be settled a priori. The proof is in the pudding. If philosophical tools make significant contributions to constitutional theory, then constitutional theorists must master them.[53]

Solum's observation seems sensible and sound, and it raises important questions that I cannot hope to resolve here. After all, theoretical sophistication in originalism is a relatively recent phenomenon; indeed, some of the most theoretically ambitious work – Solum's own article in particular – has not even been published yet. So the final results are not yet in. In addition, although Solum may be right that "[t]he proof is in the pudding," it is not entirely clear how the pudding is to be tasted, or tested, or what would count as "proof." What if the importation of philosophy makes for a lively set of high-toned discussions among select academics, for example – but also renders originalism less congenial, and more intimidating, to lawyers, judges, and less philosophically disposed academics? Would that result count as proving that philosophy had been helpful or not?

I do not know the answers to such questions. So my goal in what follows is simply to raise doubts that ought to be noticed before we give an affirmative answer (as Solum seems to imply that we should) to the question whether theoretical sophistication is good for originalism.

[53] Solum, *supra* note 13 at 130–1.

III. DARKENING DISTINCTIONS?

Analytical philosophers, as should not be surprising, analyze: They break down positions, claims, arguments into smaller parts and then focus attention on these parts. What was or at least seemed to be one becomes two – or many. *E Unum Pluribus.* (Forgive the bad Latin.) The purpose of this distinguishing project, it seems, is, as Solum says, to "illuminate" – to take what is confused (that is, "fused together") and clarify it by unfusing it into its parts, which can then be examined in their own right.

This process of analysis – of drawing distinctions – surely does often succeed in shedding light on a subject. But it also presents risks. For present purposes, we may distinguish four such risks (though I do not warrant that these are wholly distinct).

One risk is that the articulation of a distinction may lead us to suppose that the distinction describes reality when in fact it may not. The distinction may be a false or at least contestable dichotomy ("Does exempting religious objectors from general laws 'accommodate' religion or 'advance' it?"), as Balkin says the distinction between originalism and "living constitutionalism" is.[54] The terms may in fact be different ways of naming essentially the same thing. ("Look up in the sky: Is that the 'evening star,' or the planet Venus?") Or one term may refer to a subset of what the other term describes. ("Is this figure a circle or a shape?") Or a term may refer to something that does not exist at all in the sense that the term implies. ("Are you talking about two-dimensional or three-dimensional triangles?")

Whether a proffered distinction is deficient in one of these ways, of course, is something that can be ascertained only by examination (and even then only imperfectly and contestably, sometimes). And so the risk may seem to call for *more* philosophy and more analysis, not less. The risk, though, arises out of a common human tendency to suppose that if something can be named, then there must in fact be something that the name is naming.[55] And whether philosophy makes people more or less susceptible to this tendency is . . . well, debatable.[56]

[54] Balkin, "Abortion," *supra* note 28 at 296.

[55] *Cf.* Francis Bacon, "The New Organon," in *The Complete Essays of Francis Bacon* (1963) 179 at 202 (observing that our language contains "names of things which do not exist (for as there are things left unnamed through lack of observation, so likewise are there names which result from fantastic suppositions and *to which nothing in reality corresponds*). . . . ") (emphasis added).

[56] *Cf.* Ludwig Wittgenstein, *Philosophical Investigations* (G.E.M. Anscombe tr., 1958) 47 (109) [Wittgenstein, *Philosophical Investigations*] ("Philosophy is a battle against the bewitchment of our intelligence by means of language.") Wittgenstein's observation is ambiguous, perhaps,

Does this risk present itself in debates about originalism? For now, it is enough to say that it may. For example, at the center of developments in originalist theory is a supposed distinction between "sentence meaning" (or "utterance meaning") and "speaker's meaning" (or "utterer's meaning"). This distinction is well entrenched in contemporary speech act theorizing, it seems, so theorists like Solum confidently import it into discussions of originalism.[57] But it might be, as thinkers like Larry Alexander and Stanley Fish argue,[58] that "sentence meaning" does not actually exist as something independent of speaker's meaning. If they are right, the distinction misleads us, and thus introduces not light but rather darkness at the heart of originalism.

Or someone might go along with the "public meaning" of stage-two originalism but wonder whether the more idealized or hypothetical or almost Platonic meaning of stage three[59] is simply a sort of "transcendental nonsense." In this judgment, the distinction, devised to separate stage two from stage three, in fact leads its proponents to affirm something (like the man "upon the stair" who "wasn't there" in the familiar rhyme) that does not exist.

A second risk is that even if a distinction describes something real, the distinction may not be helpful. We *could* distinguish constitutional provisions containing an odd number of words from provisions with an even number of words. But that distinction would serve no apparent purpose; if it became fashionable, it would operate merely to clutter up our conversations and put a drag on our thinking. I pick for illustration an extreme example, of course, which might provoke the objection that we would never in fact be misled by that sort of pointless distinction anyway. Maybe not. But a distinction may do valuable work in one area or with respect to one set of questions, and so we might mistakenly suppose that the distinction should do valuable work in another area or with respect to a different set of questions. The distinction might thus become merely an obstacle and a distraction.

Does this sort of thing happen in discussions of originalism? Again, I will only say that it may. My own suspicion, for example, is that even if there is a viable distinction for some purposes between "sentence meaning" and

but he seems to have believed that the "bewitchment" occurred – and hence needed to be battled – *in* philosophy as much as outside and *by* it. See, *e.g.*, *ibid.* at 24 (49) ("Here we might say – though this easily leads to all kinds of philosophical superstition . . . ").

[57] Solum, "Semantic Originalism," *supra* note 13 at Part III.C. See also Lawrence B. Solum, "Constitutional Texting," 44 U. San Diego L. Rev. 123 (2007).

[58] See Larry Alexander, "Simple-Minded Originalism," and Stanley Fish, "The Intentionalist Thesis Once More," in this volume.

[59] See *supra* note 8 and accompanying text.

"speaker's meaning,"[60] and thus between "textualism" and "intentionalism," this distinction will have little practical significance in the interpretation of legal texts. "The public" presumably will interpret a legal text by trying to figure out what its authors intended; conversely, the enactors of a legal provision will want to communicate as clearly as they can, and so they will do their best to conform to the linguistic conventions used by the relevant public. (To be sure, legislators may sometimes choose to be deliberately ambiguous or vague, but they will communicate their favored ambiguity or vagueness as precisely as possible; they will want the courts and the public to have the blessing and burden of *their* preferred ambiguity, not somebody else's ambiguity.) And so intended and conventional (or perceived, or public) meanings will, in practice, tend to converge.[61]

If this is right, then the long-standing controversy between intentionalism and textualism has been much ado about . . . not *nothing*, exactly, but about very little of practical consequence. Meanwhile, that debate has served as a cover for the largely unexamined and unreflective importation into interpretation of an elephant – or maybe a cobra – named "principle." It is, after all, the pervasive assumption that the purpose of interpretation is to find and apply the "principle" within a constitutional provision that threatens to collapse the distinction between originalism and "living constitutionalism." But what a "principle" even is remains, to my mind anyway, utterly obscure.[62]

Are we to understand "principles" in a merely formal way? A principle, perhaps, is a proposition that is general in form – a proposition that indicates the correct results in a range of cases? If so, then it is hard to imagine the judicial decision that would *not* be "principled." Judges virtually always give some sort of reason for their decisions – where is the judge who says "Plaintiff wins . . . for no reason at all," or "because I said so"? – and those reasons will almost inevitably have some extension beyond the particular case. It would seem to follow as well that any constitutional provision will be susceptible, like the Gadarene demoniac, of being the host not to *a* principle, but to a legion

[60] I discuss the question in Steven D. Smith, *Law's Quandary* (2004) at 115–18 [Smith, *Law's Quandary*].

[61] The argument is a bit more developed in *ibid.* at 144–5. See also Greenberg & Litman, "The Meaning of Original Meaning," *supra* note 16 at 583 ("The choice between original intent and original meaning is relevant only in cases in which the private intentions of the legislature diverge from the publicly understood meaning of the legislative text. Since words are generally chosen in order to implement legislative intent, intent and meaning largely overlap . . . ").

[62] I attempted to consider what seemed to me the mysteries of the nature of "principles," discussing what I thought of as "formalist," "conventionalist," and "realist" accounts, in Steven D. Smith, "Idolatry in Constitutional Interpretation," in Campos, *Against the Law*, *supra* note 10, 157 at 180–6.

of principles. On this view, the demand for "principle" – in adjudication, in constitutional interpretation – comes to look so lenient as to be next to useless. It is as if someone were to insist gravely that legal reasoning is illegitimate unless conducted in *words*. Well, okay. . . .

So perhaps we need to impose some *substantive* or *content-based* restrictions – not merely restrictions of *form* – on what can count as a "principle"? Even though general in form, reasons or propositions cannot qualify as "principles," perhaps, unless they can satisfy a set of eligibility requirements, or maybe unless they can be found on some approved inventory of certified principles. So maybe one interpreter proposes to interpret a constitutional provision as implementing – or "adopting," or "embracing"– a "utility maximization" principle, whereas another interpreter proposes an "antisubordination principle." We run through the inventory, perhaps, and then tell the first interpreter, "Your proposition isn't on the list. It's not a 'principle.' We're very sorry. Go away." But finding the second interpreter's proposition ("Ah, here it is – half an inch down in the 'equal dignity' section"), we smile and say, "You may enter."

But then where does this inventory come from? What supplies its substance? Social conventions? Objective moral reality? What sort of moral reality?[63]

And is there even any reason to suppose that "principles" are necessarily benevolent or admirable? How can we be sure that the world of principles is not more dualistically Manichean in nature? There are dark princes, after all, so why can there not be dark principles? (The "hierarchy principle," maybe? Or the "patriarchy principle"?) Is there any reason to assume that a constitution (which, after all, may have been drafted and adopted, as its critics so often remind us, by a white, male, partly slave-holding aristocracy) might not contain such malign principles? And if so, what is a court's professional obligation with respect to provisions containing such principles?

It would seem that these matters lie at the heart of any "principle"-oriented originalism – which is to say of most forms of originalism that claim respectable defenders.[64] Yet theorists like Balkin occupy themselves – and their

[63] For discussion of the difficulties with each type of answer, see *ibid*. For further critical discussion, see Larry Alexander & Ken Kress, "Against Legal Principles," 82 Iowa L. Rev. 739 (1997).

[64] This fondness of originalists for "principles" may owe something to the approach's modern origins. An early modern champion of originalism, Robert Bork, presented the position as an extension of Herbert Wechsler's argument that legitimate constitutional adjudication needs to be based on "neutral principles." Herbert Wechsler, "Toward Neutral Principles of Constitutional Law," 73 Harv. L. Rev. 1 (1959). Wechsler was right, Bork argued, but he did not go far enough: The principles need to be not only neutrally applied but neutrally derived; Robert H. Bork, "Neutral Principles and Some First Amendment Problems," 47 Ind. L.J. 1 at 7–8 (1971),

readers – making nice distinctions among kinds of meaning, and between "meanings" and "applications," while evidently feeling at liberty merrily to advocate an originalism of "text and principle" without ever pausing to clarify just what sort of thing a "principle" is.[65]

My worries about these risks – namely of false or illusory dichotomies, and of unhelpful and distracting distinctions – may seem to call not for *less* philosophy, but rather for *more*. And perhaps this is ultimately the right conclusion. (Though the conclusion may implicitly pre-suppose some substantial likelihood that more philosophy will actually succeed in allaying such risks – a supposition that is far from being self-evident). The third and fourth risks that I want to notice are closely related – or maybe just different descriptions of the same risk: I'm not sure – and they reflect a more deep-seated suspicion of the contribution that philosophy in an analytical vein can make to a human enterprise like law.

It may be that the world, or some things in the world, and especially things associated with human beings, though in a sense composed of distinguishable parts, are inherently relational in character. Husband and wife. Parent and child. Mind and body. Form and substance. And a possible risk is that the method of analysis and distinction, by insisting on breaking matters into their component parts and then examining those parts, may work to distract us from perceiving and adequately understanding the inherently relational reality. The distinctions seem real – *are* real, maybe, in some sense – but by treating the terms as referring to separate and separately examinable items, we may render ourselves unable to perceive the true character of the thing, which is constituted by the components-in-relation. So we try to talk about the nature of "uncles" without confusing our reflections with references to "nieces and nephews." Or we get a town like Lake Wobegone in which *all* of the children are "above average."

Here is what may be a slightly different risk, though it is hard for me to articulate clearly. The risk is that philosophical analysis will fail to appreciate, and may even undermine, the puzzling capacity of humans *in practice* to embrace and live with both sides of an antinomy,[66] or at least with what seem on an intellectual level to be divergent or incompatible positions or perspectives.

and this came to mean something like "derived from the original meaning of a constitutional provision." Hence, in Bork's work, the assumption that originalism seeks to find "principles" is pervasive. See, *e.g.*, Bork, *The Tempting of America*, *supra* note 9 at 143–60. Other originalists, it seems, have for the most part cheerfully accepted this assumption.

[65] Larry Solum does consider this question briefly, though not in these terms, when he discusses whether it would matter to constitutional interpretation if we believe in "moral kinds" analogous to "natural kinds" such as gold. Solum, "Semantic Originalism," *supra* note 13 at 82.

[66] The point has been suggested to me by Larry Alexander, who nonetheless should be exonerated from all responsibility for the confused and no doubt misguided way in which I present it here.

Are we free or causally determined? Is morality consequentialist in nature or deontological? Such antinomies abound in law. Should criminal law be animated by consequentialist concerns of deterrence or by more deontological concerns of retribution? Should tort law be governed by considerations of economic efficiency or corrective justice? Should public law be understood and promoted by individualist or communitarian commitments?

When considered on a theoretical level, such questions may present what appear to our finite and language-limited minds to be radically dissimilar or even incompatible alternatives. And yet it seems that in practice, and particularly in the practice of law, humans manage to embrace such incompatible alternatives in ways that arguably are more productive and beneficial than the single-minded commitment to either alternative would be. Retribution *and* deterrence (in some inarticulable but somehow sensible mix). Personal accountability (presupposing free will) *together with* excuses (some of them seemingly grounded in more deterministically causal assumptions). The practice may accordingly appear to the theoretical eye to be deeply confused. And perhaps it *is* confused (fused together) – and the better for it.

Are these risks – of distorting or debilitating distinctions – realized in the more sophisticated versions of originalism? Once again, for present purposes, I will limit myself to saying that they might be. Take for example the familiar distinction between "meaning" and "expected application." "Expected application," it is said, may be relevant *in an evidentiary way* to "semantic meaning," but the two things are distinct and should not be conflated.[67] A jurist like Scalia is said to be confused because he does not grasp the distinction, or does not adhere to it consistently.[68] Theorists do a great deal of work with this supposed distinction: They argue for preferred conclusions on particular constitutional questions (like capital punishment or abortion), and they defend originalism against "dead hand" objections.[69] They may also use the distinction to dissolve the differences between originalism and what were thought to be competing approaches.[70] This looming dissolution, however, might at least prompt us to ask whether something has gone wrong.

So let us ask (and we can ask the question either about the mental states of enactors or about something like public understanding): Is it actually true that "meaning" is independent of "expected applications"? At least on first

[67] See Larry Solum's contribution to this volume, ""What Is Originalism? The Evolution of Contemporary Originalist Theory," and Solum, "Semantic Originalism," *supra* note 13 at 20; Balkin, "Abortion," *supra* note 28 at 303.

[68] See, *e.g.*, Dworkin, Comment, *supra* note 20 at 119–22.

[69] See, *e.g.*, Bradley, "Beguiled: Free Exercise Exemptions," *supra* note 52; Greenberg & Litman, "The Meaning of Original Meaning," *supra* note 16.

[70] See, *e.g.*, Balkin, "Abortion," *supra* note 28 at 291–6.

inspection, the distinction *seems* plausible. We can imagine legislators agreeing, for example, on a provision prohibiting "invidious discrimination," say, but differing about whether the prohibition forbids distinctions based on sex or sexual orientation. In such an instance, we might say, "They agree on the *meaning* but disagree on the *application*."

But is this an accurate or perspicuous description of the situation? It is a hard question, I think. But at least one possible response, I suspect, would contend that even if "meaning" and "application" are conceptually or at least verbally distinguishable, in reality the two are so inherently connected that you simply cannot understand what goes on in an enactor's mind (and even less so in something like the "public understanding") if you pull the two apart and treat one simply as "evidence" of the other. Enactors, it might be argued, do not have mental states made up of propositions like "This provision *means* X; and I expect that it will be *applied* to do A, B, and C." In their minds, rather (or in the understanding of the public that contemplates the provision), these things are all bound up together: Meaning and application are not identical, exactly, and yet they are inextricably co-mingled (perhaps along with other things, like relevant "principles," and also hopes and fears and predictions, and also connotations and vague associations, and so on). Expected applications are not *evidence* of a provision's meaning, perhaps, as much as they are *ingredients* of that amalgamation.

If this is right, then insisting on a distinction between "semantic meaning" and "expected applications" may serve not so much to clarify as to distort our understanding of the real-world situation. It distorts understanding by being at the same time *too refined* (because, as noted, "meaning" and "expected applications" are not in reality neatly distinguishable) and *not refined enough* (because if we really wanted a complete description of the ingredients of meaning, or of the dimensions of our mental states that are relevant to "meaning," we would need to add a lot more terms and concepts than these). And so someone like Justice Scalia, who can take this conceptual train for short commutes but does not commit himself to the full ride, might in fact have a more usefully realistic grasp of what happens in the world – in the minds of legislators and citizens, and in language as it is actually used – than do the theorists who criticize him for failing to consistently honor such distinctions.

Similar questions may be asked about the common distinction between descriptive and normative claims of originalism. Once again, on first inspection, the distinction seems solid enough. What a provision *means* presents one question; whether we should *follow it*, or treat it as *obligating* us, presents another. Right? Indeed, how can we decide whether we ought to follow the provision unless we first know what it means? And surely we could say of a constitutional provision – one protecting the "right to bear arms," say – that "the provision may have *meant* that government could not restrict citizens from possessing firearms, but given current realities we would be wiser *to disregard* that provision." Arguably, this is exactly what *has* happened with provisions like the "no impairment of contracts" clause in the United States Constitution.

Still, it is worth noting that discussions of originalism once did not, and perhaps still typically do not, notice or make much of this distinction. And it would seem odd and perhaps impudent for a judge, say, to separate the question of "what the constitution means" from the question of whether to follow that meaning. So, are these interpreters just being careless, or innocent, or worse? Or, conversely, might their apparent fusion of the "fact" of meaning and the "moral" issue of authority or obligation reflect a wisdom, or at least a permissible point of view, that the descriptive/normative distinguishers overlook?

To my mind, there is no obviously correct answer to that question. But it seems at least plausible to think that *in this context*, a distinction between the meaning of a text and its authority is artificial. After all, at least when we are acting as lawyers or judges, we typically read the Constitution not out of idle historical curiosity in the way we might read some newly discovered letter or pamphlet from the founding period. Rather, we read it *as law*. We read it because it is authoritative – and hence we read it *as* authoritative. Consequently, if there are different ways of reading or extracting meaning from the text (as even originalists acknowledge that there are[71]), and if some of those meanings are consistent with regarding the text as authoritative whereas

[71] As noted, originalists commonly distinguish, even within the general camp of "originalist" approaches, between interpretive approaches that focus on "framers' intentions" and others that focus on textual or "public meaning." They may also recognize the need to make choices about, for example, whether to allow resort to legislative history, or whether and how to make use of canons of construction. While arguing for an "authors' intention" account of meaning, for example, Larry Alexander and Sai Prakash acknowledge (although they criticize) the possibility of restricting evidence of that intention or of "idealizing" the author in various ways that might alter conclusions about meaning. Alexander and Prakash, "Is That English," *supra* note 10 at 982–9. Even though any individual originalist may believe that particular answers to such questions are more defensible or coherent than others, the acknowledgment of alternatives implicitly concedes that there is more than one way to extract meaning from a text and hence, at least in an important practical sense, more than one possible "meaning."

To be sure, the originalist might insist that only one of these is actually *the meaning* of the text and that the others are phonies or counterfeits. There seems little to be gained, however, by insisting on this semantic point. Indeed, the originalist who presses this point risks falling into self-contradiction, because it seems clear that the term "meaning" *is* used, conventionally and by many speakers, to include more than any one narrowly defined candidate. See, *e.g.*, Berman, "Originalism Is Bunk," *supra* note 15 (arguing for pluralism in meaning).

other meanings are not, then it seems that we might opt for the meanings that support or square with authority. And so the descriptive question of *what the provision means* and the normative question of *whether it obligates* us would not be neatly severable, and insisting on separating them would only distort the nature of what actually happens when we engage in constitutional interpretation.[72]

IV. JUST SAY "NO"– OR IS IT "YES"?

Larry Solum is still right: Whether philosophical sophistication will do more to illuminate or obfuscate the issues associated with originalism cannot be determined *a priori*. The proof *is* in the pudding.[73] And at this point, it is not entirely clear (to me, anyway) what sort of proof the pudding gives us.

More specifically, it seems to me contestable whether greater theoretical sophistication has improved originalism or impaired it. Quite likely some of both. But the threat that sophistication will have the result of dissolving originalism as a distinct position should at least give originalists pause before they rush blissfully down the primrose path of theoretical sophistication.

In the end, my own conclusions are tentative, modest, and, I hope, tolerant. Philosophers will no doubt continue to do what they do. They will make distinctions. Some of these distinctions will be helpful, sometimes, for some purposes. On the other hand, it is not clear that philosophers at this point have good grounds to demand that others imitate their methods or adopt their distinctions, or to convert the conditional in Solum's prescription ("*If* philosophical tools make significant contributions to constitutional theory, then constitutional theorists *must* master them"[74]) to an unqualified imperative. It is at least a defensible judgment, for now, that the array of terms and distinctions that have recently entered into discussions of originalism have neither strengthened the position nor produced a net gain in illumination.

My own view, for what it is worth, is something of a hybrid. Legal interpreters are looking for semantic meanings, I think, and semantic meanings are always the meanings intended by authors. It makes no sense to talk about semantic intentions except with reference to an author. Up to this point, I agree with Alexander, Prakash, Fish, Campos, and Kay (*supra* note 10). However, we can and often do interpret texts to ascertain the semantic intentions not of the flesh-and-blood historical authors, but rather of constructed or hypothetical authors. This method is problematic, to be sure (see Alexander & Prakash, "Is That English," *supra* note 10 at 988–9), but it is *possible* – and it is practiced. So in a sense, we have power to choose which authors to look to. And this choice might be described as a sort of choice among "meanings." For the more elaborate explanation, see Smith, *Law's Quandary, supra* note 60, chs. 5 and 6.

72 For a critical exploration of these issues, see Adam Samaha, "Dead Hand Arguments and Constitutional Interpretation," 108 Colum. L. Rev. 606 (2008).

73 See *supra* note 53 and accompanying text.

74 Solum, "Semantic Originalism," *supra* note 13 at 130 (emphasis added).

And so what should we do when confronted with the philosophical originalist's (or antioriginalist's[75]) questions? What should Sally say when, just as she is about to make an argument about the original meaning of the cruel and unusual punishment clause, the theoretical inquisitor interrupts to demand that she clarify her position by confessing what denomination of originalism she professes? Is she a "textualist" or an "intentionalist"? Does she hold to the "text and principle" kind of originalism, or the "expected applications" kind, or the "original methods" kind? Is she a "hard" or "soft" originalist, or something in between?

Sally *might* find these questions intriguing, and so she might try to answer them, or at least to enter into discussion with the theorist. But I also think that Sally has every right, at least for now, when confronted with the theorist's list of alternatives and distinctions, simply to say, "Yes. Those." Or to just say no – as Wittgenstein put it, to "reject the question."[76] Or to declare, without embarrassment: "That old-time originalism . . . it's good enough for me."

V. POSTSCRIPT: IS PHILOSOPHY INEVITABLE?

And yet. It is not clear whether Sally *can* actually reject the question, or whether she can adhere to this innocent version of originalism. Suppose she concludes that capital punishment violates the original meaning of the cruel and unusual punishment clause. Critics will point out that the enactors of that provision quite obviously drew a different conclusion. In responding to these critics, won't Sally necessarily have to say that what matters is not the specific conclusions that the enactors drew – their "expected applications," if you like – but rather something more like . . . well, maybe, the "principle" that they adopted? Or just the "meaning"? Meaning . . . what?

Or maybe Sally concludes, with Justice Scalia,[77] that given the clear evidence that the framers (as well as the "public" of the founding generation) thought capital punishment was permissible, we simply cannot now reach the opposite conclusion on the basis of original meaning. But then she will have to answer the Dworkins and Balkins and Perrys and Greenbergs who argue that these specific expectations are not decisive. She may also have to explain why the framers' (or the founding generation's) specific expectations are determinative with respect to the death penalty but not with respect to other punishments that they also did not intend to prohibit – cropping of ears, perhaps.

[75] Berman, "Originalism Is Bunk," *supra* note 15.
[76] Wittgenstein, *Philosophical Investigations*, *supra* note 56 at 23 (47).
[77] Scalia, *A Matter of Principle*, *supra* note 20 at 145–6.

Either way, as soon as Sally gives these explanations, won't she already have seated herself on philosophy's conceptual toboggan and begun descending the conceptual hill? And once she has started down that treacherous slope, it seems, there is no natural stopping point before the bottom (if there is a bottom).

It may seem that Sally's plight – and that of "old-time originalism" – is very much like that of the old-time religious believers who, distressed by all of the wrangling and theological complexities produced by the fragmentation of Christendom, determined to shun denominational distinctions and to call themselves simply "Christians."[78] It is easy to appreciate their motivation. But then a particular issue would arise. A baby is born: Should she be baptized or left to decide for herself upon reaching adulthood? And when a person *is* baptized, must it be by immersion? Or a loved one dies – a wayward believer, maybe, or a virtuous nonbeliever – and someone asks, "Has he gone to hell? To heaven? To purgatory?" Even to answer that we cannot know is to say *something* about a theological issue: It is to reject those positions that insist that we *can* and do know.

In short, once theological controversy has arisen, it is hard for anyone affected to remain innocent of it. And so a leading historian observes that "[i]nstead of calming sectarian strife and restoring edenic harmony, the Christians engendered controversy at every step and had to put up with chronic factionalism within their own ranks."[79]

Still, it would plainly be a mistake – wouldn't it? – to go to the other pole and conclude that because a religious believer cannot evade theological issues, every believer accordingly must master the discourse of theology. That conclusion would clearly misdescribe reality, and it also puts before us a less-than-happy picture. Even among the devout, who really wants a world crawling with theologians?

The working reality seems to be that even if believers are constantly acting on some sort of implicit theology, most of the time the theology can slumber peacefully beneath the surface; and when an issue does occasionally force itself on people's notice, they will borrow or spontaneously construct the theological tools needed to address the issue and then, having resolved or at least deflected it, will revert back to their theologically untroubled existence. Meanwhile, the theologians will carry on their own lofty conversations, ensconced away in their divinity schools. These conversations will occasionally have some value for the practicing believers. More often they will not.

[78] Nathan O. Hatch, *The Democratization of American Christianity* (1989) at 69–81.
[79] *Ibid.* at 80.

The same is true, arguably, of philosophy. We all – originalists included – have our implicit philosophies, no doubt, but for the most part we manage to live and even flourish without giving them much notice. We *could* perhaps try to make all of our philosophical assumptions and commitments explicit and to confront them self-consciously. But we would not succeed in this effort, and in any case, it is not clear that we would do better by confronting matters explicitly than we do by leaving them implicit: It is not obvious that philosophers as a class live more virtuous, or happy, or truthful, or even coherent lives than ordinary mortals do.

Even so, occasionally an issue will arise, calling for more direct confrontation with philosophical concepts and distinctions. If the philosophers can help us in these situations, we should be humbly grateful to them. Meanwhile, and most of the time, we manage to live – and to argue about law, including the "original meaning" of particular laws – without mastering the discourse of philosophy. In this way, there can be commerce between law and philosophy without, as Solum puts it, "colonization."

11 Reflective Equilibrium and Constitutional Method: Lessons from John McCain and the Natural-Born Citizenship Clause

Mitchell N. Berman*

INTRODUCTION

Partisans to the debate over originalism press their respective positions on diverse grounds. Originalists variously argue, for example, that fidelity to the original meaning of the constitutional text (or to certain intentions of framers or ratifiers) is demanded by proper respect for the rule of law, or follows from the correct understanding of the nature and objective of interpretation generally, or best promotes values like stability, predictability, and democratic accountability. Their opponents challenge these claims and argue further that a commitment to originalism is unworkable, produces bad or unjust results, or furnishes insidious cover for the naked policy choices of its proponents.

Yet as varied as these (and other) argumentative strategies are, they do not exhaust the set of plausible ways to argue for or against a theory of constitutional interpretation. In particular, it might be possible to argue productively about candidate theories of constitutional interpretation by assigning a more prominent role than is customary to purportedly shared convictions about the proper legal resolution of particular cases. In this essay, I aim to explore that possibility by adapting the Rawlsian method of reflective equilibrium to the constitutional domain and by focusing, as a case study, on the specific question of whether Senator John McCain is constitutionally eligible to serve as president of the United States, consistent with the natural-born citizenship clause of the United States Constitution, which provides that "[n]o person except a natural born Citizen . . . shall be eligible to the Office of President."[1]

*For very helpful comments on an earlier draft, I am indebted to Mike Dorf, Mark Greenberg, Kevin Toh, and participants at a constitutional theory workshop at Vanderbilt Law School. I am also grateful to Guha Krishnamurthi and Casey Duncan for excellent research assistance, and to Grant Huscroft for inviting me to contribute to this volume.

[1] U.S Const. Art. II, Sec. 1, cl. 5.

Very generally, the idea is this. The method of reflective equilibrium maintains that our beliefs in a range of domains will be better justified if we seek coherence among different sorts of considered judgments, or considered judgments about different sorts of claims or propositions. In ethics, for example, the method instructs that we should work back and forth among our considered judgments about the rightness or wrongness of particular actions in particular contexts, the general articulable principles that govern our conduct, and the yet more abstract theoretical considerations that shape or determine the principles. Crucially, none of these different types of judgments is uniquely epistemically privileged; in principle, all judgments are revisable in light of all others. If this model applies to the constitutional domain, then the direction of argument between constitutional theory and constitutional case holdings ought not to be wholly unidirectional. While the correct outcomes in constitutional cases will often simply follow from application of the correct constitutional theory, the constitutional theory we deploy should itself be answerable to whatever strong considered judgments we may have about the correct outcomes in particular cases – judgments about their *legal* correctness, mind you, not (merely) of their *moral* correctness.

Now, the ambition to use strong intuitions or convictions about particular cases to drive (necessarily provisional and rebuttable) conclusions about how to interpret the Constitution might seem circular on the supposition that those case-specific convictions themselves will be informed or infected by our interpretive theories. Put more strongly, we might expect our legal judgments about cases to be the products, not the grounds, of our constitutional theories. The possibility I am raising is that this need not always be true. And it is not true, I will suggest, with respect to the question of McCain's eligibility for the presidency.[2]

Assuming (as was generally accepted prior to provocative recent work by Jack Chin)[3] that McCain, who was born in the Panama Canal Zone, was a citizen at birth by virtue of his being born to citizen parents but not by virtue of being born in the United States, his eligibility for the presidency would seem to

[2] I am not the first to think that the McCain case can generate lessons about constitutional method well beyond its narrow context. A brief but insightful analysis of the way that the case reinforces the significance of extrajudicial constitutional interpretation is Peter J. Spiro, Commentary, "McCain's Citizenship and Constitutional Method," 107 Mich. L. Rev. First Impressions 42, online: http://michiganlawreview.org/firstimpressions/vol107/spiro.pdf (2008) [Spiro, "McCain's Citizenship"].

[3] Gabriel J. Chin, Commentary, "Why Senator John McCain Cannot Be President: Eleven Months and a Hundred Yards Short of Citizenship," 107 Mich. L. Rev. First Impressions 1 (2008), http://michiganlawreview.org/firstimpressions/vol107/chin.pdf [Chin, "Why Senator John McCain Cannot Be President"].

depend on the legal question of whether the constitutional term "natural born Citizen" is limited to that subclass of birthright citizens who were born in the territorial United States. I argue that an overwhelming majority of participants in legal practice have the strong conviction that McCain is eligible – which is to say that the clause is not so limited – that there are grounds for this conviction, and that those grounds are not contingent on beliefs about the historical facts of what the phrase "natural born Citizen" meant in 1787 or what the framers or ratifiers intended it to mean or to accomplish. The depth, breadth, and character of this case-specific conviction are thus inconsistent with a commitment to originalism as a constitutional theory. Admittedly, I do not expect my argument to carry much weight with committed originalists: Whatever limited ability work in constitutional theory ever has to change minds, coherentist arguments of the sort presented here might be of a character especially unlikely to sway the faithful. I am principally addressing myself, then, to the agnostic or the uncommitted. Even with them, however, I do not pretend that my argument will amount to a decisive refutation of originalism. (Such a contention would be incompatible with the very method of reflective equilibrium I invoke.) Quite the contrary, I view it more as piling on. It bolsters additional reasons to conclude that, although the original public meaning of the constitutional text and the original semantic intentions of its authors are relevant, they do not constitute the sole touchstones of correct constitutional interpretation, as originalism claims.

* * *

The chapter proceeds in six parts. Part I starts by defining originalism, for if we are to intelligently assess this theory, we need to be clear on just what it maintains. Part II presents a brief typology of principal existing arguments for originalism. It also argues that the dominant contemporary form of originalism is better understood as a metaphysical or conceptual theory of a constitution's contribution to the content of the law, and not as a normative theory of what judges should do. Part III introduces reflective equilibrium as a distinct method for reasoning about theories of the relationship between legal texts and legal content or law. Part IV employs the method in the particular context of addressing the case-specific question of whether McCain is a natural-born citizen within the meaning of the Constitution. As already explained, I will contend that analysis of this question causes trouble for originalism.

Parts V and VI introduce and respond to challenges to the argument of the preceding parts. Part V focuses attention on two other cases based on the Natural Born Citizenship clause – the case of a naturalized foreign-born citizen like Arnold Schwarzenegger or Jennifer Granholm; and the case of a native-born citizen delivered by Caesarian section, like Warren Harding. The cases are presented to suggest that the non-originalist arguments that appear to be doing work in Part IV commit us to conclusions in one or both of these adjacent cases that fly in the face of our considered case-specific convictions. And if this is true, then we have reason to doubt either that reflective equilibrium can be transplanted to the constitutional realm in the manner that Part IV assumes or that the specific arguments advanced in that part are sound. I propose, however, that, rather than undermining the analysis of Part IV, the cases explored in Part V provide helpful further basis for believing what most of us already grasp: An attractive and defensible theory of constitutional interpretation is likely to be more complex than snappy slogans or pithy labels can capture. Part VI is a more direct reply to one of my critics.

I. WHAT ORIGINALISM IS – A FIRST PASS

Let us start by getting clear on just what originalism is – what is the proposition that originalists and their opponents debate. We can subdivide this single question into two components: What sort of thesis is originalism (or what is its subject matter), and what is its content?[4]

Originalism is customarily understood to be a normative thesis about how some participants in American constitutional practice – judges, crucially, but possibly other persons as well – ought to behave, or about what they ought to do. Originalists commonly formulate their thesis in deontic terms, most frequently asserting what judges should, ought, or must do, or what they are required or bound or obligated to do. And what judges are required or obligated to do, according to originalism, is to interpret the Constitution in accordance with some specified aspect or feature of its original character – usually its original "public meaning" or the meaning originally intended by its framers or ratifiers – at least unless a decision by the United States Supreme Court has advanced a contrary interpretation and there exist sufficient reasons to abide by that judicial precedent. In other words, and putting aside for the moment the special problem of continued adherence to non-originalist judicial precedent, judges should interpret the Constitution *solely* in accordance with some feature of the original character of the constitutional provision at issue.

In the next section, I will highlight a critical but widely unappreciated ambiguity at the heart of contemporary originalism. Here, I wish only to

[4] Much of the analysis in this Part is drawn from Mitchell N. Berman, "Originalism Is Bunk," 84 N.Y.U. L. Rev. 1, 1–37 (2009) [Berman, "Originalism Is Bunk"].

emphasize three features of this initial and orthodox statement of the originalist thesis.

First, the thesis is very demanding. As it functions in contemporary debates over constitutional interpretation, originalism is not the weaker thesis that, for example, judges ought to pay serious attention to the original meaning or that they ought ordinarily to follow the original meaning. This point cannot be emphasized strongly enough. Virtually nobody denies that the original meaning of a constitutional provision is always relevant to the interpretive task, and few theorists deny that it is frequently a weighty consideration. What makes originalism so controversial is precisely the position it takes on what I have called in other work the dimension of interpretive *strength*. Non-originalists do not deny that the original meaning constitutes a reason, possibly even a weighty reason, in favor of a given contemporary constitutional interpretation; they only deny the originalist contention that original meaning (or the like) is a conclusive or exclusive reason to adopt a particular interpretation.[5]

Second, I am assuming that the question of what originalism is is an empirical one. I am not trying to smuggle in my own views about how originalism should be conceived to render it most plausible or attractive, but nor am I trying to make it more demanding than its champions espouse, thus to render it more vulnerable to attack. I maintain that this is how it is most often understood in the contemporary constitutional theory literature, by its proponents and opponents alike. As two prominent originalists have recently and succinctly put it, originalism "requires that judges interpret the document based only on its original meaning."[6] To be sure, I do not insist that all self-described

[5] It is true that several scholars have claimed over the years that "we are all originalists now." I believe that most scholars who advance this claim are non-originalists – they believe that the original meaning does not always decisively determine the content of constitutional law, even absent controlling non-originalist judicial precedent – and they fail to appreciate the extent to which self-described originalists maintain the more demanding thesis. *See ibid.* at 29 n.72.

[6] John O. McGinnis & Michael Rappaport, "Original Interpretive Principles as the Core of Originalism," 24 Const. Comment. 371 at 374 (2007). For just a tiny sample of similar characterizations by other originalists, see Randy E. Barnett, *Restoring the Lost Constitution* (2004) at 4 ("[B]y committing ourselves to a written constitution, we commit ourselves to adhere to the original meaning of the text and any later amendments."); Steven G. Calabresi & Saikrishna B. Prakash, "The President's Power to Execute the Laws," 104 Yale L.J. 541 at 551–2 (1994) ("[T]he text of the Constitution, as originally understood by the people who ratified it, is the fundamental law of the land. . . . The meaning of all . . . legal writings depends on their texts, as they were objectively understood by the people who enacted or ratified them. Originalists do not give priority to the plain dictionary meaning of the Constitution's text because they like grammar more than history. They give priority to it because they believe that it and it alone is law.") (footnotes omitted); Gary Lawson, "The Rise and Rise of the Administrative State," 107 Harv. L. Rev. 1231 at 1250 (1994) ("[O]riginalist interpretivism is not simply one method of interpretation among many – it is the only method that is suited

originalists understand their thesis in precisely this way. Moreover, because change is a constant, I would expect originalism to morph into a more modest (and therefore more plausible) form over time. But this notably strong thesis presents the most accurate snapshot of originalism *simpliciter* at the time of this writing.

In any event, I am quite explicit about the thesis that I will hold up for scrutiny. If you believe that I get it wrong, then you might well find that the arguments I claim to muster against it do not squarely hit their target. If you believe that I get it very wrong, then you are unlikely to find anything that follows of much interest at all, except perhaps as a curiosity.[7]

Third, while I maintain that this is the thesis that self-described originalists most commonly advance and that their critics – the non-originalists – oppose, I fully recognize variation within the originalist camp. I intend my definition of

to discovering the actual meaning of the relevant text"); Vasan Kesavan & Michael Stokes Paulsen, "The Interpretive Force of the Constitution's Secret Drafting History," 91 Geo. L.J. 1113 at 1142 (2003) ("[O]riginal meaning textualism is the only method of interpreting the Constitution."); Saikrishna B. Prakash, "Unoriginalism's Law Without Meaning," 15 Const. Commentary 529 at 544 (1998) ("When we accept some text as law, we also commit to the law's original meanings.... Indeed, to embrace the legitimacy of words as law without their original, ordinary meanings is to embrace nothing."); Michael J. Perry, *The Constitution in the Court: Law or Politics?* (1994) at 32 ("The constitutional text *as originally understood* should be deemed authoritative for purposes of constitutional adjudication."). Originalist icons Raoul Berger and Robert Bork conveyed just the same claim. See, *e.g.*, Raoul Berger, *Government by Judiciary: The Transformation of the Fourteenth Amendment* (1977) at 3 (contending "that the 'original intention' of the Framers... is binding on the Court"); Robert H. Bork, *The Tempting of America: The Political Seduction of Law* (1990) at 5 (arguing that a judge "is bound by the only thing that can be called law, the principles of the text, whether Constitution or statute, as generally understood at the enactment"). See also, *e.g.*, *Office of Legal Policy, Original Meaning: A Sourcebook* (U.S. Dept. of Justice 1987) at 2 ("[C]ourts must construe the Constitution according to its original meaning.").

[7] In his contribution to this volume, "What Is Originalism? The Evolution of Contemporary Originalist Theory," Larry Solum contends that my characterization of originalism is "surely mistaken" (at 28). But his support for that contention consists (in addition to Randy Barnett's accurate observation that Scalia doesn't really walk the talk) only of citations to self-proclaimed originalists who would allow original meaning to be trumped by judicial precedent. Yet I have consistently and explicitly defined originalism to accommodate that position – including in the very passage of mine that Solum quotes. See also "Originalism is Bunk," at 20–21, 33. Furthermore, and contra Solum, defining non-originalism "as the view that 'original meaning' in any form can never be considered in constitutional interpretation or construction" is not at all equivalent to my proposed definition of originalism. As the name suggests, non-originalism just is the denial of originalism. And as the previous footnote demonstrates, many originalists do appear to describe originalism in the very strong form that I attribute to them. Indeed, I think that the fair reader will find my definition entirely consistent with the definitions offered by most other contributors to this volume. Yet I know of no self-described non-originalist who maintains that original meaning is irrelevant to constitutional interpretation.

originalism – that, putting aside for the moment the special problem of continued adherence to non-originalist judicial precedent on the particular question at issue,[8] judges should interpret the Constitution *solely* in accordance with some feature of the original character of the constitutional provision at issue – to be agnostic with respect to those matters that most divide the originalists. Let me highlight just two.

Originalist object. As is well known, originalists divide over which aspect of the original character demands present-day fidelity: the meaning intended by the framers or ratifiers of a provision, or the "public meaning" that an ordinary, reasonable person at the time of ratification would have understood the provision to bear, or some similar such idea. I have used the phrase "original character" to encompass these distinct interpretive objects, and I will use the term "original meaning" going forward to accommodate either original public meaning, or original intended meaning, or any other broadly similar notion.

Originalism and stare decisis. I have already said that self-described originalists disagree over whether judges act properly in rejecting the original meaning in favor of intervening judicial precedent. While the formulation I advance might appear to take sides on this dispute, carefully read, it does not. Originalists who make no exception for *stare decisis* still agree that the original meaning is binding if there is no intervening contrary judicial precedent; they just deny that the existence of intervening judicial precedent alters the judicial obligation (that is, they accept *if*, but not *only if*).

II. TWO TYPES OF ARGUMENT FOR ORIGINALISM – AND TWO CONCEPTIONS OF CONSTITUTIONAL INTERPRETATION

Originalism is a controversial thesis. Many and diverse arguments have been advanced for and against it. For example, some originalists rely heavily on the claim that only originalism is consistent with respect for democracy, or that it best advances the legal system's interests in stability and predictability of decision making. Critics argue, among other things, that originalism relies on a naïve faith in the possibility of historical reconstruction, or that it produces substantively bad results. This is not the place to comprehensively catalog, let

[8] I believe that originalists who recognize an exception for judicial precedents overwhelmingly limit that exception to judicial holdings (usually of the highest court in the jurisdiction) that are directly on point; they would not allow judges to depart from the Constitution's original meaning to better accommodate implications from those judicial holdings. My own view is that such grudging or restrictive accommodation of judicial precedents threatens the coherence of the law to a far greater degree than theorists who would qualify originalism with a dash of *stare decisis* recognize. But that must be a topic for another day.

alone to critically assess, all of the extant arguments. Instead, let us move up one level of generality. Is it possible and useful to identify types of arguments for and against originalism? That is, can we profitably classify the different sorts of arguments at play in the originalism debate? Of course, there exist an almost limitless number of possible classificatory schemes. The question is which, if any, help us think more productively about problems of constitutional interpretation.

In previous work, I suggested that the arguments for originalism fall into two types, what I called "hard" and "soft." Soft arguments for originalism, I claimed, contend (in effect, if not explicitly) that judicial fidelity to the Constitution's original meaning is contingently optimal, that it produces a better overall state of affairs, given current (and, perhaps, foreseeable) conditions, than any alternative. Hard arguments endeavor to ground originalism more deeply and securely. As a first pass, they maintain either that originalism can be derived from one or another conceptual truth or that it follows logically from a set of premises that, while not themselves conceptually or necessarily true, are in fact non-controversial. Soft and hard originalist arguments provide different answers to the question of whether, or to what extent, the originalist claim is subject to empirical investigation and to reasonable disagreement about the shape and strength of competing values. If the claim is understood as hostage to empirics and evaluative disagreement (as per soft originalism), then, given the most plausible accounts of our present state of knowledge about the relevant facts and of the prospects for consensus about matters of value, it might seem to follow that soft originalist theses will be far more provisional and tentative than hard originalist theses.[9]

The most familiar and clearest example of a hard argument for originalism is intentionalist. Very simply, intentionalists argue or assume that the practice of constitutional interpretation is what it seems on the surface to be: the interpretation of the constitutional text. And interpretation, they argue further, just is – in all contexts – the effort to discern or ascertain the meaning that the

[9] Larry Solum has taken me to task for this distinction, suggesting that it depends on a naïve pre-Quinean embrace of conceptual a priority: Lawrence B. Solum, "Semantic Originalism," (November 22, 2008). Illinois Public Law Research Paper No. 07–24, online: http://ssrn.com/abstract=1120244 [Solum, "Semantic Originalism,"] at 8–9 n.22. I don't believe that is so, for the point of the distinction is only to mark differences in the texture and structure of argumentative strategies and assumptions, not to endorse any particular contested position in logic or metaphysics. For essentially this same reason (indeed, it is not clear to me that views about, e.g., the nature of interpretation are entirely a priori), I am disposed to resist Kevin Toh's suggestion, in personal communication, that my proposed distinction between "hard" and "soft" arguments would be more intuitively rendered as a distinction between "a priori" and "a posteriori" arguments.

text's author intended to communicate. Therefore, constitutional interpretation just is the effort to discern the meaning that the Constitution's authors (conceived either as framers or ratifiers) intended their text to communicate. A second hard view (much simplified) holds that originalism follows from the fact that a written constitution is designed to be authoritative or normatively binding. Law can have this authoritative character, the argument goes, only by dint of the authority of its authors. Therefore, our Constitution can in fact be authoritative, and our decision to treat it as authoritative can be intelligible only if we strive to interpret it in accordance with the meaning that its authors intended to convey.

Most of the remaining arguments for originalism are soft: They invoke one or more values that any legal system, or our legal system in particular, ought to advance or instantiate – rule of law values like predictability, stability, and transparency; democratic values like popular sovereignty and majoritarian preference-satisfaction; liberty, justice, and welfare – and maintain that strict fidelity to the original meaning promotes or realizes the relevant set of values better than any alternative interpretive approach. The arguments are soft in my terminology because, despite occasional claims by originalists to the contrary, it should be reasonably clear that the claims cannot be successfully maintained without making empirical or predictive assumptions. Indeed, that originalist interpretation is neither part of the concepts of democracy or the rule of law or the like, nor logically entailed by a commitment to such ideals, seems adequately proven by the facts that, though the United States has never had a strictly originalist judiciary, we do have democracy and the rule of law.

That is a thumbnail sketch of my previous classification of originalist arguments. I'd like now to suggest that the hard/soft distinction closely corresponds to (although is not equivalent to) a more fundamental difference in originalist theories – namely a difference in conception about the nature of constitutional interpretation.

Let us start with the idea that constitutional adjudication involves more than simply determining what the law already is, and then applying that pre-existing law to the facts of the case at hand. Plausibly, constitutional adjudication often involves at least two additional activities. First, in the course of adjudicating constitutional disputes, courts sometimes (perhaps very often) make and announce law when either no law exists on point or the court is unable to determine what the preexisting law is. Indeed, on an orthodox Hartian account of law, this is probably the fairest description of most constitutional decision making by the U.S. Supreme Court. Legal norms are secured by criteria of validity that are themselves established by a convergent practice of officials; in the "hard cases" in which practice-certified modalities of constitutional argument point in different directions, none of the contested norms is validated as law, and whatever norm the court ends up announcing is inescapably the product of judicial lawmaking. This appears to be the view as well of constitutional "pragmatists" like Judge Richard Posner, who urges that, when operating in "the open area" where "orthodox legal materials run out," judges should make law based on a clear-eyed assessment of the consequences of alternative decisions.[10]

Second, courts craft implementing doctrine to supplement pre-existing law that is not well suited to efficient judicial administration because, say, it is too vague or turns on predicates (like legislative purposes) that courts are not good at ascertaining. The *Miranda* doctrine is a frequently invoked example: Pre-*Miranda* decisions had held that the Sixth Amendment barred the introduction into evidence of extra-judicial statements by the accused that had been compelled. However, because courts had proven unable to assess whether a statement given out of court had been compelled, the Court fashioned a prophylactic rule that directed courts to exclude from the prosecutor's case in chief custodial statements that had been elicited from defendants who had not been furnished the now-canonical warnings.[11]

Although not wholly uncontroversial, this picture I have just sketched of three distinct activities that occur in the space of constitutional adjudication – finding law, supplementing law that is found, and making law where none exists – is increasingly well accepted, at least in broad strokes. Regardless of the precise way we carve the logical structure of constitutional adjudication, however, the crucial point for now is that lawyers, judges, and theorists do not consistently employ the label "constitutional interpretation" to refer to the same thing. The phrase is often used narrowly to refer only to the activity of trying to discover, as Chief Justice Marshall put it in *Marbury*, "what the law is."[12] On this view, constitutional interpretation might well be supplemented by other activities, such as what "new originalists" call "constitutional construction,"[13] where construction is creative while interpretation aims only at discovery. But the phrase is also used more broadly to refer to the collection

[10] Richard A. Posner, *How Judges Think* (2008) at 15, 324.

[11] There is a long-standing debate over the legitimacy of *Miranda* in particular, and of judge-crafted doctrine that bears a prophylactic relationship to constitutional norms that the doctrine is designed to implement. For critical discussion of the relevant literature and case law, along with a defense of such implementing doctrines, see my "Constitutional Decision Rules," 90 Va. L. Rev. 1 (2004).

[12] *Marbury v. Madison*, 5 U.S. (1 Cranch) 137 at 177 (1803).

[13] "New originalists" who emphasize the distinction between "constitutional interpretation" and "constitutional construction" include Randy Barnett, Larry Solum, and Keith Whittington.

of varied activities that, in Dick Fallon's helpful phrase, constitute "constitutional implementation."[14] As Kent Greenawalt observed, lawyers often use the term "interpretation," in both statutory and constitutional contexts, to encompass "all the considerations that move judges to develop an understanding of [enacted] provisions as they apply in practice."[15] In short, "constitutional interpretation" can be a near-synonym for constitutional implementation or can refer to the central activity involved in implementation – namely the activity of trying to discover pre-existing law.

Simplifying a messier reality, we might reasonably view hard originalism as essentially a theory of constitutional interpretation in the narrow sense: a theory of how judges should ascertain what the law is that pre-exists the interpretive activity. Soft originalism is principally a theory of constitutional interpretation in the broad sense: a theory of the considerations on which judges should rely when crafting law where it does not exist, is undiscoverable, or requires refinement or supplementation to work well in a system of judicial enforcement. It follows that hard originalists view constitutional interpretation as an exercise in theoretical reasoning; soft originalists view it as an exercise in practical reasoning.[16]

It also follows that we need now to revise our initial provisional characterization of originalism as a normative thesis. Soft originalism – originalism as

I discuss and criticize their view of constitutional construction in Mitchell N. Berman, "Constitutional Constructions and Constitutional Decision Rules: Thoughts on the Carving of Implementation Space," 16 Const. Comment. 39 (2010).

[14] Richard H. Fallon, Jr., Implementing the Constitution (2001).

[15] Kent Greenawalt, "Constitutional and Statutory Interpretation," in Jules Coleman & Scott Shapiro (eds.), *The Oxford Handbook of Jurisprudence and Philosophy of Law* (2002) at 268, 274.

[16] To be sure, many or most originalists who have espoused soft arguments were probably unaware that they were arguing (only) about what judges should do, and not about what the law *is*. Still, this is possibly the more charitable way to understand their arguments. Consider, for example, John McGinnis and Michael Rappaport's argument that judges should be originalist because originalism produces better legal outcomes. John O McGinnis & Michael B. Rappaport, "A Pragmatic Defense of Originalism," 101 Nw.U. L. Rev. 383 (2007). That originalism produces better outcomes, if true, would be an obvious reason (though not an obviously decisive reason) for judges to adjudicate cases in accordance with original meanings. It is far less likely that McGinnis and Rappaport themselves believe that the substantive goodness of originalist decisions constitutes a good reason to believe that the law already is just what the original meaning of the constitutional text was. McGinnis and Rappaport might believe that latter claim to be true, but its truth would have to be grounded on different sorts of considerations.

Jeffrey Goldsworthy astutely observes in this volume that (non-originalist) "pluralists" often fail to distinguish among different conceptions of constitutional interpretation. See Jeffrey Goldsworthy, "The Case for Originalism," in this volume at 45. I am claiming that the same is true of originalists.

a theory of proper constitutional interpretation in the broad sense – is plainly normative. But hard originalism is a conjunction of three theses: first, that judges should engage in constitutional interpretation; second, that constitutional interpretation is the activity of trying to ascertain what the constitutional law is; and third, that (again putting aside the legal relevance of judicial decisions purporting to interpret the Constitution) the norms and propositions of constitutional law just are some fixed communicative or semantic content of the Constitution.[17] Although the first thesis is normative, the second and third are metaphysical or conceptual, and it is the latter two – particularly the third – that prove controversial in the debate between originalists and their opponents. So insofar as we are focused on hard originalism – or, put another way, insofar as we are interested in originalism as a theory of constitutional interpretation in the narrow sense – it is more felicitously characterized as a metaphysical or conceptual thesis about the constituents of legal content, and not a normative thesis about what judges should do.[18] This is why self-described originalists can disavow any claims about how judges should adjudicate cases,[19] without putting their originalist credentials at risk.

I have argued elsewhere that soft originalism – understood for present purposes as an account of what judges should do when implementing the Constitution, not as a theory of what the law is – is implausible.[20] It is also

[17] Solum's claim that originalists "disagree about the role that semantic content plays in determining legal content," [this volume, at 34] would appear to contradict this third proposition. I believe, however, that Solum's analysis risks conflating two distinct issues. One issue concerns the content of the law that it is the purpose of constitutional interpretation (in the narrow sense) to discover. The second issue concerns whether it is permissible for courts to supplement, refine, or displace the pre-existing legal content that emerges from the interpretive activity when they proceed to make and announce implementing "doctrine." Solum is quite right that originalists defend different answers to this second question. But they converge on an answer to the first question: Again putting aside the thorny problem of intervening judicial precedent, they maintain (almost without exception) that the semantic content of the constitutional text exhausts the Constitution's contribution to the content of the law. So if Solum is prepared to accept that original meaning merely contributes to, but does not fully constitute, the legal content that interpretation in the narrow sense aims to discover (again putting judicial precedent aside), then his view, I submit, lies outside the boundaries of contemporary originalism. Or, if that verdict be thought too tendentious, let us just say that such a position is not one that self-described non-originalists dispute.

[18] I am here bracketing questions about the nature of the conceptual.

[19] Gary Lawson is a good example. See, *e.g.*, Gary Lawson "On Reading Recipes . . . and Constitutions," 85 Geo. L.J. 1823 (1997). Like most commentators, Lawson distinguishes between normative and descriptive constitutional theory. I am arguing that the "normative" theorizing he takes himself to be engaged in is better described as "metaphysical" or "conceptual."

[20] Soft arguments for originalism – or arguments for originalist interpretation in the broad sense – typically maintain that strict adherence to original meaning (again, contrary judicial precedents possibly excepted) promotes diverse values like democracy, stability, justice, welfare, and so on

in substantial decline, mostly a relic of now-discredited faith in the ability of originalism to constrain willful judges. So I will focus for the remainder of this chapter on originalism as a theory about the content of constitutional law, not as a theory about the considerations that should guide judges when making, refining or, supplementing law.[21]

III. HOW TO CHOOSE A CONSTITUTIONAL THEORY: THE METHOD OF REFLECTIVE EQUILIBRIUM

Once we reconceptualize originalism as a theory of the legal content that constitutional interpretation aims to discover, not (chiefly) as a normative theory of what judges ought to do, we can better appreciate that originalists need to say something more general about a theory of law.

This need presents a challenge for originalists, because the dominant contemporary theories of law – Hartian positivism and Dworkin's theory of law as integrity – seem inhospitable to originalism as an account of the content of constitutional law in those countries in which originalism is actively debated.[22]

better than would any alternative "interpretive" approach. But, critics object, once we recognize that one alternative to originalism would be an interpretive approach that pays substantial but not conclusive respect to the Constitution's original meaning – allowing interpreters to depart from that meaning for good and weighty reason – then the extremism and thus the implausibility of originalism becomes patent. Surely it is not true that *in every single case* the relevant values would be optimized by judicial enforcement of the original meaning: when a generally obscure original meaning runs counter to long-standing practice and popular expectations, stability, and predictability might favor the non-originalist interpretation; when circumstances have changed in ways not foreseen by the framing generation, interests in justice, welfare, and democratic accountability might all militate in favor of a non-originalist interpretation that better meets contemporary needs and widespread preferences and judgments; and so on. To be sure, originalists try to meet these objections by emphasizing the value or virtue of the judiciary following more easily articulated and sharper-edged rules. But in the absence of an effective mechanism to enforce judicial obedience to the supposed obligation of strict fidelity to the original meaning, the originalists run up against the familiar and powerful challenges to rule consequentialism. For all these reasons, then, it seems unlikely that soft considerations can effectively support a thesis as strict and demanding as is contemporary originalism.

[21] The shift from soft to hard originalism goes some considerable distance, I think, toward explaining a fact that puzzles Steven Smith – namely "that originalist theory has grown more theoretical and sophisticated than it once was." See Steven D. Smith, "That Old-Time Originalism," in this volume at 226. As originalism morphed from a (normative) theory of what decisions judges should reach (possibly on the implicit assumption that there is no law on the question to discover, or that what law as did exist was undiscoverable) to a (metaphysical or conceptual) theory about what the law already is that interpretation aims to discover, it would necessarily be answerable to general theories of the relationship between legal texts and legal content. And such theories are unavoidably theoretical and sophisticated.

[22] I think it largely uncontroversial that Hart's account of law is not friendly to originalism as a theory of the present content of law in, for example, the United States, Canada, or Australia precisely because judges demonstrably have not converged on a practice of interpreting

To be sure, originalism might sit comfortably with an Austinian command theory of law, but that theory boasts few defenders today. So originalists who are pressing a view about the content of the law cannot simply help themselves to a congenial theory of law straight off the rack.

This is not the place to argue for or against candidate theories of law. Instead, let us move up one level of abstraction and think about how to reason more generally about constitutional theories, by which I will mean theories of the content of constitutional law. I think that there are two basic strategies: coherentist and foundationalist.

Coherentism is an approach to epistemic justification across domains of inquiry. It maintains that a belief is justified by its inclusion in a system of beliefs that are mutually consistent and supportive. Its rival, foundationalism, provides that one or another set of these judgments provides the grounds for arguing for others, but not vice versa. Foundationalism, but not coherentism, treats some judgments as "bedrock," not revisable in light of others. The most familiar way to discover or develop a maximally coherent set of beliefs is the Rawlsian method of reflective equilibrium, which comes in both "narrow" and "wide" forms.[23] Narrow reflective equilibrium directs that we work between our case-specific judgments or intuitions and our judgments about general reasons or principles. In wide reflective equilibrium, we expand our field of inquiry to encompass yet more general or comprehensive theoretical frameworks. In ethics, where the method is arguably most plausible (although this was not Rawls's own view), wide reflective equilibrium directs us to seek coherence among our case-specific intuitions or judgments of what is right, wrong, or permissible (like whether it is permissible to switch the trolley under carefully specified circumstances), general reasons or principles (like that it is impermissible to intentionally kill an innocent person), and comprehensive moral theories (like Kantianism or classical utilitarianism).

their constitutions in an originalist mode. In contrast, there is some dispute regarding whether Dworkin himself can count as an originalist, given his occasional avowals of "semantic originalism" (in contrast with "expectation originalism"). See, *e.g.*, Keith E. Whittington, "Dworkin's 'Originalism': The Role of Intentions in Constitutional Interpretation," 62 Rev. Politics 197 (2000); Jeffrey Goldsworthy, "Dworkin as an Originalist," 17 Const. Comment. 49 (2000). But Dworkin is notoriously a moving target, and even commentators who might welcome Dworkin the man to the originalist camp agree that Dworkin's theory of law as integrity, as principally explicated in *Law's Empire*, is resolutely non-originalist. *See ibid.* at 56–78.

[23] Rawl's best known discussion of reflective equilibrium appears in *A Theory of Justice* (1971) 48–51. He introduced the distinction between "narrow" and "wide" reflective equilibrium in "The Independence of Moral Theory," 47 Proceedings and Addresses of the American Philosophical Association 5 (1974). For a good overview of the process, see Norman Daniels, "Reflective Equilibrium," *Stanford Encyclopedia of Philosophy*, online: http://plato.stanford.edu/entries/reflective-equilibrium.

This image of clearly distinct levels of inquiry is no doubt overly stylized. Still, it is a useful guide when trying to transplant the method to other domains, for it compels us to attend self-consciously to the range of different types of judgment we might reasonably hope to bring into coherence. Obviously, decisions regarding how to demarcate a domain of inquiry and how to identify and classify the types of judgments that constitute the domain will be contestable. That said, I propose that, applied to the realm of American constitutional theory, reflective equilibrium would require coherence among judgments at the following three levels, at a minimum: about particular cases (i.e., about the constitutional status of token events), about the correct jurisdiction-specific account of the determinants of the content of constitutional law, and about a general jurisprudential account of the nature or concept of law. To introduce this last and most general level of judgment is not to assume that the correct theory of law will uniquely determine the correct approach to constitutional interpretation. The much more modest (two-part) assumption is only that any theory of constitutional interpretation on which we settle must be at least consistent with our theory of law, and that not all initially plausible theories of the two types (of law and of constitutional interpretation) can be made to adequately cohere.

Hard originalists tend to be foundationalist: They appear to believe that originalism follows as a matter of course from some other belief that they take, even implicitly, as foundationally true. This characterization is probably most clearly apt of the intentionalist-originalists. They operate from an implicit belief that law is something like the semantic meaning of an authoritative pronouncement,[24] and the semantic meaning just is the meaning intended by the author. Either or both views seem often to be accepted as foundationally true.

Against foundationalism, coherentism supposes that the correct theory of constitutional interpretation does not simply flow from a theory of law but rather that the two sorts of theories answer to each other, as well as to other judgments, like those about specific cases. The broad jurisprudential or methodological suggestion of this chapter is that we might come to better warranted views about the determinants of constitutional law – and thus about "normative theories of constitutional interpretation," insofar as we continue to find this way of putting things helpful – by self-consciously employing the method of wide reflective equilibrium, and therefore by paying more systematic attention to how particular theories of constitutional interpretation fit together with theories of law and with case-specific judgments of constitutionality.

[24] Mark Greenberg has dubbed this the "standard picture" of law, and has argued that it is mistaken. See Mark Greenberg, "The Standard Picture and Its Discontents," 1 Oxford Stud. Phil. L 1 (2010).

Of course, engaging in a project of wide reflective equilibrium is no mean undertaking. I cannot advance the project very far in the remainder of this chapter. Instead, I hope to take two steps down that path. I start in the next Part by identifying what Rawls called a provisional "fixed point" – a judgment that, albeit revisable, strikes us on reflection as very hard to shake. This is our judgment that John McCain is constitutionally eligible to be president. (In starting with a case-specific judgment, I follow Michael Dorf's wise observation from a decade ago that, whereas many theorists appear to assume "that the choice of a constitutional theory precedes the formulation of answers in particular cases . . . in practice, matters typically proceed in the opposite direction."[25]) This case-specific judgment might not itself tell us much about the proper constitutional theory, but it will substantially undermine originalism – or so I will argue. In so doing, I will address the criticism that the case-specific judgment regarding McCain many of us have is not actually a judgment that he is constitutionally eligible to be President regardless of the original meaning of the Natural Born Citizenship Clause. Instead, a critic might propose, it is a judgment that, if it turns out that McCain is not constitutionally eligible to be President, the courts should not enforce the law. I will provide reason to resist this recharacterization of judgments that appear on their face to concern what the law is.

IV. TAKING CASE-SPECIFIC JUDGMENTS SERIOUSLY: JOHN MCCAIN

Take One

John McCain III was born to two U.S. citizens in 1936 in the Panama Canal Zone where his father, an admiral in the U.S. navy, was stationed. Because he was not born in the territorial United States, McCain's candidacy for president was seen by many to raise anew the question of what the natural-born citizen clause means.[26] The issue had arisen before – the 1964 Republican presidential nominee Barry Goldwater had been born in the territory of Arizona three years prior to its formal grant of statehood, and George Romney, a candidate

[25] Michael C. Dorf, "Create Your Own Constitutional Theory," 87 Cal. L. Rev. 593 at 594 (1999). See also S.L. Hurley, "Coherence, Hypothetical Cases, and Precedent," (1990) 10 O.J.L.S. 221.

[26] Although the issue had been discussed in the blogosphere for some time, it did not attract significant mainstream media attention until a February 2008 article in *The New York Times*. Carl Hulse, "McCain's Canal Zone Birth Prompts Queries About Whether That Rules Him Out," New York Times (Feb. 28, 2008) A21 [Hulse, "McCain's Canal Zone Birth"]. The online companion to the Michigan Law Review then ran a symposium on the subject two months before the general election. See "Senator John McCain and Natural Born Citizenship," 107 Mich. L. Rev. First Impression, online: http://www.michiganlawreview.org/first-impressions/volume/107 (2008).

for the Republican party's nomination in 1968, had been born to American missionaries in Mexico – but had never been authoritatively resolved by the courts. The scholarship to date has reached no consensus on the clause's original meaning. All commentators agree that persons born in the United States (except for children of foreign ministers or enemy combatants) are "natural born citizens." Beyond that, however, scholars have concluded variously (1) that the founding-era technical legal meaning of "natural born" was the same as "native born," and extended only to persons who enjoyed citizenship under the principle of *jus soli* (right of the soil), and not by *jus sanguinis* (right of the blood);[27] (2) that "natural born" had a broader meaning than "native born" and encompassed both *jus soli* and *jus sanguinis*;[28] (3) that the framers intended the phrase to cover whoever was deemed a citizen at birth by operation of subsequently adopted naturalization statutes, possibly with the sole proviso that Congress could not grant "natural born" citizenship retroactively;[29] (4) that the framers intended to delegate to Congress the power, not to reconfigure the content of "natural born citizenship" whenever it chooses, but to "clarify" or "declare" the meaning of the term so as to "fix" it once and for all;[30] and (5) that the original meaning may have been ambiguous or is opaque to us.[31] As one scholar who has researched the question fairly summarized, while "there are powerful arguments that Senator McCain or anyone else in this position is constitutionally qualified . . . it is not a slam dunk situation."[32]

[27] 113 Cong. Rec. 15,875, 15,880 (1967) (Brief of the Hon. Pinckney G. McElwee introduced by Mr. Dowdy); Randall Kennedy, "A Natural Aristocracy?" 12 Const. Comment. 175 at 175 (1995).

[28] Charles Gordon, "Who Can Be President of the United States: The Unresolved Enigma," 28 Md. L. Rev. 1 at 1 (1968); Christina S. Lohman, "Presidential Eligibility: The Meaning of the Natural-Born Citizen Clause," 36 Gonz. L. Rev. 349, 359 (2001) [Lohman, "Presidential Eligibility"]; Alexander Porter Morse, "Natural-Born Citizen of the United States: Eligibility for the Office of President," 66 Alb. L.J. 99 at 99 (1904).

[29] Jill Pryor, "The Natural-Born Citizen Clause and Presidential Eligibility: An Approach for Resolving Two Hundred Years of Uncertainty," 97 Yale L.J. 881 at 893–6 (1988).

[30] Although this is not Pryor's own view, it is at least suggested by some of the older authorities she cites. See *ibid.* at 884 notes 13 & 14. For a general discussion of the founder's views on "fixing" meaning, see Caleb Nelson, "Originalism and Interpretive Conventions," 70 U. Chi. L. Rev. 519 (2003).

[31] See Lawrence B. Solum, "Originalism and the Natural Born Citizen Clause," 107 Mich. L. Rev. First Impressions, online: http://www.michiganlawreview.org/articles/originalism-and-the-natural-born-citizen-clause (2008) [Solum, "Originalism and the Natural Born Citizen Clause"](concluding that, for a "new originalist," the meaning of the term, and in particular its application to the question of John McCain's eligibility, might depend on constitutional "construction," not "interpretation").

[32] Hulse, McCain's Canal Zone Birth," *supra* note 26 at A21 (quoting Sarah Duggin).

In short, then, the question of McCain's eligibility has arisen in a context that we rarely see today: a constitutional text that bears no clear contemporary meaning, controverted historical meaning, and intentions; and very sparse judicial precedent.[33] Given the prominence of text, original understanding, and judicial precedent as modalities of constitutional argument, we might expect opinions on the subject to be diverse and equivocal. However, neither expectation is borne out. To the contrary, there appears to be an extraordinary degree of consensus across diverse sectors of society – among lay people, law professors, and elected officials – that McCain is eligible, along with a robust conviction in the correctness of this answer.

In April 2008, for example, the U.S. Senate unanimously passed a bipartisan resolution "recognizing that John Sidney McCain, III, is a natural born citizen."[34] The stated grounds for this conclusion included that "there is no evidence of the intention of the Framers or any Congress to limit the constitutional rights of children born to American citizens serving in the military nor to prevent those children from serving as their country's President"; that "such limitations would be inconsistent with the purpose and intent of the 'natural born Citizen' clause . . . as evidenced by the First Congress's own statute defining the term 'natural born Citizen'"; that "the well-being of all citizens of the United States is preserved and enhanced by the men and women who are assigned to serve our country outside of our national borders"; and that "previous presidential candidates were born outside of the United States of America and were understood to be eligible to be President." As Patrick Leahy, the resolution's principal sponsor, explained, the conclusion reflected the "common sense" of all senators. "Because he was born to American citizens," Leahy added, "there is no doubt in my mind that Senator McCain is a natural born citizen."[35]

[33] The most relevant judicial precedents – none of them close to directly on point – include *Elk v. Wilkins*, 112 U.S. 94 (1884) (holding that members of Indian tribes are not birthright citizens under the Fourteenth Amendment because not "subject to the jurisdiction" of the United States); *United States v. Wong Kim Ark*, 169 U.S. 649 (1898) (holding that, by force of the Fourteenth Amendment, a child of Chinese subjects born in the United States is a U.S. citizen); *Weedin v. Chin Bow*, 274 U.S. 657 (1927) (holding that, under the governing statute, a child born abroad is not a U.S. citizen if his father, albeit a citizen under principles of *jus sanguinis*, had not resided in the country prior to the child's birth); and *Montana v. Kennedy*, 366 U.S. 308 (1961) (interpreting governing statute to confer birthright citizenship on principles of *jus sanguinis* only through paternal citizenship).

[34] S. Res. 511, 110th Cong. 2008.

[35] Statement of Sen. Patrick Leahy on the introduction of Senate Resolution 511 (April 10, 2008).

Theodore Olson and Laurence Tribe had reached the same verdict a month earlier in a jointly authored white paper.[36] Supporting their conclusion in a bare two pages of analysis, Olson and Tribe reasoned that Congress had "recognized in successive federal statutes since the Nation's Founding that children born abroad to U.S. citizens are themselves U.S. citizens," and particularly observed that the naturalization statute passed by the First Congress expressly referred to foreign-born children of U.S. citizens as "natural born citizens." This, they added, was consistent with the British statutes in effect at the time. They also identified "a second and independent basis" for their conclusion, namely the "substantial legal support for the proposition that the Panama Canal Zone was indeed sovereign U.S. territory when Senator McCain was born there in 1936," thereby granting him citizenship on principles of *jus soli*. "Historical practice [Goldwater's receipt of the Republican Party's nomination for President in 1964, and the fact that Charles Curtis served as Vice President to Herbert Hoover despite being born in Kansas one year before it achieved statehood] confirms that birth on soil that is under the sovereignty of the United States, but not within a State, satisfies the Natural Born Citizen Clause." Noting that Barack Obama was born in Hawaii only two years after its admission to statehood, Olson and Tribe deemed it "inconceivable that Senator Obama would have been ineligible for the Presidency had he been born two years earlier." For these and other reasons, they concluded, "based on the original meaning of the Constitution, the Framers' intentions, and subsequent legal and historical precedent, Senator McCain's birth to parents who were U.S. citizens, serving on a U.S. military base in the Panama Canal Zone in 1936, makes him a 'natural born Citizen' within the meaning of the Constitution."

As best I can tell, legal academic opinion largely accords with this conclusion. On the most frequented blawgs, for example, Michael Dorf, James Lindgren, and Larry Solum all weighed in in McCain's favor, whereas Jonathan Turley was perhaps the lone dissenter.[37] Even Jack Chin (who, as we will see, contends that McCain was not in fact a U.S. citizen at birth – let alone a "natural born" U.S. citizen) seems to agree that if the relevant statutes had

[36] Opinion of Laurence Tribe & Theodore B. Olson (Mar. 19, 2008) (included as an appendix in Chin, "Why Senator John McCain Cannot Be President," *supra* note 3 at 19–21).

[37] *Dorf on Law*, online: http://michaeldorf.org/2008_02_01_archive.html (Feb. 29, 2008); Posting of Jim Lindgren to *The Volokh Conspiracy*, online: http://volokh.com/posts/1204265246.shtml (Feb. 29, 2008); *Legal Theory Blog*, online: http://lsolum.typepad.com/legaltheory/2008/07/gabriel-j-chin.html (July 14, 2008); *Jonathan Turley*, online: http://jonathanturley.org/2008/02/28/does-john-mccain-have-an-alexander-hamilton-problem-a-constitutional-challenge-may-loom-over-mccains-eligibility-for-president/ (Feb. 28, 2008).

conferred citizenship on McCain at birth, then he would have been a "natural born citizen" for constitutional purposes.[38]

On this matter, finally, lay opinion and elite opinion appear to coincide. It is hard to find any expression of dissent in the blogosphere, whereas fervent affirmations of McCain's eligibility abound. The following postings are representative of both the strength of conviction on the subject and the reasoning embraced:

> Anyone who has served in the US military knows that any children they have are 'natural born' citizens no matter where they are actually born. Just think if that wasn't so. The military would consist of nothing but single men and women. Since much of our military are married we'd lose all of them.[39]

> I can't even believe there is any debate on whether or not someone who risked his life in Vietnam, was held in Hanoi's infamous POW camp and was awarded a Silver Star, a Bronze Star, a Legion of Merit, a Purple Heart, and the Distinguished Flying Cross while serving his country is eligible as president because he was born on foreign soil while his parents were serving his country. Seriously, he may not be my candidate, but it sure as shit isn't because of any doubt of him being an "eligible" American.[40]

In short, armchair empiricism suggests that the conviction that McCain is a natural-born citizen within the meaning of the law is broadly shared and robustly held. Moreover, it rests, or is said to rest, on a wide variety of arguments.

Importantly, though, and for several different reasons, many of the common argumentative maneuvers do not withstand scrutiny.

Some are just fallacious. For example, Olson and Tribe's argument that McCain probably enjoyed citizenship just by virtue of having been born in the "sovereign U.S. territory" of the canal zone overlooks, as Chin has pointed out, that persons whose sole claim to citizenship is birth in the canal zone are not treated as citizens under existing law; they are routinely deported.[41] In reaching the contrary conclusion (albeit with some equivocation), not only do Tribe and Olson overlook this fact, they also ignore the well-settled

[38] Chin, "Why Senator John McCain Cannot Be President," *supra* note 3 at 2.

[39] Comment responding to posting of Matt Margolis to *Blogs for Victory*, online: http://blogsforvictory.com/2008/02/28/the-inevitable-natural-born-citizen-debate/ (Feb. 28, 2008).

[40] Comment responding to posting of McCullough to *Dvorak Uncensored*, online: http://www.dvorak.org/blog/2008/02/28/is-john-mccain-a-%E2%80%9Cnatural-born-citizen%E2%80%9D/ (Feb. 28, 2008).

[41] Posting of Jack Chin to *PrawfsBlawg*, online: http://prawfsblawg.blogs.com/prawfsblawg/2008/07/page/2/ (July 12, 2008).

distinction between incorporated territories – those destined for statehood – and unincorporated territories.[42] Even putting aside this distinction, that Olson and Tribe would find it "inconceivable" that a two-year difference in birth might spell the difference between eligibility and ineligibility for presidency is itself, if "conceivable," more than a little surprising. That is just the way rules (as opposed to standards) work: They impose substantially different consequences for conduct or phenomena that reside on different sides of a line whose precise location is sometimes arbitrary. Hawaii was annexed by the United States in 1898 and made a territory in 1900. Surely there was *some* point in time at which it is true that a person born as a U.S. citizen in Hawaii would not have been a U.S. citizen had he or she been born there a year earlier.

Other arguments, while perhaps strictly true, are substantially misleading. Consider, for example, the Senate Resolution's observation that "previous presidential candidates were born outside the United States of America and were understood to be eligible to be President." Well, some were understood to be eligible – Goldwater, for instance. But the eligibility of many others was deeply questioned. George Romney's eligibility was challenged in a legal opinion published in the Congressional Record, and Franklin Delano Roosevelt, Jr., who served in Congress and was once considered a possible presidential candidate, was deemed ineligible because of his birth in Canada.[43]

Most significantly, though, many of the most often expressed reasons for finding McCain eligible are not self-evidently good arguments of constitutional law. Consider the kindred but distinct arguments that a contrary result (1) would be unjust to McCain himself (especially given his distinguished service to this country); (2) would be unjust to Senator McCain's father, Admiral McCain; (3) would be unjust to all foreign-born children of service members; (4) would be unjust to all service member parents of foreign-born children; and (5) would imprudently discourage military service. My claim is not that arguments of justice and prudence are not legitimate modalities of constitutional argument, but only that the arguments are much too underdeveloped to suggest a worked-out constitutional theory: It is not clear that all those who advance these arguments in defense of McCain's eligibility would acknowledge that arguments of the same type have any force at all across all contexts. The point is well illustrated by the remarks of Senator Lindsay Graham, who

[42] Sarah Helene Duggin & Mary Beth Collins, "'Natural Born' in the USA: The Striking Unfairness and Dangerous Ambiguity of the Constitution's Presidential Qualifications Clause and Why We Need to Fix It," 85 B.U. L. Rev. 53, at 89–96 (2005).

[43] *Ibid.* at 57.

appears to consider himself a "strict constructionist."[44] McCain's father was posted to the Canal Zone "on orders from the United States government," Graham observed. If he is deemed ineligible for president, "we need to tell every military family that your kid can't be president if they take an overseas assignment."[45] Precisely how Graham himself understands this observation to function as an argument for McCain's eligibility is not wholly clear. I accept that this would be a bad result. But surely Graham is not assuming, as a general premise or theory of interpretation, that the goodness or badness of a particular outcome constitutes the touchstone for the truth or falsity of a proposition of constitutional law. As a "strict constructionist," presumably he is not advocating that the Constitution should presumptively be interpreted to avoid bad results. In just the same way, we might reasonably doubt that all those who appear to derive the conclusion that McCain is eligible from the fact that a contrary judgment would be unjust to him or his father proceed from the general premise that the Constitution must always be interpreted to avoid injustice, or even that the avoidance of injustice is always a valid *pro tanto* reason in support of a candidate interpretation.[46]

I hope you do not suppose that, in criticizing some of the arguments given for the near-universal judgment that McCain is legally eligible to be president, I aim to cast doubt on that conclusion. Not at all. I share the conviction. Furthermore, I am disposed to accept that at least some of the reasons given for that conclusion are good reasons of constitutional interpretation. My point is to suggest that people's conviction that McCain is eligible (assuming that he was a birthright citizen) is very likely prior to any particular theory they may

[44] See, *e.g.*, "Bush Confident of Securing Senate Confirmation," Boston Globe, Oct. 8, 2005; Confirmation Hearing on the Nomination of Samuel A. Alito etc, S Hrg 109–227 (2006), at 429.

[45] Hulse, McCain's Canal Zone Birth," *supra* note 26 (quoting Lindsay Graham).

[46] Many commentators also place seemingly excessive weight on the absence of evidence that the framers intended to exclude foreign-born children of U.S. service members. See, *e.g.*, S. Res. 511, 110th Cong. 2008 (enacted) ("Whereas there is no evidence of the intention of the Framers or any Congress to limit the constitutional rights of children born to American citizens serving in the military nor to prevent those children from serving as their country's President, . . . John Sidney McCain, III, is a 'natural born Citizen' under Article II, Section 1, of the Constitution of the United States."); Opinion of Tribe & Olson, *supra* note 36 ("It goes without saying that the Framers did not intend to exclude a person from the office of the President simply because he or she was born to U.S. citizens serving in the U.S. military outside of the continental United States. . . . "). Generally, that is not how originalist arguments run. For expectation or application originalists, an intent that X obtain might be constitutionally dispositive. And meaning originalists (whether focused on intended meaning or public meaning) would likely take an intent that X as weighty evidence that the text has a meaning that permits X. But the absence of an intent that X ordinarily has substantially less probative weight; it may be that the framers lacked an intent concerning X because they never thought about the situation.

have about the proper way(s) to interpret the Constitution: Most commentators are more certain of their case-specific conclusion than they are of the general soundness of the particular considerations on which they purport to rely.[47] The method of reflective equilibrium advises us to take this conviction seriously – seriously, but not intransigently. Any theory of constitutional interpretation that would not yield this case-specific conclusion is to that extent undermined or thrown into doubt. Our theories of interpretation are answerable to this judgment.[48]

Originalism is such a theory – but not because I assume that the original meaning or intent of the natural-born citizen clause was strictly limited to *jus soli*. The McCain case undermines originalism because our conviction is not contingent on the historical facts that originalism would make dispositive.[49]

[47] Because the epistemic significance, on coherentist thinking, of the fact that a particular judgment is shared by others may not be entirely clear or noncontroversial, perhaps I should say that you should take the conviction seriously if you in fact hold it, and that you may allow the fact that others share it (to the extent that they do) to strengthen your own conviction on this point. (I am grateful to Kevin Toh for provoking this clarification.)

[48] This might not be true if our case-specific judgments, though not purporting, or initially appearing, to rely on any particular interpretive theory, are in fact traceable to a prior embrace of a particular interpretive theory by ourselves or by others. Suppose, for example, that the judiciary, or the broader society, accepted as true some proposition of constitutional law, *p*, and did so on originalist grounds. You might be influenced by this general acceptance or endorsement of *p* in coming to believe that *p* is in fact the correct legal meaning or significance of the relevant constitutional text, T. Later, historians might persuade you that the original meaning of T was not *p*. If *p* generates some case-specific judgment "c" not itself consistent with the original understanding of T, your conviction that "c" is legally sound might be unreliable against originalism to the extent that others' commitment to an originalist interpretation was causally responsible for your case-specific judgment of "c", notwithstanding your unawareness of that fact. Be this as it may be, it strikes me as not remotely likely that qualifications of this sort contaminate whatever convictions we might have about whether McCain is a natural-born citizen within the meaning of Article II.

[49] I am puzzled by Larry Alexander's denial "that one does or can have constitutional or legal intuitions that pre-exist and provide the grist for building our theory of legal interpretation." See Larry Alexander, "Simple-Minded Originalism" in this volume at 97. It sure does seem, after all, that some people *do* have strong legal intuitions that pre-exist their embrace of a theory of legal interpretation or of legal content. (And perhaps it is revealing that nobody, to my knowledge, has similarly strong intuitions, not easily defeated, about the height in feet of Mt. Cook.) So I take Alexander really to be denying, not that such intuitions might exist, but only that we should credit such intuitions when trying to develop a theory of legal content. Perhaps not. But one might think that the fact that philosophers of law have not yet converged on a theory of legal content should give him more pause before dismissing the possibility. Incidentally, I share Alexander's doubt that many (or any) of us have case-specific intuitions about, for example, whether states can issue "letters of marque and reprisal" or the length of the statute of limitations for fraud in Alabama. I am not sure why Alexander would think that this should cause any embarrassment for my thesis. Possibly, though, it stems from his apparent belief that I advocate reflective equilibrium as a "method of constitutional interpretation." *Ibid.* at 98. Not quite. I advocate it as a method for settling on a theory of law or legal content: Our theory of legal content should be drawn from the set of theories that yield the particular legal

For shorthand, let us say that our conviction about this case is that McCain is "non-contingently eligible" for President, by which I mean, of course, not that his eligibility is contingent on nothing, but only that it is not contingent on any particular facts about the original character of the natural-born citizen clause. Put very simply, originalism makes the correct judgment about McCain's eligibility contingent on some facts about the late eighteenth century – even, I would think, if we are mistaken about those facts. If the original meaning of "natural born Citizen" was limited to birthright citizens born in U.S. territory, then McCain is not legally eligible, says originalism, no matter what any of us – or all of us – might believe. Indeed, if sufficient historical evidence that the original meaning was limited to the native-born were to be unearthed, then we would seem compelled to conclude that McCain is ineligible to be president even if the evidence were to be discovered after his election, or deep in his first term.[50] Furthermore, if this hypothetically compelling historical evidence were to arise some years after a McCain presidency, and if another candidate were to present the same issue, and if a court were to deem a legal challenge to that candidate justiciable, then it would seem that the McCain precedent would be, for an originalist, entirely without legal relevance: While self-described originalists differ mightily over whether to recognize an exception for judicial precedents, very few would also recognize an exception for non-judicial precedents – which is not surprising given the difficulty of then insisting that no other social and political developments could bear on constitutional meaning.[51] All of these originalist conclusions conflict with our non-contingent conviction about McCain. So much the worse for our case-specific conviction, says the foundationalist-originalist.[52] So much the worse for originalism, says the coherentist.[53]

propositions of which we may be confident on reflection. The fewer such propositions as may exist, the less constraining is this coherentist approach to legal theorizing. *Cf.* Michael C. Dorf, "The Coherentism of Democracy and Distrust," 114 Yale L.J. 1237 at 1257–8 (2005) (pointing out that to embrace coherentism as a way to justify theories of constitutional interpretation does not entail that the theory that emerges as most justified or warranted must itself direct judges to engage in Dworkin-style coherentist analysis as the way of determining what the law is).

50 Admittedly, exactly what we should do about his ineligibility would be a separate question.

51 For a discussion of the difficulty originalists confront when they accept an exception for *stare decisis*, see Berman, "Originalism Is Bunk," *supra* note 4 at 33–6.

52 To his credit, this, I believe, would be Solum's response. See Solum, "Originalism and the Natural Born Citizen Clause," *supra* note 31. But as noted in the Introduction, I expect most committed originalists to respond this way (this is a comment on how coherentist arguments operate, not a questioning of my opponents' good faith), which is why I hope mostly to reach the presently unaffiliated.

53 We could run essentially the same argument by relying on *Brown v. Board of Education* 347 U.S. 483 (1954). On this view, *Brown* undermines originalism so long as we are strongly committed to the proposition that *Brown* was correct in holding that de jure racial segregation in

Take Two

In claiming that many of us are durably convinced, on reflection, that McCain is a natural-born citizen within the meaning of Article II, thus constitutionally eligible to be president, I mean to be saying more than that many of us believe that a challenge to his eligibility should be nonjusticiable. The claim is that he and his supporters could correctly contend that a McCain presidency would have been wholly constitutional (assuming satisfaction of any other legal requirements), that members of the legislative and executive branches of the national government and of the states could support a McCain presidency consistent with their constitutional obligations. I'd like now to briefly consider whether that judgment might be less secure than first appears, because we, or many of us, are mistaking for a conviction of non-contingent eligibility the distinct but neighboring convictions that, although McCain would *not* be constitutionally eligible were the constitutional history to come out the wrong way, either (a) the judiciary should nonetheless not intervene or (b) nobody (judges and others) should feel any moral compunction about disregarding the fact of McCain's legal ineligibility. The difference between (a) and (b) is that the former view leaves open the possibility that relevant actors in the legal drama other than judges – like McCain himself and his electors – should feel duty-bound to act in accordance with the conclusion that he is ineligible. The latter position, in contrast, maintains that, while McCain would not be legally eligible to be president were the original meaning of "natural born citizen" limited to birthright citizenship by *jus soli*, such a legal conclusion would confer no moral obligation on anyone.

public education is unconstitutional, and even without establishing that the original meaning of the Equal Protection Clause cannot accommodate that result. Rather, *Brown* undermines originalism just because, or insofar as, we believe it was non-contingently correct. Although I believe this argument has substantial force, I think that the McCain case makes the point even more effectively for at least two reasons. First, it might be harder than we appreciate for those of us not alive in 1954 (or alive but too young to have attended to constitutional debates) to separate our convictions regarding whether *Brown* was rightly decided in 1954 from our intuitions regarding what the correct statement of the law is now. That is, from the standpoint of the early years of the twenty-first century, contemplating *Brown* introduces the variable of intervening judicial precedent that the contemplation of McCain's eligibility does not. Second, because racial segregation offends principles of justice to a far greater degree than would the possible constitutional ineligibility of John McCain and similarly situated others, we might worry that our convictions related to *Brown* are as much about what the Court should have done as about what the constitutional law was. That is, we might risk confusing a moral conviction that the Court should have done justice regardless of what the constitutional law (correctly understood) might have been, for a conviction about what the constitutional law (correctly understood) actually was.

Here is a roundabout way to test the suggestion that I have mischaracterized the case-specific considered judgment that I observe in myself and in others. I have assumed thus far that McCain was a citizen at birth, albeit by virtue only of the principle of *jus sanguinis*, not by *jus soli*. But Jack Chin's recent scholarship reveals that this is not so obviously true as to be accepted without argument. As Chin explains, the statutory framework in effect at the time of McCain's birth in 1936 conferred citizenship on persons born "out of the limits and jurisdiction of the United States" if one or both parents was a U.S. citizen.[54] The problem for McCain, Chin argues, is that limits and jurisdiction were understood at the time to refer to different concepts. The limits of the United States is a straightforward territorial concept: By being born in the Canal Zone, McCain was born out of the limits of the United States within the meaning of § 1993. Jurisdiction, however, refers to the legitimate exercise of sovereign power: Because the Panama Canal Zone was within U.S. jurisdiction, McCain was *not* born outside of the jurisdiction of the U.S. Therefore, he was not granted citizenship by § 1993. Because no other constitutional or statutory provision granted him citizenship, and because the United States had abolished common-law principles of citizenship, McCain was not a citizen at birth. Instead, he was granted citizenship *after birth* by virtue of a 1937 revision to the immigration laws that expressly conferred citizenship on "any person born in the Canal Zone on or after February 26, 1904, and whether before or after the effective date of this Act, whose father or mother . . . was or is a citizen of the United States."[55] Thus, although McCain is a citizen by virtue of his birth, he was not a citizen at birth, Chin concludes, and surely cannot be a "natural born Citizen."

Now, Chin's argument is not impregnable. McCain's status as a "natural born citizen" could possibly be restored in a variety of ways: if "limits and jurisdiction" is best interpreted as a mere doublet – a redundancy, like "cease and desist" or "metes and bounds" – rather than as marking distinct concepts;[56] or if, contrary to Chin's contention, common law principles of citizenship have remained effective; or if "natural born citizenship" is interpreted to mean "citizenship *by* birth" and not "citizenship *at* birth,"[57] let alone some

[54] 8 U.S.C. § 1993. The statute added two qualifications: first, the citizen parents must have resided in the United States at some point; and second, if only one parent was a U.S. citizen, the child must reside continuously in the United States for five years prior to his or her eighteenth birthday, and must take an oath of allegiance.

[55] 8 U.S.C. § 1403.

[56] See Stephen E. Sachs, Commentary, "Why John McCain Was a Citizen at Birth," 107 Mich. L. Rev. First Impressions 49 at 51–3 (2008), online: http://www.michiganlawreview.org/firstimpressions/vol107/sachs.pdf.

[57] See Solum, "Originalism and the Natural Born Citizen Clause," *supra* note 31 at 28.

subset thereof. But none of these paths for rebutting Chin's argument is a clear winner.[58] So let us assume *arguendo* that Chin's analysis is correct: John McCain was not an American citizen at birth. The instant question is whether this supposition affects our initial conviction that McCain would have been non-contingently eligible to be president had he been born a year later, or if the relevant statutes had been amended a year earlier.

Chin presented his scholarship after McCain had effectively sewed up the Republican nomination. Yet I'd bet that few readers of his paper, or of reports of his paper in the mainstream media,[59] thought: "Wow! This could change everything!" Few readers, in other words, predicted or would have urged that McCain be excluded from the ballot or that, were he to prevail in the general election against the Democratic candidate, Barack Obama, he should step aside in favor of his own vice presidential nominee. I'd also doubt, however, that this is because many readers would accept that the correct legal interpretation of "natural-born citizen" extends to cover persons not citizens at birth. If all this is correct, then the predictably apathetic response to Chin's fascinating paper might best be explained by readers' judgments that, while McCain would *not* be constitutionally eligible to be president if Chin's analysis were correct, his ineligibility should not be enforced by the courts, or would be due to a legal technicality that all of us may comfortably disregard. And if this is so, we might suspect that a similar judgment is at work even if Chin is wrong. That is, if we believe, contra Chin, that McCain was a U.S. citizen at birth, we might *not* believe, as I contended in Section IV.A., that this makes him non-contingently eligible to be president. Instead, we might believe that one of two things is true – either that he is *legally* eligible to be president or that, if he is not, the *moral* grounds for disregarding his technical legal ineligibility are overwhelming – and that which is the case depends entirely on facts about the late eighteenth century.

Although this is possible, my own guess is that reflection on the Chin wrinkle does more to bolster the argument from the preceding section than to undermine it. Unfortunately, this is hard or impossible to demonstrate. About all I can do is avow that my own reactions to the two variants of the McCain case differ, to report that other readers of a previous draft of this paper have had similar reactions, and to invite the reader's own introspection. The Chin thesis discomforted me when I first encountered it prior to the November election, because, while I surely did not feel that his research, if sound, would justify

[58] One scholar of immigration law adjudged Chin's analysis "compelling as a matter of positive law." See Spiro, "McCain's Citizenship," *supra* note 2 at 44.

[59] See, *e.g.*, Adam Liptak, "A Hint of New Life to a McCain Birth Issue," New York Times (July 11, 2008) online: http://www.nytimes.com/2008/07/11/us/politics/11mccain.html.

judicial action or even that it should compel McCain to stand aside out of respect for the Constitution, I could not fully shake the sense that it would cast a legal stain or taint on a McCain presidency: all would not be quite right, legally speaking. Reflection on doubts about the original meaning of the Natural Born Citizen Clause, in contrast, caused me no similar disquiet. Had McCain been born a citizen and had he defeated Obama in November, I believed he could have assumed the presidency without apology or asterisk no matter what the framers intended to capture by the phrase and no matter how the hypothetical reasonable citizen might have understood it at the time of ratification. The Chin variant on the McCain case teaches that we need not be slaves to the law; the pre-Chin variant teaches that the Constitution is not enslaved to the deep past.

V. OBJECTIONS AND FURTHER ANALYSIS

Originalists can respond to the foregoing argument in several ways. Of course, they could abandon originalism or soften it into a more moderate form. (As I have argued elsewhere,[60] "moderate originalism" – a collection of views that consider the original meaning highly relevant, though not necessarily constraining, even putting judicial precedent aside – describes a plausible swath of originalist logical space but does not fairly lay claim to the label originalism *simpliciter*: "originalism" is a highly controversial theory of constitutional interpretation; "moderate originalism" is not.) Alternatively, they can continue to insist that McCain's constitutional eligibility does depend on historical facts about the late eighteenth century. If they do bite this bullet, they could either reject reflective equilibrium as a viable method for reasoning about constitutional theory, or they could accept the method but disclaim the case-specific conviction that McCain is non-contingently eligible. Here I pursue a line of argument designed to avoid having to choose between these latter two options.

Quite generally, the strategy shall be to marshal other strong case-specific intuitions that are consistent with originalism and that cannot be brought into coherence with any plausible theory of interpretation that would be supported or suggested by our case-specific conviction that McCain is non-contingently eligible. One way to carry out this strategy involves two other cases involving the Natural Born Citizenship clause: one involving the eligibility of a naturalized American citizen (call this the Arnold Schwarzenegger case), and a second involving the eligibility of a birthright citizen born in the United States by caesarian section (call this the Warren Harding case). The claims

[60] See Berman, "Originalism Is Bunk," *supra* note 4 at 16–27.

will be that we have strong convictions that Schwarzenegger is not eligible for President and that Harding is. The argument that builds on these claims holds that we cannot bring into reflective equilibrium these two case-specific convictions and the case-specific conviction that McCain is non-contingently eligible, along with any plausible non-originalist theory of interpretation. Put another way, any non-originalist theory of interpretation that would seem to yield the intuitively correct result in the case of John McCain commits us to the intuitively incorrect results in one or both of the cases of Schwarzenegger and Harding. Originalists would advise that we abandon either the coherentist method of justification or the conviction of McCain's non-contingent eligibility, either of which moves would leave originalism remaining unscathed.

Arnold Schwarzenegger and the Constraining Force of Text

Arnold Schwarzenegger was born in Austria, to Austrian parents, in 1947. He became a U.S. citizen in 1983. Because his American citizenship is by naturalization, not by birth, we share a strong conviction that he is not eligible to be president. To be sure, we recognize strong arguments that barring qualified and potentially very popular candidates like Schwarzenegger (and like Michigan Governor Jennifer Granholm and former Secretary of State Madeleine Albright) might be both unjust and unwise. But, we say, that is what the Constitution requires. Schwarzenegger's ineligibility is not contingent on an assessment of the strength of the arguments of principle and policy that seem to weigh so heavily in our evaluation of the McCain case. Schwarzenegger's non-contingent ineligibility thus might appear, at first blush, to be in tension with whatever non-originalist theory of interpretation our conviction of McCain's non-contingent eligibility might seem to support. Surely, by the method of reflective equilibrium, Schwarzenegger's non-contingent ineligibility causes trouble for a rigorously justice-seeking theory of constitutional interpretation[61] – in either the narrow or the broad sense.

Of course, defenders of the analysis pursued in Part IV are not likely to find this argument troubling. In this case, they might reason, the plain language of the text is sufficient to resolve the issue against Schwarzenegger. A naturalized citizen is not "natural born." We can accommodate the conviction of Schwarzenegger's non-contingent ineligibility just by granting that the plain

[61] The idea of a "justice-seeking theory" comes from Larry Sager. See Lawrence G. Sager, "Justice in Plainclothes: A Theory of American Constitutional Practice," ch. 5 (2004).

language of the text must play a prominent role in the best account of constitutional law.[62] We do not need to be originalists to reach this conclusion, they might say.

Warren Harding and the Puzzle of Fortuitous Changes in Meaning

That is true. But enter now the case of Warren G. Harding, who is said to have been born by caesarian section. (Let us assume that this is both true and adequately proven.) Imagine that, in 1920, the phrase "natural born" had come widely to mean "born by vaginal delivery."[63] The argument is thus pressed that Harding is not a "natural born Citizen," hence ineligible to be president. Surely the argument is risible. We all have the strong conviction that Harding (a native Ohioan) is eligible, and that his eligibility is non-contingent on whether the meaning of words and phrases used in the Constitution have or have not changed in any accidental ways. Like McCain, Harding is non-contingently eligible (although their eligibility is non-contingent on different circumstances). The Harding case, then, demonstrates that the non-originalist response to the Schwarzenegger case is not secure. Because we do not think that the correct case-specific resolution of constitutional questions is hostage to the fortuity of changed meanings, the text can provide the firm constraint that the Schwarzenegger case assumes it does only if the meaning of the text is fixed – either by its original public meaning or by the meaning intended by its authors.

This argument neither compels originalism nor undermines application of the method of reflective equilibrium to the constitutional domain. What it teaches is that a good theory of constitutional interpretation is likely to be complex. This does not mean that we are destined to say nothing more helpful and determinate than that many different modalities of argument are legitimate, and that wielding them appropriately in a given case requires good judgment. It could well be that existing and normatively attractive practices of constitutional interpretation involve reasoning that can be described not

[62] Some might also deny the case-specific conviction of Schwarzenegger's non-contingent ineligibility; they find it plausible that equality principles (constitutionalized by the later-enacted Fourteenth Amendment, and then reverse-incorporated against the federal government) can be relied on to defeat Article II's discrimination between birthright and naturalized citizens. But I will put this counterargument aside at present and focus only on those who share the conviction that Schwarzenegger is non-contingently ineligible.

[63] *See* Lohman, *supra* note 28 at 350 (noting that some have "poked fun at the clause with tongue-in-cheek assertions that individuals born by cesarean section are not viable presidential candidates").

only by reference to the relative weights of the reasons we deploy, but to their structured interaction as well. Furthermore, as I have recently proposed elsewhere, such an account might cohere well with our best understanding of law itself as an argumentative practice.[64]

To offer just one possible piece of a larger picture (which piece I hold out at arm's length, for purposes of illustration), perhaps arguments of text are sound arguments (of not-conclusive weight, of course) even when not couched in terms of original meaning, but that when we believe to a sufficiently high confidence level that the putatively plain meaning attributed to the text was *not* originally intended or understood, then the argument from text alone is not just overridden, but canceled, and the original meaning carries the day unless overridden by arguments of a different sort – for example, arguments of policy, principle, or shared contemporary social understandings. Recast in the language of reasons, the suggestion is something like this: The fact that the plain or ordinary present meaning of a constitutional provision, T, is *p* constitutes a sound reason (of some weight) to interpret the law to be *p* in the absence of confident belief regarding whether the original meaning of T was *p*; but a confident belief that the original meaning of T was not *p* is a "protected reason"[65] that constitutes both a sound first-order reason (of some weight) to interpret the law to be *p*, and a second-order exclusionary reason not to entertain the otherwise available textualist reason in favor of *p*.

In other words, when we believe that some candidate interpretation of a portion of the text was not originally intended or understood, then the mere fortuity that this interpretation fits a present meaning of the text is itself no reason to support that legal interpretation, although other considerations could constitute sound reasons for such an interpretation. (An illustration: If we believe to some requisite confidence level that the original meaning of "domestic violence" in Article IV[66] was roughly synonymous with "insurrection" – referring to a revolt against civil or political authority – then the happenstance that, in

[64] I take a first stab at developing an account of law as a complex argumentative practice in Mitchell N. Berman, "Constitutional Theory and the Rule of Recognition: Toward a Fourth Theory of Law," in Matthew D. Adler & Kenneth E. Himma (eds.), *The United States and the Rule of Recognition* (2009). Larry Alexander and Jeffrey Goldsworthy have criticized that piece in their contributions to this volume. Their thoughtful challenges deserve a reply – but not, I'm afraid, in this already long chapter.

[65] On "protected reasons" and "exclusionary reasons," see Joseph Raz, *Practical Reason and Norms* (1999) at 35–48, 190–4.

[66] "The United States shall guarantee to every State in this Union a Republican Form of Government, and shall protect each of them against Invasion; and on Application of the Legislature, or of the Executive (when the Legislature cannot be convened) against domestic Violence." U.S. Const. Art. IV, § 4.

American English circa 2011, the term commonly means "private violence between intimates" would not *itself* be a reason to interpret the Constitution to compel the national government, on application from a state, to protect the state against an epidemic of spousal assaults, though it is conceivable that *other* reasons would support such an interpretation – reasons that, most likely, would not support a different result were the state to appeal for protection against ordinary street crime.)[67] I do not know how plausible this particular suggestion may turn out to be, on fuller reflection. My point is only to disabuse us of the naïve assumption that any pluralist or eclectic approach to interpretation must amount to nothing more structured and rigorous than a catalog of legitimate argumentative modalities. Our existing argumentative legal practice might have (in Llewellyn's words) a "bony structure"[68] that careful attention could help excavate.

VI. REBUTTING THE INTENTIONALIST THESIS ONCE MORE

In his contribution to this volume, "The Intentionalist Thesis Once More," Stanley Fish relitigates, against me and others, his familiar "simple and categorical" contention that "a text means what its author or authors intend."[69] I here advance three claims in response. First, Fish conflates the questions of what the speaker or author meant and what the text he uttered means. Much of the force of Fish's argument comes from mistakenly attributing to his opponents a non-intentionalist answer to the first question, when, instead, they are giving a non-intentionalist answer to the second question (and thereby driving a wedge between the two). Second, stripped of some effective defenses of propositions not in dispute and his characteristically enviable rhetoric, Fish's sole argument in support of the intentionalist thesis is what I elsewhere termed "the argument from rationality." Third, that argument is not sound.

Author meaning and text meaning. Non-intentionalism, as the negation of intentionalism, provides only that it is not the case that the meaning of all texts is the meaning that the text's author(s) intended to convey. Given the relationship between interpretation and meaning that I take Fish and I

[67] For a recent discussion of the Domestic Violence Clause that seeks to problematize the assumption that its original meaning was limited to insurrections and the like, but which is not inconsistent with anything I say here, see Mark S. Stein, "The Domestic Violence Clause in 'New Originalist' Theory," 37 Hastings Const. Con. L.Q. 129 (2009).

[68] Karl N. Llewellyn, *My Philosophy of Law* (1941) 181 at 187 (describing "practice" as "the bony structure of a legal system"), quoted in Dennis M. Patterson, "Law's Practice," Book Review of *The Caselaw System in America*, by Karl N. Llewellyn, 90 Colum. L. Rev 575 at 593 (1990).

[69] Fish, "The Intentionalist Thesis Once More," at 100 [Fish, "The Intentionalist Thesis"].

to share, this proposition is equivalent to the proposition that interpretation, rightly understood, is not always a search for authorially intended meaning; the object of an activity can be something other than the authorially intended meaning and that token would still qualify as an instance of the act-type *interpretation*. So, on the non-intentionalist view, there are (at least) these two things that we can ask about a text: (1) what does the text mean? and (2) what did the text's author intend to convey through this text? Question (2) can be, and often is, reformulated as (2) "what did the text's author mean to convey through this text?", and as (2) "what did the text's author mean?" Non-intentionalism denies that (1) is conceptually reducible to (2), although it grants that, as an empirical matter, the answer to (2) is often the correct answer to (1). Intentionalism maintains that questions (1) and (2) are the same.

In "Originalism Is Bunk," I hypothesized a public announcement that included the phrase "12:00 a.m." under circumstances in which the conventional meaning was midnight and the author's intended meaning was noon. I argued that there are good reasons – reasons having to do with the particular functions of public announcements – to interpret this utterance in accordance with its conventional meaning and not with its authorially intended meaning. I also said, in an earlier unpublished draft of that article, that things would likely be different if a friend had written "12:00 a.m." in a personal communication. In that context, you would properly interpret the communication in accordance with intended meaning even if that intended meaning were inconsistent with conventional meaning.

This analysis, says Fish, is wrong:

> The 'you' in this example reaches the conclusion that her friend meant noon rather than midnight independently of any goal she might have. She would have reasoned the same way if she had been given the example as an academic exercise, if a teacher had said to her, let's say that you got this message and knew those things about the sender; what would you conclude about what he meant?[70]

All that Fish says here is correct. Unfortunately (for him, not for me), it is not relevant to the dispute, because he has not read my passage as carefully as he might have. I did not say that your goals determine or even shape what you should conclude your *friend meant* (i.e., intended his utterance to mean); I said that your goals shape what you should interpret *his utterance* to mean. That is, it is a consequence of your goals that you choose to seek the authorially intended meaning. What you believe to be the authorially intended meaning

[70] *Ibid.* at 103.

is independent of your goals, but whether you seek that meaning – whether the better target of interpretation in this case is authorially intended meaning or conventional meaning (or, perhaps, something else) – *is* goal-dependent.

It bears emphasis that I have not caught Fish in an uncharacteristic slip here. Time and again he attributes to his opponents a view about what an author intended that is both implausible and not at all what they advance. For example, when charging me with confusing and conflating "(1) the formation of meaning and (2) its communication," Fish insists that "having your meaning misunderstood doesn't mean that your meaning is something other than what you have determined it to be," and that "what you meant by the sounds you uttered is what you meant, no matter what happened to those words when they entered the circuit of communication."[71] But naturally I agree, for I have neither said nor suggested that "your meaning" (in the sense of the meaning that you formed, or had in mind, or wanted to communicate) is other than what you formed (or had in mind, or wanted to communicate). Nor have I taken issue with the tautology that what you meant is what you meant. In denying intentionalism, I deny only that what *your text means* must be what you meant.

To be clear: Nothing I have just said purports to be an argument against intentionalism or (equivalently) for non-intentionalism. I aim only to show that Part I of Fish's chapter obscures as much ground as it clears. I speculate that the reason Fish falls into this error is that, because (being an intentionalist) he believes that what a text means just is what the author intended it to mean, he consistently fails to recognize that that equation is precisely what is in dispute between intentionalists and their opponents. Now, perhaps non-intentionalists are wrong. But if so, it is because they are mistaken in failing to appreciate that *the text's* meaning must be the author's meaning, not because they mistakenly fail to appreciate that *the author's* meaning must be the author's meaning. Put another way, nobody denies that "speakers and writers are free to mean anything they like by the words they deploy."[72] The matter in dispute is whether they have the power to make it the case that the text they utter has only one meaning, namely the meaning they endeavored to give it.

Fish's argument for intentionalism. Well, do they? In virtue of what is it the case that a text always and only means what its author(s) intended it to mean? Why can't at least some texts bear more than one meaning and why can't a proper target of interpretation of such texts sometimes be other than the authorially intended meaning?

[71] *Ibid.* at 101–2.

[72] *Ibid.* at 111.

Portions of Fish's essay hint at this answer: intentionalism is true because (a) non-intentionalism is committed to the claim that the relationship between meaning and mark is natural, not artificial (in Hobbes's sense), and (b) that view is absurd. Yes, that view is absurd. But are non-intentionalists committed to it? Or, to put things a little more personally, am I? Fish seems to think so. Thus does he contend that "*[p]ace* Berman, words don't 'have meanings prior to their deployment' in the sense that the meaning they have belongs to them naturally."[73]

Pace Berman? Hardly. My claim was that words have meanings prior to their deployment in the sense that the meaning they have belongs to them by convention, *not* by nature. That is why, in the very sentence from which Fish quotes, I made clear that a speaker is always free to coin new words. Yet more plainly, consider the very next sentence, which introduces what Fish calls my "main example" – concerning "salt" and "gas." Trying to illustrate that conventions supply meanings to signs prior to their use in a particular context, I claimed that "you know that my utterance of the word 'salt' in this context is evidence of my wanting salt because of the meaning *that our conventions have assigned to the word prior to my usage*."[74] That, Fish says, is "wrong" because what you really know "is that in the present company *there is a conventional correlation between that sound and an object*."[75] Well, yes. And consider Fish's further caution: "salt" does not mean what it means "by virtue of some essential relationship between the sound and the concept." Again, true. One might say that the error of uttering "gas" when you mean salt is an error "not because saltness is naturally excluded from the combination of sounds or markings that constitute 'gas,' but because of common usage and understandings" – which, in fact, is precisely what I *did* say.[76] It is unclear to me whether Fish really believes that we are disagreeing on this point, or is just inviting me to play Bud Abbott to his Lou Costello.

In short, intentionalists and non-intentionalists do not disagree regarding whether any non-intended meanings of texts that the latter might recognize are conventional or natural. We all agree that they are conventional. The disagreement is this: Most non-intentionalists maintain that texts often possess, carry, or bear more than one type of meaning and that a meaning other than the authorially intended one can sometimes be the proper target of interpretation; intentionalists deny either the first or second of these propositions. So the

[73] *Ibid.* at 3 (quoting Berman, "Originalism Is Bunk," *supra* note 4 at 44).
[74] Berman, "Originalism Is Bunk," *supra* note 4 at 44 (emphasis added).
[75] Fish, "The Intentionalist Thesis," *supra* note 69 at 102 (emphasis added).
[76] Berman, "Originalism Is Bunk," *supra* note 4 at 44–5.

question remains: What reasons do the intentionalists have for denying what their opponents affirm?

In "Originalism Is Bunk," I observed, and dubbed "the argument from rationality," the crucial intentionalist move in the debate. It runs like this: "[If] we aren't searching for the authorially intended meaning, we're just making it all up, and whatever interpretation *is*, one thing it's clearly *not* is *that*."[77] That remains the core of Fish's argument for intentionalism. Intentionalist interpretation, he says, "belongs to an inquiry guided by the desire and determination to get things right." Nonintentionalist interpretation, in contrast, "belongs to an inquiry guided only by desires, even if they are called 'goals' and 'reasons'."[78]

The argument from rationality is not sound. In my earlier work, I thought I had demonstrated the falsity of "the argument from rationality" by showing that, in many contexts, non-intentionalist interpretation remains substantially constrained.[79] "The Intentionalist Thesis Once More" does not respond to that argument. Fish does not explain which step in my argument was mistaken. In fact, far from undermining confidence in my rebuttal to the intentionalist argument from rationality, Fish's contribution to this volume does more to bolster it.

Take Fish's nice example of the airport sign that announces hot sandwiches now being served.[80] One might think the sign ambiguous: It could mean "they are served even at the late hour that one is reading the sign" or "they had not previously been available, but these days are (during regular serving hours)." Fish denies the ambiguity, however. Once you understand that the intent of those who installed it was to boast of the new additions to the menu, he says, the meaning is clear.

Possibly. But let us take a variant. Suppose the sign said "all our sandwiches are now vegetarian." Suppose too that Fish is a vegetarian and, surveying the menu, is disappointed to see that all the sandwiches are named obscurely after airplanes ("The Boeing 747," "The Airbus A380," etc.) without the benefit of any description. Worse, the sales associate has too poor a command of English to convey what is in any of the sandwiches. Fortunately, Fish eats and likes just about everything – other than meat. On a whim, he orders the DC-8 and hopes for the best. At first bite, however, he realizes that something is wrong: What the Euro Café calls a "DC-8" is what you and I would call a "ham and swiss." Irate, Fish demands to see the manager. "This is outrageous!" he

[77] *Ibid.* at 51.

[78] Fish, "The Intentionalist Thesis," *supra* note 69 at 105.

[79] Berman, "Originalism Is Bunk," *supra* note 4 at 52–9.

[80] Fish, "The Intentionalist Thesis," *supra* note 69 at 112.

complains. "This sandwich isn't vegetarian." "Oh, yes," explains the manager calmly. "We now only use meat from animals fed on a strictly vegetarian diet. Whereas, as you know, most pigs are omnivores, the pig that gave up his life for that there sandwich was fed only corn. There are no carnivores or omnivores in our sandwiches. All our sandwiches are now vegetarian."

So what do you think? Does our hypothetical Fish say, "Oh, gosh, my mistake. If that's what you meant by the signifiers you employed, then that's what your sign means. Sorry for making a scene."? No, I don't think so either. As all of us would, he points out that a "vegetarian sandwich" does not mean a sandwich consisting of vegetarians, but a sandwich consisting of no meat or meat products and therefore suitable for a vegetarian diet.

The first thing to note about this story, of course, is that our hypothetical Fish is a non-intentionalist, for he can press his case even without doubting the manager's sincerity. (And why doubt it? The hamness of one of the two main ingredients in the DC-8 not having been concealed, the owners and operators of the Euro Café would not have thought that customers would long be fooled into believing that the sandwiches were vegetarian in the conventional sense.) Our hypothetical Fish does not argue merely that the manager's apparently made a mistake about the meaning that Standard English assigns to "vegetarian sandwich"; he argues that the manager is mistaken *about what the sign means*. It is precisely because the sign promises what the café does not deliver that certain consequences follow. At the least, the manager owes Fish his money back, along with an apology.

The second lesson is perhaps less obvious but equally important. Recall the real Fish's insistence that non-intentionalist interpretation "belongs to an inquiry guided only by desires," and that (as he put it elsewhere), "[t]he only object of interpretation that makes it a rational activity rather than a free-for-all is the intention of the author."[81] And yet we cannot imagine our hypothetical non-intentionalist Fish contending that "all our sandwiches are now vegetarian" really means "Milton scholars eat free" or "We promise $10,000 to every customer who orders the DC-8." That is not because hypothetical Fish is limited either in imagination or desires. It is because even if there is no objective, fixed truth prior to the act of interpretation, it does not follow that anything goes: Interpretation is answerable to, and therefore constrained by, reason. What the norms of reasoned argumentation permit likely vary across types of texts and the purposes to which we put them.

[81] Stanley Fish, "Intention Is All There Is: A Critical Analysis of Aharon Barak's *Purposive Interpretation in Law*," 29 Cardozo L. Rev. 1109 at 1138 n.98 (2008) (citation omitted).

This is not a decisive argument for non-intentionalism. Perhaps intentionalism is true after all. But if it is, it will not be on the strength of the argument from rationality. It is simply false that the non-intentionalist enterprise is pointless or unconstrained. And because the argument from rationality is the best argument in the intentionalist arsenal, intentionalists still do not have what they will need.

CONCLUSION

Most arguments for normative theories of constitutional interpretation assume that their persuasiveness depends on the cogency and force of the general considerations and theoretical desiderata appealed to. And whatever those considerations may be, they are rarely thought to include our convictions about the proper legal outcome of particular cases. Our theories of interpretation (or of "implementation") are the grounds, not the product, of any case-specific judgments we may have. The method of reflective equilibrium advises that this is a mistake: Our convictions about the principles that properly guide how we ought to interpret the Constitution, about the concept or nature of law, and about how particular cases should come out (and perhaps much else besides) inform, and are answerable to, each other.

Of course, even if this is true, it might also be true that there are few case-specific judgments to which we hold firm, prior to an embrace (even if revisable) of correct principles of constitutional interpretation. Given the prevalence of basically positivist jurisprudential outlooks, we simply may not have many strong convictions about particular case-specific legal questions, as we do about particular case-specific moral questions.[82] But that does not mean we have none. I have argued that most of us have a firm conviction that John McCain satisfies the Constitution's eligibility requirements for the presidency – in particular, the requirement that the president be a "natural born Citizen" – notwithstanding the obscurity of the phrase and our acceptance, as a nontrivial possibility, that the phrase was understood at the time of the Constitution's drafting and ratification to refer to persons who were born in the United States, as McCain himself was not. Reflection on this case thus undermines contemporary originalism – the theory that (judicial precedent to one side) the legal norms that judges seek when engaged in constitutional interpretation just are the norms originally intended by the Constitution's authors or that correspond to the original public meaning of the constitutional

[82] *See supra* note 49.

text. The case does not, however, dictate that we adopt any particular theory of constitutional interpretation or any particular account of the determinants of constitutional law. Our best such theories remain to be articulated. As we continue to work them out, coherentism counsels that we pay more attention than we often do both to more abstract theorizing about the concept of law and to more concrete judgments about individual cases.

12 Constitutions, Originalism, and Meaning

Brian H. Bix*

INTRODUCTION

Originalism constitutes a group of approaches to interpreting the United States Constitution, or perhaps constitutions generally.[1] For a long time, "originalism" meant a focus on the intentions of the Constitution's Framers.[2] However, this approach was sharply criticized on a variety of grounds.[3] More recently, the "new originalists" have offered an important repackaging of the originalist approach to constitutional interpretation. Part of what has made these newer versions of originalism more powerful than their predecessors has been their more modest claims and focus, which has included an emphasis on the

*I am grateful for the comments and suggestions of the other participants at the Originalism Colloquium.

[1] E.g., Steven G. Calabresi, (ed.), *Originalism: A Quarter-Century of Debate* (2007); and Steven G. Calabresi, "A Critical Introduction to the Originalism Debate," 31 Harv. J.L. & Pub. Pol'y 875 (2008). Lawrence Solum has argued that what all originalist theories seem to have in common is the view that the meaning of a constitution was set at a particular time – the Founding (or, in the case of amendments to the constitution, at the time those amendments were written and/or ratified). Lawrence B. Solum, "Semantic Originalism," http://papers.ssrn.com/sol3/papers.cfm?abstract_id=1120244 (draft of November 22, 2008) [Solum, "Semantic Originalism"].

Christopher Green gives a sense of the possible range of "originalisms" in his seven variations of what could be meant by the "interpretively supreme 'Constitution'": (1) original expected applications; (2) original ultimate purpose; (3) original textually expressed meaning; (4) a collection of evolving common law concepts; (5) current linguistic meaning; (6) moral concepts according to the best current understanding; and (7) a collection of non-binding recommendations. Christopher R. Green, "'This Constitution': Constitutional Indexicals as a Basis for Textualist Semi-Originalism," 84 Notre Dame L. Rev 1607 at 1607 (2009).

[2] E.g., Robert Bork, "Neutral Principles and Some First Amendment Problems," 47 Ind. L.J 1 (1971); Raoul Berger, *Government by Judiciary* (1977).

[3] E.g., Paul Brest, "The Misconceived Quest for the Original Understanding," 60 B.U. L. Rev 204 (1980); H. Jefferson Powell, "The Original Understanding of Original Intent," 98 Harv. L. Rev. 885 (1985).

meaning of constitutional terms, and the distinction between questions of the text's meaning on one hand and the derived legal rules on the other hand.

In this chapter, I will use Larry Solum's elaboration and defense of originalism – his "Semantic Originalism"[4] is one of the most detailed, sophisticated, and well-defended versions of ("new") originalism – as a useful starting place.[5] I want to focus on two narrow, but important, aspects of new originalism. First, in Part I, I will focus on semantic meaning, an important element in Solum's version of originalism (and that of a number of other originalism theorists). For Solum, determining the semantic content of a constitution, or constitutional provision – as understood at the time of ratification – is the first step in determining what the text requires. In particular, I will suggest that semantic content needs to be understood differently in a normative, or legal normative context (compared to conventional, assertive propositions), in particular that the tie between meaning and application may be closer.

Secondly, in Part II, I will consider a basic, though underdiscussed, aspect of the originalism debate: whether the claim for originalism could, or should, be understood universally, as applicable to all current, and all possible, constitutions, or parochially, with its application to constitutional texts to be considered on a case-by-case (jurisdiction by jurisdiction) basis, with due consideration to the particular circumstances of each legal system.

I. ORIGINALISM, SEMANTIC VALUE, AND NORMS

Solum divides his approach to constitutional interpretation into two overlapping, but separate and equally significant, claims (the following are the article's early "rough approximations," which he refines later in his article):

1. "[T]he semantic content of the text of a constitution is (roughly) the original meaning of the text as it was fixed at the time of framing and ratification"; and
2. "Constitutional practice should be substantially guided by the original public meaning of the text."[6]

[4] Solum, "Semantic Originalism," *supra* note 1; Lawrence B. Solum, "A Reader's Guide to Semantic Originalism and a Reply to Professor Griffith," http://papers.ssrn.com/sol3/papers.cfm?abstract_id=1130665 (draft of June 19, 2009).

[5] I do not mean to imply that Solum's is the only possible, or the only defensible, version of originalism. And while I believe that my comments would be equally applicable to other new originalist approaches, I realize that my discussion remains vulnerable to the claim that there is some better version or better understanding for which my arguments are inapplicable or ineffective.

[6] Solum, "Semantic Originalism," *supra* note 1 at 30.

Solum's version of new originalism emphasizes the distinction between interpretation and construction, between what a constitution means and how it applies in particular cases. He asserts: "The distinction between semantic and normative originalism is a fundamental building block of the argument of this Article."[7]

In discussing the semantic part of his analysis, Solum goes on to introduce important analytical moves: the distinction between semantics and pragmatics, the distinction between speaker's meaning and sentence meaning, and the possible importance of special categories of terms – essentially contested concepts and natural kind terms.[8]

Solum asks, "What does the constitution mean? To be more specific, what is the fact of the matter with respect to the linguistic meaning of the constitutional text?"[9] The focus of this section is to raise some questions regarding the "meaning," the "semantics" of legal (and other) norms.

The conceptual structure on which "new originalism" is built is that there is a meaning to the (words of the) constitution, which is to be separated from the ultimate rules that are applied, but that meaning is the necessary starting point of analysis. The idea of distinguishing in legal interpretation between meaning or interpretation on one hand and construction and application on the other goes back at least to Francis Lieber in the nineteenth century,[10] and was emphasized in one of the earliest texts of the "new originalism," a book by Keith Whittington.[11] For Whittington, however, judges are to be confined to declaration ("interpretation") of the original meaning of the text; only democratically elected officials are authorized to elaborate the meaning of the constitutional text ("construction").[12]

Solum's version of new originalism does not similarly restrict judges; his judges are to start with the semantic meaning of the constitutional text, but there are various reasons offered why the final constitutional rule might vary from that content. Some readers sympathetic to (certain versions of) originalism might think that this guts the basic point of ("old") originalism: to have *the application* of constitutional provisions be determined by the original

[7] *Ibid.*, at 28.

[8] *Ibid.*, at 31–67, 93–103.

[9] *Ibid.*, at 27 (footnote omitted).

[10] Francis Lieber, *Legal and Political Hermeneutics, Or, Principles of Interpretation and Construction in Law and Politics with Remarks on Precedents and Authorities* (1839; reprinted 1970). However, for Lieber, "interpretation" was always the recovery of the lawmaker's original intentions, and his focus was more on statutes than constitutional provisions.

[11] See Keith E. Whittington *Constitutional Interpretation: Textual Meaning, Original Intent, and Judicial Review* (1999) e.g., at 5.

[12] *Ibid.* at 9, 110–59; see also Keith E. Whittington, *Constitutional Construction: Divided Powers and Constitutional Meaning* (1999).

intention or understanding.[13] If the great benefit of ("old") originalism was the constraint of judges who might otherwise be tempted to enforce their own policy preferences, the argument would go, creating a gap between constitutional meaning and constitutional law would only seem to feed that judicial temptation to stray.

In any event, my concern in this chapter is elsewhere. Where "new originalists" divide the tasks of constitutional interpretation between determining the meaning of the text (interpretation) and the application of the text – which can, does, and should go beyond the meaning – I believe that more attention should be paid to the first part of that task, determining the meaning of the text, with its assumption that meaning is easily separable from the context or process of legal application.

Let us first go back one step and look generally at the division between meaning and application of legal norms. The idea that what a legal norm means may vary from how that norm is applied to a particular dispute is not new, but the gap has been explained or characterized in a variety of ways. In part, this is because the distinction between meaning and legal effect may encompass a number of different concerns. In other contexts, one can see how, for example: (a) the right understanding of a statute or even a judicial decision may have to be put aside if significant precedent (and reliance) have surrounded a contrary reading; (b) the likely interpretation of the norm is affected by the need to make it consistent with other norms in that area of the legal system, or the values held to underlie the rules in the area; and (c) the current legal norms need not determine the resolution of a case, as courts generally have the authority (and sometimes the legal or moral duty) to modify the law in its application to a new case – for example, to avoid injustice or absurdity.

Solum's basic position is that there are three distinct stages in constitutional law: the linguistic (semantic) meaning of the constitutional text, the creation (construction) of law from that meaning, and the moral question of whether we owe any obligation to that law.[14] Certainly, there is a helpful clarity in dividing up the questions that way, and that division does, as Solum rightly points out, avoid certain confusions in discussions about originalism (and about constitutional law generally) that are otherwise too common. Still, one

[13] However, even at the level of determining the original semantic meaning, some might doubt that there will be significant consensus as to important terms in contested cases. See, e.g., Mark Tushnet, "*Heller* and the New Originalism," 69 Ohio St. L.J. 609 (2008) [Tushnet, "*Heller* and the New Originalism"].

[14] Solum, "Semantic Originalism," *supra* note 1 at 2–9, 127–8.

might want to look more closely at the idea of the linguistic or semantic meaning of the constitution (or of individual constitutional clauses).

The argument in this section is that discussion of the "meaning" of a term from a legal norm – whether located in a constitutional provision, a statute, an administrative directive, or some other legal source – differs in important ways from a similar discussion in the context of descriptive propositions, and that this difference may have implications for how one constructs a "new originalist" theory. In particular, the argument is (a) that terms often carry different meanings when part of (legal) norms than in other contexts; and (b) that the gap between meaning and application is far smaller in normative contexts (thus including morality as well as law), such that the view that "meaning is use"[15] is a good, though not flawless, guide.

Here, there are parallels to the classic debate between H.L.A. Hart and Lon Fuller, where they differed on whether the "meaning" of the legal norm, "no vehicles in the park," turns on the meaning of the individual terms or on something else entirely.[16] As Fuller pointed out, in this domain, the proper approach is not to focus on what "vehicle" means in the abstract, but to consider the term in the context of the (actual or likely) purpose of the enactment. Fuller gave an even better example, reflecting how the meaning of the terms of an instruction, "all improvements must be promptly reported to . . . ," could only be understood if one knew the whole statute of which that was a fragment, and the purpose of that statute (or group of laws of which the statute were merely a part).[17]

Fuller's point is that one does not determine the meaning of a legal norm through a process that focuses on ascertaining the acontextual meaning of each of the norm's terms. The argument is, in part, that the meaning of terms is changed by the context of norms – or, perhaps, by the particular context of *legal* norms.[18] This is a commonplace comment, when applied to terms that are legal "terms of art" – where the law has created new concepts or modified existing terms in distinctive ways. "Actual malice" in libel law[19]

[15] The reference, of course, is to the position, associated with Ludwig Wittgenstein, that "meaning is use." In particular, Wittgenstein wrote: "For a *large* class of cases – though not for all – in which we employ the word 'meaning' it can be defined thus: the meaning of a word is its use in the language." (Ludwig Wittgenstein, *Philosophical Investigations* (G. E. M. Anscombe, trans.1958), § 43.

[16] H.L.A. Hart, "Positivism and the Separation of Law and Morals," 71 Harv. L. Rev. 593 (1958); Lon L. Fuller, "Positivism and Fidelity to Law – A Reply to Professor Hart," 71 Harv. L. Rev. 630 (1958).

[17] Fuller, *ibid.* at 666–7.

[18] One could argue further, by even more specific contexts – *e.g.*, criminal prohibitions.

[19] *New York Times v. Sullivan*, 376 U.S. 254 (1964).

means something different from what that term means in conventional speech, as well as "consideration" in contract law; a similar argument has also been made for "to keep and bear arms."[20]

However, the phenomenon is broader than that. For example, as A. M. Honoré pointed out,[21] in the context of norms, terms that denote universals in conventional propositions – "all," "no," "never," and the like – are not treated as absolutes, but rather as strong presumptions or generalizations, with the understanding that there will be exceptions for extreme cases. Justice Black to the contrary,[22] "no law" does not mean no law.[23]

One might similarly argue that the meaning of terms might differ, at times significantly, when one moves from descriptive to normative contexts. What is distinctive about normative contexts – like law and morality – is a complication regarding reference. With natural-kind terms (like "gold" or "water") used in descriptive propositions, there appears to be something objective in the world (the "real nature" of gold and water) that determines what does and does not ("really") count as gold and water. However, with legal concepts (for example, "legal right," "valid contract," "contractual consideration"), the referent – what it is in the world that makes the application of a term correct or incorrect – is far less certain, and the topic far more controversial.[24]

To be clear: This line of argument is certainly not intended as a denial that one can sensibly distinguish "semantics" and "pragmatics" in discussing meaning generally, nor even a denial that the distinction might sometimes have a place in normative contexts, but as a question of whether that distinction might be more misleading than helpful when discussing the proper understanding of legal norms. This relates to, but is separate from, the argument that the prevailing political-legal theory may require that terms in a constitutional or statutory text be interpreted (understood and applied) according to the

[20] *District of Columbia v. Heller*, 128 S. Ct. 2783 (2008) see also Mark Tushnet, "*Heller* and the New Originalism," *supra* note 13.

[21] In conversation with the author, Oxford, 1988.

[22] See, *e.g.*, *New York Times v. United States*, 403 U.S. 713 at 717–8 (1971) (Black, J., concurring).

[23] Like Gilbert & Sullivan's "H.M.S. Pinafore" – "'What, never?' 'Well, hardly ever.'"

[24] Brian H. Bix, "Ross and Olivecrona on Rights," 34 Australian J. Legal Phil. 103 (2009). In moral theories that deny that moral terms describe special sort of Platonic ideas, there is a similar tendency to equate meaning with application. The suggestion that meaning might be strongly connected with use in normative contexts is thus sometimes associated with non-cognitivist, expressivist views of morality, like those of Gibbard and Blackburn. See, *e.g.*, Alan Gibbard, *Wise Choices, Apt Feelings* (1990); Simon Blackburn, *Spreading the Word* (1984). In general, the "semantics" of terms in normative contexts remains an underdeveloped area of study, and likely no quick or sure conclusion can be justified.

lawmakers' intentions even when those conflict with the semantic meaning of the terms used.[25]

The idea that the meaning of terms may depend on their context – specifically, that it depends on whether the term is in a descriptive proposition or a norm – needs to be distinguished from other claims. For example, it is distinct from the insight that we need to keep separate what the (existing) law requires from the question of how a case under that law should be decided. It is also different from Ronald Dworkin's interpretive approach to law,[26] under which the process for determining "what the law is" seems inseparable from deciding particular cases (thus, largely denying the distinction mentioned in the previous sentence).[27]

I also note that there is a parallel between the argument I am making and one offered in Hans-Georg Gadamer's work – where he expressly states, in his best-known text, that "discovering the meaning of a legal text and discovering how to apply it in a particular legal instance are not two separate actions, but one unitary process."[28]

What follows for Solum's approach if the suggested modification or critique is correct? Perhaps the necessary changes would not be that significant. Solum's originalism seems to be consistent with a wide variety of practices. It appears sufficient for originalism, as he portrays it, that the semantic content of a constitution is taken seriously and is not deviated from without some reason being given. And perhaps this approach could be maintained even for an approach to legal interpretation in which meaning and application were more closely bound.

At the same time, the sharp separation of meaning and application in Solum's version of "new originalism" is central to the flexibility of that approach, and an important element of its persuasive power. At a minimum, if the meaning of terms in (legal) norms requires a different approach than the semantics of descriptive propositions, and especially if the meaning of normative terms cannot be easily separated from their application, then part of the analytical structure of new originalism may need some readjustment (though perhaps no radical restructuring).

[25] Brian H. Bix, "Can Theories of Meaning and Reference Solve the Problem of Legal Determinacy?" 16 Ratio Juris 281 (2003).

[26] Ronald Dworkin, *Law's Empire* (1986) [Dworkin, *Law's Empire*].

[27] Though it may be that Dworkin's interpretive approach significantly overlaps or converges with the idea that the meaning of legal texts is largely determined by their application.

[28] Hans-Georg Gadamer, *Truth and Method* (2nd rev. edition. Trans. J. Weinsheimer and D. G. Marshall, 1989) 310. I do not agree with much of Gadamer's views on meaning, but I include this reference to his work because I am aware that many people do find his views persuasive.

II. ORIGINALISM FOR ALL CONSTITUTIONS OR ONLY FOR OUR CONSTITUTION?

The discussions about originalism, in all its different forms ("old," "new," and others), are not always clear about the scope or subject of the claims being made. To what extent does the theory purport to be (only) about how to determine the true meaning or application of the United States Constitution, and to what extent, by contrast, are these theories meant to apply to all past, current, and possible constitutions?[29]

Justice Antonin Scalia may be a good example of a local or contingent originalist, in this sense, though he is by no means the only example.[30] Scalia's argument for originalism is primarily that it avoids problems for *American* judges, applying *their* constitution, that other interpretive strategies encourage.[31] In particular, his argument is that the United States Constitution does not expressly authorize judicial review of legislation; the justification for judicial review offered by Chief Justice Marshall in *Marbury v. Madison*[32] was based on the judiciary's role *to declare what the law is*, which requires a resolution when two laws conflict – in this case, the conflict between the lesser law (state or federal legislation) and higher law (the Constitution).[33] For Scalia, this analysis only works if the United States Constitution is in fact like a law, in having "a fixed meaning ascertainable through the usual devices familiar to those learned in the law."[34] Note, though, that the argument would not apply, on its own terms, if one were dealing with a constitution (as is the case with many current constitutions in other countries) that expressly authorized the judicial review of legislation (though, of course, there might still be other arguments to offer in favor of originalism in those countries). Scalia also argued that originalism was less likely than non-originalist approaches to encourage the existing danger of judges mistaking their own preferences for the law.[35]

[29] Mitch Berman offers a similar distinction between "hard originalism" and "soft originalism" where the former refers to necessary or conceptual claims about constitutions and the latter refers to arguments based on the relative merits of different interpretive strategies. See Mitchell N. Berman, "Originalism Is Bunk," 84 N.Y.U. L. Rev. (2009) 1. For a criticism of Berman's formulation and argument, see Solum, "Semantic Originalism," *supra* note 1 at 8–9 n. 22.

[30] See, *e.g.*, John O. McGinnis & Michael B. Rappaport, "A Pragmatic Defense of Originalism," 101 Nw. U. L. Rev. 383 (2007).

[31] Antonin Scalia, "Originalism: The Lesser Evil," 57 U. Cin. L. Rev. 849 (1989) [Scalia, "The Lesser Evil"].

[32] 5 U.S. (1 Cranch.) 137 (1803).

[33] See *ibid*. at 177.

[34] Scalia, "The Lesser Evil," *supra* note 31 at 854. *Cf.* Antonin Scalia, *A Matter of Interpretation*, Amy Gutmann ed., (1997) at 47: the objective of "a rock-solid, unchanging Constitution" [Scalia, *A Matter of Interpretation*].

[35] Scalia, "The Lesser Evil" *supra* note 13 at 863. Scalia's other main objection to non-originalist theories is that non-originalists cannot agree on an interpretive approach (beyond their

This argument would seem to be one more generally applicable, though whether it was universal might depend on whether one thought this danger of judges applying their own preferences is universal.[36] In the following sections, I will discuss what a general or universal argument for originalism might look like, and offer some tentative thoughts on the likely success of such arguments. I divide the possible proposals into arguments based on the nature of (all) constitutions and arguments based on the nature of (legal) interpretation.

All Constitutions

From one angle, what we need might be a sense of what it even means to say that some attribute or approach is "true for all constitutions." We first would need to make sense of the idea that there is a category "constitutions," perhaps defined by necessary and sufficient criteria, or perhaps corresponding to some Platonic idea or natural kind of a constitution, or the like.

There have been occasional efforts to define what qualifies a legal document as "a constitution."[37] Among the criteria suggested is that there be a written text (with the famous problem of Britain's purported "unwritten constitution"[38]), that it deal with foundational or structural elements of society and governance,[39] that it have priority over conventional law, that it be "entrenched" (require special procedures and/or supermajorities to modify), and so on.

It would seem unlikely that any theory about the nature of (all) constitutions would be separate from a broader political theory, which would speak to the criteria of legitimacy for government, the role of laws in general and foundational laws in particular, and so on. For it seems probable that to have

objection to originalism), and this means any attempt to use non-originalist approaches will increase the risk for unpredictable and diverging case outcomes (*Ibid.* at 854, 862–3).

[36] As discussed further in this chapter, there might be societies, presently existing or easily imagined, where the society's conventions, understandings, and training made it extremely unlikely that judges would impose their own preferences as law.

[37] See *e.g.*, Larry Alexander, "Constitutions, Judicial Review, Moral Rights, and Democracy: Disentangling the Issues," in Grant Huscroft (ed.), *Expounding the Constitution: Essays in Constitutional Theory* (2008) 119; Joseph Raz, *Between Authority and Interpretation: On the Theory of Law and Practical Reason* (2009) at 323–9 [Raz, *Between Authority and Interpretation*].

[38] As Adam Tomkins, *Public Law* (2003) 7–8, and others have pointed out, it is not so much that the English Constitution is unwritten as that it is not all written down in one place; instead, much of it is scattered across a large number of historical agreements and statutes.

[39] Raz suggests a possible "thin sense" of constitution, which would cover whatever *functions* to establish the foundational laws of society, whatever other structural features it might have. (Raz, *Between Authority and Interpretation*, *supra* note 37 at 324. This is similar to Michael Moore's discussion of a "functional kind" for law. See Michael S. Moore, "Law as a Functional Kind," in Robert P. George (ed.), *Natural Law Theory: Contemporary Essays* (1992) 188.

a view about the nature of (all) "constitutions" is to have a view about the structure of a legal system, the need to constrain electoral and official power, and the value of placing basic structural decisions within a separate process, prior to and/or relatively protected from conventional political pressures. (It remains controversial whether one needs a similar view of the role of law within society prior to having a general theory of law. Arguably, a number of significant theorists – for example, John Austin[40] and Hans Kelsen[41] – did not ground their theories of law on broader political theories. However, many modern theorists, in particular theorists in the Hartian legal positivist tradition,[42] focus their theories on ideas about the role of law within society or what is most important about law within society.)

In determining what it would mean for originalism (or "new originalism") to be true of all constitutions, we would need a sense of what it would mean for it to be false (for any constitution, or for all constitutions). The alternative to "new originalism," understood as broadly as Solum has proposed, would be some sort of "living constitution" or "living tree constitution."[43] Those approaches are conventionally considered the opposite of originalism because they emphasize the *changing* meaning or requirements of a constitution rather than its stable meaning.

However, as Solum points out, whereas a changing constitution may have been rejected by the "old originalists," it may be consistent with the broad constraints of "new originalism."[44] For example, consider the U.S. Supreme Court's well-known comment, regarding the "cruel and unusual punishment" language of the Eighth Amendment to the U.S. Constitution, that "the words of the Amendment are not precise, and that their scope is not static. The Amendment must draw its meaning from the evolving standards of decency that mark the progress of a maturing society."[45] Comments of this form could be read as simply stating (if not in the clearest way) that moral terms are to be understood according to our best current understanding of what morality

[40] John Austin, *The Province of Jurisprudence Determined* (Wilfrid E. Rumble, ed., 1995).

[41] Hans Kelsen, *Introduction to the Problems of Legal Theory* (Bonnie Litschewski Paulson & Stanley L. Paulson, trans., 1992).

[42] See *e.g.*, H.L.A. Hart, *The Concept of Law* (2nd ed., 1994); Joseph Raz, *Ethics in the Public Domain: Essays in the Morality of Law and Politics* (1994) [Raz, *Ethics in the Public Domain*].

[43] W.J. Waluchow, *A Common Law Theory of Judicial Review: The Living Tree* (2007). See *Rummel v. Estelle*, 445 U.S. 263, 307 (1980) (Powell, J., dissenting) ("We are construing a living Constitution."). Many American commentators sympathetic to a "living constitution" approach also point to the Chief Justice Marshall's language in *McCulloch v. Maryland*, 17 U.S. (4 Wheat.) 316 at 415 (1819): "This provision is made in a Constitution intended to endure for ages to come, and consequently to be adapted to the various crises of human affairs."

[44] Solum, "Semantic Originalism," *supra* note 1 at 161–2.

[45] *Trop v. Dulles*, 356 U.S. 86, 101 (1958) (footnote omitted).

requires, even if this is different from how the drafters or ratifiers of the Constitution thought about those moral terms. For Solum, it is not the case that all moral terms should be interpreted in this natural kinds or deference sort of way, but it is appropriate if *that is how the terms were generally understood at the time of ratification*.[46]

There would clearly be much work to be done to create a political theory within which to claim an essential nature to (all) constitutions. Once established, though, that argument could well make claims about how interpreting foundational documents in line with original understandings (or, for "old originalists," lawmakers' intentions) is required for the resulting legal system to be legitimate. At the least, though, one should note that no originalist theory (of which I am aware) has offered such a grand and far-reaching theory.

However, on the whole, an argument that all constitutions must be interpreted the same way seems an even harder persuasive task than the broader argument (discussed in the next section) that all (legal) interpretation must be done the same way. For assuming that the broader argument *cannot* be made, it would be difficult to say why *constitutions* would have to be interpreted in one single way.

To make a claim about the essential nature of constitutions would be to say that any country that did not follow an originalist approach to interpretation would be making a basic mistake – regardless of the local history, current conventions, or public preferences. Alternatively, perhaps, such a theory might conclude that where non-originalist approaches are used, the text(s) being interpreted would not be (*could* not be) a constitution. It is hard to see how such claims could be made persuasive.

All (Legal) Interpretation

In thinking about justifying originalism as the proper, best, or only interpretive approach for all constitutions, the alternative to focusing on what is common or essential to constitutions is to focus on what is common or essential to interpretation in general, or legal interpretation in particular.

The first option could probably be rejected quickly. One would not likely want to ground one's theory of universal "new originalism" in the nature of interpretation generally. Too much of what we consider "interpretation" does not follow, and would not comfortably fit, a sort of "original public meaning" approach. For interpretation applies to a wide variety of art and literature as well as law. Would one take an "original public meaning" approach to

[46] Solum, "Semantic Originalism," *supra* note 1 at 93–6.

understanding Cezanne? "Hamlet"? Beethoven's Ninth Symphony? "Ode to a Nightingale"? While such an approach is not unthinkable, it does not seem persuasive either as a description of current practices or as a prescriptive reform for those practices.

Traditional originalism, focusing on original intentions, might be a somewhat better candidate to be part of a general theory of interpretation. A number of prominent theorists have argued for intentionalist approaches to artistic interpretation,[47] focusing primarily or exclusively on the artist's intentions, and it has even been argued that it is essential to interpretation that it be intentionalist (that a reading should not count as an interpretation if it were not intentionalist).[48] At the same time, intentionalism has serious critics regarding artistic interpretation,[49] whatever one might think of its merits for legal interpretation.

A more likely strategy would be to argue that original public meaning is the proper, essential, or necessary approach to all *legal* interpretation, covering the interpretation not only of constitutions, but also of statutes (and perhaps also contracts, wills and trusts, though these raise special issues, and could, individually or collectively, be justifiably excluded from one's theory of "legal interpretation"). Indeed, one might characterize Scalia's approach[50] as advocating the use of "plain meaning" or "original public meaning" for legal interpretation generally.

One objection that might arise to "original public meaning" (or a similar approach) as a universal theory of legal interpretation is that one can find many instances of jurisdictions that use alternative approaches to legal interpretation (including, at least in some parts of legal interpretation, and at some periods of its history, the United States). This objection would be fatal if the theory of legal interpretation was purely descriptive, but a conceptual claim is, or can be, different.

One might (without speaking nonsense) say that jurisdictions that use (say) intentionalist approaches or current plain meaning approaches to legal interpretation are in error. One could even claim that what those jurisdictions call "legal interpretation" is not in fact legal interpretation, because to be legal

[47] See, *e.g.*, E. D. Hirsch, *Validity in Interpretation* (1967).

[48] See Stanley Fish, "The Intentionalist Thesis Once More," earlier in this volume. See also Stanley Fish, "Intention Is All There Is: A Critical Analysis of Aharon Barak's *Purposive Interpretation in Law*," 29 Cardozo L. Rev. 1109 (2008).

[49] See *e.g.*, William K. Wimsatt, & Monroe C. Beardsley, "The Intentional Fallacy," 54 Sewanee Review 568 (1946); Dworkin, *Law's Empire, supra* note 26; and Raz, *Between Authority and Interpretation, supra* note 37 at 241–322.

[50] In particular, Scalia, *A Matter of Interpretation, supra* note 34.

interpretation, the process must follow the (original public meaning) approach new originalism prescribes.

Of course, most of the arguments that claim that jurisdictions that use intentionalism or "living constitution" approaches are in error are *not* making conceptual claims about the nature of legal interpretation, but rather are making claims about consequences: that new originalism will lead to less (bad) judicial activism, better legislative drafting, more democratic control over law, and so on. These look like contingent claims: that these are the consequences in *our* country, responsive in part to *our* legal and social culture, the way *our* judges are selected and trained, our processes of legislative drafting, and so forth. One might possibly argue, however, that what causes original public meaning to have the best consequences in our country will also cause it to have the best consequences in every (or nearly every) other jurisdiction, because it turns on general truths about human nature, strategic behavior, and the like.

If one were to have a theory of originalism as necessarily the right interpretive approach to (all) constitutions, a good grounding – or at least a useful analogy – might be Joseph Raz's authority-based theory of law. Raz's theory of law is grounded in the claim that law necessarily claims authoritative status.[51] What follows from this is that law must be the sort of thing that *can be* authoritative. This is then combined with Raz's "service conception of authority," under which it is appropriate to submit to a purported authority when "the subject would better conform to reasons that apply to him anyway . . . if he intends to be guided by the authority's directives than if he does not."[52] The result, Raz argues, is that for law to be the type of thing that *can be authoritative*, citizens must be in a position to determine what the law requires without consulting the underlying reasons – including the underlying moral reasons – for the ultimate choice.[53] This grounds Raz's "Sources Thesis," that "the existence and content of every law is fully determined by social sources,"[54] which in turn has been a highly contested claim in the debates within legal positivism,

[51] Raz, *Ethics in the Public Domain*, *supra* note 42 at 199.

[52] Raz, *Between Authority and Interpretation*, *supra* note 37 at 136–7 (footnote omitted). Raz adds that excluded are "matters . . . such that with respect to them it is better to decide for oneself, unaided by authority" than to conform to reason (*ibid.* at 137).

[53] Raz, *Ethics in the Public Domain*, *supra* note 42 at 201–4.

[54] Joseph Raz, *The Authority of Law* (1979) at 46; see also Raz, *Ethics in the Public Domain*, *supra* note 42 at 202–4. Raz does not assert that these are the *only* essential truths about law. To the contrary, Raz's view hints at a long list of essential characteristics. He writes: "While the law has many essential features we are not aware of all of them. They come to light as we find reason to highlight them, in response to some puzzle, to some bad theory, or to some intellectual preoccupation of the time" (Raz, *Between Authority and Interpretation*, *supra* note 37 at 97–8).

and between legal positivism and its critics, regarding the role of morality in law.

A roughly comparable argument might be built, grounded on Raz's theory or analogous to it. The argument would be that for a constitution to be authoritative, the choices made in that constitution must be treated as supplanting the reasons for action that apply to the citizens subject to that constitution. That (the argument continues) could only be the case if constitutional interpretation followed the original intentions embodied in the text (or at least the meaning of the words chosen by the drafters and approved by the ratifiers).[55]

As noted, intentionalism has its advocates, both as regards artistic and legal interpretation, though there are also well-known critics and equally well-known criticisms. For the new originalists, who are not intentionalists, a general theory of legal interpretation might be even harder to make out. Certainly, as Scalia has pointed out, there are distinct "rule of law" virtues to this approach, but the argument that it is the only possible approach to legal interpretation, in all countries and all contexts, seems a heavy burden to carry.

CONCLUSION

In this chapter, I have focused on "new originalism," and Larry Solum's version of it, as a starting point for suggesting two modest reflections on the new originalist project. First, I have argued that any reference to the "semantic content" of a constitution, or a constitutional provision, needs to be cautious and consider the possibility that language can change its shape and meaning in a (legal) normative context, in contrast to descriptive propositional contexts. At the least, one should be aware of the different meanings of terms in the different contexts, where terms in legal norms might carry meanings quite different from the same terms in other contexts. This concern, however, would require only small adjustments in the distinction the "new originalists" urge between the meaning and construction of constitutional texts. Potentially more problematic for the "new originalist" project is the possibility that no sharp divide is possible in a normative context between meaning and application. (Though, as pointed out in the text, one is still left with the analytical move, noted in conventional legal analysis, between what the existing law requires and how the judge should decide the next case – even if the decision in the next case "changes the law.")

[55] Raz himself emphasizes only the minimal intention of the lawmakers – the intention to create law – and does not argue that we must follow their intentions for the meaning or application of the rules they promulgated (Raz, *Between Authority and Interpretation*, *supra* note 37 at 279–85).

Second, I considered whether, or how, a "(new) originalist" view of constitutional interpretation could be understood as a general or universal theory rather than one dependent on contingent claims about our/one nation's constitutional text, history, and politics. I showed that such an option would be difficult, though perhaps not impossible or untenable. A universal theory of constitutional originalism would focus either on the nature of constitutions, the nature of interpretation, or the nature of *legal* interpretation. The last may be the most promising, but, at least as an initial guess, it would seem hard to show how a single approach to interpretation *must* be used, regardless of the politics, culture, practices, or understandings of the constitution's home country.

Index

www.ingramcontent.com/pod-product-compliance
Lightning Source LLC
LaVergne TN
LVHW011525200926
848484LV00001B/161